Countercultures instruct us about ourelves, more profoundly than many have een able to realize. "Every society gets the ounterculture it deserves," Yinger writes. nd his book is an invaluable new perspecve for those who seek to stand back from the olemics surrounding today's religious sects, olitical "radicals," and cultural movements -in order to see what they suggest about the ocial transformations that will shape our uture. Rich in theory, rooted in history, and ensitive to both permanence and change, *Countercultures* promises to become one of he major sociological studies of our time.

. **MILTON YINGER**, Professor of Sociology nd Anthropology at Oberlin College, has eld fellowships from the Guggenheim Foun-lation, the National Endowment for the Hu-nanities, the East-West Center and from Clare Hall, Cambridge University. A former Presilent of the American Sociological Associaion, he has written or edited many books, ncluding *Racial and Cultural Minorities* with George E. Simpson), *Toward a Field Theory of Behavior, The Scientific Study of Religion, Religion, Society, and the Individual,* and, with Stephen E. Cutler, *Major Social ssues: A Multidisciplinary View* (The Free Press).

COUNTERCULTURES

Also by J. Milton Yinger

Religion in the Struggle for Power
Racial and Cultural Minorities (with George E. Simpson)
Religion, Society, and the Individual
Toward a Field Theory of Behavior
Sociology Looks at Religion
A Minority Group in American Society
The Scientific Study of Religion
Middle Start: An Experiment in the Educational Enrichment of Young Adolescents (with Kiyoshi Ikeda, Frank Laycock and Stephen Cutler)
Major Social Issues (co-edited with Stephen Cutler)

COUNTERCULTURES

The Promise and the Peril of a World Turned Upside Down

J. Milton Yinger

THE FREE PRESS
A Division of Macmillan Publishing Co., Inc.
NEW YORK

Collier Macmillan Publishers
LONDON

The Free Press
A Division of Macmillan Publishing Co., Inc.
866 Third Avenue, New York, N.Y. 10022

Collier Macmillan Canada, Inc.

Library of Congress Catalog Card Number: 81-17276

Printed in the United States of America

printing number

1 2 3 4 5 6 7 8 9 10

Library of Congress Cataloging in Publication Data

Yinger, J. Milton (John Milton)
Countercultures.

Bibliography: p.
Includes index.
1. Subculture. 2. Social change. 3. Social problems.
4. Religion and culture. 5. Minorities. I. Title.
HN17.5.Y55 306'.1 81-17276
ISBN 0-02-935890-6 AACR2

These men who have turned
the world upside down
have come here also.

ACTS 17:6

Contents

Preface

The study of countercultures may seem strangely out of place during a period widely acclaimed, or lamented, as conservative. The title of this book may suggest to some readers a period piece, an effort to reconstruct a picture of the 1960s or some earlier generation. If that is still their impression after they have read the book, I will have failed. I hope to show that countercultures are not simply bizarre and marginal sets of standards and activities, but important elements in the process of social change. Their influence may be creative or destructive. Failure to take them seriously, to study them comparatively and in depth, is to squander the creative and to increase the destructive potential.

Several disciplines share an interest in the dualities, inversions, contradictions, oppositions, and reversals that characterize many aspects of life. Thus I have been led from my home base in sociology and anthropology into the relatively familiar territories of the other social sciences, psychology, history, religion, and philosophy, but also into fields where I have wandered before only as visitor or tourist or consumer. My training in art and literature, to put the best face on it, is modest; such training as I have in music is close to Bach, not rock.

Undoubtedly I have stumbled, in the choice of illustration, in interpretations, in examining the range of views. This I shall regret. What would be a source of much deeper regret, however, would be a failure to demonstrate the need to examine countercultures from many perspectives, to begin to bring integration to the topic, and to demonstrate its continuing relevance.

Although this is primarily an analytic work, I have not hesitated to express my own preferences. I am not "value free," and to pretend to be would only make me uncertain when I was engaged in analysis, when evaluating. Few readers will have any difficulty making the distinction. By making my values reasonably explicit, however, I may make it easier to judge the extent to which and the ways in which they affect the argument.

This book began to form in my mind several years ago as an essay in sociological and anthropological theory—a theme that continues to be the dominant one. As the final draft emerged, however, its implications for the crises of the day loomed larger and larger. As all can see, three interlocking problems of enormous proportions are upon us: How increase the range of justice among nations, classes, races, ethnic groups, sexes, ages? How attain peace, the elimination of the use of organized and official violence as the way to attempt to settle disputes? And how protect the environment against overcrowding, the depletion of irreplaceable resources, and pollution? Humankind has made a few tentative gestures, indicating awareness of these problems; but our social systems seem incapable of the major transformations that are required. Do they have to be turned upside down? Or are efforts to do so—the drastic reversals of recent decades—major causes of those very problems? It is my hope that the study of countercultures will lead us to pose these questions in a less stereotypical, a more creative way.

Many readers will observe that I have taken part of the subtitle—A World Turned Upside Down—from the Bible. That ancient phrase, so prominent in the sketches and cartoons of protest movements in the Middle Ages, has already been used to excellent advantage by Christopher Hill in his study of the English Revolution, *The World Turned Upside Down*. And even as I write this Preface I have seen an advertisement for a book by Daniel Yankelovich entitled *New Rules in American Life: Searching for Self-Fulfillment in a World Turned Upside Down*. Despite its frequent use, the phrase has not become a cliche but remains a clear reminder that cultural challenges and changes are powerful forces that we will do well to try to understand. It is my aim to give this ancient and dramatic phrase systematic and analytic treatment.

Another part of the subtitle—The Promise and the Peril—has been borrowed from Harvey Cox's valuable essay entitled *Turning East: The Promise and Peril of the New Orientalism*. The phrase captures for me, as it did for him, the ambivalence one feels toward many of the countercultures. To put the contrast in literary terms, which so often express life's contradictions and inversions, one cannot forget, in the 1980s, that the Ministry of Truth, in George Orwell's *1984*, was in charge of official lying. Its slogans were: War is Peace; Freedom is Slavery; Ignorance is Strength. Such inversions will seem all too similar to some of the countercultures I shall be discussing. But perhaps others will seem more promising than perilous, even those close in spirit to Dale Wasserman's *Man of La Mancha*: "When life itself seems lunatic, who knows where madness lies? Too much sanity may be madness. . . . And maddest of all, to see life as it is and not as it should be."

Work on this book has for several years been carried on alongside or in alternation with other projects. I am deeply grateful that during that time I have been granted a Fellowship for Study and Research by the National Endowment for the Humanities, a Visiting Fellowship to Clare Hall, Cambridge University, and leaves of absence from Oberlin College. In addition to conversations with scores of persons involved in or interested in contemporary countercultures, I have had the opportunity to work in the splendid libraries of the Universities of California—Berkeley, Cambridge, Hawaii, and Oberlin College. I hope that the footnotes and bibliography will not only express my appreciation to the hundreds of counterculturalists and scholars—not necessarily mutually exclusive terms—on whose works I have drawn, but may also prove to be of value to readers seeking additional descriptions and commentary.

Special thanks are due to Ada Macarthy who managed, somehow, to decipher the manuscript and put it in legible form. I am also grateful to the American Sociological Association for permission to use a number of paragraphs from two papers that I wrote for the *American Sociological Review*: "Contraculture and Subculture," 1960, and "Countercultures and Social Change," 1977. I have profited by the insights and suggestions of many colleagues and friends who have read parts or all of the manuscript. In particular I appreciate the comments of George E. Simpson, Stephen Cutler, Ronald Casson, Susan Y. Johnson, John Yinger, Nancy Yinger, Marc Blecher, and Robert Longsworth. Above all, Winnie Yinger, in ways beyond measure, has contributed to this book.

J. M. Y.
Oberlin, Ohio
May, 1981

Chapter One

Countercultures: Promise or Peril

People take for granted that law and order are intrinsically good. We fear anarchy, things getting out of control. "But if we were logical it would be order, not chaos, which would now fill us with alarm." For the world is changing so fast that clinging to orderliness shows that we are out of touch, unable to adapt successfully to the situation we face.

Edmund Leach, *A Runaway World*

One of the sloppier public myths . . . during the 1960's was the one about the counter-culture. The myth told us that somehow the young people of those years were unique: a cultural mutation that was breaking the course of Western history. They had mastered the weapon of refusal, and were forging a new society that would be non-competitive, anti-materialistic, charged with a sense of community and, of course, drenched with love. . . . They were innocent. They were pure. They were different. The times, they were-a-changin' . . . And . . . the hype goes on.

Pete Hamill, *The New York Times Book Review*, Nov. 11, 1975: 32

Countercultures and the many types of intentional communities they commonly create are not social aberrations. For thousands of years there have been attempts to provide alternatives for the existing social order in response to the perennial grounds for dissent: hierarchy and privilege, distrust of bureaucracy, disgust with hedonism and consumerism. . . . A decline in the quality of life coinciding with an increase in economic affluence symbolizes the trend toward the absurd in technological societies. Present-day countercultures probably are the expressions of a deep-seated, almost subconscious social wisdom capable of generating protective responses against this trend.

René Dubos, *The New York Times*, Sept. 24, 1972: E-13

The so-called counter-culture was a children's crusade that sought to eliminate the line between fantasy and reality and act out in life its impulses under a banner of liberation. It claimed to mock bourgeois prudishness, when it was only flaunting the closet behavior of its liberal parents. It claimed to be new and daring when it was only repeating in more raucous form—its rock noise amplified in the electronic echo-chamber of the mass media—the youthful japes of a Greenwich Village bohemia of a half century before. It was less a counter-culture than a counterfeit culture.

Daniel Bell, *The Cultural Contradictions of Capitalism*

One could quote such conflicting statements almost endlessly. For years I have carried on the same "debate" within my own skull—as perhaps you have also. At times I have felt akin to Midas: Everything I touched turned into a countercultural topic. Some twenty-five years ago, when I began to discuss countercultures in lectures, the referent was fairly narrow. At first the concept proved useful in the analysis of the sharp challenges to dominant values made by some religious sects, and useful in interpreting the meaning of heresy, charisma, antinomianism, and gnosticism. It also proved of value in the study of delinquency and other forms of deviation, since there were times when dominant standards were not simply violated but turned upside down.[1]

It soon became apparent that other themes could well be examined from the same perspective. It is unnecessary to give a full list of topics that took on added dimensions and significance when viewed counterculturally. In addition to sectarianism and delinquency, however, several others should be noted, since they will recur in the pages that follow. Simply to list them here may suggest some of the issues with which we will be dealing:

Alienation and anomie—the causes and effects of normative voids and of individuals' experiences thereof

Freudian and other depth psychologies, with their conceptions of a characterological underworld, filled with impulses and tendencies in sharp contradiction with the conscious life of the ego and the normative order of the superego

Socialization and social control—particularly the forces that interfere with socialization and increase or decrease the intensity of social control

Youth groups, and age groups generally; generation conflicts, their causes and effects

Mass society; the return to communities; communes; utopias

Protest movements; revolutions; modernization and countermodernization

Social stratificaiton, prejudice, and discrimination—and the protests against them made by dominated groups.

Rites of rebellion and rituals of reversal in tribal societies; saturnalia, feasts of fools, and "Abbeys of misrule" in feudal societies

The sociology of knowledge, and of literature, art, and music

And, of course—and most importantly, in such a melange—social change.

What these topics have in common, despite their enormous differences, is reference to the tension between the established and the marginal. To deal with their diversity, what is needed is a unifying theme, a concept that can focus attention on the problems common to the segments.

"Counterculture" serves that purpose well. I will define it briefly here as a set of norms and values of a group that sharply contradict the dominant norms and values of the society of which that group is a part. Similar terms occasionally have appeared in the literature. In *World Politics and Personal Insecurity* (1935) Harold Lasswell spoke of "countermores"—"culture patterns which appeal mainly to the *id*." Referring to the ideological aspects of a subculture, Talcott Parsons wrote: "In such cases of an open break with the value-system and ideology of the wider society, we may speak of a 'counter-ideology.' " And in a later passage: "If, however, the culture of the deviant group, like that of the delinquent gang, remains a 'counter-culture' it is difficult to find the bridges by which it can acquire influence over wider circles."[2]

Although these were passing references, they were undoubtedly in my mind as I sought to develop the concept in a systematic way. I preferred and used the Latin prefix, hence "contraculture." But the voice of the people has spoken, and the usual spelling by about three to one is now counterculture. To my ear, contraculture is more mellifluous. It also avoids the suggestion of a close parallel with counterrevolution and Counter Reformation, with their rather specific connotations of returning to an earlier situation. Yet, like Mark Twain, I have no sympathy for those ignorant people who know only one way to spell a word. In referring to others' work, I will use the spelling she or he employed; otherwise I will use counterculture.

Power, Reciprocity, and Culture: The Foundations of Order—and of Disorder

It is a bit paradoxical to use such a "disorderly" set of topics as those listed above in an effort to extend our knowledge of social process and human experience. The central questions of social theory have typically been: How can we account for social order? And how is change from one system of order to another brought about? I am proposing that we approach these questions in a different way, that we look for explanations of disorder in the hope that we can increase our understanding by seeing those in a new light. This light will also cast its shadows, of course, and leave dark places; so it is best used in conjunction with, or in alternation with, other perspectives. It may be well, therefore, to glance at the basic questions in the more usual light before seeing them counterculturally.

Social order is problematic because many of the goods, services, and rewards that human beings value are in scarce supply; some, in fact, are zero-sum: What some gain, others lose. Although altruism is deeply rooted, not only in ethical systems but also in our inheritance, a large measure of egocentricity also governs our actions. However one combines explanations of the sources of the problem of order, one needs to account for the fact that human societies exist, that much of the time human actions and interactions follow predicatable patterns.

Social theorists have developed, of course, four partially competing theories of social order.

1. It is a product of reciprocity and exchange, of perceived mutual advantages. Behavior occurs in anticipation of rewards from others.
2. It is a consequence of the power of some to command the compliance of others—the reciprocal of power being the fear of sanctions, of loss or pain or death. Behavior occurs in response to various forms of coercion.
3. It is a product of culture, of a mutually shared normative system—a blueprint for action that has been internalized by a set of persons in interaction. Behavior occurs in harmony with values and norms to which one has been socialized.
4. It is an expression of our inheritance. In the evolutionary process of selection, those groups among our early ancestors capable of altruism and social organization were better able to survive. Behavior occurs as a manifestation of our genetic make-up.

Statements such as these are best seen as analytic. A given interaction, a specific social situation is likely to be a product of all four factors, although one may predominate. Each of the factors, moreover, has a "disorderly" side.

In making analytic distinctions among these four bases of order, we must not fail to recognize their empirical mixtures. Assuming a near constancy in the genetic influence, one should note the interactions in the three social factors: Norms may be exploited to increase power (legitimate leaders may acquire illegitimate wealth and other resources that expand their power); exchange arrangements may get "frozen" into culture (concepts of a "fair price" or a "living wage" influence the bargaining); and power long execrcised may take on the trappings of authority—a cultural concept.

These mixtures influence the nature of the targets against which countercultures direct their opposition. Although they are, in the first instance, in conflict with the dominant normative system, or some part of it, this usually means opposition to the power distribution as well. Those elements of power that have been transformed into authority—that is, have been legitimated by culture, indeed have become part of culture—are among the prime targets of countercultures. The authority of governments, of university administrations or faculties, of religious leaders, of employers, and of parents is challenged. Authority truly rests, to counterculturalists, in the self or in some new leader or some new group; it rests with those who profess and will protect the new values.

Countercultures often express opposition to exchange arrangements also, because the terms of the social bargains we strike are not simply individual, they are partly cultural. What is a "fair exchange" becomes challenged.[3]

Thus countercultures combine three forms of protest: direct opposition to the dominant values, but opposition also to the power structures and opposition to patterned exchanges that are entangled with those values.

Quarrels among theorists over the "true" or "basic" source of order seem pointless. The task is to measure the range of empirical mixtures of culture, power, reciprocity, and inheritance and then to explore the conditions under which these mixtures occur. The mixtures undergo continual change, hence the study of social order must at the same time be a study of social change. Any one of the three social sources of order—or more commonly some combination—may be involved in the process of change: Normative agreement may break down; power balances, or more precisely stable power imbalances, may shift; or individuals and groups may gain or lose in what they have to offer in exchange. Under these conditions, expected satisfactions are unfulfilled and newly envisaged satisfactions are kept tantalizingly out of reach.

This is where countercultures come in. Some individuals and groups, living under sets of conditions that we shall try to explain and illustrate, feel particularly strongly that the social order is unable to bring them the accustomed or the hoped-for satisfactions. Depending on their social location and their personal tendencies, they attack, strongly or weakly, violently or symbolically, the frustrating social order—that is, the normative-power-reciprocity system. The nature of the attack varies widely, with some believing that they have been caught in very bad bargains, others that they are being exploited by unjust and unwise leaders or rulers, and still others emphasizing that they are surrounded by a shoddy system of norms and values. All three elements are found in most protest movements, even though they can be distinguished analytically. Giving the terms sharper and more limited meanings than they ordinarily carry, we can say that reform movements are efforts to change the social bargains—the exchange rates; rebellions are attempts to change the rulers; and countercultural movements are attempts drastically to reorganize the normative bases of order, the culture. Perhaps it is more satisfactory to say that although a movement can be characterized by the *primary* focus of opposition, the others are likely also to be involved. Revolutons, which are rare and usually require several decades to complete, include all three.

Our concern here is with normative systems in sharp opposition to the prevailing culture, and with the groups and individuals who are proponents and carriers of the oppositional culture. Attention to social organization and social structure must be complemented, it is now generally agreed, by attention to the fact that conflict is endemic, presenting a need for synthesis. Similarly, the emphasis on normative integration, on culture as a governing blueprint, must be modified by *continuous* attention to countercultures, while working toward synthesis. I am suggesting not simply a philosophical dialectic, but a cultural dialectic: Every normative system contains the seeds of its own contradiction. This is not propounded as a truth, but is suggested as a point of departure, a fruitful way to study societies.

In each of the several topics mentioned at the start, the cultural-countercultural dialectic has appeared; only by dealing with it will we be able to resolve pressing problems of analysis and interpretation. Ideological as well as evidential factors have tended to make it difficult to attain a perspective that continuously and simultaneously examines structure and change, culture and counterculture. This is not to deny the importance of cultural integration, whether as fact or as value, but to emphasize that we need to study it alongside its reciprocal.

At the same time, I do not agree with those who see the social world as essentially without meaning except as meaning is shaped in day-by-day encounters, where bargains are struck. With the spotlight thrown continuously on conflict and deviation, one is tempted to overlook the steady stream of behavior, from others and ourselves, that fits the cultural model. "Contemporary societies," Alaine Touraine writes, "can no longer be situated historically, because they produce their history." "For a long time we have been accustomed to define social sciences as a study of society and to conceive society as a functional system organized around values and norms, and creating order and civilization. This 'classical view' should be abandoned and the very concept of society dropped."[4]

In my judgment, this carries a good point too far. We need a dialectical view, one concerned with structure and with anti-structure. We need a theory that guides us to the study of the persistence of values and norms but also to the study of their reversals. A central task is to explore the causes and consequences of the interaction of these social poles.

Insofar as they are trying to enrich the study of society by adding attention to "the absurd," and not trying to replace attention to the mundane, the regular, the traditional, one can agree with Lyman and Scott when they write: "The puzzle, the mystery of how social order somehow emerges from the chaos and conflict predicated by the inherently meaningless is the motive for the study of the social phenomena."[5] Certainly social life is more "loose-jointed," open-ended, and emergent than was described in much of the earlier work in sociology and anthropology. Role-making, and not simply role-taking, is an important process. To overlook the continuing influence of social structure and cultural patterning, however, is to attempt to build a social theory out of a segment of observations, a segment highlighted precisely by its contrast with the expected and the usual.

A key problem for any society is the process by which authority is transferred, whether by hard bargaining among a small group, with different factions seeking to demonstrate their greater power; by military coup; or by open elections in which a large proportion of the population joins. A related issue is the degree of diversity in the control structure that is possible under various conditions, and the effects of various patterns. Who's in control here, we often want to know. Regionalism, ethnic autonomy, states' rights, and devolution are important political problems in many societies.

Much less attention has been paid to the question of the succession of cultures. How does a society move from one cultural system to another? How much cultural pluralism is possible under various sets of conditions, and what are the results of various amounts of cultural diversity? The study of countercultures is a way of examining these normative aspects of social change.

A few decades ago, most Western economics was devoted to the analysis of "the free market." Perhaps a chapter or two at the end of a volume would discuss monopoly and, by the mid-1930s, oligopoly and imperfect competition. In a similar way, much of modern sociology has been criticized for emphasizing order and integration, while treating change, conflict, and disorder as bothersome exceptions. In my judgment, some of this criticism is exaggerated, not only out of a desire to emphasize the importance of change, deviation, and conflict but also out of an ideological need to emphasize their value. (A reciprocal ideological need to stress the value of consensus and integration influenced the neglect of disorder and deviation.) Despite the exaggerations, the emphasis on change, disorder, and conflict is an important enrichment of social analysis.

Conflict is less likely to be downgraded in interpretations of international relations. Shared values may be seen as among the sources of cooperation among close allies; but other influences are more likely to be seen as determining in many international contacts. "They respond only to force," an American diplomat said of the Soviet Union, "and if force cannot be applied, then to straight Oriental bartering or trading methods."[6]

It has taken some time, however, for students of society to give sufficient attention to the persistent influence of force and conflict, the struggle for power, within as well as between societies, despite the influence of Marx, Weber, Simmel, Gumplowicz, Gluckman, Dahrendorf, Coser, and others.[7]

In this essay I am attempting to develop a parallel idea, to document and discuss the continuous tension in the cultural order, the normative system. Although I support the current emphasis on power and exchange, as complements to, but not as replacements for, cultural analysis, that emphasis tends to leave us largely unaware of the deeply nonrational forces at work in all societies, forces that are built around symbol, ritual, and myth. Most of us are ready to recognize the unconscious and nonrational aspects of individual life but pay too little attention to the counterpart on the societal level—the shared myths and rituals by which we collectively strive to avert crises or deal with them if they come. We can think of culture on its most abstract and mythical level as a paradigm that selects, interprets, and powerfully affects our impressions and feelings and desires. When culture begins to leave many questions unanswered and many needs unfilled, when individuals suspect their own emotions and experience only a blurred identity, the cultural system may be pushed aside.[8] Periods of cultural crisis are periods not simply of loss of faith but of struggle toward some new way to deal with the threat or reality of crisis and chaos.

Today's counterculturalists can be thought of as the shamans of urban society, dreaming new dreams, formulating new myths, forging alternative paradigms. They are different, analytically, from the eccentric and the deviant, because they set off some resonant tone in others (few or many). I am not entirely comfortable with Devereaux's formulation,[9] but I see an essential truth in his description of the shaman, as contrasted with the psychotic or deviant, as one who is working through a crisis that is duplicated in the lives of many others. The ritual acts through which he expresses his symptoms, though evolved as defenses for himself "are found to be reassuring to his fellows. . . . He tells us what we want. By contrast, the psychotic tells us of the content of his untypical or idiosyncratic unconscious. He tells us what we fear."[10]

From one point of view, then, countercultures can be seen as calls for help in stressful times, in periods when the cultural support systems, the myths and symbols, are operating inadequately, when faith in them is gone and seems unlikely to be regained.

Perspectives in the Study of Countercultures

An analytic statement about countercultures faces all the problems of similar statements about art or religion. To subject what is basically an aesthetic, moral, and emotional experience to examination seems, to the believer, the devotee, to take the heart out of it. Phenomena that involve values, feelings, and color seem woefully impoverished by analysis. How can one truly see a stained glass window from the outside?

The opponent or disbeliever may be equally unwilling to examine countercultures with some measure of objectivity. To reserve one's judgment on what are seen as foolish or dangerous beliefs and practices may give them credence or leave a suspicion that one is not a dedicated opponent.

Thus, he who is not for me is against me, or in its contemporary version, if you're not part of the solution you're part of the problem, is an argument that cuts both ways. In the vast literature on countercultures, on cultural reversals and inversions, a few studies examine, but most of the works applaud or lament, celebrate or attack, in the belief that one ought to take a stand. I think it is true that one ought to take a stand, but it is not exclusively true. Until we know a great deal more than we do about the sources of countercultures and the full range of their consequences, we may be applauding fads or irrelevancies or seriously destructive standards; we may be lamenting and opposing essential new values or inconsequential small-scale deviations.

The very importance of the cultural-countercultural dialectic now requires that we step back from it for a time. There is truth in Flaubert's remark, "If you participate actively in life, you don"t see it clearly: you suffer from it too much or enjoy it too much."[11] This implies far too much withdrawal for my taste, however, and too little of what might be called "Quakerly concern": involvement without intolerant assertion of one's own truth. This is not far from the anthropologist's effort to attain a humane neutrality. Having studied different cultures firsthand, Levi-Strauss remarks, the anthropologist has a sympathetic feeling for them. At the same time, "the method peculiar to anthropology is marked by that 'distantiation' which characterizes the contacts between representatives of very different cultures. *The anthropologist is the astronomer of the social sciences*: His task is to discover a meaning for configurations which, owing to their size and remoteness, are very different from those within the observers' immediate purview."[12]

We shall be dealing mainly, however, not with remote cultures but with those in which we live, where "distantiation," however sympathetic, is both less adequate and more difficult to attain. The need is for an alternation between involvement and contemplation, or a vital blend of the two. Wordsworth saw poetry as "the spontaneous overflow of powerful feelings: it takes its origin from emotion recollected in tranquillity."[13] Something of the same thing can be said of social analysis. If I can indulge a bad habit to tamper with the poetical statement, my hope here is not only to draw upon emotion (experience, involvement) recollected in tranquillity, but to cultivate tranquillity (quiet contemplation and study) recaptured in the midst of involvement. It is the schism from which we suffer.

Some of those to whom I have talked are made unhappy by the suggestion that countercultures are a continuing part of social life. Most of them have been participants in some alternative life-style, which they consider a great and unique breakthrough. To see it as only one of a series of related although different cultural reversals seems to them to degrade it, to minimize its significance. Their response is a "religious" objection to any doubt cast on the uniqueness of their experience. They are implicitly supported by the host of writers who, in recent years, have discussed "the" counterculture.

A few of those who reject the idea that countercultures have occurred in many times and places are opponents of the countercultures they see around them. To such persons, the suggestion that contemporary value inversions are part of a long history is to give them more credence, more dignity than they deserve.

Although one can sympathize with these beliefs, I think they are not well founded. That there has been a succession of countercultures throughout history neither deprives current ones of their significance nor proves their importance. Each interacts with a specific setting and is a comment on that setting as well as on the human condition. Each can be judged in terms of its effect—good or bad—on that setting. One ought not disregard their differences; every counterculture has unique elements that for some purposes are appropriately the focus of attention. The similarities among them in their relationships to the surrounding society, however, are also important. To take a comparative, ahistorical approach, Adler notes, "implies the possibility that one can learn from history and that man can transcend and remake himself."[14]

The flow of countercultures is now a torrent, now a trickle, at one time underground, at another fully visible. There are continuous sources in personality and in social process, as we shall see. In literate societies there is also, paradoxically, a tradition of antitraditions on which new movements can build. Directly and indirectly, Winstanley, Blake, Marx, and Lawrence—to cite a diverse list—have been drawn upon by recent and current counterculturalists.

Countercultures have been studied from many different perspectives. To put this in terms of the sharpest contrast, one can ask, reflecting widely different modes of thought: How do snowflakes differ, each from the other? Or one can ask: How are whales, lions, and bats alike? There are hundreds of rich ethnographic descriptions of specific countercultural groups and events, the aim being to portray them in their full particularity. There are also numerous discussions of "the counterculture," sometimes designed to comment on events scattered widely in space and time, to emphasize their similarities, but more often referring to events of the last few decades—religious cults, rock music, changing sexual norms, inverted economic values, and many other phenomena that I will be discussing—that are seen as part of a common movement.

Each of these approaches has its value. A combination of approaches, however, is most powerful. Although we often don't act upon it, most of us support the great insight of Kant's statement: "Perception without conception is blind; conception without perception is empty." It is my aim to supply an abundance of percetions of specific countercultures, not because of an interest, in this essay, in ethnographic description, but in the hope that our conceptions about them will not be empty, devoid of relevance to specific events. I will also be developing a number of concepts, not because they are important in themselves, but because they can help us see things about countercultural events that we otherwise would miss.

The task of the scientist, particularly one with interest in systematic theory, is similar to that of the poet, as Aristotle saw the poet, or of writers more generally. Northrop Frye skillfully develops the Aristotelian view:

> The poet's job is not to tell you what happened, but what happens: not what did take place, but the kind of thing that always does take place. He gives you the typical, recurring, or what Aristotle calls universal event. You wouldn't go to *Macbeth* to learn about the history of Scotland—you go to learn what a man feels like after he's gained a kingdom and lost his soul. When you meet such a character as Micawber in Dickens, you don't feel that there must have been a man Dickens knew who was exactly like this: you feel that there's a bit of Micawber in almost everybody you know, including yourself. Our impressions of human life are picked up one by one, and remain for most of us loose and disorganized. But we certainly find things in literature that suddenly co-ordinate and bring into focus a great many such impressions, and this is part of what Aristotle means by the typical or universal human event."[15]

Some take Aristotle's point of view as a sign of sharp conflict between writers and social scientists. I see it as an indication of their colleagueship. Their methods and the kinds of material they employ differ; their purposes are similar. I shall be attempting to describe and analyze not what happened but what happens, to use Frye's words. My aim is to design a paradigm (a prototype, a grammar, a pattern, a model—to use various connotations of paradigm) for the study of countercultures. It is based on my assessment of existing theories and the ways they can be brought together. Thus I shall try to consolidate and codify something of what we think we know about the "structures" of a fascinating part of human life. It is also a task of theory, however, to *imagine* the structures of nature, to make tentative sense out of conflicting, paradoxical, and incomplete observations, thus to guide the continuing process of investigation. It is my hope in this essay, both to consolidate and to guide.

As a guide to the study of countercultures, a kind of field manual, the chapters that follow suggest: If you should wander into some strange place or time—certainly not excluding the present—here are some gentle hints about what you might look for. Of course, as Kenneth Burke has said, and many others in different words, a way of seeing is also a way of not-seeing. In suggesting that you put on the special countercultural glasses, I am hoping and assuming that you have and will continue to use other pairs.

Analogies. The cultural-countercultural contrast has many analogues, some of them quite far-fetched, but each of which can stimulate our imaginations. During the last few decades, physicists have discovered that for every kind of matter there is a corresponding form of antimatter. Every electron has its positron; for every type of neutrino there exists an inverted match in the form of an antineutrino.

In a more instructive analogy, which I shall discuss more fully later, the biological process of genetic transmission is interrupted, under some circumstances, by mutations. "Counter-genes" appear that create unexpected deviations. In a more easily observed analogy, gardens produce not only flowers or vegetables or grains but also "weeds"—a kind of counter-crop—plants where they ought not to be. What is crop and what is weed, however, depends on the person and the time. Cigarette and pot smokers play with the distinction, and their own ambivalence, by asking for a weed. Not long ago, tomatoes were "poisonous." Marijuana is a poisonous weed to many but a multimillion-dollar crop to others.

On the psychological level, the normal civilities and disciplines required during all our social interactions, Freud asserted, were possible only because they were balanced out by dreams, projection, and displacement—psychological counter-civility, one might call them. In the process, secret wishes that ran counter to socially acceptable norms could be privately gratified. In a larger sense, negative identities may develop on the conscious as well as the unconscious level. In setting themselves openly against the world around them, persons with negative identities, as we shall see, become one of the sources of countercultures.

Probably the most instructive analogy can be drawn from philosophy. Every theoretical argument, in Hegel's interpretation of the dialectical process, is self-generating: every thesis contains the germ of its own contradiction. In his view, the dialectic was an internal thinking process. Any development has its positive aspect—growth—and its negative aspect—rejection. Negativity is essential to thinking. While using dialectical thinking extensively, Marx emphasized external structures rather than ideas. "My dialectic method," he wrote in the second Preface to *Capital*, "is not only different from the Hegelian, but is its direct opposite." For Hegel, the "real world" was the outward form of the idea; for Marx, the ideal was the material world transposed inside the head[16]

Insofar as there has been a theoretical element in recent countercultures, it has been shaped to a significant degree by the dialectical thinking of Marx and Hegel and by the agreements as well as the disagreements between them. Much of this has come through the work of Herbert Marcuse and the "Frankfurt school" generally. Hegel's contemporary opponents called his system a "negative philosophy," "for in it every immediately given form passes into its opposite and attains its true content only by so doing." "Positive" philosophy, Marcuse wrote, facilitated the "surrender of thought to everything that existed"[17]

Thus in dialectical thought the accent is on the negative, on the refutation of that which exists. The contradictions between various aspects of any phenomenon create tensions that are the major source of change.

The idea of a dialectical process, whether or not under that name, is widely used in social analysis. Gennep used it in his discussion of "Rites of Passage," which involve a stage of "liminality" during which normative demands are lifted and contrary behavior made possible. Victor Turner has emphasized the importance of this alternation between culturally structured situations and open-ended situations. In the interim of "liminality," it is possible to stand aside from social positions to formulate "a potentially unlimited series of alternative social arrangements." Recognizing the danger in this, from the dominant view, tribal societies have many taboos by which they "hedge in and constrain those on whom the normative structure loses its grip." And in industrial societies, legislation and custom restrict those who "utilize such 'liminoid' genres as literature, the film, and the higher journalism to subvert the axioms and standards of the *ancien régime*."[18] Turner sees this cultural alternation as a necessary source of adaptability, similar to the variability in the biological process that allows for genetic modification under conditions of radical environmental change.

One can find similar paired comparisons in the work of Freud, Weber, George Herbert Mead, and many others. In each, one finds discussions of phenomena that can be simultaneously opposed and interdependent, a kind of "unity of opposites" that is the core of dialectical processes. This paradoxical relationship "results in tension and the ever present potential for movement away from one polar position toward the opposite."[19]

The culture-counterculture relationship fits this pattern closely. We will be wise to use a dialectical perspective in examining the normative reversals that are the object of our interest.

Since this is an essay about "the world turned upside down," an inverted, reversible world, it is appropriate for me to state my conclusions in the introductory chapter. I'll come back to them, however, and not only at the end.

Any culture that will permit humankind to survive on this planet beyond the next few generations must have absorbed substantial countercultural elements—a set of values and norms significantly different from and often in direct contrast with the dominant values and norms that prevail today. This is true whether one is thinking of specific societies or of standards widely shared around the world. A society without countercultures is a vulnerable society today, as so often in the past; it is inflexible and poorly equipped to deal with the rapidly changing conditions.

Alongside that I must quickly put another statement: Most countercultures of the recent past and the present are woefully inadequate. They are cries of pain, accidental mutations, awkward reactions to, rather than replacements for, the imperfections of the dominant order. The great gulf: Criticism flows over us in a huge and often refreshing wave. Countercultural movements that are mindful of competing goals, to be optimized, however, and of conflicting interests, of biological, psychological, and social constants that can be disregarded but not avoided—these are rare.

In the discussion that follows it will be apparent that there seem to me to be some exceptions to this rather sweeping and pessimistic statement, exceptions that we may learn how to increase. Some past countercultural movements have transformed their worlds for the better (although never unambiguously). Some contemporary value reversals hold the promise of a new order or, more probably, of a successful blending with immutable elements of the old.

The great need: A continuous process of change, of step-by-step adaptations to the transformations of human experience, rather than drastic swings, powered by one-sided ideologies.

Notes

In the "Notes" sections, each first citation consists of authors' full names, title of work, date, and in some cases page numbers. Later mentions of the same work are shortened. A citation falling ten or more numbers beyond the last previous citation of the same work will refer to the first citation of the work as follows: (note 2 above). For fuller publication data, see the Bibliography.

1. J. Milton Yinger, "Contraculture and Subculture," 1960.

2. Talcott Parsons, *The Social System*, 1951; pp. 355, 522.

3. On social exchange, see, for example, Peter Blau, *Exchange and Power in Social Life*, 1964; Marcel Mauss, *The Gift*, 1954; George Homans, *Social Behavior: Its Elementary Forms*, rev. ed., 1974; Anthony Heath, *Rational Choice and Social Exchange: A Critique of Exchange Theory*, 1976; Peter Ekeh, *Social Exchange Theory: The Two Traditions*, 1974; Kenneth Gergen, Martin Greenberg, and Richard Willis, editors, *Social Exchange: Advances in Theory and Research*, 1980; William Goode, *The Celebration of Heroes*, 1978; and Richard Emerson, "Social Exchange Theory," in *Annual Review of Sociology*, Vol. 2, 1974, Alex Inkeles, James Coleman, and Neil Smelser, editors.

4. Alain Touraine, "The Voice and the Eye: On the Relationship Between Actors and Analysts," 1980; pp. 5, 3.

5. Stanford Lyman and Marvin Scott, *A Sociology of the Absurd*, 1970, p. 9.

6. St. Petersburg *Times*, February 2, 1977, p. 10.

7. On social conflict, see, for example, Karl Marx, *Eighteenth Brumaire of Louis Napoleon*, 1963; Georg Simmel, *Conflict*, 1955; Ralf Dahrendorf, *Class and Class Conflict in Industrial Society*, 1959; Lewis Coser, *The Functions of Social Conflict*, 1956; *idem*, *Continuities in the Study of Social Conflict*, 1967; Anthony Giddens, *The Class Structure of Advanced Industrial Societies, 1973; Randall Collins, Conflict Sociology*, 1975; and Max Weber, *From Max Weber*, 1946.

8. Edward A. Tiryakian, *On the Margin of the Visible: Sociology, the Esoteric, and the Occult*, 1974, pp. 1-15.

9. George Devereux, "Normal and Abnormal: The Key Problem of Psychiatric Anthropology," 1956, pp. 3-32.

10. Weston LaBarre. *The Ghost Dance: Origins of Religion*, 1972, pp. 207-8.

11. Francis Steegmuller, editor, *The Letters of Gustave Flaubert*, 1980, p. 132.

12. Claude Lévi-Strauss, *Structural Anthropology*, 1967, p. 376; emphasis in original. See also his *Tropical Sadness*, 1974, chap. 6.

13. William Wordsworth, from the Preface to *Lyrical Ballads*, 1926.

14. Nathan Adler, *The Underground Stream: New Life Styles and the Antinomian Personality*, 1972, p. xxiii.

15. Northup Frye, *The Educated Imagination*, 1964, pp. 63-64. This book was first brought to my attention by Clifford Geertz, "Deep Play: Notes on the Balinese Cockfight," 1972.

16. See Karl Marx, *Capital*, 1906, p. 25, and his *Early Writings*, 1964; pp. 195-219. See also G. W. F. Hegel, *Science of Logic*, 1929.

17. Herbert Marcuse, *Reason and Revolution: Hegel and the Rise of Social Theory*, 2d edition, 1954, pp. 325, 327. See also Susan Buck-Morss, *The Origin of Negative Dialectics*, 1977.

18. Victor W. Turner, *Dramas, Fields, and Metaphors*, 1974, pp. 13-14.

19. Jay Meddin, "Human Nature and the Dialectics of Immanent Sociocultural Change," 1976, p. 392. For other discussions of the dialectic in recent social thought, see Richard A. Ball, "The Dialectic Method: Its Application to Social Theory," 1979; Jackson W. Carroll, "Transcendence and Mystery in the Counter Culture," 1973; and Louis Schneider, "Dialectic in Sociology," 1971.

Chapter Two

The Definition of Countercultures

Particularly in times of cultural stress, some terms take on unusual salience. Critical words are revived or new ones invented that seem to help us deal both emotionally and intellectually with the flood of challenging or disturbing experiences and observations. A few "big" concepts become the code words of an intellectual tradition and are used as explanations rather than as labels for complex situations requiring explanation. These words take on a great variety of meanings as they spread from their original base to one related phenomenon after another. In the end they may refer to vast problem areas; they may be more indicative of a mood of the times and of an intellectual tradition than of a specified referent.[1]

Too often we illustrate the truth of Walter Kaufman's appraisal that as it becomes increasingly difficult to keep up with events in a field of study, many people feel a need for "bargain words that cost little or no study and can be used in a great variety of contexts with an air of expertise."[2] This risk is the greater because our key terms have both value-laden and objective components; they are critical appraisals of society and of individual tendencies at the same time that they are attempts to describe.

Any analysis of countercultures faces this problem. Some use it as a word of opprobrium, an indication of incivility, depravity, heresy, or sedition. For others, counterculture means hope and salvation, a unique and perhaps final opportunity to get humankind off the road to destruction. We need, therefore, to define counterculture with great care and draw as clearly as we can the boundaries that limit its domain.

Several explicit and dozens of implicit definitions of counterculture have been offered since I proposed the term more than two decades ago. We can begin to sketch its parameters by examining some of these definitions.

Westhues refers to ideology, behavior, and social structure in his definition:

> On the ideological level, a counterculture is a set of beliefs and values which radically reject the dominant culture of a society and prescribe a sectarian alternative. On the behavioral level, a counterculture is a group of people who, because they accept such beliefs and values, behave in such radically nonconformist ways that they tend to drop out of the society.[3]

The statement that countercultural groups tend to drop out of society is problematic, as Westhues recognizes. Some do; others stay engaged, hoping to change society and its values; others look inward, searching for their souls, but not leaving society.

It has become nearly standard to use the term counterculture, as Westhues does, to refer both to the norms and values and to the groups with which they are identified, after the fashion of may anthropological uses of "culture." This is not my preference. I think it blurs distinctions that are often essential to clarity. Yet I do not want to carry the burden of another neologism—countergroup or countersociety—to serve as a parallel concept. Therefore I will use various circumlocutions to make the distinction between culture and society, between normative systems and the groups that carry them; and on occasion will refer to both by "counterculture" when the context prevents misunderstanding.

Some definitions proceed mainly by illustration. Contrast minor variations on a cultural theme, Fred Davis suggests, with sharp variations:

> The gang boy configuration . . . fits nicely Yinger's notion of a contraculture; its very meaning and existential quality inhere in its members' patterned deviation from the dominant American cultural pattern . . . hippies, too, are an instance par excellence of a contraculture whose *raison d'être* . . . lies in its members' almost studied inversion of certain key middle class American values and practices.[4]

Davis then spells out these contradictions of value and practice in some detail:

> . . . *immediacy* contra past preoccupation and future concern; the *natural* . . . contra the artificial . . . ; the *colorful* and *baroque* contra the classical, contained, and symmetrical; the *direct* contra the mediated, interposed, or intervening . . . ; the *spontaneous* contra the structured; the *primitive* contra the sophisticated; the *mystical* contra the scientific; the *egalitarian* contra the hierarchical; the *polymorphous* and *androgynous*

> contra the singular; the *diffuse* contra the categorical; the *communal* contra the private."[5]

There is a tendency to stereotype both the dominant and the hippie standards in Davis's description, as in many discussions of countercultures, in order to draw the sharpest possible contrast; but he does skillfully capture the ideological tone of many recent and contemporary countercultures. Many interpreters draw just this kind of extreme difference in order to praise or condemn.

"There are an almost infinite number of polarities," Philip Slater writes, "by means of which one can differentiate between the two cultures. The old culture, when forced to choose, tends to give preference to property rights over personal rights, technological requirements over human needs, competition over cooperation, violence over sexuality, concentration over distribution, the producer over the consumer, means over ends, secrecy over openness, social forms over personal expression, striving over gratification, Oedipal love over communal love, and so on. The counterculture tends to reverse all of these priorities."[6]

In a later sentence Slater expresses the epitome of the countercultural view, at least in its American form at the time of his writing: "Americans continually find themselves in the position of having killed someone to avoid sharing a meal which turns out to be too large to eat alone."[7]

Such sweeping generalizations should not be read simply as the products of empirical study. They are resonant with faith. Countercultural ethnocentrism is no less likely to be loaded with stereotypes and exaggerations than other forms of ethnocentrism. It tells us a great deal about the times to which it refers as well as about the inverted values.

Some descriptions proceed from an opposite perspective:

> Today's pop counterculture, especially among the young, is an awesome mix of maximum mindlessness, minimum historical awareness, and a pathetic yearning for (to quote Chico Marx) strawberry shortcut. To hell with established religions, with science, with philosophy, with economics and politics, with the liberal arts—with anything that demands time and effort. Dig the rock beat, kink up your sex life, meditate, tack a photo of Squeaky Fromme on the wall.[8]

Although the language is quite different, a contemporary Marxist definition and interpretation of "Counter-culture—a symptom of development or an indication of decay" has much in common with conservative views. The general outlook of the current Western counterculture, Davidov writes, is that of the negation of idealism, of intellectualism, and of anything seen as objectively necessary, rational, or governed by law. It is the negation of traditional theology, the ethic of labor and responsiblility, and Christian rigor regarding family and sex. It is the negation of the principle of individualism central to Western cultures. Altogether, the contemporary counterculture represents one of the deepest crises of Western capitalism, in her judgment, having "affected its mechanism of socialization and of transmission of vital, moral and ideological values from one generation to another."[9]

The rich descriptions of recent and current countercultures reveal both unique qualities and qualities that have appeared frequently in protest movements. In their study of "freak" culture in the United States, Wieder and Zimmerman base their discussion on Karl Mannheim's concept of the generation. This is not simply a group of persons of similar age, but one that has experienced distinctive social changes. Those changes give them a vision and knowledge of society differing significantly from the vision and knowledge of their predecessors and successors. With information from lengthy interviews and from questionnaires, Weider and Zimmerman draw a picture of countercultural norms that "all but turn middle class standards on their heads." Freaks reject conventional economic and occupational success norms, seeing them as repressive and destructive of spontaneity. Immediate consummatory values, not deferred gratification and instrumental activism, are their goals. Life should be a continuous free flow of satisfactions.[10]

The details are different, but the relationship to the dominant culture was similar among *les Bouzingos* in France in the 1830s. *Bouzingos*, meaning noisy, undisciplined, and extravagant, was an epithet that young protestors proudly wore "as they pledged with their obscene songs to fight the philistines. They saw themselves as a camp of Tartars and used skulls as drinking vessels and danced wildly and nakedly in the streets or sat naked in their gardens to outrage the neighborhood . . . they were obsessed with sadism, rape, satanism and werewolves."[11]

The 1911 edition of the *Encyclopaedia Britannica* described some of the Russian students of the 1870s and 1880s as

> a new and striking orginal type—young men and women in slovenly attire who called in question and ridiculed the generally received convictions and respectable conventions of social life. . . . They reversed the

> traditional order of things even to the trivial matters of external appearance, the males allowing the hair to grow long and the females cutting it short, and adding the additional badge of blue spectacles.[12]

These descriptions are similar to but not identical with the picture of hippies drawn by many observers. They too are antiroutine, anticonventional. In a time of plenitude, they ask, why defer gratification if there is abundance; and if it all may be blown away by atomic war tomorrow, there is even less reason to defer.[13] The widespread use of drugs and the lifting of restraints on sex are expressive of these values. Some of the themes emphasized by hippies, however, differentiate them from the freaks described by Wieder and Zimmerman. Hippies are to some degree anticonsumption: We can live happily on less. There is an emphasis on community, as opposed to the anonymous city; on peace and love, as opposed to a society that they see as riven by conflict;[14] and on egalitarian participation, as opposed to virtuoso standards for the few combined with passive spectatorship for the many.

With schedules, planning, and deferred gratification set aside as dull routine, there is no simple time trajectory of the present into the future. In such a context, some hippies find a millennial view congenial; one can hope for the imminent transformation of the world.[15] This perspective helps to account for the ease with which some hippies moved into mystical or fundamentalist religious groups.

In his influential *The Making of a Counterculture*, Roszak emphasizes opposition to technocratic society as the major theme of the counterculture of the 1960s. (Since both Adam Smith and Karl Marx worried about the corrosive effects of technology, recent countercultures have a rather diverse set of predecessors on that topic.) Other themes are closely connected: Society is corrupted by its overemphasis on "repressive rationality" to the neglect of the importance of the irrational in human experience, by its oppressive bureaucracies, and by its exaggerated dependence on science as the only road to truth.

Amid an abundance of such descriptions and definitions, indicating widely varying attitudes pro and con, it is difficult to reestablish "counterculture" as a term that can be used with some agreement. By examining several questions that I have often been asked, or have asked myself, I think we can bring some precision into the word. First, a fairly formal definition may furnish a standard against which the comments on the questions can be measured. The term counterculture is appropriately used whenever the normative system of a group contains, as a primary element, a theme of conflict with the dominant values of society, where the tendencies, needs, and perceptions of the members of that group are directly involved in the development and maintenance of its values, and wherever its norms can be understood only by reference to the relationship of the group to the surrounding dominant society and its culture.[16]

The term "values" in this definition can be understood as the states and objects toward which behavior is preferentially directed. Values are "conceptions of the desirable" that serve as major guidelines for behavior.[17] They can be identified by asking what a group is most willing to spend scarce resources to obtain. (There are also individual values, but these are not, by definition, part of culture or counterculture.) As Williams notes, these conceptions of the desirable state of affairs are used "as *criteria* for preference or choice or as *justification* for proposed or actual behavior."[18] Norms are the culturally approved procedures and objects believed necessary to optimize the realization of values in particular sets of condition. This distinction between norms and values is similar to that drawn by Rokeach between intrumental and terminal values.[19] It is close to the familiar distinction between means and ends. In each instance the contrast should be kept fluid, because today's values or ends strongly affect, and may in fact become, tomorrow's means.

A countercultural movement is both behavioral and symbolic. It grows out of a combination of deviance and criticism of the social order, as suggested in Figure 2.1, page 24.

These two streams are never entirely separate, of course. Some individuals will be both the exemplars and the theoreticians of the cultural inversions—the gurus, charismatic leaders, or prophets. Others are identified primarily with the symbolic stream or with the behavioral stream. It is when the two merge, however, as in the United States and Western Europe during the 1960s, in England in the 1640s and 1650s, or in the Roman Empire in the second century A.D., that major countercultural movements occur.

Tracing the Boundaries of Countercultures

Only the essay as a whole can adequately define countercultures. Brief comments on several questions, however, can mark out the parameters.

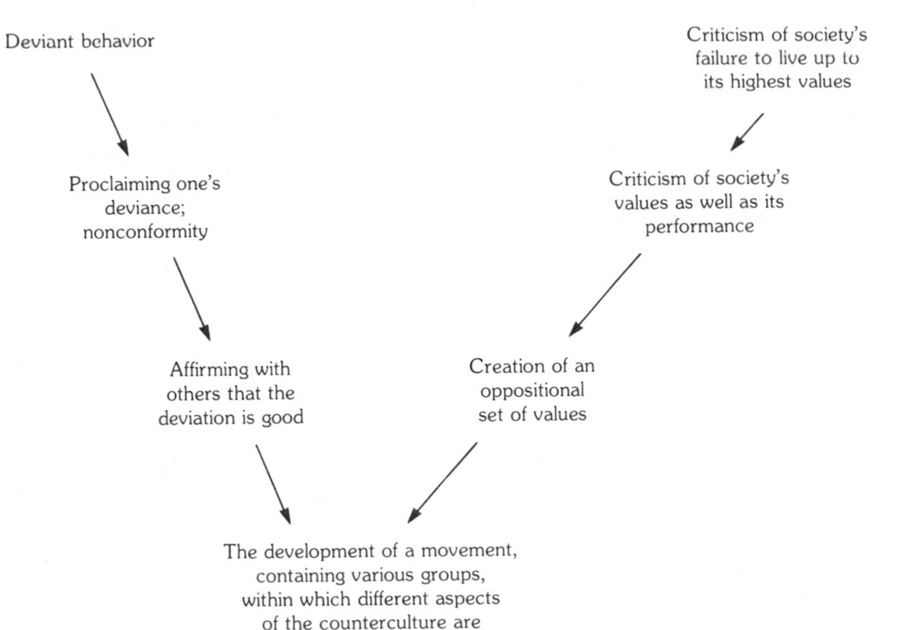

Figure 2.1

1. Should we speak of countercultures when second-level or subterranean values of a society are raised by some segment of that society to a primary place? The apocalyptic visions, populism, and evangelical fervor of American student radicals, Matza notes, are part of the dominant tradition. When these "counterthemes" are carried to an extreme, however, they are "publicly denounced." Delinquent youth can also draw on a subterranean tradition of the dominant society. The search for a thrill, the use of "pull," and aggression are scarcely limited to delinquents; they are secondary values of the dominant society, particularly of the leisure class, in Veblen's usage.[20]

At some point an exaggerated emphasis on a value becomes a countervalue by virtue of the exaggeration. "A society may accept or even applaud a pattern that is used to a limited degree while condemning its extravagant use. And the meaning of the pattern in the life of the individual when found in culturally approved degree differs from what it is when the pattern becomes a dominant theme."[21] We are dealing with a variable, and only careful study can tell us at what point an exaggerated value becomes countercultural, as indicated by the behavior and attitudes of both the proponents and the opponents.

Related to the presence of "subterranean" values is the fact that many societies, perhaps most, have more explicit contradictions and ambivalences built into their cultures. At least since Goethe there have been discussions of the "two Germanys." Similarly, from Tocqueville's observations a century and a half ago down to the present, examination of the tension between the values of equality and of liberty in the United States has been crucial to cultural analysis. In *Childhood and Society*, Erik Erikson observed that a culture is much more richly defined by such point-counterpoint tensions than by a list of mutually consistent values.[22]

These various polarities are not indications of cultural-countercultural conflict so long as they remain in dynamic relationship. One or the other may be emphasized at particular times, but so long as its opposite modifies that emphasis and is generally accepted as normative under appropriate conditions, both are part of culture. When these long-established polarites are torn apart, however, with one part being given almost exclusive support, the value thus supported, although drawn from the larger culture, is countercultural.

Two illustrations may help to clarify this relationship. Pacifists affirm values that break apart the patriotism and preparedness/peace and brotherhood polarity, emphasizing only the latter part. Even in societies where pacifists have at least a marginal legal position, and more religious support, they are widely regarded not as occupying an uncommon but acceptable alternative cultural position but as deviant. By stressing only one part of an unstable yet persistent dualism, they take a cultural stand in contrast with the standard. However much military considerations seem to dominate public actions, ordinarily they are not given exclusive valuative emphasis. Indeed, military action is usually defended as necessary to secure peace and to promote brotherhood. Of course, there are those (caricatured by the movie *Dr. Strangelove*) who emphasize only the patriotism-preparedness side of the polarity, as value as well as policy. They too can be regarded as counterculturalists.

Law-and-order and anarchy are bound together in another polarity. At least a little anarchy is thought appropriate by most Americans,[23] but we are also quick to affirm that "there ought to be a law." When the latter becomes "law and order" without notions of law, *justice*, and order, or without being qualified by "when needed for the larger public good," the cultural polarity is destroyed and the seeds of counterculture planted. When the anarchic side is empasized, "do your own thing" breaks free from such qualifications as, "so long as similar rights to others are not denied" and "within limits set by the long-run public good." Thus a contrasting counterculture is promoted. (Almost every reader will be unhappy with one or the other side of these illustrations.)

In a similar way, Merton has discussed the ways in which social structures generate social conflict by being differentiated into strata, organizations, and communities with potentially conflicting interests and values. Thus what he calls "sociological ambivalence" is built into normative structures in the form of incompatible expectations and a "dynamic alternation of norms and counternorms."[24]

2. How many values and norms must be challenged before we speak of a counterculture? The term culture implies a blueprint for the whole range of life's activities. Should not a counterculture be seen in the same way? Many persons have observed that during the last few decades inverted values have been affirmed for almost every aspect of life—familial, religious, economic, political, and educational.[25] Antilanguage, anti-psychiatry, and artistic inversions abound.

Nevertheless, I think we should treat the term as a variable. We need analogues of analytic chemistry, ways to detect "trace elements" in complex compounds, not just to identify "pure substances." It is the mixtures that are most common. The values of a group can be moderately or extensively countercultural; a few, several, or a large number of the institutional patterns can be opposed. Undoubtedly there are vast differences in the causes and effects of minimal and maximal countercultures, and these should be made the subject of study, not dismissed by definition.

This suggestion has drawbacks. We realize that individuals may be stereotyped, as a result of one act or a few acts, as criminals or as heroes, even though most of their actions are law-abiding or are commonplace. Preferably we say: They have diverse tendencies; they behaved criminally, or heroically, in certain situations. It would be useful to think in a similar way about countercultures, with attention to the extent to which countercultural elements are mixed into a group's normative system. Even a few such elements may be of great significance in the self-definitions of the members and the attitudes and actions of the surrounding society, with consequent importance for social interaction.

3. Has authenticity or sincerity been taken into account in describing a countercultural group and designating its values? Many new movements have their hangers-on who participate not out of belief in the new set of values but for excitement or profit or other reasons extraneous to the counterculture. Those who have been called "plastic hippies"[26] are out for a weekend's fun more than a new way of life. Some students who join a protest are closer to fraternity highjinks than to revolution. Highly deviant fads may flourish briefly as a result of a

desire for attention and variety rather than a desire to promote an inverted value.

In *Radical Chic and Mau-Mauing the Flak Catchers*, Tom Wolfe described the "extra dividend" and "creamy dessert" (financial and emotional) that came to some Blacks out of confrontation tactics. They discovered that by doing the "savage number," it was no longer necessary "to play it cool and go in for pseudo-ignorant malingering [that beautiful phrase of Charles S. Johnson] and put your head into that Ofay Pig Latin catacomb code style of protest. Maumauing brought you respect in its cash forms: namely, fear and envy."[27]

Just as some Blacks played on the threat of violence (some of course *were* violent) and on fear among Whites, some wealthy Whites played "radical chic" at parties for the Black Panthers and others. This is not an uncommon pattern (one thinks of how Thorstein Veblen was lionized in New York in somewhat the same way). Nor was it clearly a matter of *nostalgie de la boue* (nostalgia for the mud) or "romanticizing of primitive souls," to use Wolfe's phrases, for there was also sincerity and conviction. But style and radical chic played an important part.

In addition, "there are those 'swingers' who hide behind the sexual revolution to justify the plain old-fashioned sort of infidelity that their parents' generation practiced with more discretion."[28] Every movement has its charlatans, Gerlach and Hine go on to note. Some persons who took the lead in proclaiming counter values have discovered that the power and glory and income were more attractive than the new world they first envisaged. It is sometimes difficult to sort out the religious con artists from the prophets. Some of the new psychotherapies, based on principles that contrast sharply with those more widely accepted, have proved to be quite old-fashioned in their greed and cruelty.

Of course, it is easy to challenge someone else's authenticity, to label them charlatans, especially if they are acting out values that one finds repugnant. While trying to avoid this error, we must at the same time recognize that countercultural groups are not likely to be able to escape these tendencies found so widely in the dominant society.

4. Is not the whole concept of counterculture riddled with class and ethnic bias in pluralistic societies? There is a growing tendency to view urban societies as so diverse culturally that each segment is, at the most, countercultural to the other segments. To some, we observed in Chapter One, the world seems almost entirely lacking in cultural coherence; anomie is endemic. Lyman and Scott describe a new

wave of thought they see sweeping over sociology. They call it "the sociology of the absurd," within which they include a number of perspectives—ethnomethodology, labeling theory, new developments in symbolic interactionism, and others—that proceed from the assumption that "the world is essentially without meaning" except as meaning emerges from interaction and bargaining.[29] In contrast are those who say that all societies are centered upon shared values and beliefs, with associated roles.[30]

As is often true with conflicting perspectives, a good case can be made for both, although each is qualified by the other. The degree of cultural fluidity and diversity, however, varies among societies and through time. Countercultural theory must deal with the wide range of social situations, from those where value coherence and agreement are high to those where the common core is small.[31] *To the degree that* the total society has a shared culture, there can be reciprocal countercultures. And each subsociety can also have countercultures. Punk rock is not just a blue-collar deviation from upper-class music; it also drastically contradicts the musical and other values of the working class from which it springs.

Because departures from the norm are newsworthy, because societies need their deviants, and because those involved in a "cultural revolution" want to emphasize their strength, there is a tendency to exaggerate cultural deviation. Empirical study of Western societies tends to support the view that most youths hold to the values of the larger society. From their study of Danish and American high schools, Kandel and Lesser conclude that "far from developing a contraculture in opposition to that of adult society, the adolescents we have studied express the values of adult society." A report on Britain's sixteen-year-olds found that most of a sample of sixteen thousand were thoroughly traditional. Studies by Yankelovich and Wattenberg show wider deviations, especially among college youth, but the total impression is one of fairly close identification with the values of society.[32]

Berger skillfully calls our attention to the tendency to create a cultural myth out of one segment of a generation while at the same time he notes the need to recognize cultural diversity. Our diagnoses of cultural generations tell us little about the actual distribution of experience in age groups:

> "Youth" is not James Dean rebelling with plenty of cause and choking us up with poignance, just as "age" is not snow-white Robert Frost barking his eccentric wisdom to students in search of a sage. My father was a

young man in the 1920s, but he never drank bathtub gin, nor leapt into the fountain at the Plaza, nor Charlestoned to jazz, and he certainly was not beautiful and gay and damned. But my bet is that his experience, such as it was, was actually more representative than that of those who captured the myth of the twenties. Culturally speaking, however, it is as if he never lived; history as myth ignores him. Until we free ourselves from this myth of homogeneous generations, we shall continue to be innocently surprised and troubled when surveys of adolescents reveal lots of young people to be quite ordinary reflections of their parental milieux.[33]

5. How counter must a statement or action be (assuming it to be expressive of some norm or value of a group) before we shall consider it countercultural? In the most limiting sense, we might say it has to be specifically a *reversal* of the established value. There is a long tradition of commentary and popular art on "The World Turned Upside Down." Note the use of such terms as "polarity," "reversal," "inversion" in the definitions I have cited. Berger and Berger speak of "diametric opposition" and Yablonsky of the "total rejection," among hippies, of the American social system. Indeed, these ideas are central to the original concept of counterculture.[34]

We have no way of saying with certainty, however, that sharply oppositional norms, statements, and actions are 180 degrees different from prevailing values. In the absence of ways of demonstrating their polarity, the use of the "upside down" and "reversal" themes is best seen as metaphorical rather than metrical. I do not mean by this statement to minimize the importance of cultural contrasts nor to suggest the lack of substantial agreement among persons with widely differing perspectives on the completeness of cultural reversals. When members of dominant groups say, "They are diametrically opposed to basic values," counterculturalists are likely to respond: "Yes, we are." These perceptions of an inverted cultural world, as well as independent measurements, are critical indicators of countercultures.

6. How is deviant behavior distinguished from countercultural behavior? Countercultural behavior is only one form of deviation; it is nonconformist and not aberrant, in Merton's terms.[35] The nonconformist believes he is right; he announces his deviancy, challenging the legitimacy of the established ways. The aberrant typically tries to hide his deviancy, accepting the prevailing norms but seeking to escape the penalties for violating them.

Whether a deviation is announced or hidden is not, we should note, a definitive distinction between nonconformity and aberrancy. There are times when the aberrant confesses his deviation, perhaps even seeks punishment. There are times when the nonconformist hides his deviation, perhaps to wait for a more strategic time to proclaim it or to avoid punishment. Several individuals or groups may claim credit, from hidden locations, for a deviant act that only some of them could have committed. The definitive distinction, then, is that the nonconformist takes pride in his deviant acts and believes they are moral, and the aberrant feels guilty and believes his acts are immoral or wrong. Empirically, of course, many actions fall between the poles. Guilt expressed in deflected ways or pride disguised by qualified support indicates the mixtures.[36]

In addition to being nonconformist, countercultural behavior is group-supported. Every form of culture is inherently a group phenomenon; it is a shared normative system. Although an individual nonconformist may lead the way to a counterculture, his deviancy lacks the essence of culture until it is accepted as normative by a group. Even more, individual descriptions of what an inverted life is, should be, or will be are not countercultural. The picture of unrestrained self-indulgence drawn by the Marquis de Sade, for example—an anarchic world of individuals pursuing unlimited pleasure—may affect the development of shared norms, but it is not itself normative. We know little about the behavioral influence of such writing, despite strong claims and counterclaims. Like other utopias and dystopias, it is important to the student of countercultures only as it influences the development of inverted norms or becomes part of symbolic tradition.

When counterculture is used to refer to deviation whether or not it is group-supported and nonconformist, rather than aberrant, we are prevented from distinguishing among behaviors which, although sometimes similar on the surface, are different in their causes and consequences. The shared quality, among other things, influences individuals' feelings about the guidelines; it strengthens convictions.[37] In the modal case, the deviants do not overtly feel guilty, although an unrecognized ambivalence is usual.

The quality of aberrancy or nonconformity is not determined wholly by the actor. Societal definitions and responses are also involved. I may feel aberrant, judging myself by personal or subcultural standards, while my behavior is seen as acceptable in the society at large. An Amish young person may feel guilty for riding in a car, but the non-Amish will not regard the behavior as aberrant. In a similar way, nonconformity may be proclaimed—an assumed deviation from dominant codes—only to have responses that say: Your nonconformity is within acceptable limits. A deviation is countercultural only when it is expressive of a group's nonconformist values or norms and at the same time is seen as aberrant when judged by the prevailing standards.

Given acts are not inevitably fixed in one or another of these categories. In a important paper, Ralph Turner has examined the fact that "collective acts of disruption and violence are sometimes viewed as expressions of social protest and sometimes as crime or rebellion [and often, in our terms, countercultural], leading to different community reactions."[38] The definition of a given act of disruption may be pushed in the direction of a counterculture by some persons, both opponents and supporters, who want to make it appear as violent and contranormative as possible, and pushed in the direction of "social protest," a form of communication, by other supporters and by those who want to limit the conflict, form a coalition, or use the protest designation in a bargaining process. Countercultural deviation, then, is partly defined situationally and politically. The cultural blueprint of a society—smudged by much handling—is sometimes ambiguous and difficult to decipher.

Horowitz and Liebowitz have made a similar point in their discussion of the changing relationship between social problems and the political process.[39] The distinction, in their view, "is becoming obsolete." They assume that a permanent one-way shift toward the removal of the distinctions between social problems and political questions is taking place—an issue that ought perhaps to be left open. I would prefer to say that, under certain circumstances, standards of behavior that had been considered deviant are pushed into the political arena by proponents who claim the right to have those standards recognized as political alternatives; and other forms of behavior that had been regarded as political alternatives are pushed out—or strong efforts are made to push them out—because they have been labeled countercultural or aberrant. Thus both the designation of what is deviant and the nature of the control mechanisms are partly determined by the political process.

When the distinction between deviation and political competition is easily drawn, we have:

1. Illegitimate deviation according to the powerful majority, and therefore Control by administrative means.	*and*	**2.** Legitimate dissent accepted as such by majority and minority and therefore Decision by political competition.

But when the decisive power of the majority or consensus suddenly breaks down:

1. Powerful minorities rise to say, "our view is legitimate," and try to push it into the political arena. E.g., pot smokers may join in protests or "smoke-ins" to have the use of marijuana legalized or to get the control procedures decriminalized.

and

2. Powerful groups arise to say of formerly accepted political dissent, "your view is illegitimate," and try to push it out of the political arena into the deviation category. E.g., "right to lifers" may proclaim that abortion is categorically evil and seek to have it criminalized or, at the least, removed from public support.[40]

In emphasizing the public process by which deviation is defined, Turner, Horowitz, Liebowitz, and others are making a valuable observation. Although they do not use these terms, for our purposes here we can translate that observation to read: What is countercultural is not determined by the intrinsic qualities of given acts but is partly determind by definitions that emerge from a political process. This observation can be interpreted in various ways. From a strictly empirical point of view, "the sociologist of deviance can only locate those violations of the norms that evoke sanctions of one kind or another." Alternately, Lyman observes, the sociologist can become an advocate "of an allegedly oppressed group, or of history itself," seeking "to define and locate evil in just those official elements that move against and demoralize his chosen people or trajectory of history."[41] That is the position taken by Gouldner. The powerful, in his view, are those who are able to "conventionalize their moral defaults," while subordinate groups find their deviations stigmatized.[42]

I do not intend, by these references, to indicate agreement with a thoroughly relativistic position. To attain a full definition of counterculture we need to explore the implications of relativism and of its repudiation.

Most social scientists have been strongly influenced by Sumner's view that "the mores can make anything right" and, more recently, by the argument that social events are what they are, and are evaluated as they are evaluated, because of the power that some persons have to label them in given ways. I read "the mores can make anything right" to mean: If the customs of the societies of the world are studied comparatively they will be seen to vary enormously. What is seen in one society as evil will be mandatory in another. Somewhere or other, anything—well, almost anything—goes. That is not to say that one applauds the fact. Sumner was making an empirical not a moral observation; and with a moment's thought it is clear to anyone that it should not be taken literally. Some practices, if built into the mores, would destroy a society. This leaves plenty of room for cruel, perverse, and harmful standards, as well as for creative, sustaining, and helpful ones. And the cultural relativist rightly reminds us to judge the former in the context of the life conditions of the people involved, not against some absolute standard.

Labeling theory also has implications for the definition of counterculture. In its extreme form it affirms that the power to label an event is the power to create it. To match the rhythm of Sumner's phrase: Labeling can make anything wrong. More moderately it is argued: Labeling enters into a process, along with other factors, to influence who will be considered, and will become, mentally ill or intellectually competent or deviant. Applied to countercultures, labeling theory would suggest that what is to be considered countercultural is not a system of values that are intrinsically different from, the inversion of, dominant values; it is a normative system so labeled. And those who carry out that system have been selected to do so by a labeling process. The central fact, Becker writes, is that deviance "is created by society . . . by making the rules whose infraction constitutes deviance, and by applying those rules to particular people and labeling them outsiders."[43]

Is countercultural deviation, then, defined solely by reference to a given society's values, or is it designated only by a process of labeling? Or, to suggest a third possibility, are larger human standards also involved? One can think of answers that range from the purely relative to the absolute, from "what is considered deviant is determined by a process of pulling and hauling among contending groups and by successful labeling" to "what is deviant is the violation of fundamental standards of good and evil." If the former is true, one can scarcely speak of a counterculture, since the culture to which it might be counter is inauthentic, the happenstance of political and economic power. If the latter is true, one has little reason to study countercultures, because they are inevitably inauthentic—contradictions of basic standards. Quite clearly I find both of these positions uncongenial.

To the purely relativist argument I would reply that on the social and psychological levels there are limits and constraints analogous to those on the biological and physical levels. Alexander Goldenweiser once remarked that canoes around the world have a great deal in common, not because of diffusion but because the properties of water and of available building materials set limits to the variation. Who wants a square canoe that sinks, however much the denial of that option limits one's freedom and creativity? In a similar vein, Charles Horton Cooley observed that "primary group ideals" were similar around the world—they emphasized loyalty, lawfulness, and freedom—because intimate small-group interaction could not successfully continue, over time, without such ideals. Not all values are cultural accidents; some seem to be built on the accumulated evidence of the consequences.[44]

Cooley was far from arguing that all values are the necessary projection of social and individual constants. His point, which is often neglected today, is that there are limits to cultural variability. Only when this observation is made into the one fundamental cultural principle does it become cultural absolutism, which can be stated in this way: Opposition to the "seven deadly sins"—or whatever set of principles one wants to declare as basic—is fundamental to all cultures; values that qualify that opposition are inevitably countercultural.

To the absolutist argument I would reply that circumstances change, that population grows or declines, that norms often reflect given levels of ability to satisfy needs, and that those levels change. Institutional structures get frozen until sometimes, as we shall observe, they produce the opposite results from those for which the structures seem designed. Society needs deviants not only because they furnish opportunities, as Durkheim noted, for reaffirming established values (or in the way described by Mandeville in his *Fable of the Bees*, where "Private Vices, Publick Benefits" are ironically linked), but also because new values are required when the conditions of life are significantly altered.

7. Is illegal behavior countercultural by definition? The answer is clearly no when the violation is aberrant rather than nonconformist. Nor is illegal behavior countercultural in those cases where a law does not represent the prevailing norms, when it is a "dead letter," a nearly forgotten survival of an earlier time, or when it has been adopted as a result of pressure from a small group with large interests, despite prevailing standards opposed to the law.

The question is more complicated when large groups of people, often drawing on earlier norms, regard a law as offensive and quite openly violate it, as was the case with the Eighteenth Amendment in the United States, 1920-33. This may be simply "the hallmark of a society with marked internal social differentiation," as Robin Williams puts it. Violation of marijuana laws can perhaps be regarded in the same way, except that in the minds of many people use of marijuana is identified with a larger complex of countercultural activities, in contrast with the traditional uses of alcohol more often envisaged during the period of Prohibition. This identification is likely to be reduced in the years ahead. In my view, illegal activities are not best regarded as countercultural if they are accepted by a large minority and are only lightly or symbolically punished. These two characteristics are not easily measured, of course, leaving us with an ambiguous line between the illegal-quasi-cultural and the illegal-countercultural.

An even more complicated relationship exists between counterculture and the law when it is prescisely the full acceptance of the law that is regarded as deviant, if not fully countercultural. Williams describes this situation with reference to the moral code, but it applies also to the overlapping legal code. Those who insist on the full enforcement of the law with reference to air and water pollution or strict adherence to rules opposed to racism, sexism, and ageism may be regarded as fanatics and troublemakers. As Williams observes, "institutions may thrive upon a relatively large amount of passive conformity and discreet deviation, but are often allergic to full and energetic conformity to their more 'utopian' norms."[45]

With these various qualifications in mind, we still need to remark that, yes, laws are part of culture and illegal behavior is countercultural if it is nonconformist, if it is accepted by a group as an expression of its normative system, and if it does not have substantial support, overt and covert, from the larger society. Terrorism as a way of life, for example, is countercultural. Pacifists who not only use the law to establish their own conscientious objection (which, I have suggested above, may be regarded as deviant despite the law) but burn the offices of the draft board are clearly countercultural. Because of the emotional weight of these two illustrations, we might forget that to call something countercultural is not to applaud it or lament it. Such judgments have to be made in each instance, in the light of particular values. To balance the case here, perhaps I ought to observe that Robin Hood—or the legend of Robin Hood—was also countercultural, as were the participants in the civil rights movement who sought to get a cup of coffee in a "legally" segregated restaurant.

8. Is there any sense in which "reactionary movements" (in the literal, nonpejorative meaning of a "return to earlier values") can be

considered countercultural? Such a return emphasizes opposition to the dominant culture of the time; but for its criticism it looks to earlier, fundamental, "primitive" elements. These may still have a place in the "official" culture, celebrated in song and story, although they are perhaps more utopian than traditional. The past to which reactionary movements appeal is partly imaginary (things are not as good as they used to be—and they never were) and partly historical. This is as true of the "return to the land" communes of contemporary America as of the traditional Old Believers of Russia.

Yet such movements may have strong countercultural elements. They invert many of the values of the dominant society, and they revive dormant values that, although once widely acepted, are now believed outmoded. These qualities are found in some of the varieties of "revitalization movements." In his influential paper on that subject, Anthony Wallace defined a revitalization movement as "a deliberate, organized, conscious effort by members of a society to construct a more satisfying culture."[46] Of the six varieties he described, only "revivalistic" is specifically characterized by efforts to recover values and customs that are presumed to have existed earlier; most of the others (nativistic, millenarian, and messianic, for example) mix such revivals with new utopian and imported elements.

In a later discussion of revitalization movements, Wallace develops a useful chemical analogy to suggest how the old can be mixed with the new to form a compound out of disparate elements. Substances may exist in separate form within the same solution, but when a catalyst is added and the temperature raised (by analogy, when a prophet or charismatic leader appears in the heat of societal disorder), new compounds may be formed. Thus "mutually contradictory beliefs and customs" combine into a new structure.[47] Some countercultures, I suggest, may have reactionary qualities. These are blended, however, with new elements and utopian elements to produce standards sharply at odds with the dominant contemporary system of values.

9. Is society moving toward some of the norms and values of oppositional groups? The time perspective is critical in defining counterculture. Just as previously accepted but now defunct or dormant values may be seen as countercultural, so contemporary reversals of norms may in the future be absorbed into the dominant culture. (Others, of course, die out or continue as oppositional cultural elements.) The perception and the reality of this process of absorption affect the survival of countercultural groups and influence their recruit-

ment processes. At a distance in time or space, we are likely to see the similarities of a group to its cultural environment and its roots in that environment. Close up, we see the differences.

In the 1930s some "premature antifascists" were jailed or denied jobs or otherwise ostracized, some of them for supporting actions that a few years later, during the war against facism, were embodied in official policy. Leaders of the Puritan Commonwealth in England in the 1650s were certain that the Ranters and the Diggers were countercultural—premature democrats, one might say—and undoubtedly they were, in religious, economic, political, and other ways. It is difficult to describe precisely the culture against which the radical religious sects protested; but royalist, aristocrat, and Presbyterian of the commonwealth alike agreed on respect for property, the reality of God, the literal truth of the Bible and of heaven and hell, and the validity of a hierarchical society. "New Presbyter is but old Priest writ large, " John Milton wrote. It is not difficult to imagine the response of the full range of conservative Englishmen to the Ranter Christmas carol (1650):

> They prate of God; believe it, fellow creatures,
> There's no such bugbear; all was made by Nature.
> We know all came of nothing, and shall pass
> Into the same condition once it was,
> By Nature's power; and that they grossly lie
> That say there's hope of immortality.
> Let them but tell us what a soul is, then
> We will adhere to these mad brain-sick men.[48]

A generation earlier, the Puritans themselves were seen as deviants by the royalists. The Puritans were premature republicans, as it turned out. They worked for the interests of the emerging middle classes against the nobility (and against the landless wage-earner) in the name of a divine mission to establish the City of God. It was not only that the power base of the King was threatened, but many fundamental beliefs were challegned: The Anglican doctrine of free will was replaced by belief in predestination. Altars were removed from churches and the rites and symbols of the Anglicans were attacked as "popish superstition." It is not surprising that political leaders (e.g., King James I and King Charles I) and religious leaders (e.g., Richard Bancroft, Bishop of London and later Archbishop of Canterbury), sought to make heresy and sedition synonymous. Martyrdom, however, seemed only to strengthen the Puritan opposition.

We shall be wise to try to discover ways to identify those countercultural elements that seem likely to persist and to be absorbed, for they are diagnostic of important societal needs and trends.

10. Are cultural conflicts across societal lines indicative of the presence of a counterculture? As I use the term, counterculture refers to normative and value conflicts within a society, not to those among societies. Ethnocentric judgments of other peoples—beliefs that the standards of other societies are foolish, evil, and ugly—are widespread.[49] Frequently, in fact, they are seen as the inversions of the right ways of doing things, and in this sense they can be considered substantively as countercultural. The first Europeans to come to East Africa, Middleton tells us, were believed by the Lugbara literally to be physically inverted. More than that, all of those distant, in a mythical or social sense, were believed characterized by "physical inversion, cannibalism, incest, miracle-working, absence of bridewealth, no fighting, living outside the bounds of society."[50] To regard such contrasts as the Lugbara draw between themselves and outsiders as indications of countercultures, however, would be to extend the meaning of the term far beyond my intent. Countercultures emerge *within* a society as expressions of deeply experienced personal frustrations and group conflicts. They represent efforts to create a cultural world in which new identities can be formed or tenuous ones validated and strengthened around congenial values and norms.

The distinction between external culture conflict, often expressed as ethnocentrism, and internal culture conflict, indicated by the opposition to countercultures, is sometimes difficult to draw in practice. Before one can say that the values of a group are countercultural, one needs to know the extent to which that group is fully participant in the society in question. It is one thing to set a group's culture sharply against a dominant society to which one scarcely belongs; it is something else to set a culture against a society of which one is—or could be—fully a member. When one thinks about it, "membership in a society" becomes a complicated concept, not easily measured. Here I want only to suggest the need for considering it as a variable in any full definition of counterculture.

The values and norms of the Ghost Dance among the Plains Indians, 1870-90, were sharply in conflict with those of the dominant American culture. Black power protests now rising among young South Africans are based on the conviction that official values are repugnant. Black Muslims in the United States until at least the mid-

1960s proclaimed a set of values many of which reverse those of the larger society. Members of the Hare Krishna movement, often from middle- and upper-class background, accept a mode of life contrasting in many ways with the one in which they were raised. These four groups, I am suggesting, are progressively more fully participants in the society within which they lived or live—those in the Ghost Dance least, in Hare Krishna most. By the same token, their value systems can be regarded as progressively more countercultural:

Intersocietal culture conflict					Intrasocietal countercultures	
X	Ghost Dance	Black Power in South Africa	Black Muslims before 1965	Hare Krishna		X

The placement of these illustrations may be off the mark, but the brief comments may help to indicate that intrasocietal cultural conflicts vary widely in the degree to which they are countercultural, because some are, in an important sense, intersocietal.

There will be occasion to refer to some of these ten questions from time to time in the chapters that follow. It is unlikely that they draw the boundary around the territory of countercultures with sufficient clarity or completeness. They may, however, help us move toward some degree of consensus.

Culture, Subculture, and Counterculture

We need to be clear on what is cultural about counterculture. Among the numerous definitions, I prefer those that focus on culture as a blueprint, a system of normative guidelines. In the words of Kluckhohn and Kelly, culture is "all those historically created designs for living, explicit and implicit, rational, irrational, and nonrational, that exist at any given time as potential guides for the behavior of men."[51]

In parallel terms, then, counterculture is all those *situationally* created designs for living formed in contexts of high anomie and intrasocietal conflict, the designs being inversions of, in sharp opposition to, the historically created designs.

Defined in this way, both terms draw a distinction between norms and behavior. This distinction seems clear enough, but there is a strong temptation to think of culture as "the way of life" of a people or group and then to be ambiguous about whether "way of life" means the way things are in fact done or the way things ought to be done according to the standards of the group in question. Linton tried to reduce this ambiguity, but may have contributed to it, by distinguishing among "real culture" (the actual behavior of members of a society), "culture construct" (the mode of the real series), and "ideal patterns" (the consensus of opinion on how people should behave).[52]

Behavior is partly caused by, and partly congruent with, culture, but it is also caused by the interacting situation and by individual tendencies. These distinctions are obscured by thinking of "real culture." It is equally important to keep clearly in mind the distinction between counterculture as a blueprint for behavior and the actual behavior of those who accept that blueprint as a model. Some people behave in ways that correspond with countercultural guidelines but don't accept them as normative. Their violations of the dominant norms are aberrant, in Merton's sense of the term; they are not based on commitment to the countercultural norms. Other persons may have such a commitment, yet behave according to dominant standards.

Perhaps these distinctions can be clarified by indicating the various possible combinations of belief and behavior, as shown in Figure 2.2. Such a model overly simplifies the situation, of course, by disregarding ambivalence and borderline cases, which may be the most numerous; but it emphasizes the need to distinguish between behavior

		Belief in the Countercultural Blueprint	
		yes	no
Behavior According to the Countercultural Blueprint	yes	counterculturalists	aberrant deviationists
	no	potential or hidden counterculturalists	culturalists

Figure 2.2

and norms. The combinations in the model represent very different sets of causes and consequences.

Most contemporary societies are divided to some degree along ethnic, regional, class, occupational, and other lines. It is useful to think of these divisions, if they are persistent enough and deep enough, as marking off subsocieties. Paralleling these structural lines are cultural differences of varying strength and range. An ethnic group that is lingually and religiously different, geographically concentrated, and economically differentiated is likely to be characterized by norms, values, artifacts, shared memories, and other items that differ in many ways from the dominant culture. Other groups may have fewer links, as for example the vocabulary, emphasis on particular skills, and shared perceptions of an occupational group. Whatever the range, the subculture becomes meaningful insofar as it is expressive of a network of social relationships.

I will not comment further on the concept of subculture here,[53] except to examine its relationship to counterculture. Quite clearly subculture cannot be subsumed under counterculture. The religious views, speech patterns, preferred foods, or other normative characteristics of an ethnic group are primarily the product not of conflict with the larger society but of socialization and interaction within a subsociety. The personal tendencies of children born into such a subsociety have not gone into the process of shaping its normative system.

It is not quite so clear whether the relationship might be reversed, with countercultures being considered a subset of subcultures. Ones decision rests largely on whether it seems wiser to emphasize the similarities or the differences between the two terms. Both refer to normative systems that are less comprehensive than and to some degree separate from the total culture. One is defined primarily by its reversal of the dominant norms, however, whereas this characteristic is incidental or lacking in the other.

In my judgment, we understand the processes involved better by keeping the two terms analytically separate, while recognizing that the phenomena they refer to are sometimes empirically mixed. Countercultures are emergent phenomena, not rooted in traditional subsocieties, ethnic communities, occupational groups, or other fairly stable social structures. Normally, a change in the surrounding society leads to quite rapid change in countercultures; subcultures evolve more slowly. As expressions of norms and values sharply at variance with those of society at large, countercultures tend to be defined, both by themselves and by others, as much by what they are set against as by their own normative system.

The behavior of the members of a group may manifest cultural elements, subcultural patterns (reflecting sharp class boundaries or different ethnic backgrounds), and aberrant acts of some individuals, as well as countercultural values. In his fascinating collection of essays *Cony-Catchers and Bawdy Baskets: An Anthology of Elizabethan Low Life*, Salgãdo brings together descriptions not only of "an anti-society with its own rules and rulers" but also of class variations and individual deviations. This empirical mixture, which is not uncommon, should not cause us to fail to make necessary analytic distinctions.

In a later chapter I shall discuss the concept of "anti-language." In his paper by that title, Halliday remarks that an anti-language is nobody's mother tongue. It is an emergent form of speech that separates the users from a hurtful, hated society; it is used to oppose that society. Typically it is a second language. Similarly, a counterculture is nobody's native culture. Although another culture has been learned, an inverted normative system develops out of the conflict and frustration of some of those who have been socialized to the values of the larger society. Despite their training, they have been thwarted in their efforts to achieve those values, have seen them regularly denied in practice, or have come to see them as shoddy.

Another way to make this same contrast is to note that counterculturalists are heretics, not aliens, using these terms in a purely descriptive sense.[54]

A comment on one additional concept may be helpful here. The term "alternative culture" is now quite widely used, partly to avoid using counterculture (some persons not liking the way it ties new normative systems into a dialectic with the dominant culture) and partly to subsume it among various divergent choices. Subcultures as well as countercultures can be considered, in this latter sense, alternatives.

We will be wise, in my judgment, not to use alternative as a synonym or a replacement for counterculture. An alternate route, in a familiar usage, is a different road to a destination served also by another, perhaps more familiar, road. A countercultural road leads to a different destination—in the opposite direction.

Linton used the term alternative in a more limited way to refer to modes of action that are not common and are not preferred according to dominant standards but are at least acceptable and seen as part of the larger culture.[55] It is in that way that I will use the concept of alternative.

The distinctions among these several terms can be drawn together as in Figure 2.3 to indicate their relationships.

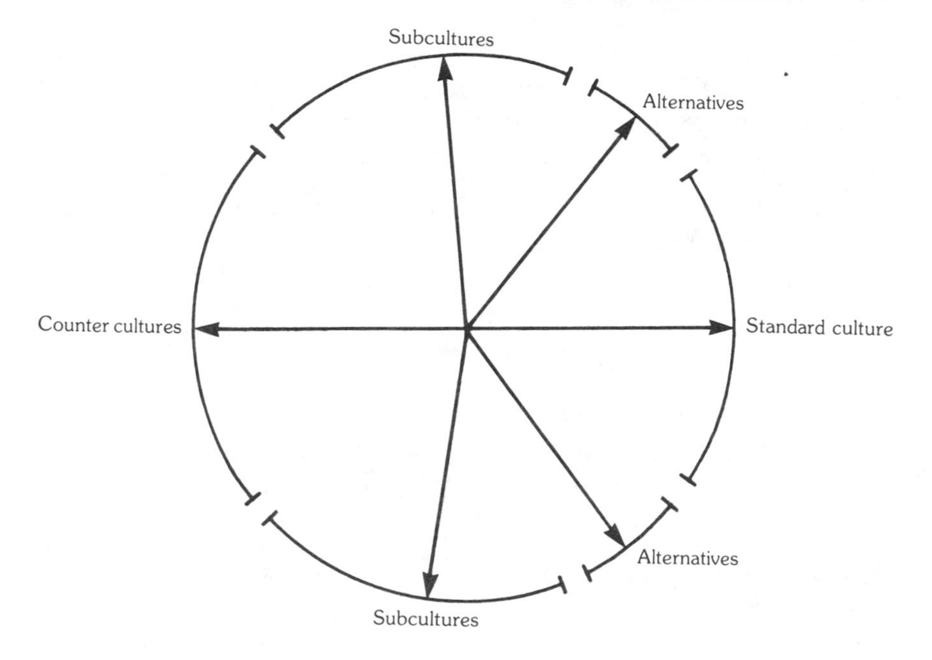

Measurement of Countercultures

We can develop an adequate theory of countercultures only when we have identified the essential elements and have learned how to measure them. Measurement is refined definition. Without more precision in our measurement of the several dimensions of countercultures, we cannot attain the clear definitions required. Measurement is not a substitute for but a complement to full ethnographic description. It makes comparisons possible across space and time.

Some devotees are doubtless aghast at these statements, measurement being so out of harmony with their views of the world. So also are some humanists, who see attempts to measure human behavior as just one more cause of disenchantment.[56] In a less analytic mood, I would also be aghast. It is easy to affirm that values are to be lived, not examined. My dominant mood, however, resists the separation of analysis from life and action. Until we examine contexts and the range of choices, we cannot be confident that our values are well based and well served.

Viewing the problem of identifying and measuring countercultures from the perspective of the sociology of knowledge, we see the differing positions from which they can be observed. No one position is likely to furnish a rich description.[57] Throughout this essay I shall rely on at least four sets of observations to identify and measure countercultures:

1. Perceived: Outsiders, those who hold to the dominant culture, see a set of values as sharply oppositional.
2. Experienced: Participants see their values as sharply at odds with the establishment.
3. Measured: Observers systematically record and compare the values both of oppositional groups and of the majority.
4. Interpreted: Informal observations form the basis of judgment. Although not readily scaled or replicated, such judgments can enlarge the more precise but thinner descriptions obtained by measurement.

The degree of correspondence—or lack of correspondence—among the pictures drawn from these different perspectives is itself an important sociological fact. It is not certain that all of the blind men together can fully describe an elephant, but we need not see it only as a spear or a snake. Most of what we know about late medieval and early modern radical sects was written by opponents. A great deal of what has been said and written about contemporary countercultures has come from dedicated opponents or from participants and admirers. Only by comparing the range of views and trying to complement them with more systematically gathered evidence can we enlarge our understanding.

We have the beginnings of a sociometry of dominant values[58] and of measurement of countercultures.[59] Systematic content analysis of the underground press, of statements by participants in oppositional groups, and of authors' appraisals can help us deal more critically with the exuberant statements, both pro and con, that are the more common form of definition.

From such sources, Musgrove has designed scales of countercultural values that are valuable illustrations of efforts to measure inverted standards. Respondents were asked to indicate their agreement or disagreement with a series of forty-eight statements. When the responses were analyzed, five factors, which he treats as indicative of basic countercultural values, emerged. Three factors were quite clear-cut, at least in the mathematical sense: support for a fun ethic and uninhibited relationships and opposition to hierarchies and constraint; for a simple, nautral life, against boundaries; and for pop art, mysticism, handicraft, and the communal rearing of children, against organizational regulation.

The other two factors were more complex. One reflected concern with runaway technology, pollution, and depersonalization. The relevant statements formed what Musgrove called the Ruskin-Southey scale. The other he called the Godwin-Shelley scale: "It is non-deferential, anarchist, reformist, activist; it is opposed to rules and law-enforcement agencies; it is critical of the family because of its power structure. It is against boundaries. It rejects the work ethic. It supports obscenity, drug-use and communal living."[60]

Here is a sample of the statements used to form the Musgrove scales:

> Poets and mystics are of more value than scientists and engineers.
> We all need vivid, exciting and exotic experiences which expand our minds.
> The contemplative Eastern life has many attractions.
> The present family structure is outmoded.
> Education should be unending gaiety.
> Work should be done when it's fun.

And, of course, there were some that require reverse scoring:

> It's pitiable that people need artificial stimulants to "turn on."
> We must have respect for authority.
> Legal marriage must be preserved.
> Pop art and pop poetry are a huge confidence trick.

The themes contained in Musgrove's scales are similar to those that appear in a comparative content analysis, by Spates and Levin, of the "underground" press and middle-class journals. Although significant overlap appears from the sentence-by-sentence analysis of more than a dozen journals, a clear instrumental-expressive contrast is the decisive finding. The instrumentalism of the middle-class journals is shown in the emphasis on achievement, rationality, and economic-occupational effort. The underground press saw emphasis on achievement as the rat race, rational behavior as a narrowing of goals, economic behavior as exploitation—all leading to the repression of more vital needs and expressive values. Self-expression, concern for others, a need for affiliation, and a mystical, often Oriental religious and philosphical outlook were major themes in the underground journals. Seventy-five per cent of the items fitted the expressive categories, indicating "a well-established contra-culture"; but it should be noted that such items were not lacking in the middle-class journals, either in the late 1950s or the late 1960s.[61]

An additional content study of 1970-72 issues (some Canadian and English underground and "straight" journals having been added), revealed no shift toward more emphasis on expressive values in the middle-class journals—a shift that Roszak, Reich, and others had predicted. The underground journals did change in the 1967-69 to 1970-72 period, with expressive themes appearing much less frequently in the later issues, while instrumental and political themes appeared more frequently.[62]

The American cultural scene is quite volatile in this "post-industrial" era, however. A recent Harris Survey shows strong support for what seem more nearly expressive than instrumental values: 89 per cent say they are seeking "experiences that make you peaceful inside"; 81 per cent want to be involved in activities "where people cooperate rather than compete"; 91 per cent want "ample opportunities to use their creative talents"; 72 per cent prefer "breaking up big things and getting back to more humanized living."[63] What is countercultural today may also be tomorrow, or it may disappear, or it may flow into the dominant cultural stream.

Perhaps we can hope for a time when continuities and shifts in basic values will be monitored as carefully and fully as the weather and the stock market—monitored in such a way that we can compare four sets of responses: the values of straights; their perceptions of the values of counterculturalists; the values of counterculturalists; and their perceptions of the values of straights. Such information would allow us to build on the increasingly rich data available from research centers and polling agencies by adding comparative perspectives. Of course, the value questions would remain. Detection of a falling barometer and probable rain can mean the likelihood of a ruined picnic for some and a better crop for others.

Notes

1. See J. Milton Yinger, "Anomie, Alienation, and Political Behavior," 1972, p. 172.

2. Walter Kaufman, in *Alienation*, Richard Schacht, editor, 1971, p. xlix.

3. Kenneth Westhues, *Society's Shadow: Studies in the Sociology of Countercultures*, 1972, pp. 9-10.

4. Fred Davis, *On Youth Subcultures: The Hippie Variant*, 1971, p. 4.

5. *Ibid.*, pp. 14-15.

6. Philip Slater, *The Pursuit of Loneliness: American Culture at the Breaking Point*, 1971, p. 100.

7. *Ibid.*, p. 103.

8. Martin Gardner, review of *Powers of Mind*, by Adam Smith, *New York Review of Books*, Dec. 11, 1975, p. 46.

9. Y. N. Davidov, "Counter-Culture—A Symptom of Development or an Indication of Decay?" unpublished manuscript, 1978, p. 19.

10. D. Lawrence Wieder and Don H. Zimmerman, "Generational Experience and the Development of Freak Culture," 1974; see also Karl Mannheim, *Essays in the Sociology of Knowledge*, 1952.

11. Nathan Adler, *The Underground Stream: New Life Styles and the Antinomian Personality*, 1972, p. 44; see also Richard Miller, *Bohemia: The Protoculture Then and Now*, 1977, chap. 3.

12. Quoted by S. M. Lipset in *Technology, Power, and Social Change*, Charles A. Thrall and Jerold M. Starr, editors, 1972, p. 86.

13. See Davis, 1971; Richard Mills, *Young Outsiders: A Study of Alternative Communities*, 1973; and Lewis Yablonsky, *The Hippie Trip*, 1968.

14. Jerold M. Starr, "The Peace and Love Generation: Changing Attitudes Toward Sex and Violence Among College Youth," 1974.

15. Mills, 1973, pp. 104-8.

16. J. Milton Yinger, "Contraculture and Subculture," 1960, p. 629. This is a field theoretical definition: Countercultures can be fully defined only by taking into account cultural, characterological, and structural elements and, most importantly, their interaction. On the cultural level there are values in conflict. On the characterological level the definition refers to the individual tendencies that directly influence the rise of countercultures. There is a sense in which an infant is "born into" a culture, although we all influence our cultural milieu to some degree. One is not born into a counterculture, however, but moves into it and helps to shape it, in protest against his native culture. The third element in the definition is the social structure and the interactions that go on within it. One cannot define a counterculture without continuous reference to its relationship with the larger society and its culture. It emerges from and develops in the context of that relationship.

17. Clyde Kluckhohn in *Toward a General Theory of Action*, Talcott Parsons and Edward Shils, editors, 1962, pp. 395-96.

18. Robin Williams, Jr., *American Society*, 1970, p. 442; emphasis in original.

19. Milton Rokeach, *The Nature of Human Values*, 1973.

20. David Matza and Gresham Sykes, "Juvenile Delinquency and Subterranean Values," 1961.

21. Yinger, 1960, p. 633.

22. Erik Erikson, *Childhood and Society*, rev. ed., 1963, pp. 285-287. Kai Erikson has skillfully used this theme in *Everything in Its Path*, 1976, pp. 79-93. The term culture, he notes, refers both to the ways a people induce conformity in behavior and outlook and to "the ways in which they organize diversity."

23. See David DeLeon, *The American as Anarchist*, 1979.

24. Robert Merton, "Structural Analysis in Sociology," in *Approaches to the Study of Social Structure*, Peter Blau, editor, 1975, p. 35.

25. See, for example, Joseph Berke, editor, *Counter-Culture: The Creation of an Alternative Society*, 1969; Charles Glock and Robert Bellah, editors, *The New Religious Consciousness*, 1976; Theodore Roszak, *The Making of a Counter Culture*, 1969; and Robert Wuthnow, *The Consciousness Reformation*, 1976b.

26. Yablonsky, 1968 (note 13 above).

27. Tom Wolfe, *Radical Chic and Maumauing the Flak Catchers*, 1970, p. 120.

28. Luther Gerlach and Virginia H. Hine, *Lifeway Leap: The Dynamics of Change in America*, 1973, p. 184.

29. Stanford Lyman and Marvin Scott, *A Sociology of the Absurd*, 1970.

30. Edward Shils, *Center and Periphery: Essays in Macrosociology*, 1975.

31. See David Aberle, "Shared Values in Complex Societies," 1950, and Williams, 1970 (note 18 above), chap. 10.

32. Denise B. Kandel and Gerald S. Lesser, *Youth in Two Worlds*, 1972, p., 168; National Children's Bureau, *Britain's Sixteen-Year-Olds*, 1976; Daniel Yankelovich, *The New Morality: A Profile of American Youth in the 70's*, 1974; and Ben Wattenberg, *The Real America: A Surprising Examination of the State of the Union*, 1974.

33. Bennett M. Berger, *Looking for America: Essays on Youth, Suburbia, and Other American Obsessions*, 1971, p. 41.

34. Barbara Babcock, editor, *The Reversible World*, 1978; Peter Berger and Brigitte Berger, "The Blueing of America," 1971, p. 20; Yablonsky, 1968, p. 320; and Yinger, 1960 (note 16 above).

35. Robert Merton and Robert Nisbet, editors, Contemporary Social Problems, 1966, chap. 15.

36. Gresham Sykes and David Matza, "Techniques of Neutralization: A Theory of Delinquency," 1957.

37. Frank Young, "Reactive Subsystems," 1970, and Rosabeth Kanter, *Commitment and Community: Communes and Utopias in Sociological Perspective*, 1972.

38. Ralph Turner, "The Public Perception of Protest," 1969. See also Marvin Olsen, "Perceived Legitimacy of Social Protest Actions," 1968, and Michael Lipsky, "Protest as a Political Resource," 1968.

39. Irving Horowitz and Martin Liebowitz, "Social Deviance and Political Marginality: Toward A Redefinition of the Relation Between Sociology and Politics," 1968.

40. Adapted from George E. Simpson and J. Milton Yinger, *Racial and Cultural Minorities*, 1972, p. 666.

41. Stanford Lyman, *The Seven Deadly Sins: Society and Evil*, 1978, p. 3.

42. Alvin Gouldner, *The Coming Crisis of Western Sociology*, 1970.

43. Howard S. Becker, *Outsiders: Studies in the Sociology of Deviance*, 1963, pp. 8-9. His full discussion is more qualified.

44. The limits to cultural variability have been widely observed in cultural anthropology for some time. I shall add only one reference, from Robert Lowie: "Notwithstanding undeniable differences in outward manifestations, savagery and civilization display the same sentiments with reference to basic human relations. Not unbridled self-indulgence, but restraint; not brutality, but kindness; not neglect of one's neighbors, but regard for them, are prescribed as proper goals of social conduct. What differs is essentially *the extent of the group* to which these sentiments are applied." (From *Scientific Aspects of the Race Problem*, H.S. Jennings *et al.*, 1941, 233. Italics mine.)

45. Williams, 1970 (note 18 above), p. 420.

46. Anthony Wallace, "Revitalization Movements," 1956, p. 265.

47. Anthony Wallace, *Religion: An Anthropological View*, 1966, pp. 210-1.

48. From Christopher Hill, *The World Turned Upside Down: Radical Ideas During the English Revolution*, 1975, p.184.

49. See William Graham Sumner, *Folkways*, 1906; R. A. LeVine and Donald T. Campbell, *Ethnocentrism: Theories of Conflict, Ethnic Attitudes and Group Behavior*, 1972; and Vittorio Lanternari, "Ethnocentrism and Ideology," 1980.

50. John Middleton, *Lugbara Religion: Ritual and Authority Among an East African People*, 1960, p. 236.

51. Clyde Kluckhohn, *Culture and Behavior*, 1962, p. 54.

52. Ralph Linton, *The Cultural Background of Personality*, 1945, pp. 43-53.

53. See David Arnold, editor, *The Sociology of Subcultures*, 1970; Gary Fine and Sherryl Kleinman, "Rethinking Subculture: An Interactionist Analysis," 1979; and Michael Clarke, "On the Concept of 'Sub-Culture'," 1974.

54. See Keith Roberts, "Toward a Generic Concept of Counter-Culture," 1978, p. 120; M. A. K. Halliday, "Anti-Languages," 1976; and Gamini Salgado, editor, *Cony-Catchers and Bawdy Baskets: An Anthology of Elizabethan Low Life*, 1972.

55. Ralph Linton, *The Study of Man*, 1936, chap. 16.

56. See Max Weber, *From Max Weber*, 1946, chap. 5; see also Berger, 1971 (note 32 above), for a valuable discussion of this issue.

57. Robert Merton, "Insiders and Outsiders: A Chapter in the Sociology of Knowledge," 1972.

58. See, for example, Rokeach, 1973 (note 19 above); Yankelovich, 1974 (note 31 above); Robin Williams, Jr., "The Concept of Values," 1968; and William McCready, with Andrew Greeley, *The Ultimate Values of the American Population*, 1976.

59. In addition to the works of Starr, 1974 (note 14 above); Wattenberg, 1974 (note 31 above); Wieder and Zimmerman, 1974 (note 10 above); and Wuthnow, 1976b (note 24 above), see Frank Musgrove, *Ecstasy and Holiness: Counter Culture and the Open Society*, 1974; James Spates, "Counterculture and Dominant Culture Values," 1976; and James Spates and Jack Levin, "Beats, Hippies, and the Hip Generation and the American Middle Class: An Analysis of Values," 1972.

60. Musgrove, 1974, p. 91.

61. Spates and Levin, 1972, p. 342.

62. Spates, 1976.

63. Cleveland *Plain Dealer*, May 17, 1979, p. 22A.

Chapter Three

The Sources of Countercultures

The form and intensity of specific countercultures can be explained in part by particular circumstances—in the contemporary world by disillusionment following World War II (and, in the United States, the Vietnam War); by the impact of television and the mass media generally; by affluence, urbanization, and the increase in education; by the availability of illegal drugs in societies that consume enormous varieties and amounts of legal drugs; or by other factors in different settings. To such particular sources, however, should be added those that are recurrent or are endemic to humanity. These latter will be the focus of attention here. By identifying those sources of most general significance, those that can be observed in many times and places, I seek to advance our understanding of countercultures as a continuous part of human experience.

Although one can distinguish analytically between the sources of countercultures and their manifestations, some of the latter flow back into the sociocultural environment from which they came, becoming sources of an ongoing countercultural process. That process is, in the first instance, an indicator of social change, of a society experiencing severe stress. Certain conditions, which I shall attempt to summarize, create individuals who are particularly likely to invent, embrace, and expound countercultural values. If those most likely to be influenced by such conditions are in communication with others who are vulnerable, although not so strongly susceptible to oppostional values, the situation is created for the appearance of a countercultural group. If the conditions are severe and the number affected is large, the group or groups not only will symbolize social change but can help to precipitate a social movement that effects change.

In this chapter, however, we shall be dealing with countercultures simply as consequences. Many kinds of social change upset the moving equilibrium of a social order, the structural-cultural-characterological balance of a given time, and make the appearance of countercultural movements more likely. Among the factors discussed, none is a sufficient cause, although some may be necessary. For purposes of exposition, I shall divide them into structural and interactional, cultural, and individual sources. This is an analytic distinction, however, that should not be allowed to obscure their interdependence.

Structural and Interactional Sources of Countercultures

1. Economic factors. Drastic reorganization of the ways in which people make their living. The promises and frustrations of economic abundance.

These conditions are bound up not only with the power distribution and with accustomed reciprocities but also with shared values and norms. Rapid economic growth and related political changes, whether in industrialized or developing societies, are closely connected with occupational changes and magnify their destabilizing impact.[1] The development of bureaucratic and impersonal work situations is one of the critical economic shifts that, in the course of history, have been associated with countercultures. In his examination of six periods of economic change and growth, Musgrove found countercultural tendencies associated with all but one.[2] Perhaps the Renaissance period seems not to have fitted the pattern, Musgrove suggests, because it was not a period of extensive migration and population growth—as the others were—thus indicating the interdependence of the influencing factors.

The nature of the linkages between economic changes and the development of countercultures is complex. A rapidly expanding economy promises abundance, even as the related occupational changes impose difficult problems of adjustment. It is well documented that a high proportion of those who have opposed the established economic system during recent years in the West have come from advantaged families. In addition, as Richard Flacks, David Westby, and others have shown, the families have tended to be non-Protestant and humanist. They have stressed critical thought, autonomy, and left-of-center political views. Parents have been much less likely to be in business than in the professions. The students most often have been in nonvocational programs, in courses of study farthest from the economic base of the corporate structure, matching their parents' relative independence from the structure. Their independence is partly illusory, however, because employment opportunites that match their level of training, particularly for those outside the technical fields, were shrinking even as the number of candidates was increasing.[3] Perhaps for the first time in American history a substantial proportion of middle-class youths faced the possibility of being less well off than their parents.

The impact of being on the "periphery" is not solely a result of the occupational changes. Values and interests derived from their families inclined some students toward courses of study that made them particularly vunerable to the changes.

There are other, more general influences. A "Catch-22" is connected with the abundance. It may require, along with luck and fortunate parentage, hard work and skill, which some of those in an affluent society are not prepared to furnish. Some critical resources prove to be nonrenewable just when a society has come to depend upon them. And most importantly, desires run ahead even of rapidly increasing resources. Although needs are more fully satisfied, wants continue to expand; the feeling of deprivation grows despite steadily improving economic circumstances. For some, economic success proves to be a fraud and a disaster, either for promising much while furnishing little, considering the expanding appetites, or for the ugliness and rapacity that follow in its wake. Musgrove speaks of the "anarchism, attacks on authority and the family, the rejection of the work ethic and deep interest in communes (and drugs)" that characterize some counterculturalists, and of others who are "far from being anarchists, but their interest in the environment, their distaste for technology, their concern that work should be 'expressive' and human" lead them to repudiate the economic order.[4] This is a description of protests associated with economic growth and industrialization in England in the early nineteenth century.

Similar protests appeared in an affluent America a century and a half later. A pro-environment and antitechnology movement proclaims that the prevailing economic order is based on twisted values. At the same time a hedonistic version of the counterculture, focusing on the promise rather than the costs of affluence, attacks the economic order from the opposite side. "The core of the old culture," Philip Slater writes, "is scarcity."

> Everything in it rests upon the assumption that the world does not contain the werewithal to satisfy the needs of its human inhabitants. From this it

> follows that people must compete with one another for these scarce resources—lie, swindle, steal, and kill, if necessary. . . . The key flaw in the old culture is, of course, the fact that the scarcity is spurious—man made in the case of bodily gratifications and man-allowed or man-maintained in the case of material goods. . . . The new culture is based on the assumption that important human needs are easily satisfied and that the resources for doing so are plentiful. Competition is unnecessary and the only danger to humans is human aggression. There is no reason outside of human perversity for peace not to reign and for life not to be spent in the cultivation of joy and beauty.[5]

If Slater had wondered whether wants as well as needs could be easily satisfied, and had puzzled over the ingenuity and toughness of human perversity, his opposition to the "old culture" might have been different. Its very productivity might have been the subject of criticism because of the human and environmental costs. Instead, ironically, the "economy of abundance" has released in him, and in others, an abundant optimism. In a strange way, Slater sounds like a countercultural Norman Vincent Peale. Our problems are not deep. Here are seven easy steps to salvation. Needless to say, their steps are on different paths, but their moods are similar.

2. Demographic factors. Changes in the size, location, age distribution, and sex ratio of a population.

> *Bliss was it that dawn to be alive, But to be young was very heaven.*
>
> William Wordsworth, *The Prelude*

In writing of his youthful enthusiasm for the French Revolution, Wordsworth suggests to our minds that most revolutionary and countercultural movements are led by young people, particularly young men. What the television camera tells us today, historical records tell us about the past. Most of the radical sectarians during the English Civil War, for example, were still under thirty when the war ended. Leaders of the Bolshevik Revolution made their commitments to the revolution at an average age of seventeen, although they were much older when they attained power.[6]

Societies or communities with a concentration of young persons are likely, if other factors support the trend, to experience oppositional movements.[7] Such a concentration almost always reflects a period of rapid population growth that lowers the average age. The English population grew rapidly between 1600 and 1640, a period of increasingly important religious and political protests. The average age of the German population fell steadily from 1880 until 1930. "By the time the Depression struck, the labor market was glutted with young people, who made up the largest potential work force in German history."[8]

A brief period of growth followed by lower birthrates creates what demographers call "disordered cohort flow." This results in a population bulge that moves up the age ladder, rather than there being successively smaller age groups in older cohorts. Thus in the United States in 1980 there were several million more persons between the ages of fifteen and thirty than there were under fifteen or between thirty and forty-five years of age.

It is not the numbers *per se* that create the tendency toward oppositional movements. When the percentage of youth increases, it is usually more difficult to absorb them into the institutional structure, particularly into occupations, because of imbalance in the people-role equation. As cohorts grow older, Joan Waring emphasizes, they not only successively occupy and vacate age strata "but also succcessively assume and relinquish spaces in an age-stratified system of roles."[9] If, when a hundred positions are vacated, one hundred and fifty persons rush in to fill them, something has to give. This effect of disordered cohort flow is influenced, of course, by any concomitant changes in the varieties of jobs available, in the educational system (with their effects on aspirations and preparation), and in the individuals considered eligible (women and minorities may be added to the list, for example). Such changes can reduce the people-role imbalance; but when the young adult cohort is larger than usual, rather than smaller, they are more likely to increase that imbalance.

Why the powerful antifamily sentiments and numerous religious heresies, Herlihy asks, in medieval societies in Europe? Population growth was rapid, although erratically so, from the eleventh century up to the twentieth. The cultural ideal was a stable society, with sons replacing fathers in smooth succession. But when there were more sons than fathers, more persons demanding places than there were places to fill, the cultural ideal was unobtainable.[10] Movements demanding drastic changes in the social order are fostered by such demographic facts.

The demographic impact is not felt equally in all parts of a society. Young people may be more heavily concentrated in particular settings. More than half of the residents of Soweto, the black township in South Africa, are under twenty-five years of age, and they have experienced almost all of the violence and legal repression. Some of them have moved to the left and far left politically; others support a highly puritanical life style, in contrast with prevailing patterns, and try to enforce it by argument and coercion.[11] The average age in

"Blackstone," a black community in an Eastern U.S. city, is under eighteen.[12] Nonconformist as well as aberrant behavior is common. Numerous universities in Europe, Japan, and America have enrollments of over 20,000 students. Even on smaller campuses, contact between older and younger persons has been reduced by residential and other changes. Since there is only a low correlation, however, between the development of countercultural groups and the size of the student bodies, the direct influence of numbers on a particular campus is small. It is the size of the total cohort that is most critical.

That the impact of the comparative size of age groups is highly interactive with other factors is clearly show in the distinctions drawn among age (life cycle), generation (or cohort), and period effects.[13] Persons twenty to twenty-four years of age, for example, are influenced by the position, and the associated role, of that age group in a society; but they are continuously replaced in the group as they move along in the life cycle. They are also influenced by the generation to which they belong as they grow older. And they are influenced by period effects that condition the lives of all age groups—increasing affluence, perhaps, or the experience of anomie. When all three of these influences are destabalizing to a group, a powerful countercultural movement is likely to appear.

This can perhaps best be shown by viewing the situation from the generational perspective.[14] Countercultures are much more likely to occur under conditions that increase the sense of "my generation" and reduce the sense of belonging to a kin group, a community, a status group, or a nation. Rapid social change, physical and social mobility, disordered cohort flow, major economic, technological, and military events during ones youth—these are among the conditions that increase the feeling that one belongs to a generation. Many such conditions powerfully influenced young people in many parts of the world during the 1960s and 1970s. In the United States, for example, major changes on college and universtiy campuses, the Vietnam War, the spread of television, the ready availability of "the pill," affluence, and the threat and promise of the atomic age were powerful influences. Although several of these were period effects, with implications for everyone, they had a particular significance for youth, giving them a generational quality. Persons born since World War II have never known a world without atomic bombs or television. For many, affluence is a state of nature. Although the greatest burdens of war have always fallen on the young, they are experienced as especially heavy when the war is morally ambiguous or repugnant.

Such generational influences, Wuthnow shows by his analysis of national and regional poll data and interviews, are significantly related to participation in recent countercultural activities.[15] The generational concept also informs the analysis by Wieder and Zimmerman of a densely packed university neighborhood, inhabited mainly by students. Of those who were living unconventionally, substantial proportions endorsed "freak" values. They rejected conventional attitudes toward the importance of occupational success and financial security—careers mean self-repression; they were antiplanning—plans inhibit spontaneity; conventional manners and morals require repressive impulse-control; it is virtuous to seek continuous satisfactions. These attitudes and values, and the accompanying behavior, which "all but turn middle-class standards on their heads," are "related to distinctive generation-based experiences of middle class youth born after World War II, the first middle class generation which consumed on the open market long before it earned or produced."[16]

That only a minority of the young people supported the deviant values, even in a neighborhood described by the authors as "uniquely suited" to the development of a flourishing counterculture, warns us against overemphasizing the generational influence.

Although he mentions various generational experiences, Bennett Berger relies most strongly on the age factor to explain the value divergences of youth—whether they be applauded or lamented. Societies seem almost to have designed a division of labor in which the role of "moral organ" is assigned to the young, "what with all the grown-ups being too busy running the bureaucracies of the world (with their inevitable compromises, deals, gives and takes) to concern themselves with 'ideals.' " The young, being relatively unfettered by ties to family, community, and career, are perhaps best qualified, Berger suggests, to serve this role of "idealist" "in the same sense and for the same reason that Plato denied normal family life to his philosopher-kings and the Roman Catholic Church denies it to their Priests."[17] While some applaud this role for the young, seeing it as an essential resource for moral development, as Berger notes, others lament it precisely because detachment from institutional responsibilities means unaccountability and freedom for idealism to become violent and terroristic, propelled by moral zealotry.

Age- or life-cycle-related transitions vary from society to society. They tend to be quite discontinuous in industrial societies, Eisenstadt observes. There is a shift, as a child moves from the family, where *who* he is counts (judgments are particularistic) to the occupational world and society at large, where *what* he can do is more critical (judgments are universalistic). The "youth culture" serves as a bridge[18] over these sometimes troubled waters. The more drastic the discontinuity, the more likely that the standards of youth will contradict the standards of society.

Oppositional norms based on age tend to be set aside when persons move into the roles of a new age group. The countercultural standards serve as a "rite de passage," aiding the transition into adult roles. When those standards express more or less unique generational experiences, however, they are less likely to fade. They are based on experiences that are significant sources of ones identity throughout life. One does not remain a nineteen-year-old; but a member of the "Depression generation" or the "Vietnam generation" carries this identity throughout life. In this sense, there may be several generations within one age group. One is likely to be dominant, however, or more visible. It is when discontinuous age-transitions, powerful generational influences, and stressful period effects combine that the demographic impact on countercultures is at a maximum.

For the last quarter of a century, age distribution in most countries of the world has been favorable to the development of oppositional movements. In a large proportion of the developing countries, China being an important exception, a low average age will almost certainly continue to be the case for the next several decades. Much of the opposition in those countries has been directed abroad, against imperial powers and developed societies seen as exploitative. With the collapse of empires, however, and the curtailment of opportunities for exploitation, internal opposition has grown and is likely to grow further. New and unstable regimes need outside enemies, which they can readily create out of a combination of historical memories, myths, their own hostile acts, and the old and new modes of domination used by developed countries. Yet it will become less easy, or so it seems to me, to project hostility abroad. Internal dissension will grow, some of it conflict over power and some of it countercultural.

The situation in the most highly industrialized societies is quite different, and insofar as age distribution is a factor, they can expect a reduction of countercultural inventiveness, for better and for worse. About 1965 it was widely observed that soon half of the population of the United States would be under twenty-five years of age. Almost at that moment the trend was changing. By 1980 the average age was over thirty and it will be about thirty-five by the end of the century if present trends continue. The graying of America may prove to be a more accurate prediction than the "greening of America." This does not mean that the effects of disordered cohort flow will disappear, because they are not limited to the time when the largest cohorts are young. One can foresee that when, about 2020, 16 or 17 percent of the population is over sixty-five, the relatively moderate "gray panthers" will make way for more radical movements among the elderly. Although these are most likely to focus on the attainment of a larger share of political power and economic resources, countercultural movements—challenging the values of a youth-oriented society—are not improbable (sustained, paradoxically, by fifty-year-old memories and legends).

Meanwhile, the effects of current population trends will be more moderate. Although he may exaggerate the effects of the demographic situation, Richard Easterlin shows that a number of social ills—crime, suicide, unemployment, divorce—rise and fall, to put it overly simply, with the ease of entering the job market.[19] The rates are all likely to fall, therefore, in the 1980s. Although he does not make this connection, insofar as difficulty in obtaining desired educational and occupational placement is a factor, we will also see fewer countercultural movements in the years immediately ahead.

3. Relative deprivation. Sharp increase in life's possibilities, hopes, dreams, and actualities, followed by a plateau, actual loss, or serious threat of loss.

Such a sequence of events has long been recognized as a factor in revolutions, which, I have suggested earlier, typically contain countercultures as well as structural and personality changes. Countercultural movements, whether or not part of larger revolutionary changes, do not ordinarily occur at the end of a period when needs have become more difficult to satisfy and prevailing values more difficult to achieve, although that is likely to be the perception of those propounding the new standards. They are more likely to appear when needs have been more fully satisfied and the prevailing values have been more fully attained. These gains, however, have come at a rate slower than the increase in expectation and demand. This is particularly true when a fairly long period of improvement in need and value satisfaction is followed by a time of retrenchment. Hopes and expectations continue to soar; the gap between them and reality grows. The result is a strong sense of relative deprivation, even if the extent of "absolute" deprivation has fallen.

American students in the 1960s, for example, were certainly faced with some serious actual losses or threats of losses: life- threatening military service in a war many considered immoral, crowded and bureaucratized universities, severe competition for places in the professions. At the same time they were better off in many ways than their predecessors, except that the gains were seen against even higher expectations and aspirations. They were more affluent, on the average, had greater freedom in life style, and lived by a more open sexual ethic (the result of a decades-long transition). Rapid improvement, however, inclines one to look forward for standards of comparison, not backward. Seen against the promises and images of a sexual paradise, for example, the contemporary scene could be pictured as hypocritical and uptight. With Lawrence, Miller, Mailer, and others promising us salvation through orgasm, a promise distorted, glossed, and packaged as the "Playboy philosophy," the intricacies in attaining rich sexual relationships and integrating them with other values seemed burdensome. Moreover, many felt ambivalent about the more extreme versions of the new standards. Easy roads to salvation often seem like detours after a little experience proves that they too are bumpy. For a while one can repress the ambivalence by idealizing the stronger force and caricaturing the weaker, creating a countercultural-cultural contrast.

One particular form of relative deprivation, the experience of status inconsistency, deserves special attention. I will not examine the large body of literature that uses this concept but will only note its implications for the appearance of countercultures.[20] Although a variety of measures are used by various scholars, with resulting disagreements, the concept itself is quite simple: Each person's placement in the social hierarchy is the result of a combination of attributes—income, power, and prestige, in the classic formulations, or occupational and educational attainments, income, and ethnic status, in various recent uses. It is one thing for an individual to be consistently placed, whether at a high, medium, or low level, according to the criteria used; it is something quite different, so far as self-conception and the conceptions of others are concerned, to be inconsistently placed. The implications of high educational level are quite different for the person of high income and high status than for those of equal educational attainment whose incomes are modest or low or whose ethnic group suffers discrimination.

The processes through which the effects of status inconsistency are carried are not well understood, but they seem to be of two sorts: Individuals who experience status inconsistency tend to believe that rewards ought to be determined by their highest measure. The lack of such rewards is seen as injustice. The structure of opportunities, however, may reflect the influence of the lower measures more fully. Or I may interact with a person whose own status inconsistency is the reverse of mine, so that his justice is my injustice. A wealthy person of modest educational attainments is less likely to stress the entitlements due the educated person than those due him, for his business acumen and risk-taking or for the sheer fact of his wealth. The university graduate of modest income is likely to reverse these criteria. Each may experience deprivation, one of status the other of income, relative to the criterion he or she considers fundamental.

Different patterns of status inconsistency have different effects. Put overly simply, well-educated persons of little power and income tend to be liberal or radical; the poorly educated wealthy, especially if they are in positions of some power, tend to be conservative or reactionary, the strength of the effect depending upon many other factors besides the degree of inconsistency.

Some students, particularly in the highly selective colleges and universities, experience rather severe status inconsistency, mainly of the kind predisposing them to political and cultural radicalism. Most of them have been in the top one-third of their high school classes. Two-thirds of them are in the bottom two-thirds of their college classes. Most of those who stay on top do so only as a result of steady effort, something they have not been fully prepared for in high school. They have been promised a playful world by the media or, in some instances, by their own experience in affluent families. And the world out there that one has to work so hard to join seems not only lacking in playfulness but almost a shambles.

At home, before attending these selective schools, many of the students, perhaps unknowingly, shared the advantages of the high status accorded their parents. Although there are rudimentary signals of parental status still available in some of the colleges and universities, in the form of fraternities, sororities, clubs, cars, holidays, and the like, these have been democratized or equalized to a significant degree. The student culture does not allow one to draw heavily on the family status account, and professors tend to be stubbornly universalistic—partly out of lack of knowledge of their students' backgrounds, no doubt—in their requirements and in their distribution of unflattering assessments.

Although of little importance by themselves as sources of inclinations toward countercultures, such status inconsistencies reinforce the other sources we are discussing.

The experience of relative deprivation and status inconsistency varies quite widely from group to group. Since I will discuss countercultures among minorities in a later chapter, I want here only to note the special ways in which that experience helps to account for such strong opposition as the Black Power movement. It is not the result of a steadily deteriorating situation. Most of America's black population at the turn of the century, indeed through the next several decades, was uniformly low in income, power, education, and other status variables. Beginning in 1944, to pick the symbolically important date when the Supreme Court declared the "white primary" unconstitutional, and culminating in the Civil Rights Acts of 1964 and 1965, a civil rights movement of unprecendented strength significantly altered the educational, political, and economic positions of black Americans. I shall not try to document that statement at any length here[21] but will only note that political participation increased rapidly, in the form both of voting and office holding; the discrepancies between Whites and Blacks in income and in the holding of high-status jobs decreased by about one-third (two-thirds remained!); and the gap in educational attainment levels was dramatically narrowed, especially after the *Brown v. Board of Education* decision by the Supreme Court in 1954 and the Civil Rights acts of the 1960s.

Many forces in addition to legal and judicial actions were involved in bringing about these changes, of course: The black population migrated to cities of the North, West, and South in unprecedented numbers; after the small gains between 1935 and 1940 were slowed by World War II, industrial labor unions began to gain strength again in the late 1940s; the national conscience was aroused by the war against Nazism; private civil right groups showed great skill and won strong support; and each of these forces helped to reinforce the others.

It was in this context that the Black Power movement and some of the harsher antiwhite groups began to appear, carrying messages of cultural reversal, powered by that volatile mixture of success and failure. The failure was more easily seen after 1965, because the move toward equality of status went forward at a slower and slower pace. The easier gains were used up, particularly those related to national, public actions and to the removal of the symbols of discrimination. The more difficult problems, associated with institutionally embedded privileges and the attitudes that supported them, remained. The Vietnam War consumed vast resources, deflected the country's attention, and divided it morally. Energy shortages and other economic problems, political corruption in high places, continuing international tensions, and high rates of crime pushed the civil rights movement to a low place on the national agenda.

The aspirations and expectations of the country's black population did not, however, rise and then fall with this series of events. They continued to rise after 1965, propelled by the gains of the preceding generation. Although much better off than before World War II, their feelings of relative deprivation became powerful. The leveling of gains, the stubbornly high rate of unemployment (twice that of Whites), and the persistence of discrimination convinced some black Americans—although only a small proportion—that only a drastic change in American institutions and an inversion of the dominant values would bring justice. Some took the route of religious protest or of separatist and militant political action, as illustrated by the drastic changes of policy of the Congress of Racial Equality (CORE), an offshoot of the Fellowship of Reconciliation, and the Student Nonviolent Coordinating Committee (SNCC), an offshoot of the Southern Christian Leadership Conference. Harshly critical writing appeared, such as Julius Lester's *Look Out Whitey, Black Power's Gon' Get Your Mama*. It would be a mistake to forget, however, that the words of CORE, SNCC, and others spoke much more loudly than their actions so far as violence is concerned. For the most part, protests were nonviolent.

The feelings of relative deprivation among members of a minority are increased by a kind of status inconsistency not generally taken into account. It is not only income, power, and prestige that a society distributes among its population, however equally or unequally, but also hope and aspiration. Small improvements on the objective scales may lead to soaring hopes and to dreams of dramatic changes. Those improvements release the imagination. The result may be a split between the objective and the subjective aspects of status—a split as significant as inconsistency among the various objective standards.[22] A ruling group that wants to keep a minority group in subservience has not only to prevent the decrystallization of their low levels of income, power, and education but also to suppress their hopes. Failing that, they will be confronted with protest movements and, if they are only marginally successful as judged by the criteria of relative deprivation, by countercultures that proclaim the dominant value system, not just its power system, an abomination.

American soldiers used to sing: How you gonna keep 'em down on the farm now that they've seen Paree? Chinese rulers, faced with enormous problems of modernization, are doubtless wondering how they're going to keep several hundred million peasants on farm communes once they've seen Shanghai (or the flood of goods from relatives in Hong Kong). The South African government is hoping to keep some black South Africans down on the farm (in "tribal homelands") and others in the city only during the hours of their industrial labor; but both groups have "seen Paree." In the United States, the question is no longer relevant. Here the research and the moral question coincide: Can the elimination of discrimination against minorities proceed rapidly enough so that soaring hopes encourage achievement; or will a growing sense of relative deprivation lead to such disillusionment and cynicism, not just among a few but among many, that inverted values will prevail?

One additonal comment on the implications of status inconsistency for the appearance of countercultural tendencies is needed. Although the evidence is not conclusive, it generally supports the view that Jews in the United States, and probably elsewhere, are "overrepresented" among those who support countercultural values.[23] This is partly a statistical quirk, a simple correlation, since they are also "overrepresented" among the highly educated middle- and upper-class group from which many oppositional movements spring. It is partly, however, a matter of the cultural history of Jews. For generations, indeed centuries, they needed great collective and individual ingenuity to adapt to and survive in hostile environments. They developed a skillful "culture of opposition." (As a liberal-to-radical non-Jew, I shudder at the thought of the size of the loss if this great resource were not available—therefore I also shudder at the desertions that occur here and there.) This culture of oppsition draws some Jews, in my judgment, into countercultural currents.

It is not the purely statistical association, however, nor Jewish traditions that I am mainly concerned with here. Status inconsistency is also involved. Anti-Semitism, now much abated in the United States but certainly not lacking, separates social status from income and from occupational and educational attainment. And the *memory* of the anti-Semitism so powerful in Europe in the recent past reinforces the impact of the current levels of discrimination and prejudice. That memory creates a dread that acts as a psychological element in the status-inconsistency compound: One may be consistently medium to high today in education, occupational status, income, and power; but don't count on this as a stable situation; do not forget how quickly circumstances can change. This feeling among Jews, continually reinforced by such things as the violence at the 1976 Olympic Games, by anti-Semitism in the Soviet Union, by Arab-Israeli conflict (although much of that is geopolitical), and by lingering discrimination in the United States, tends to decrystallize status and to create a sense of injustice. Like the hope, as well as dread, among black Americans, this psychological aspect of status inconsistency makes some Jews responsive to alternative and oppositional life styles.

4. Isolation. Lower participation in intimate and supporting social circles—families, neighborhoods, work groups.[24]

> *. . . the results of our study suggest that the most clearly and directly noxious aspects of sociocultural disintegration are those that affect the achievement of love, recognition, spontaneity, and the sense of belonging to a moral order and of being right in what one does.*
>
> Dorothea Leighton *et al*, *The Character of Danger*

Counterculturalists range from the utterly deprived to the "poor little rich kids," but they share in common a high likelihood of a broken bond between parents and children that predisposes the latter to many forms of negativism. When parents combine warmth and discipline, children identify with them and internalize their standards.[25] To put it too neatly: If a child experiences warmth without discipline he has no need to identify with parents; if he experiences discipline without warmth he has no desire to identify. These relationships are strongly modified, of course, by the situation within which they occur. For example, disciplined training that is contradicted by patterns in the community and society—contradictions visible to the child—is likely to be seen as unfair and coercive. Warmth that turns out to be neglect in the guise of permissiveness is likely to be experienced as desertion.

Some turn the negative impulses that grow from the broken bond inward, which in our time has meant a sharp increase in rates of anxiety and suicide.[26] Others find group support for turning the hostility outward. Musgrove found that students on an American campus who had high scores on a counterculture "scale" had a strong sense of social dislocation and uprootedness; "the self concepts of high scorers were devastatingly negative and harrowingly lonely."[27] Feuer speaks of the de-authorization of the older generation as the major cause of the coalescing into a shared revolt of what he sees as basically individual oedipal problems.[28] He is imprecise in his discussion of the sources of such de-authorization, which itself requires explanation, since it seems unlikely to be the starting point for a counterculture building process. De-authorization does, however, seem to be an important ingredient, interacting with the other sources we have noted.

Although it carries several messages, with reference to the point under discussion "don't trust anyone over thirty" means: How can we trust you? You deserted us. Parents can be de-authorized by drastic social change; they can also de-authorize themselves. Driven to succeed, to amass money, or to enjoy life, some of the rich and successful were "doing their own thing" before a younger generation invented the phrase.[29]

The effects of rejection and emotional isolation appear in societies of many types. In a study that included, among other methods, a cross-cultural survey of 101 societies, Ronald Rohner found that certain "developmental tendencies" exhibit, everywhere, the effects of the experience that *They Love Me, They Love Me Not*, to use the words of his title. The evidence "converges on the conclusion that parental rejection in children, as well as in adults who were rejected as children, leads to: hostility, aggression, passive aggression, or problems with the management of hostility and aggression; dependency; probably emotional unresponsiveness and negative self-evalutation (negative self-esteem and negative self-adequacy); and, probably, emotional instability as well as a negative world view."[30]

Rohner's study is not without difficulty for the student of countercultures. I applaud his effort to discover whether there are universal qualities to the experience of socialization; but several of his terms are difficult to define without reference to particular cultures. His reference to the "malignant" effects of rejection ought perhaps to be qualified by the observation that the responses to rejection may include creative efforts to deal with it—efforts that can be of value to others and can include the seeds of new cultural standards adapted to changing circumstances. Whatever the mixture of malignant and creative effects, the lack of emotional support from intimate social circles is an important source of countercultural tendencies.

The loss of intimacy between generations does not seem to have been overcome by the "love" generation, whose children are sometimes neglected in the name of permissiveness, much as they themselves were neglected.[31]

Individual Sources of Countercultures

But it's perfectly delicious!
What a pity it isn't forbidden!

Stendhal on ice cream

When my mother took me to see "Snow White," everyone fell in love with Snow White; I immediately fell for the Wicked Queen.

Woody Allen *in "Annie Hall"*

Are some persons particularly attracted to inverted norms, to the negation of whatever is standard? Or are such tendencies universal, the result of the inevitable constraints and frustrations of social life? Or, perhaps, do such inclinations abound in certain sets of social conditions, symptoms of the stress associated with rapid social change or anomie? The answer to all three questions, I believe, is yes. Becoming "well socialized" to prevailing standards is inherently problematic; some circumstances heighten the difficulty for large segments of a population, perhaps for the members of a "generation," as we have used that word; and certain individuals, because of their distinctive experiences, are especially attracted to the forbidden and the inverted.

Once again, I neither applaud nor lament, as a general principle, this wealth of individual sources for countercultures. One can say, thank God for our misfits; what a rigid and dull world it would be without them; they are the truly creative. Or one can say, good God, why the misfits? What a perverse and sorry lot they are; they are tearing us apart. Most of us probably find both exclamations necessary, to be used on alternate days. Our task here, however, is to try to identify the experiences, ranging from the universal to the unique, that predispose individuals to invent, propagate, or accept inverted standards.

Statements that individual tendencies are among the sources of countercultures require careful scrutiny. Unless they are made in a field-theoretical context that emphasizes the interdependence of structural, cultural, and individual factors, such statements are easily misinterpreted. It seems to me a great oversimplification to interpret major social events by reference to the turmoil and talent of a few persons, or even by reference to the shared anxieties of many. To a substantial degree these individual tendencies are effects before they become causes: they are products of major social, demographic, economic, and other changes. That argument can, however, be pushed too far. We need to examine those theories that hold that all persons have reservoirs of hostility. We need also to examine theories which, leaving open the question of biopsychological universals, explore the casualties of socialization (casualties from the point view of the dominant order) that predispose some to oppositional life styles. Whether or not antinomians (literally, persons opposed to the obligatoriness of the moral law) can be found in all times and places, one cannot doubt that in our era plenty of raw material exists for the making of countercultures. Why are some people drawn to the new standards while others are repelled by them? A theory of countercultures must examine the range of connections between oppositional normative movements and individual personalities.

Many writers have suggested an analogue, on the psychological level, of countercultures. Throughout his work, Freud explored a reality hidden within the person that is set over against the visible person, at odds with expressed views and values and overt behavior. Freud saw us all as good candidates for behavior that contravenes the norms because, as he put it "what we call our civilization is largely responsible for our misery" by blocking strongly motivated activities. "If civilization imposes such great sacrifices not only on man's sexuality but on his aggressivity, we can understand better why it is hard for him to be happy in that civilization."[32]

Although Freud wrote that about 1930, he still held to the now outmoded notion that "primitive man was better off in knowing no restrictions of instinct." He immediately qualified that statement, however, by noting the insecurity of primitive life; and he then almost revoked the statement by asserting "that in the primal family only the head of it enjoyed this instinctual freedom."[33] Thus to Freud, hostility to civilization is endemic. The qualification extends his view to include most of the people in tribal societies. Moderns compare themselves with primitives, whom they suppose to be much freer, and they observe that technology has not increased their satisfactions in life. In fact we are dealing not just with "Civilization and Its Discontents" but with humanity and its discontents.

Just as Marx saw the whole institutional superstructure of a society built upon the foundation of coercive productive relations, Freud saw the superstructure of culture built upon instinctual repression, designed to hide a presumed primaeval oedipal guilt. This judgment inclined him toward a reluctant conservatism. Anthropological and sociological theory confirms the fact of sexual and aggressive "repression" in all societies. If it is seen as "control by cultural standards," however, different connotations appear. From the Freudian perspective, "in the beginning was the individual," a view also accepted by some sociologists.[34] From this point of view, countercultures are formed when repressed tendencies break through social constraints that have become vulnerable.

In my judgment it is more accurate to say, with Cooley, that self and society are twin-born. This does not mean that they are the same phenomenon, seen from two different perspectives, but that they emerge together. No less real than our individual natures are our group natures, based on such factors as the long period of infancy and dependency, the lack of instinctual answers to survival problems, and our reliance on language—an intrinsically group phenomenon. Alexander Goldenweiser somewhere wrote that a weight that is not felt is only half a weight. In times when a cultural system is splitting apart and the declicate balance between individual and group needs is upset, the weight of the social controls is felt. Indeed it becomes burdensome. Carrying it does not bring the accustomed rewards and expected reciprocities. In such contexts, countercultures may arise that say, referring to the burdens emphasized by Freud: release the controls on aggression; violence is purifying. Or, release the controls on sex; inhibition is stultifying.

In his discussion, Freud stated a principle that today we call hedonic relativism, a term similar to relative deprivation. "We are so made," he wrote, "that we can derive intense enjoyment only from a contrast and very little from a state of things. Thus our possiblilities of happiness are already restricted by our constitution. Unhappiness is much less difficult to experience."[35] Durkheim, although he does not locate the cause in the individual psyche, had earlier made a similar point. One can only be disillusioned he remarked, if one moves toward a point that "recedes in the same measure that one advances. . . . This is why historical periods like ours, which have known the malady of infinite aspiration, are necessarily touched with pessimism."[36] Both Freud and Durkheim referred to wants, not needs, as Aristotle used those terms. Wants are, indeed, "infinite," and our enjoyment of them is relative. Societies that have the capacity to satisfy needs shift attention to wants, increasing the likelihood that insatiable demands will arise.

We all know, from experience and experiment, how readily we accommodate to new standards of enjoyment, so that what seemed pleasant yesterday is now unacceptably bland. "Where pleasure is concerned, humans are insatiable animals, shifting their criterion level upward when the level of pleasurable input increases, so that once again experience is scored as one-third pleasure, one-third pain, and one-third blah."[37] We do not make equally quick adaptation to any downward pull of experience. There is nothing more painful, as Veblen noted, than a retreat from a standard of living. Perhaps we need only to generalize that to say, "retreat from a standard of pleasure."

Granted this principle, a society that enormously raises the aspirations but only modestly raises the pleasures of its members, or some of its members, is furnishing an essential ingredient of protest. Even if there are gains in some objective sense, many will feel cheated by society and disenchanted with its values. These are perhaps the conditions under which a shift occurs, in Ralph Turner's terms, from institutional defintions of "the real self" toward impulse definitions. Some persons will experience their own deviations as a threat to their "real selves." Others will see such actions as the real self breaking through institutional constraints. Contemporary conditions, in Turner's view, increase the latter experience. "Perhaps the greatest impact Freud had on the modern world was to discredit normative behavior and conscience as manifestations of our true selves and to elevate impulses to that position."[38] I would see Freud more as a symbol of a situation within which institutional selves have come to be felt as unsatisfying by more persons. What Turner calls impulse selves also require social validation and support from others. What start out as impulse selves may be collectively validated as the partially institutionalized selves of a counterculture.

The criteria by which Turner defines the impulse self are similar to those used by Keniston and others to describe alienation. Living for today, rejection of "success," emphasis on "being" rather than on "doing," self-expression and the lowering of inhibitions are tendencies that Keniston sees as point-by-point denials of the established values and replacement by their opposites.[39]

Narcissism is another word that has been widely used in recent years to describe, usually in critical terms, tendencies similar to the impulse self. In *The Fall of Public Man*, Richard Sennett described the contemporary situation as one in which intimate feelings, not the social structure and a shared culture, are the measure of reality. Tom Wolfe labeled the 1970s the "Me" decade, emphasizing the "most delicious look inward" of the new religions and psychotherapies. Or in Christopher Lasch's words: "To live for the moment is the prevailing passion—to live for yourself, not for your predecessors or posterity."[40]

This use of the concept of narcissism departs rather widely from its psychiatric meaning and tends to blur the distinction between individual tendencies and cultural contexts (as in the title of Lasch's book: *The Culture of Narcissism*). Read with due caution, however, the literature on narcissism adds to our understanding of the tendencies toward "deinstitutionalized" selves, inclined toward new and in many instances inverted standards.

In addition to impulse self, alienated self, and narcissism, other terms can be used to help us examine the individual counterpart of countercultures. Adler discusses the antinomian personality, Kavolis the underground personality, Trilling the opposing self in literature, and Erik Erikson, using perhaps the most useful psychological analogue for counterculture, develops the term "negative identity." In an often desperate choice between being a failure, a nobody, an "invisible man," and being a shockingly visible antihero, a person to reckon with, some choose the latter, expressing their frustration" in a scornful and snobbish hostility toward the roles offered as proper and desirable in one's family or immediate community." It is not simply that standard roles are abrogated. "They choose instead a *negative identity*, i.e., an identity perversely based on all those identifications and roles which, at critical stages of development, had been presented to them as most undesirable or dangerous and yet also as most real."[41]

Erikson tends to assume that a negative identity is pathological. It may be wiser to reserve ones judgment on that issue, asking in each instance what a person is being negative against, what balance of creativity and inanity is found in the available positive identities, and what the consequences are for the individual and society in the various choices. Nietzsche, for example, is quite forthright about his negativism. "My taste," he writes, "which may be called the opposite of a tolerant taste, is even here far from uttering a wholesale Yes: in general it dislikes saying Yes, it would rather say No."[42] Or, at another place: "*Not* contentment, but more power; *not* peace at all, but war; *not* virtue, but proficiency (virtue in the Renaissance style, virtu, virtue free of moralic acid)."[43]

Once a negative identity has become dominant, it needs confirmation. If others don't furnish confirmation spontaneously, by their opposition and condemnation, persons negatively inclined provoke it by their own behavior, perhaps by flunking out of school or by violence. The behavior is not wisely evaluated simply in terms of its origins. Revolutionary students, Hendin observed, have been plagued by a lifetime of emotional invisibility and rejection. "The inner turmoil of these revolutionary students," however, "in no way invalidates their critique of society."[44] Their indictment requires assessment on grounds independent of this emotional source, which, in fact, has become salient because of its convergence with other sources in society.

Erikson's use of the concept of negative identity is based on his work as a psychiatrist, and there may indeed be some neurotic element in many cases of negative self-identification. Yet such feelings may be part of the character not only of the neurotic but also of the prophet or the highly creative person who finds the proffered identities too closely bound to an unacceptable society. It is not only that individuals may be alienated, societies may be alientating. One psychiatrist, "when asked what he thought the best therapy was for students who had been severely alienated by the Vietnam war, replied, 'Stop the damn war!' "[45]

To reduce the risk that the concept Erikson labeled negative identity would necessarily imply only its unfortunate aspects, counter- or countraidentity might be a preferable term. Adler creatively uses the old term antinomian but cannot thereby easily suggest the norms upheld as well as those opposed. I shall use negative identity and antinomian, nevertheless, as rough synonyms that overlap the meaning of the concept of counter-personality.

Whatever the balance of individual and social factors, the choice of a negative identity reflects extremely difficult circumstances, "a desperate attempt at regaining some mastery in a situation in which the positive identity elements cancel each other out. The history of such a choice reveals a set of conditions in which it is easier for the patient to derive a sense of identity out of a total identification with that which he is least supposed to be than to struggle for a feeling of reality in acceptable roles which are unattainable with his inner means,"[46] or in roles, one might add, that are blocked by the lack of outer resources.

A tentative negative identity is part of the effort of self-discovery and the behavior of young children. They explore the physical world, discovering the boundaries, the rough places and the smooth. And they explore the social world, testing for the boundaries of the possible and the permissible. At first the behavior is random, so far as the social norms are concerned, but quickly they begin to learn, from the responses of other, what the social world is like. The lessons are not entirely favorable from their point of view: Random behavior must be curtailed; strongly instigated activity proves to be off limits according to those powerful giants—three times as tall and five or six times as heavy—upon whom one depends. For example, that gentle hug of baby sister, with an especially hard squeeze at the end for editorial effect, seems to send a message the adults don't want to hear, that baby sister is a nuisance at best, demanding most of the parents' time and affection, and at worst a usurper. In time, having given up the hope that the competitor is a temporary visitor, an older child may turn to strategies other than direct attack. He may demand things selfishly, seeking for a sign that he is still loved; he is "bad" by the parents' definition in order to test them; he regresses, hoping that by acting like a baby he can win the same attention. If these powerful adults give reassurance and affection, the tendency toward negative identity will be set aside in favor of the greater satisfactions that come from a positive identity. If only punishment and further neglect follow this "bad" behavior, however, a child may embrace a negative self-image. This releases him, at least, to enjoy the discomfort he brings to those who, as he sees it, so abuse him.

I do not intend, by this illustration, to imply that the position of the older or oldest child is particularly likely to reinforce tendencies toward negative identity. There is a huge literature on "sibling location," which I shall not examine. But if any firm conclusion can be drawn from that literature it is that the oldest child, on the average, is more likely to be the closest to parental values, more responsible, more conservative. One further observation will indicate the complexity of this issue. In some family contexts, the younger children feel a special kind of stress. Writing about Billy Carter, William Greider observed that "the last-born feels distant, insulated from contentious emotions, such as the wrath of parents, that provoke so much smoke and flames among the older children. In many ways he fells uniquely free. . . . If the little brother gets caught, he clowns his way out of it. . . . On the other hand, the last-born also feels permanently confused."[47] Don't be too hard on the errant little brother the headline suggests, for he has a difficult time being somebody in the presence of talented, articulate older brothers and sisters. So he "zings them . . . , says something so foul and contentious that they are forced to react." And the pattern may continue into adulthood. For a while, Billy Carter drank heavily rather than moderately, paraded his irresponsibility, and, in a much publicized affair, had associations with Libya (foe of Jimmy Carter's Egypt-Israel treaty, supporter of Amin, and haven for terrorists).

All children discover who they are, in part, by pushing away from even the most nurturing adults. Some for reasons that have only been hinted at here, find it difficult to "take the role of the other," to use George Herbert Mead's famous phrase. They do not look out at themselves from the perspective of others, do not identify with them, because what they see if they do is too painful—you are ignorant, a nuisance, bad. Some children find that their first efforts at identification lead only to confusion, because they receive double, and contradictory, messages. They are caught, as Gregory Bateson expressed it, in a double bind: Go to bed, darling, a mother says, so that you can get your rest and grow up to be a strong, healthy boy. But the child sees signals that also say: Go to bed; I cannot stand the sight of you; you make me feel inadequate; yet I need you and hope that you will remain dependent upon me.[48] Although the child sees the contradiction, he cannot admit it, for this would be to doubt the love and competence of his mother, the very source of self. The child is punished for understanding, rewarded for blocking his understanding. Thus the parent gets no correction, and the child becomes, in Bateson's words, "an accomplice of the parent's unconscious hypocrisy." In severe cases, such blockage of communication is a source of schizophrenia. Far more commonly, the blurred messages that many of us send to our children from time to time are stumbling blocks in the way of reaching a positive self-image.

Some of the sources of negative identity are most influencial during adolescence. If rewards from a somewhat tenuous positive identity—love, appreciation, participation in respected groups—are lacking, some of the experiences during adolescence may lead a person to believe that a negative identity would be more satisfying. If one lives in a society where, he begins to see, the values he has been taught in childhood are not much honored; if generational differences in experience are marked; if social setting or individual circumstance have made the learning of a sex role difficult; if racial or ethnic discrimination threatens self-confidence—such conditions increase the likelihood that a negative self-image will be adopted.

The intimate, interpersonal sources of negative identity, particularly in the family, shade off toward macrasocial sources. In the latter cases, the identity is as much an outside label as an inner experience, as attested by two-known essays: Howard Becker's *Outsiders*, and Erving Goffman's *Stigma: Notes on the Management of Spoiled Identity*. Stereotyped minority-group members may have strong interpersonal and subcultural resources that help them to resist the negative self-definitions implicit in the images of them and the treatment they receive from those in dominant groups.[49] The experience of being "invisible," however, or, as DuBois put it years ago, "inaudible" to the majority inevitably penetrates ones selfhood to some degree. The results, of course, are both positive and negative. Both creativity and hostility can flow from the experience of discrimination.

The linkage between a negative self-image and the acceptance of countercultural values is by no means direct or even necessary. Social and cultural conditions may or may not nourish the potential for normative inversions to match the characterological. Nor is it a matter of those with high potential for deviation first learning the values of a nonconformist group, then behaving in accordance with them. Behavioral change usually comes first, as Mills notes with respect to the hippies, and then some create or adopt an interpretation that brings some sense of coherence to their experience, justifying and rationalizing it.[50] "Im Anfang war die Tat," Goethe's Faust proclaimed. In the beginning was the deed; its meaning emerges only in the context of the whole field within which it occured.

Those driven to define themselves in terms quite the reverse of the standards of their time and place are often torn by ambivalence, in both the psychological sense of having mutually contradictory feelings, wishes, or beliefs and in the sociological sense of being caught between mutually contradictory expectations, between norms and counter-norms, arising from persons in their role network.[51] Keniston writes that "with potentially emulable older men, the alienated are involved in a struggle *against* their own underlying admiration and desire to emulate, a struggle which they must maintain precisely because they are so overwhelmingly drawn to men who might serve as models for them."[52]

Redl and Wineman note that although some delinquents so identify with criminal activity that they have few problems with guilt, "Others are not quite that advanced. They still have mighty chunks of their value-identified superego intact. . . . In that case, the 'delinquent ego' has the additional task of 'duping its own superego,' so that delinquent impulsivity can be enjoyed tax-free from feelings of guilt."[53] What better way is there to dupe ones superego than to raise the deviant behavior about which one feels ambivalent to a matter of high principle, while caricaturing and condemning the socially approved view, which is also ones own hidden view?

Perhaps the counterpart of this is the need a participant in the dominant society—one who is also ambiavalent about dominant values—has for duping his own id. The "long-haired ne'er-do-well pot smokers" are the hidden and repressed parts of his own life— the dreams and fantasies of freedom from routine, inhibition, and the demands of work. By making advocates of such freedoms seem abhorrent, one can more easily resist temptation.

This interpretation, however, ought not to be pushed too far in either direction. Genuine value conflicts exist, and the opponents are those who hold contrary values, not the hidden selves.

Jerry Rubin is one of several leaders of oppositional movements who have recently discovered their own ambivalence. "I always thought I was the opposite of my parents. I rebelled against them publicly, seeing the hypocrisy in my family reflected in society as a whole. After the sixties ended. . . . I discovered that though I rebelled against my parents, I had in fact reproduced their psychic structures inside me." At one point, a headline about him read: "Yippie leader tells children to kill their parents." Five years later: "I finally understood what I meant! Kill the *parents-in-you*."[54] Of course, the "parents-in-you" may win, as attested by the not uncommon return of counterculturalists, including Jerry Rubin, to positions in the "established" society.

Ambivalence is dramatically revealed by abrupt shifts from one from of opposition to the dominant culture to a drastically different form, as when Rennie Davis, a central figure in the radical protest of the 1960s becomes a follower of the fifteen-year-old ascetic Maharaj Ji.[55]

Because of their ambivalence, counterculturalists need opposition. In recent years they have needed a "police state" and have helped to intensify already existing tendencies in that direction.[56] Harsh opposition helps to justify their feelings and actions and helps to push them away from the center; win attention, sympathy, and converts; and draw sharper, value-protecting boundaries.

Ambivalence also helps to account for the contrast between the modernistic and the underground types of personality that Kavolis describes. It is his thesis that when social trends have psychological effects, "the result is *either* the precise reflection of social trends in personality structures, *or* the exact opposite—a psychological 'rejection' of ongoing social trends and the development of personality characteristics (and cultural products) expressive of such a rejection." If the trends are toward a rationalized and impersonal bureaucracy, one result is a rationally organized person concerned with the orderly application of rules; but another result is a reaction to that trend—a person "inclined toward anarchic romanticism, expressionism, mysticism, and the politics and education of 'ecstasy'."[57]

The either-or formulation of Kavolis's thesis seems to me to be an exaggeration of a valuable point. We are all affected by major social trends both by being drawn into their circle of influence and by resisting their demands and personal costs. What he calls underground personality tendencies are those expressed by those to whom the demands and costs seem excessive but who, nevertheless, have been strongly influenced by the social trends. The pull of opposite inclinations is controlled by repressing one set and affirming its opposite.

Erikson stresses the ambivalence built into the feelings of negative identity. Persons thus characterized seem to want to be everything that "society" tells them not to be. But are they truly dominated by their negative identities? Erikson does not think so. They are gratified that their parents are dismayed at their appearance or behavior, for they are seeking a positive identity distinct from their parents. Yet their nonconformity is also a plea for "fraternal confirmation," thus expressing the "paradox of all rebellious identity formation."[58]

Although persons with feelings of negative identity are symptoms of and sources of countercultures, it is necessary to distinguish the individual from the group level. Not all those with negative identities support countercultural values or groups; not all who support countercultures have negative identities. Under some conditions, however, persons struggling with problems of identity and leaning toward a negative formulation are drawn into a social movement that validates their self-definitions and thus aids in the repression of the doubt and guilt that characterize ambivalent feelings. Or, in the absence of a countercultural group that gives validity to their negative identities, individuals may make tentative and ambiguous gestures to each other suggesting counter values, but leaving room for retreat or modification if the exploratory gestures don't lead toward consensus on the oppositional values.[59] Individuals facing similar frustrations and holding similar views of the roads that are blocked to them and the roads that are open, the values worth pursuing and those that are repugnant, may then come to agree on a collective "solution" in the form of a counterculture that is tailor-made—but not necessarily with a good fit—to their negative identities.

Let me state again that the cultural products of "negative" identities are not necessarily negative when set against particular values. They seem bizarre, immoral, even mad to many contemporaries, but history may view them in a different light. Before it has become normative for some group, the effort of an abnormal person to deal with his anxieties can signal patterns that fit the needs of others. Once taken up, these patterns can become first countercultural and then cultural.[60] Certain persons experience the conflicts and contradictions of their times in particularly vivid form. The great person, or the one who later is believed to have been great, deals with those conflicts in a way that is meaningful to many others and, as Erikson says in *Young Man Luther*, becomes the vehicle of a major social change.

I do not agree with Fromm and Maccoby that the deviant personality is the "central principle" in the process of social change. It is true that persons of traditional character may be poorly adapted to new circumstances, as they emphasize, while persons of "heretofore deviant character type" are better able to make use of the new conditions.[61] The result, however, is always a product of a transaction between the tendencies of individuals and the constraints and possibilties of the situation within which they live.

Thus we cannot separate "the identity crises in individual life and contemporary crises in historical development because the two help to define each other and are truly relative to each other."[62]

Even when the influence of social factors is taken into account, we should note that the concept of identity is not without problems. It has become loaded with implications and connotations related to the uncertainties of our time. In particular, the search for identity, deemed essential by Erikson, may have unintended consequences. It may not be the way to find ones self. Ellen Goodman describes a student who had left college to find herself, "rather as if she were a set of misplaced keys. She had the notion that her mind was a collection of pockets, and if she searched in each of them long enough she would find the keys to unlock this self." She had become "a professional introspector. A very private eye." Goodman did not oppose interior travels; she lamented the fact that many people went through life without "interviewing themselves." She did puzzle over the belief, however, that people "were born with complete, coherent inner beings which only need to be uncovered and expressed." In her view, people were born with tendencies and possibilities, but they "grew" selves. "Some of the most self-aware people had taken their chance first and their temperature second. . . . After all, most people don't find themselves; they become themselves. And life has a way of interrupting the most hypnotic private eye."[63] In biblical terms: He who loses his life shall find it.

Bennett Berger, in a related comment, wonders if the sense of a lost identity might not open creative possibilities. "Who would be so fatuous," he asks, "as to announce that he has found his identity"? It is not even clear, in Berger's judgment, that finding it is a good idea. "A person who does not know who he is might *just be anybody*, and hence is fit for the unanticipateable opportunities and eventualities which rapidly changing industrial societies provide."[64] Having long thought that a dose of alienation and a dash of anomie were not only inevitable but essential in the modern world,[65] I share Berger's view to some degree. We are a long way from knowing, however, what the long-run consequences of identity diffusion and of various levels of alienation and anomie are. Whatever the case, what requires study is the interaction between given individual tendencies and countercultures, treating them alternately as causes and then as effects.

In research on this question, both character and social situations have been used as starting points. Kaplan found that "antecedent negative self-attitudes significantly increase the probability of subsequent deviant responses," but he also emphasizes that the normative structure has helped to shape the negative self-attitudes.[66] The countercultural lives of Charles Manson's family were dominated by his psychotic charisma; but that cannot be understood without knowledge of his twenty-two years in prison and the harshness of his life.

Cultural Sources of Countercultures

> *Human life is reduced to real suffering, to hell, only when two ages, two cultures and religions overlap. . . . Now there are times when a whole generation is caught in this way between two ages, two modes of life, with the consequence that it loses all power to understand itself and has no standard, no security, no simple acquiescence.*
>
> Herman Hesse in *Steppenwolf* (1963, p. 22)

Two contrasting themes are needed to discuss the cultural sources of countercultures. In some measure, the inverted standards are the direct, even if caricatured, expressions of dominant standards. They are also, however, responses to anomie, to the experience of normlessness, to the perceived inadequacies of the dominant culture, or to the absence of a coherent culture.

However much they may invert dominant beliefs and values, the antinomians cannot escape their influence. Although cultural polarities may be pulled apart, as I have suggested earlier, the new standards are formed out of pieces of the old. Technology may be abhorrent, but electrically amplified guitars are essential. It is not only Timothy Leary and those who share his views who seek to "build a better world through chemistry." Today's antinomians, Adler writes, "really believe in culture via 'great books,' music through ten easy lessons, a new personality as available as a hair tint, and they seek out multichannel sound and color, stroboscopic experiments, and drugs."[67]

In Chapter Two I cited David Matza's well-known paper on student radicalism, in which he describes several themes in the larger culture on which a protest movement can draw. The biblical picture of the apocalypse through which the evil world will be replaced; belief in the creativity and superior worth of ordinary people; and the spirit of evangelism—the recruitment of sympathizers and supporters for major social causes—are themes that have strongly traditional sources and uses.[68] They can also be used, however, as weapons with which to attack the established order in the name of a counterculture.

Although they do not escape the imprint of the surrounding culture, antinomians also appear as a result of perceived inadequacies of prevailing norms and values. I am referring here not to the belief that aberration, hypocrisy, and injustice are rife, that dominant members of society frequently violate their own values, but to the belief that the values themselves are inadequate. To be sure, high levels of deviation weaken the prevailing standards. So also, however, do rapidly changing circumstances that make those standards seem irrelevant or constricting. This is more likely to occur when, in fact, standards are changing and becoming less constricting. "In the new Spain," Barbara Solomon notes, "there is a tremendous revulsion against any kind of rigidity in culture, politics, social or sexual life. . . . Last July, members of the old Spanish left were startled when a young anarchist group, holding its festivities in Barcelona before a mass audience of over half a million young anarchist workers, cavorted nude in a Boccaccio-like setting and performed sodomy. The anarchists believe they are making a heterodoxical, anti-authoritarian statement."[69] It often happens that when changes long delayed do come, they are seen by some to be too little and too late, as indeed they often are, judged by any but modest standards.

Those who criticize a society because it fails to live up to its own values want revitalization; those who see the values themselves as poor want culture change, perhaps a counterculture. In *Growing Up Absurd*, Paul Goodman wrote that youthful deviation is not best explained as a failure of socialization. Such an explanation implies that the values are good, that it is only the ways youth are brought into adult society that are inadequate. Suppose we take an opposite tack, he asks. Suppose we ask, "Socialization to what?" "Is the harmonious organization to which the young are inadequately socialized, perhaps against human nature, or not worthy of human nature, and *therefore* there is difficulty in growing up?"[70]

Important as exaggerated expressions and direct criticisms of the dominant culture are as sources of countercultures, they are probably less influencial than the experience of anomie, of a state of normlessness, of a loss of meaning in the deepest symbols and rituals of society. We are far from knowing why a major reduction in the legitimacy of the values of a society—rather than endemic but scattered skepticism—occurs. The various other individual and social sources of countercultures I have discussed doubtless contribute to the loss of meaning, just as several are in turn strengthened by it. We can be more confident, however, in noting the fact of the loss of meaning at various times and in assessing some of its consequences. One does not need to follow Saint-Simon, or more recently Sorokin, in the belief—to use Saint-Simon's terms—that there are "organic" periods, held together by a common faith, and "critical" periods, divided and confused about their fundamental beliefs. The "excluded middle" may be the more common situation, particularly in the industrial world. There are times, however, when the loss of trust and of shared meanings becomes a decisive fact of experience. In a recent study of more than a thousand university students in six countries, I found that 60 percent believed that problems of meaning were the most fundamental issues facing humanity. (About half of these also mentioned problems of injustice, suffering, or both.)[71] Trust in our institutions has been at a low ebb in the United States in recent years, although it may have risen somewhat since about 1975.

We can think of culture at its most abstract or mythical level as a paradigm that influences the selection and interpretation of our beliefs, observations, and feelings. When there is "an interpenetration of value and fact," as Nathan Adler puts it, the regnant culture is continually confirmed as the right blueprint by which to guide our actions. When, under changed circumstances, culture seems to frustrate the satisfaction of our needs, leave our questions unanswered, our emotions suspect, our identity blurred, it may be pushed aside—or strong efforts will be made to push it aside by those most affected by the changes.

Attacks on the prevailing values and norms are often preceded by opposition to or neglect of a society's rituals, those symbolic actions that both reflect and support a group's bonds. Concomitantly, the word ritual comes to mean, as Mary Douglas shows, an *empty* symbol, a form without content, behavior without commitment. When Merton used the concept of ritualism in this way in his well-known discussion of anomie,[72] many of us found his interpretation congenial, perhaps suggesting something about our judgment of his analysis of responses to anomie.

If ritual is an empty symbol of conformity, what shall we call symbolic acts that express commitment and belief? I think Douglas put the issue too sharply when she wrote that in small, face-to-face societies "the gulf between personal meanings and public meanings cannot develop," that in primitive religions there is no "ritualized ritual."[73] The distinction she draws, however, is vital, and her judgment seems wise that we should use the term ritual neutrally, not as a synonym for either symbolic behavior devoid of commitment or a symbol of genuine conformity. Our sense of the degree to which one or the other of these tendencies prevails is a valuable clue to the cultural climate and the extent to which it is favorable to the growth of countercultures.

Insofar as the cultural situation is experienced as traumatic and the critique has gone beyond opposition to the formation of new standards, we will see the emergence of new rituals, new symbolic forms to confirm the standards and define the community of believers. The new rituals often will not be recognized as such, ritualism itself, not just irrelevant rituals, having been denounced, as Douglas notes. But a new way of seeing the world requires a new myth and the symbolic acts to support it.[74]

New rituals and the standards they confirm will often contain items borrowed from abroad. Ideas, goods, techniques, and values from "alien" societies or from earlier periods are especially likely to be imported during periods of high anomie. Those most dismayed over the values of the established culture, yet distressed over what they experience as moral anarchy, seek a contrast conception. They lower the usual cultural tariff barriers. To counterculturalists in the industrial West, the values of the "exotic Orient" or the ways of "primitives" have special appeal, because they are seen to be in sharp contradiction to prevailing standards. Most societies, of course, import goods, ideas, and values from abroad. Much importation, however, is designed to fill a specific need or to enrich a culture. Countercultural importation seeks to expose the weaknesses of the existing order and to replace it with an inverted order. Replacement seldom occurs, even when the indigenous "deviants" are supported by military, economic, and ecclesiastic support from outside. Yet under some conditions the importations can have a powerful dissolving effect on the established way of doing things.

Although we have no well agreed upon ways to measure amomie, few doubt that this is a time of cultural crisis. Hendin puts it strongly: This "culture is at war and young people are in the front lines."[75] Peter Berger sees modernity itself confronted by a dilemma. Modernity promotes secularization, yet "Secularization frustrates deeply grounded human aspirations—most important among these, the aspiration to exist in a meaningful and ultimately hopeful cosmos."[76] In Weber's terms, there is a continuing need for "theodicies"—ways of explaining and coping with suffering and evil. But they are not always available.

The present crisis of meaning is now generations old, and many feel, with Matthew Arnold that they are

> wandering between two worlds, one dead,
> the other powerless to be born. . . .[77]

Many of those caught in such a situation grasp for faith; they invent what they can (glorious religions are seldom the outcome), and they borrow meaning systems that seem uncorrupted by the society around them.

> We need a theme? then let that be our theme:
> that we, poor grovellers between faith and doubt,
> the sun and north star lost, and compass out,
> the heart's weak engine all but stopped, the time
> timeless in this chaos of our wills—
> that we must ask a theme, something to think,
> something to say, between dawn and dark,
> something to hold to, something to love.[78]

We are moved by the poet more than by prosaic facts, but I think we need to guard against pluralistic ignorance—a shared belief in pseudo facts. It may be that a moderate reduction in the sense of shared fundamental values is so threatening that we are drawn to those sensitive voices warning of imminent danger.

Countercultures and Communication

Such social, cultural, and personality factors as I have mentioned create the context in which countercultures are likely to occur, but at least one other element is needed: communication among those with predispositions and living in situations that can precipitate countercultural values. Potential members need to identify one another; leaders need audiences; powerful signals to and from the dominant society are required to help give protesters a sense of identity and to set boundaries. It is not by accident that the Diggers, Ranters, and Seekers, not to mention the more moderate Levellers, spread rapidly across England at a time when small printing presses were appearing in large numbers, when literacy was growing, and when the Puritans and the Royalists, struggling with one another, were for a brief period relatively tolerant of radical notions, each hoping to win support. It is scarcely necessary to note how much the TV camera, the mass circulation magazines and newspapers, and the movies, as well as the enormously variegated underground press, have spread the word in the contemporary Western world. More generally, the recurring conditions for countercultures are reinforced by direct lines of communication to the past and by the rediscovery and reemphasis of past leaders and movements.[79]

Countercultural groups emerge in a process of interaction between those inclined to deviate and those inclined to repress, with many in the middle shaping the outcome by what they do or do not do. Extensive publicity, even if largely negative, helps an oppositional group to define itself and brings in recruits who are attracted to the antiestablishment image. Harsh treatment can also strengthen a countercultural group. Its members, I have argued, are ambivalent. Cruelty or behavior by the authorities that can be defined as cruelty aids the repression of that part of the self attracted to the repressors' standards. If my opponents are not sufficiently harsh, I can goad them into stronger repressive measures. I cannot convince myself that I've made the right choice of values just by *calling* the agents of the establishment pigs, but if I can make them *act* like pigs, it is easier to repress my doubts.

The reciprocal of this is that the same conditions that increase tendencies toward cultural reversals create a crisis of meaning in the society at large. Just as nonconformists need their pigs, groups torn by cultural doubts and confusion need their witches to help them define their standards unambiguously by reference to the counter standards and counter behavior of the deviants.

Intragroup and intergroup communication is thus the chain by which the counter-valuative behaviors of individuals are linked—in a process involving all three of the sources we have been discussing (the structural, cultural, and individual)—into the countercultural values of a group.

Notes

1. See Max Weber, *The Protestant Ethic and the Spirit of Capitalism*, 1930; Lucian Pye, *Politics, Personality, and Nation-building*, 1962; Daniel Lerner, *The Passing of Traditional Society*, 1958; Robert Bellah, *Beyond Belief: Essays on Religion in a Post-Traditional World*, 1970; Peter Berger, Brigitte Berger, and Hansfried Kellner, *The Homeless Mind*, 1973; and Alex Inkeles and David Smith, *Becoming Modern: Individual Change in Six Developing Countries*, 1974.

2. Frank Musgrove, *Ecstasy and Holiness: Counter Culture and the Open Society*, 1974.

3. Richard Flacks, *Youth and Social Change, 1971, and David Westby, The Clouded Vision: The Student Movement in the United States in the 1960s*, 1976. For a different perspective, see Midge Decter, *Liberal Parents, Radical Children*, 1975.

4. Musgrove, 1974, p. 13.

5. Philip Slater, *The Pursuit of Loneliness: American Culture at the Breaking Point*, 1971, pp. 103-104.

6. H. N. Brailsford, *The Levellers and the English Revolution*, 1961, chap. 10, and Michael Barkun, *Disaster and the Millennium*, 1974, p. 126.

7. See Arnold van Gennep, *The Rites of Passage*, 1960; James Pruess, "Merit and Misconduct: Venerating the Bo Tree at a Buddhist Shrine," 1979; Bettylou Valentine, *Hustling and Other Hard Work: Life Styles in the Ghetto*, 1978; and Steven Smith, "The London Apprentices as Seventeenth-Century Adolescents," 1973.

8. Barkun, 1974, p. 188; see also E. A. Wrigley, *Population and History, 1969*.

9. Joan Waring, "Social Replenishment and Social Change: The Problem of Disordered Cohort Flow," 1975, p. 238.

10. David Herlihy, "Alienation in Medieval Culture and Society," in *Alienation: Concept, Term, and Meanings*, Frank Johnson, editor, 1973, chap. 5.

11. Stanley Uys, "South Africa's New Black Puritans," 1976.

12. Valentine, 1978.

13. Matilda Riley, "Aging and Cohort Succession: Interpretations and Misinterpretations," 1973, and Norval Glenn, *Cohort Analysis*, 1977.

14. For general theory of generations, see Karl Mannheim, *Essays in the Sociology of Knowledge*, 1952, and S.N. Eisenstadt, *From Generation to Generation: Age Groups and Social Structure*, 1956.

15. Robert Wuthnow, "Recent Patterns of Secularization: A Problem of Generations," 1976c.

16. Lawrence Wieder and Don Zimmerman, "Generational Experience and the Development of Freak Culture," 1974.

17. Bennett Berger, *Looking for America: Essays on Youth, Suburbia, and Other American Obsessions*, 1971, p. 106.

18. Talcott Parsons, *Essays in Sociological Theory*, 1954, pp. 89-103.

19. Richard Easterlin, "What Will 1984 Be Like? Socioeconomic Implication of Recent Twists in Age Structure," 1978. See also Easterlin, *Birth and Fortune: The Impact of Numbers on Personal Welfare*, 1980.

20. The discussion was based to some degree on Max Weber, *From Max Weber*, 1946, pp. 180-95, and was precipitated by the important work of Gerhard Lenski, "Status Crystallization: A Non-Vertical Dimension of Social Status," 1954.

21. See George E. Simpson and J. Milton Yinger, *Racial and Cultural Minorities, 1972.*

22. J. Milton Yinger, *A Minority Group in American Society*, 1965, pp. 10-14.

23. See, for example, Nathan Glazer, *The Social Basis of American Communism*, 1961; Lewis Feuer, *The Conflict of Generations*, 1969, pp. 423-25; Thomas Piazza in Charles Glock and Robert Bellah, *The New Religious Consciousness*, 1976, pp. 245-64; Stanley Rothman, "Group Fantasies and Jewish Radicalism: A Psychodynamic Interpretation," 1978; and Arthur Liebman, *Jews and the Left*, 1979.

24. See Herbert Hendin, *The Age of Sensation*, 1975, and Lauren Langman, Richard Block, and Ineke Cunningham, "Countercultural Values at a Catholic University," 1973.

25. Ralph White and Ronald Lippitt, *Autocracy and Democracy: An Experimental Inquiry*, 1960; Eleanor Maccoby, "The Choice of Variables in the Study of Socialization," 1961; and Robert Sears, Eleanor Maccoby, and Harry Levin, *Patterns of Child Rearing, 1957.*

26. Hendin, 1975, chap. 9.

27. Musgrove, 1974 (note 2 above), p. 11.

28. Feuer, 1969.

29. Robert Coles, *Privileged Ones: The Well-off and the Rich in America*, 1977.

30. Ronald Rohner, *They Love Me, They Love Me Not: A Worldwide Study of the Effects of Parental Acceptance and Rejection*, 1975, p. 168.

31. John Rothchild and Susan Berns Wolf, *The Children of the Counter-Culture*, 1976, and Yablonsky, 1968, pp. 302-5.

32. Sigmund Freud, *Civilization and Its Discontents*, 1962, pp. 33, 62.

33. *Ibid.*, p 62.

34. Dennis Wrong, "The Oversocialized Conception of Man," 1961, and George Homans, "Bringing Men Back In," 1964.

35. Freud, 1962, pp. 23-24.

36. Emile Durkheim, *Moral Education*, 1973, p. 40.

37. Donald Campbell, "On the Conflicts Between Biological and Social Evolution and Between Psychology and Moral Tradition," 1975, p. 1121.

38. Ralph Turner, "The Real Self: From Institution to Impulse," 1976, p. 998.

39. Kenneth Keniston, *The Uncommitted: Allienated Youth in American*

Society, 1965, p. 81. See also Myron Bloy, "Alientated Youth, the Counter Culture, and the Chaplain," 1969, and Donald Oken, "Alienation and Identity: Some Comments on Adolescence, the Counterculture, and Contemporarary Adaptations," in *Alienation: Concept, Term, Meanings*, Frank Johnson, editor, 1973, pp. 83-110.

40. Richard Sennett, *The Fall of Public Man*, 1977; Christopher Lasch, *The Culture of Narcissism: American Life in an Age of Diminishing Expectations, 1978, p. 5; and Tom Wolfe, "The 'Me' Decade and the Third Great Awakening," 1976.*

41. Erik Erikson, *Identity: Youth and Crisis*, 1968, pp. 172-4, See also Nathan Adler, *The Underground Stream: New Life Styles and the Antinomian Personality, 1972; Vytautas Kavolis, "Post-Modern Man: Psychocultural Responses to Social Trends," 1970a; Lionel Trilling, The Opposing Self*, 1955; and Orrin Klapp, *Collective Search for Identity*, 1969.

42. Friedrich Nietzsche, Twilight of the Idols, 1968a, p. 105.

43. Friedrich Nietzsche, *The Anti-Christ*, 1968b, p. 116.

44. Hendin, 1975 (note 24 above), 300.

45. Bloy, 1969, p. 651.

46. Erikson, 1968, p. 176.

47. William Greider, "Billy Carter: Errant Little Brother," *Washington Post*, Februrary 25, 1979.

48. Gregory Bateson *et al.*, "Toward a Theory of Schizophrenia," 1956.

49. See Robert Coles, *Children of Crisis*, 1967.

50. Richard Mills, *Young Outsiders: A Study of Alternative Communities*, 1973.

51. On ambivalence, see Robert Merton and Elinor Barber, "Sociological Ambivalence," in Merton, *Sociological Ambivalence and Other Essays*, pp. 3-31; Robin Room, "Ambivalence as a Sociological Explanation: The Case of Cultural Explanations of Alcohol Problems," 1976; and Erikson, 1968, p. 26

52. Keniston, 1965 (note 39 above), p. 96.

53. Fritz Redl and David Wineman, *Children Who Hate*, 1951, p. 144. See also M.D. Buffalo and J. W. Rodgers, "Behavioral Norms, Moral Norms, and Attachment: Problems of Deviance and Conformity," 1971, and Richard Cloward and Lloyd Ohlin, *Delinquency and Opportunity*, 1960, p. 110.

54. Jerry Rubin, *Growing (Up) at 37*, 1976, pp. 67, 128.

55. Ken Kelley, "Blissed Out with the Perfect Master," 1973.

56. Jack Douglas, *Youth in Turmoil*, 1970, p. 179.

57. Kavolis, 1970 (note 41 above), pp. 436-37.

58. Erikson, 1968, p. 26.

59. Albert Cohen, *Delinquent Boys*, 1955 pp. 59-65, and Klapp, (note 41 above) 1969.

60. Weston LaBarre, *The Ghost Dance*, 1972.

61. Erich Fromm and Michael Maccoby, *Social Character in a Mexican Village: A Sociopsychoanalytic Study*, 1970.

62. Erikson, 1968, p. 23.

63. Ellen Goodman, Cleveland *Plain Dealer*, Sept. 10, 1978, Section 4, p. 15.

64. Bennett Berger, 1971 (note 17 above), pp. 90, 97.

65. J. Milton Yinger, "On Anomie," 1964, and *idem, Toward a Field Theory of Behavior*, 1965, chap. 9.

66. Howard Kaplan, "Self-Attitudes and Deviant Response," 1976, 788. See also his "Sequelae of Self-Derogation: Predicting from a General Theory of Deviant Behavior," 1975.

67. Adler (note 41 above) 1972, p. 49.

68. David Matza, "Subterranean Traditions of Youth," 1961.

69. Barbara P. Solomon in the *New York Times Book Review*, Sept. 18, 1977, p. 3.

70. Paul Goodman, *Growing Up Absurd*, 1960, p. 11.

71. J. Milton Yinger, "A Comparative Study of the Substructures of Religion," 1977.

72. Mary Douglas, *Natural Symbols*, 1970a, and Robert Merton, "Social Structure and Anomie," in Merton, *Social Theory and Social Structure*, 1968.

73. Douglas, 1970, p. 2.

74. Suzanne Langer, *Philosophy in a New Key*, 1972.

75. Hendin, 1975 (note 24 above), p. 1.

76. Peter Berger, *Facing Up to Modernity*, 1977, p. 79.

77. Matthew Arnold, *Poetical Works*, 1907, p. 321.

78. Conrad Aiken, *Time in the Rock*, 1936, p. 2.

79. See Christopher Hill, *The World Turned Upside Down*, 1975, chap. 18.

Chapter Four

Varieties of Countercultures

The diversity of cultures is matched by the diversity of countercultures. To get some sense of the enormous range of value reversals, we need a set of organizing principles, which, fortunately, we can draw from studies of the traditional and established elements of society.

Values and norms can be examined "institutionally," with the orthodox or dominant patterns of economics, politics, education, the family, and religion seen against those that invert the prevailing standards. Although most countercultural groups oppose society in several different ways, focal concerns may be more specialized. A comparative study of inverted economic values, for example, might reveal the conditions under which countercultural protests are aimed particularly at prevailing modes of production and types of work, at dominant economic values, or at the extent of economic inequality. Of course, such protests are likely to have implications not only for economics but for all the other institutions as well.

A second method of analysis is to examine countercultural reversals of prevailing beliefs and practices concerning the true, the good, and the beautiful. Particular groups, although they may make all three assertions, are likely to emphasize that the established order is foolish (however much technical knowledge it has), that it is evil, or that it is ugly. We will find it helpful to look separately at the theories of knowledge, the conceptions of good and evil, and the aesthetic judgments of countercultural groups. Because their opposition, insofar as it is verbalized, is often stated in these terms, the assertions become three spotlights focused on the dominant society, revealing what are seen by those groups as its major weaknesses.

I shall use these two methods of analysis in later sections of this chapter and in other chapters. It will be helpful, however, prior to those comments, to look at another way of examining the varieties of countercultures. A mode of analysis that has proved useful in several other fields helps us to see how countercultures differ in the methods they use to promote their values. In her influencial book *The Neurotic Personality of our Time*, Karen Horney noted that neurotics tend to struggle with their anxieties in three ways: by attack, by withdrawal, or by a search for shelter and protection. Charles S. Johnson skillfully described the ways in which minority-group members deal with discrimination by aggression, avoidance, or acceptance. The last is typically accompanied by adaptations that downgrade the importance of the harsh reality. Turner and Killian develop a highly analogous interpretation of power-oriented, value-oriented, and participation-oriented social movements. Persons involved in power-oriented movements want to control society and perhaps to change it, or some part of it. Those who are value-oriented want above all to protect and preserve a set of values that seems threatened. They may withdraw into a protected community in the attempt to attain that end. It is the experience itself, the very fact of participation, that is of highest priority for those in participation-oriented movements. An additional close parallel to these descriptions of three methods of coping with, or seeking to change, unsatisfactory situations is found in Weber's account of prophetic, ascetic, and mystical religious sects.[1]

The Three Faces of Counterculture

Countercultural groups quite clearly fall into the same threefold pattern, not the twofold activist-versus-withdrawal categories often employed. Many observers have distinguished between the two types of protest, variously labeled, in Malcolm Cowley's terms for example, as social versus individual, political versus aesthetic, radical versus bohemian, or the revolt against capitalism versus the revolt against puritanism.[2] This is a helpful distinction, but it is incomplete. The search for individual ecstasy, for dionysian release, for mystical insight can be contrasted with the protest activities of the radical, denouncing the injustices of society and the values on which they are believed to rest. It can also be contrasted, however, with protests expressed by efforts to build a separate countercommunity. In many instances, those who withdraw from a society seen as fundamentally evil, whether into an isolated community or into a sectarian group surrounded by a social moat, are more ascetic than dionysian. They search for ways to give reality to new values, not for ways to attain new levels of experience or to achieve mystical insight.

These are analytic distinctions, of course, not empirical descriptions. Conceptually clear types are essential, however, in any effort to understand the range of empirical mixtures. Of the several sets of ways to promote values or to work toward goals that I have noted, the closest comparison of the countercultural set is with types of sects. The radical activist counterculturalist is the prophet who "preaches, creates, or demands *new* obligations," to use Weber's words. The communitarian, seen as a type, is the ascetic who withdraws into a separated community where the new values can be lived out with minimum hindrance from an evil society. Neither of these descriptions fits the mystics who are searching for the truth and for themselves. Realization of their values requires, in their view, that they turn inward. They do not so much attack society as disregard it, insofar as they can, and float above it in search of enlightenment. "The enemy is within each of us," says Charles Reich.[3]

Every countercultural group tends to be a mixture; the strains and the splits they experience often result from sharply contrasting views of the best way to realize their oppositional values. When at the 1969 Woodstock festival, Abbie Hoffman tried to generate political action by saying that the festival was meaningless until a radical "rotting in jail" was freed, a member of The Who rock band, in the words of *Rolling Stone*, "clubbed Hoffman off the stage with his guitar,"[4] a wonderfully symbolic way to express the conflict. From the perspective of prophetic counterculturalists, the tendency of many participants in the "new left" to define political problems in terms of personal issues, often in the language of alienation, seems a terrible deflection from the basic goal of achieving a society based on new values.[5] "The Yippies are Marxists. . . . We follow in the revolutionary tradition of Groucho, Chico, Harpo, and Karl."[6] Hoffman's similar effort to combine radical and hippie views is well shown in the title of one his books, *Revolution for the Hell of it*, and by the title of its first chapter, "Revolution: The Highest Trip of Them All." He has been more hippie than revolutionary, however, complaining that the new left had no sense of fun and was built too much on sacrifice, dedication, responsibility, anger, frustration, and guilt. "Look, you want to have more fun, you want to get laid more, you want to turn on with friends, you want an outlet for your creativity, then get out of school, quit your job.

Come on out and help build and defend the society you want. Stop trying to organize everybody but yourself. Begin to live your vision."[7]

A Marxist counterculturalist sees the drive to have more fun quite useless until society has been transformed: ". . . in a rotten society your fun will always be tainted anyway. That's partly why the step from Woodstock to Altamount, From Leary to Manson, or for that matter from *Hair* to *Jesus Christ Superstar*, will always be a short one when there is no attempt to understand how society works and no realistic effort to change it."[8] Those who think the main, or the first, battle is in the streets, to overturn established institutions see only weakness in the claims of Charles Reich or Timothy Leary or others who see it in the head. In theory, if not always in their own ideologically guided behavior, they share Weber's view that "he who seeks the salvation of the soul, of his own and others, should not seek it along the avenue of politics."[9]

It is difficult to support both Lenin's sternly "puritanical" approach and the "politics of joy" associated with Emma Goldman. For several years, from the late 1960s until the mid-1970s, the German magazine *Konkret* sought to combine a communist ideology with an emphasis on sex, but editors concluded that the latter deflected attention from the former. *Rolling Stone*, one of the most important countercultural journals of the 1960s and 1970s, with a similar although less extreme combination, after several years sharply reduced the more "vivacious" of its sexual material.

The tension created by efforts to combine different countercultural modes are personal as well as organizational. As a young woman, Ulrike Meinhof was a Christian pacifist and political radical. She became a coleader of the "Baeder-Meinhof gang," which moved toward an ideology justifying murder and uninhibited self-expression. Her "old-left" inclinations combined only with difficulty with the "new-left" atmosphere of the gang, with its emphasis on self-affirmation. Meinhof's suicide in 1976 reflected her searing ambivalence.

Internal conflicts over the right method to attain countercultural values can be expressed in several different ways. Eldridge Cleaver at first participated in the individually oriented protests, with emphasis on a countercultural life style; he wrote the introduction to Jerry Rubin's *Do It*. With some other black Americans, however, he shifted toward revolutionary protest, motivated by anger and, in the midst of the civil rights movement, by rising aspirations. Having helped to found the Black Panthers, he fled to Algeria during a period of severe confrontation with the law. There, in a sharp disagreement with Timothy Leary, he denounced "ego trips and the magic-wand approach . . . demanded that the white counterculture be critically reassessed, and spoke of Rubin, Abbie Hoffman, Allen Ginsberg, and Stew Albert as 'that silly psychedelic movement.' "[10] More recently, Cleaver has declared himself a "born again" Christian and a supporter of Sun Myung Moon's Unification Church, thus moving to the third method for confronting a society that is seen as basically evil.

That the activist-prophetic and mystical-experiential compound is highly unstable, both within individuals and among them, is not a new phenomenon. Although there was a powerful licentiousness to several early modern Christian sects, they sought, at the same time, drastic social change.[11] If they did not evolve into more purely prophetic or ascetic sects, however, they tended to be short-lived.

Each of the mixtures of modes of countercultural opposition and criticism can be found, historically and contemporaneously. Among recent communes there have been groups that seek to mix the mystical-experiential with the ascetic approach, until it becomes clear that the search for wisdom and the ultimate trip doesn't get the corn planted or the groceries bought, whereupon the group breaks up or some members leave for a setting more in keeping with their inclinations. In the seventeenth century many Ranters became Quakers, shifting to a more ascetic movement. In recent years, persons who had sought salvation through drugs and unrestrained sex have sometimes turned to ascetic and highly restrained religious groups—the Divine Light Mission, Hare Krishna, or Meher Baba.[12] Others have shifted from a prophetic countercultural mode to ascetic and mystical modes.

Groups break apart because some members perceive that one set of methods or one set of goals which to them is the minor set, is winning out over the major set. In one of the first articles on the hippies, Warren Hinckle wrote:

> If more and more youngsters begin to share the hippie political posture of unrelenting quietism, the future of activist, serious politics is bound to be affected. The hippies have shown that it can be pleasant to drop out of the arduous task of attempting to steer a difficult, unrewarding society. But when that is done, you leave the driving to the Hell's Angels.[13]

Despite the schismatic tendencies, two or more types of countercultural protest frequently reappear in combination. In the years between the two world wars, Cowley observed, bohemians read Marx and radicals had a touch of bohemianism, making it difficult to tell the difference between the two views. For the international groups of students in Paris, Cowley wrote, "socialism, free love, anarchism syndicalism, free verse" were all part of the same cause.[14]

The musical *Hair* also illustrates the combination of radicalism and bohemianism. Each is used to strengthen the other. Those needing more energy to overcome their sexual ambivalence, hang-ups, and inhibitions use radicalism as a motor: You see, all of this is for a high moral purpose, for justice and peace. (Many readers will suppose that I have left out a few words in the preceding sentences. Surely it was the sexual inhibitions and confusion of the larger society that were being rejected in *Hair*. That is doubtless true. It is also true, in my judgment, that the drama projects qualities onto a "puritanical," "repressed," "sexually schizoid" society in an effort to handle the sexual ambivalence of audiences and performers as well.) On the other side, those needing more energy to sustain their radical drive find it, or look for it, in the release of sexuality: You see what a world it will be—how loving and pleasurable—if the radical new world is brought about.

Countercultural groups and movements, in summary, form various mixtures of prophetic activism, communal or utopian withdrawal, and the search for ecstasy and mystical insight. Mixtures are common but unstable because of the mutually contradictory qualities of both the means seen as effective in attaining the various goals and of the goals themselves. If ones greatest desire is for a flood of raw experience, uncensored and unconstrained by an "uptight, plastic society," it is difficult to marshal the resources and maintain the disciplines necessary to alter the basic values of that society. If it is exactly a new world governed by those altered basic values that is the fundamental goal, then the protest is likely to be political and radical. Yet if one is pessimistic about success in building a world around counter values, it will seem best to create one's own community where they can be attained, hoping that the example will succeed in changing the larger society where direct attack could not. The relationships among these three types of countercultures and various mixtures can be suggested by the schema in Figure 4.1.

Most societies, in my view, give cultural support to these same three value clusters. The dominant elements, however, have accepted various compromises, some of them extremely limiting and self-contradictory, in the attempt to optimize the attainment of all three sets of values. Those who see the compromises as utterly destructive or, for reasons of their generational experiences and personal biographies, see one of the sets as uniquely important, are dismayed by the compromises and failures. The dominant culture is condemned, a counterculture affirmed.

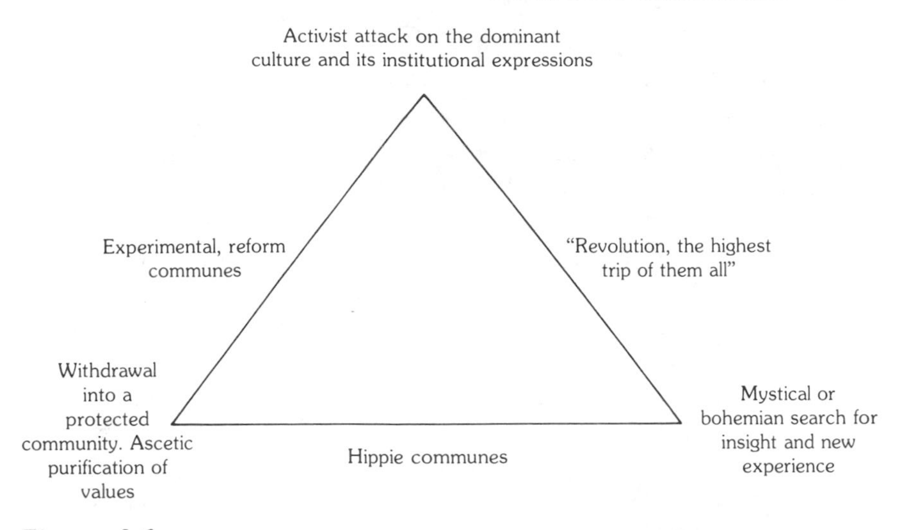

Figure 4.1

In viewing this intellectual, moral, and political struggle, one can say: Thank God for those who refuse to accept such a shoddy world and demand a better one. Or one can say: What a pity that the delicate and complicated task of building and maintaining a civilization is so crudely attacked. (Personally, I say both of these things, depending upon the circumstances being experienced or described, while struggling to find a humane blend.) What one cannot say, with any degree of realism, is that these cultural conflicts are of minor and passing interest. They are of fundamental concern not only to social science but also to the larger human enterprise.

The True, the Good, and the Beautiful

No sets of values and norms better characterize a culture, nor more clearly distinguish it from other cultures, than those which affirm: This is the truth, and this is the way we know the truth; this is good, which has been shown to us in these ways; and this is beautiful, made evident by the application of these basic standards. Despite the extensive intercultural contact of our time, we need to remind ourselves that the principles of truth, goodness, and beauty are deeply embedded in particular cultures. For most persons socialized to a culture, the criteria for making judgments are self-evident. If we are ethnocentric, it is because, in responding to another culture, we automatically use those criteria as if they were universal.

Of course, beauty—and doubtless truth and goodness also—is in the eye of the beholder. It is a pity to disturb the sentiment and the poetry of that phrase; but for most of us, individual variation is within a culturally established frame. From the other side, humanity as a whole shares some standards, which have developed out of common needs, observations, and experiences. Comparative study readily shows, however, that culture and subculture strongly influence our standards of judgment. Any traveler into an exotic land (that is, a land very different from ones own) is likely to exclaim: How can they eat that? How can they do that? How can they believe that?

The importance of culture in shaping our cognitive, evaluative, and cathetic standards, to use the somewhat larger concepts employed by Talcott Parsons, furnishes an invaluable clue to the identification and examination of countercultures. A group that leaves those standards unchallenged can scarcely be seen as countercultural, no matter the strength of its opposition to the social order. A group that inverts those standards, however, is cutting at the root of a culture. In examining normative reversals, therefore, we need to ask:

Are there drastic shifts in the criteria and the methods by which a group claims to *know* what is true, good, and beautiful?

Are there drastic shifts in the standards of what are *held to be* true, good, and beautiful?

In the traditional categories of philosophy, we can identify countercultures by their epistemologies, their ethics, and their aesthetics. The events we study will almost always combine two or more of these elements; but we can understand the blends better if we keep in mind the elements out of which they are built.

Truth, Cultural and Countercultural

One need scarcely stress that rules of evidence are cultural. Much of what people think they know depends on their society's particular way of defining evidence. If I were to declare that there is life on Mars, most readers would want to know how I knew. If I said God spoke to me and revealed it, a certain skepticism would be expressed. If I said scientists at Cambridge Universtiy, MIT, and the University of Wisconsin all have evidence from particles of matter collected in outer space, most of the skepticism would fade.[15] Nevertheless, the responses would be based on faith in certain kinds of authorities and on a world view that gives them credibility.

When a world view seems no longer to help one organize experience and deal with crises and mysteries, a drastically different one may be adopted. Though the substance of the epistemological challenge today is quite different from the one John Donne saw, we can perhaps read him with some understanding:

> New philosophy calls all in doubt;
> The element of fire is quite put out;
> The sun is lost, and the Earth, and no man's wit
> Can well direct him where to look for it.

Through the centuries since Donne wrote, the "new philosophy" continued to call all in doubt. Organized skepticism, as someone has defined science, has vastly increased our understanding of and our control over nature. Or has it? some persons are asking. And if it has, are its truths destroying greater truths? Science has brought many diseases under control, expanded the food supply, taken men to the moon—and created atomic bombs. Has it utterly neglected the need for mystery—showing how poorly human nature is understood?[16] Has it neglected roads to truth that have nothing to do with the empirical and logical processes of science? Despite the enlightenment, modernism, rationalism, and the enormous growth of science—a set of forces that have dominated thought in the West for several centuries—a not insignificant challenge has persisted. Indeed, to many person's amazement, the challenge has increased in strength in the late twentieth century, even in the face of major scientific discoveries (or perhaps one should say, precisely because of those discoveries). From William Blake, to take an arbitrary post-Enlightenment starting point, to the romanticists, the transcendentalists, followers of various religious traditions, a few experimental psychologists, and others, down to the resurgent contemporary interest in mysticism, altered states of consciousness, and the occult, science and rationalism have been held in suspicion. Counterculturalists declare that the tentative judgments of science, subject always to revision, leave our deepest needs for secure knowledge in an uncertain world unfulfilled.

Truth, today's counterculturalists declare, is attained not by arid research but by mystical insight. It is found in populist, homespun wisdom, in direct experience with the cosmos, in meditation, in chants, in drugs, in sensory deprivation, in sensitivity to the messages of the intuitive right hemisphere of the brain—all this set over against science, technology, the knowledge of the expert, and cold rationality. Roszak expresses this point of view in appropriate style: "The Old

Gnosis. Vision born of transcendental knowledge. Mysticism . . . . the exploration of magic and dreams, science and alchemy, idolatry and the sacramental awareness, visionary poetry and the tricks of perception."[17]

In Roszak's view, science can now be regarded as a school—one of various schools of consciousness—just as classic art traditions have come to be seen as schools. Following this line of thought, Adam Smith, in *Powers of Mind*, explores what might be called the "new consciousness school." It is his belief that industrial societies have overvalued the rational, cognitive left hemisphere of the brain. He wants us to get in touch with the more intuitive way of knowing, ranging from Transcendental Meditiation, to the mystical exercises in Arica, to the use of LSD, body-pummeling in Rolfing, isolation in an underwater sensory-deprivation tank, and Zen tennis lessons. Smith treats the subject in a somewhat lighthearted, perhaps even lightheaded, way. His own views are obscure, except that he thinks he sees interesting things happening that are beyond the grasp of science. Whether or not that is true, they are not beyond the efforts of some scientists to try to reach them. A group of qualified and researching physicists, calling themselves "counterculture physicists" are publishing a journal, *Foundations of Physics*, in which they explore precognition, unusual experiences of time and space, telepathy, clairvoyance, psychokinesis, and "shattering new senses of how organic and inorganic life are related through time and space. These experiences amount not to a shift of emphasis, but to a virtual dissolution of the ways that time, space, energy, light, matter, organic and inorganic life are assumed to relate."[18] They are asking questions, Heirich observes, that "would simply have served to label the participants as mentally deranged" a few years ago.

Some seekers for mystical knowledge have proceeded without the aid of technology, chemistry, and the modern media: "Standing on the bare gound—my head bathed by the blithe air and uplifted into infinite space—all mean egotism vanishes. I become a transparent eyeball; I am nothing; I see all; the currents of the Universal Being circulate through me; I am part or parcel of God." "Transparent eyeball"! Is this a full-page drawing in an underground newspaper or the name of a rock band? The phrase comes from Emerson, as does the full quotation. The imaginative explanations are those of William Hamilton.[19]

Echoes of Emerson reverberate through Charles Reich's description of "Consciousness III," although he uses less mystical language. We can grasp the truth only when we break free from the distorting images imposed on us by a coercive society. "Ultimately, what the corporate state does is to separate man from his sources of meaning and truth."[20] One who is fortunate or wise enough to have made the break attains great insight:

> . . . the Consciousness III person, no matter how young and inexperienced he may be, seems to possess an extraordinary "new knowledge." . . . He does not "know" the facts, but he still "knows" the truth that seems hidden from others. The explanation for this political sophistication is primarily the repeal of pretense and absurdity. . . . the young people of Consicousness III see effortlessly what is phony or dishonest in politics, or what is ugly and meretricious in architecture and city planning, whereas an older person has to go through years of education to make himself equally aware. It might take a Consciousness II person twenty years of reading radical literature to "know" that law is a tool of oppression, the young drug user just plain "knows" it.[21]

The wisdom of children, springing from their innocence, is an ancient theme. All parents know, to their delight and their dismay, that the absence of cultural blinders and an unblunted curiosity may help a child to see truths that are obscure to an adult. Although the ratio of delight to dismay may decrease, few parents escape the same knowledge with respect to the youths in their household. (The youths sometimes have a parallel experience a few years later: When they get to be twenty-one—or thirty—they are amazed to discover how much the old man has learned during the previous several years.) To most adults, however, these are part-truths. The absence of cultural glasses, microscopes, and telescopes, metaphorical and real, blocks or postpones the attainment of much knowledge and wisdom. That is not Reich's countercultural view. It is not the learning of skills, nor the study of a body of literature, nor experience that makes one wise. It is the "repeal of pretense and absurdity." (It is difficult not to take up the sword against pretense and absurdity, although, as Reich's discussion shows, it is a difficult weapon to use without cutting oneself.)

Countercultural beliefs about the road to truth are mixed in various proportions with an emphasis on "natural wisdom" and with more orthodox study. It is not easy to identify the countercultural element in the mixture; but it is necessary to try to do so if one wants to examine competing epistemologies. They are seldom found in pure form. This is well illustrated in a school of thought that we can call, following David Cooper, antipsychiatry.[22] This should be understood to mean opposition to the premises and methods of established psychiatry, not oppostion to efforts to attain mental health. Insofar as antipsychiatry develops explanations and offers therapies for mental illness different from the orthodoxies of the day, while keeping within the scientific mode of interpretation, there is little that can be called countercultural. Many studies of the antihealing effects of hospitals and of the importance of labeling in causing mental illness, although they disagree with the "medical model" as an explanation of mental illness, are carried out within the frame of "orthodox" epistemology.[23]

This is less true of the antipsychiatrists themselves: Cooper, Szasz, and especially Laing.[24] To be sure, they build on family theory, and therapy, to contest the medical view that schizophrenia, for example, is solely inside the patient. With Bateson they see its origins in family conflict and inconsistent communication.[25] In other ways, however, they make drastic shifts in the criteria and methods by which they claim to know what is true and in the standards of what is held to be true, to repeat the criteria we have stated earlier. Schizophrenia is not so much an illness as a healing voyage, in the interpretation of Laing in *The Politics of Experience*. It is society that is mad. Instead of looking for ways to increase normality and reasonableness in a repressive society, we should seek to learn from the "unwitting attempt by a few to cleanse themselves, literally, of the wounds of civilisation."[26]

The views of the "antipsychiatrists," based on medical training, shade off toward a wide variety of other countercultural psychotherapies that proclaim new ways to increase the use of human potential. Embraced by some with religious fervor, they are regarded by others as dangerous frauds, as indications of "man's talent for reducing, distorting, evading, and vulgarizing his own reality," as Sigmund Koch put it.[27] These various encounter, sensitivity, or meditation groups range from those close to medical forms of psychotherapy to mystical quasi-religious groups dominated by a charismatic leader.

Our concern here is not with their differing methods (which disguise a great deal of similarity) or with their effectiveness. A substantial literature examines these questions.[28] I want simply to note the extent to which they invert widely accepted therapeutic practices and build upon beliefs that contradict those based on the rationalistic tradition. By ritual manipulation of emotion (although their activities may not be seen in that light by practitioners and participants), they create a "psychic opening," a lowering of defenses that promote suggestibility. During this period "major shifts in . . . psychic configurations can occur."[29]

In sensitivity training, Back remarks, "taboos of ordinary society are reversed: frankness substitutes for tact, self-expression for manners, nonverbal techniques for language, and immediacy for responsiblility. Norms that have evolved to ensure the smooth and continual operation of society are rejected."[30]

New psychotherapies, reflecting the experiences and values of various groups, flourish in times of drastic social change.[31] They tell us a great deal about the society and about contemporary experiences, even if they tell us little about how, over the long run, to prevent or cure the widespread feelings of loneliness, the demoralization, and the sense that life is absurd.

Paradoxically, the way was paved for the countercultural epistemology of our time by the long tradition of unmasking in European and American social thought (along with other sources). Do not trust appearances or presumed objective truth, for there are deeper realities, say Hume, Marx, Nietzsche, Freud, Pareto, and many others. Truth requires that we bring these deeper realities to light.[32] If this unmasking laid the groundwork for the sociology and psychology of knowledge in the thought of some persons, it supported the search for truth through mysticism and the occult among others for whom science itself has been unmasked. (My statement itself, of course, is a hypothesis in the sociology of knowledge).

Opposition to science and a world dominated by rational calculation is also, in part, an extension of opposition to structure, bureaucratic control, and hierarchical organization. As Kavolis observes, particularly in democracies (or "people's democracies"), the images and experiences of control often seem threatening; "personality must become, to the highest possible degree, 'disorganized' and 'unsystematic' if it is not to be perceived as bureaucratization of the self. . . . Systematic restraints of any kind, from standardized clothing to logical (or scientific) categories, come to be experienced as instruments by which imposed hierarchies (or images of hierarchies) perpetuate themselves."[33]

A famous sociologist has recalled to our minds the powerful image, from Plato's *Republic*, of the enchained cavemen, with faces turned toward the wall. "Behind them lies the source of the light which they cannot see. The are concerned only with the shadowy images that this light throws upon the wall, and they seek to fathom their interrelations." One of them succeeds in breaking his fetters. He turns around and sees the sun. At first blinded, he gradually is able to see, and stammers of the marvels. The others think he is raving, but he is the philosopher. The sun is the truth of science, "which alone seizes not upon illusions and shadows but upon the true being."

Well, who today, our commentator asks, views science in such a manner?

> Today youth feels rather the reverse: the intellectual constructions of science constitute an unreal realm of artificial abstractions, which with their bony hands seek to grasp the blood-and-the-sap of true life without ever catching up with it. But here in life, in what for Plato was the play of shadows on the walls of the cave, genuine reality is pulsating; and the rest are derivatives of life, lifeless ghosts, and nothing else.[34]

Most readers have doubtless identified these statements as coming from Weber's famous essay on "Science as a Vocation," first presented as a lecture in 1918. It was one of the ways he expressed his understanding of the reaction to the growth of rationalization and bureaucratization, to the *Entzauberung*, the disenchantment of life. This goes beyond opposition to or suspicion of science to include the broader impact of the emphasis on rationality.

Donald MacRae reminds us that *Entzauberung*, disenchantment, can as readily—and more literally—be translated as "driving out magic." Weber was a friend of the poet Stefan George, who, in "Man and Satyr," has the goat-man sneer: " 'You are but man . . . our wisdom begins where your wisdom ends.' The man replies that the day of myth is over and the Satyr's time is done. Yet, says the Satyr, 'it is only through magic that life stays awake.' (Nur durch den Zauber bleibt das Leben wach.)" MacRae wisely concludes: "He might not much have liked such teaching, but it is the lesson of Max Weber all the same."[35]

What Weber may not have liked, but sought to understand, others embraced. Nietzche, whom Weber often cited, in *The Will to Power* described what he believed to be the inevitable advent of nihilism, springing from rationalism and science that destroy "unreflective spontaneity." The Order of the Golden Dawn, a group of upper- and middle-class Christian writers, of whom Yeats is the best known, was concerned primarily with magical beliefs and practices.[36] Philip Slater, in *The Wayward Gate: Science and the Supernatural*, is one of the most recent to develop a similar point of view. He believes that science is the characteristic way of looking at the world in the dominant culture. The supernatural is denied or overlooked. Science, dedicated to rationality and objectivity, is based on "the suppression of feeling, on the denial of motivation, and on the need to control,"[37] with consequent impoverishment of life.

In a time of perpetual crisis, when a great deal of scientific effort is given over to discoveries that at best might reduce the disasters caused by earlier scientific efforts, it is not difficult to understand the appeal of movements that promise instant insight or a group-supported way to the discovery of ancient and eternal truths. Such a view however, is still in sharp opposition to the prevailing one. Seventy-five per cent of a national sample of adults in the United States think that science and technology have changed life for the better. Only 12 per cent feel fear or alarm or indifference in connection with science.[38] It is often remarked that America has a strong "anti-intellectual" strain. There is good evidence for this, I believe; but to describe it precisely, we should note that the tension is often between the theoretician, academician, or thinker and the pragmatic person of "common sense." In different ways both tend to be rationalistic. The are epistemologically quite similar, and in contrast with the mystical world view. Only a minority are likely to share the view expressed by Roszak:

> It may well be that the richest symbols in human culture come down to us from an early generation of supremely gifted visionaries, shamanic geniuses touched by unique powers. Perhaps in the early evolution of consciousness mankind passed through a singular interval when the mind took fire as it never would again and the symbolic raw materials of culture were, like the phenomenon of human speech itself, generated all at once. Myth and occult tradition have more to tell us about this state of our development than science or scholarship ever will; for at least the myths are touched with a wonder that does justice to the event.[39]

Some seek to follow this countercultural road to truth with the aid of drugs.[40] Others—including many who had earlier sought salvation through drugs—have turned to ascetically inclined religious movements that promise a new age not by changing institutions but by changing consciousness, by showing the way—through meditiation, discipline, and restraint—to timeless and absolute truths. These include the Hare Krishna and Meher Baba movements, the Divine Light Mission, Scientology, and the pervasive influence of Zen and yoga.[41] Still others turn to the occult, astrology, witchcraft, and magic to find explanation of bewildering experiences and perhaps to attain some control.

Despite the enormous range in methods and symbolic forms, these various efforts to increase understanding in ways opposed to the dominant rationalism are of two major types. For some, truth is within us. If we can remove the social filters, throw off our perceptual inhibitions, and alter our consciousness, a natural wisdom will be released. Yoga, known most widely in the West as a way of "getting into shape," evolved as a disciplined way to break the hold of external constraints on understanding. Meditation, chanting, breathing and other exercises, and diet can, in the yoga view, lead to mystic comprehension and ecstasy.

Similar methods are central to the practices of the several Oriental religious groups that have taken root in the West. Mararishi Mahesh Yogi has founded the Mararishi International University in Iowa to teach the Science of Creative Intelligence, or Transcendental Meditation (TM), an exercise in deep relaxation designed to wake up dormant parts of the intellect. Like the Hare Krishna, Meher Baba, and Divine Light movements, TM does not seek to teach a formal body of doctrine but to create a new consciousness. Knowledge comes from within; it is not learned, but released. In Meher Baba's words: "I have come not to teach but to awaken."[42]

Those who are alienated from science, rationalism, and the often tedious methods of detailed study and research may turn to drugs in search of an "expanded consciousness" that they perceive as a way of opening a door to truths otherwise hidden. Drug use is, of course, much more—or perhaps I should say much less—than that. A few gurus and explorers of the mind may articulate a drug-oriented epistemology or, more broadly, road to salvation. Among the great majority of users, however, the implications range from something not very far from the Saturday night "beer bust," to the primordial search for "kicks," to protests against an authority that has lost its legitimacy, to attacks on boredom, to a desire to shut out the confusion and lower the anxiety promoted by a blurred self-image and a world in constant turmoil, and finally, for some, to a religious quest for enlightenment.

A contra-Marx might observe that in some societies opium is the religion of the people—or hashish or peyote. Drug use has been widespread among some Oriental religions, Muslim mystical orders, and various Siberian and American Indian tribes. In the industrial West, however, not many have applauded Thomas de Quincey's exclamation, "Eloquent opium . . . thou hast the keys of Paradise." (Marx's declaration that "religion is the opium of the people" has had greater support, although it has also played to mixed reviews.)

Drug use "eliminates" all of one's problems—for the moment. In some instances, it is analogous to borrowing from a high-interest loan shark to pay off all one's debts. Now there is only one debt. But the interest is exorbitant, the debt is not actually lower, and tomorrow it must be repaid.

In talking with drug users, I have somehow been reminded of the advertisement that shows a young couple strolling hand-in-hand along a beautiful beach—*because* they have borrowed money: *mirabile dictu*!

I will not undertake to examine the differences in clientele, mystique, and physical and psychic effects of the various drugs,[43] but only note here that, building on small beginnings in the nineteenth century, countercultural movements in the West since about 1950 have, in many instances, made extensive use of drugs. Our interest here is in their belief in the power of drugs to alter consciousness, to attain mystical states, to gain insight, and to be psychedelic (literally, "mind manifesting"), in Humphrey Osmond's term. Aldous Huxley applauded what he experienced with mescaline as "cleansed perception" (a phrase he drew from Blake) and a growth in powers of contemplation.

In some cases, drug use is tied to religious practice; the knowledge it is designed to attain is religious knowledge, as in Timothy Leary's "League for Spiritual Discovery"—though the acronym may be more diagnostic than the adjective. Michael Novak, expressing the antiachievement ethic of the 1960s, if not Leary's full "drop out" ethic, wrote of the " 'pelagian' prejudice that spiritual achievement is proportionate to personal effort. Those who share this prejudice cannot conceive of the possibility that the Creator may have graced his creation with drugs which, discovered in due time, might be instrumental in preparing people to understand the gentleness, brotherhood, and peace of the gospels. Spiritual achievement is not won only through will and effort; often it is grace."[44]

I'm inclined to wonder, as Huxley did in reference to his own experience with drugs, how such means for "preparing people to understand" are "to be reconciled with a proper concern with human relations, with the necessary chores and duties, to say nothing of charity and practical compassion."[45] The use of drugs by privileged persons in industrial societies to attain mystical insight seems related to our culturally powerful training in the expectation of "instant success." With respect to the religious dimension in drug use, some are inclined to ask: If we can have instant romance, instant beauty, instant wealth, why not instant religion? No self-sacrifice, no steady period of service, no intensive study of the human condition is needed. There's a religious genius—or at least a religious experience—in each of us, waiting to get out, if we can only learn how to pry off the lid.

The use of drugs, perhaps undertaken in pursuit of a religious experience, may itself become, as Needleman notes, the experience that is sought. At a Zen center he is describing, the goal is to transform desire, not to satisfy it. Those who continue to take drugs almost never continue beyond the beginning stages of practice at the Center; "those who persist gradually reduce and, eventually, stop the use of drugs."[46]

To draw an overly sharp distinction, the second major type of countercultural epistemology sees the search for truth, not as a process of turning inward to find hidden intuitions that need only to be released but as an outward journey, to make contact with the sources of understanding, to learn to read and perhaps to control them. This is the realm of the occult, the magical, the astrological. To understand what moves the world, and especially our individual fate, according to this view, we need mediums to instruct and guide us. We will not be well instructed by the teacher, doctor, lawyer, engineer, or broker—to what a sorry state they have brought the world—but will turn to tarot cards, the I Ching, and our horoscopes.

Occult beliefs and practices have a long history in virtually every civilization. In many times and places they cannot be considered countercultural, since they are part of the traditional system used by the members of a society to interpret and deal with their experience. Although pushed into the background by rationalism and science, they are not uncommon in industrial societies, both among those who express disenchantment with many aspects of contemporary cultures and also among more traditional groups. Extrapolating from a national sample, the Gallup Poll has estimated that more than one-fifth of American adults believe that stars influence our lives and foretell events.[47] In the 1960s 30 per cent of a French sample believed in astrology.[48] Using a sample from the San Francisco Bay area, Wuthnow found that commitment to astrology was strongest among the less well educated, the unemployed, and the lonely. He also found, however, that those associated with countercultural groups were more likely to be attracted to astrology than persons of similar educational and class levels not involved in the counterculture.[49]

Marty distinguishes between what he calls the "respectable and established public version," its publications widely distributed to "middle America" and aimed at their individual anxieties, from an occult underground press, the "drunken and erotic dionysian types" that get more attention. The occult "establishment" is highly critical of Satanism and other countercultural varieties of occultism.[50] Interest in the occult is one part of life for those participating in the more standard forms. It tends to become the center of life for those involved in the underground versions.

The difference between these two streams should not be overlooked. The larger one is a more direct continuation of the esoteric tradition, the smaller is one aspect of a multifaceted countercultural movement. Both express, however, a disenchantment with rationalism and science. Tiryakian has observed that, although much of modernism derives from the long stream of esoteric culture, "paradoxically, the value orientation of Western exoteric society, embodied in rationalism, the scientific ethos, the industrialism, has forced esoteric culture into the role of a marginal or underground movement. That is, modern Western civilization (dating it back to the Renaissance and Reformation) has increasingly given to esoteric culture the mantle of a counterculture, while at the same time coopting many of its values and products."[51]

It is useful, following Tiryakian, to distinguish between the occult and the esoteric. The former is a set of intentional practices or techniques that draw on hidden forces in nature or the cosmos believed to be inaccessible to scientific detection. The occult practices are designed to obtain knowledge of the course of events or to alter those events. By esoteric Tiryakian refers to religiophilosophic belief systems, the "cognitive mappings of nature and the cosmos, the epistemological and ontological reflections of ultimate reality," which underlie occult practices and techniques.[52] By analogy, he suggests, the esoteric is theoretical physics, the occult is engineering.

How does one account for the resurgence of occultism in industrial societies? In part, in my judgment, it is simply playfulness. One reads the horoscope column just before working the crossword puzzle. A few newspapers and magazines find that esoterica attracts attention, so others follow, giving the impression of a wave of interest and partly creating such a wave. That is an inadequate explanation, however. The rise in occult interest corresponds too closely to other challenges to the scientific world view. Earlier waves of renewal needed no support from the mass media. We need to look for explanations on both the individual and the social level.

Modernism has led us to believe in progress; liberalism has led us to believe in individual success; we have come to expect from science a steady reduction of our ignorance-based difficulties. Yet wars overwhelm us; choices of all sorts press in upon us for decisions; success eludes us or proves to be unsatisfying; scientific knowledge grows, but without any equivalent growth in life's satisfactions; the organization needed to maintain the modernizing process is constrictive—or so it all seems to many people. Feeling that we have lost control, it is easier to believe that the fault is not in ourselves but in our stars. Better to accommodate to what we KNOW than to struggle to learn about so capricious a world.

On the social level, we can connect the flourishing of esoteric beliefs and occult practices with periods of cultural turmoil and change. After the golden age of Pericles, which had been a period of rapidly expanding knowledge and growing rationalism, Greek civilization was overwhelmed with conflict and despair. Belief in fate, never much abated among the deprived, was widely reaffirmed. There were similar "occult revivals" during the waning years of the Roman Empire and during the time of the Renaissance and Reformation. These too were times of major shifts in cultural paradigms.[53]

Among the more moderate proponents of mystical knowledge today, the aim is not to obliterate science but to contain it, to oppose the one-valued, single-vision approach that they see dominating the urban, industrial world, as William Blake did nearly two centuries ago:

> May God us keep
> From Single vision and Newton's sleep!

Many persons share the distress that underlies these views, a distress that led H. G. Wells to say at the end of World War II that "mind is at the end of its tether." Today we see even more clearly that some of our deepest problems come from application of scientific findings. The countercultural epistemology appears in response to this predicament. "The advancing one-dimensional society alters the relation between the rational and the irrational. Contrasted with the fantastic and insane aspects of its rationality, the realm of the irrational becomes the home of the really rational—of the ideas which may 'promote the art of life'."[54] Hence, pursue a sense of mystery and fantasy, embrace the occult, meditate, unlock the truth that is in you.[55]

Sometimes the expression of this point of view is whimsical. In Abbie Hoffman's words: "Fantasy is the only truth. Once we had a demonstration at the *Daily News* building. About three hundred people smoked pot, danced, sprayed the reporters with body deodorant, burned money, handed out leaflets to all employees that began: 'Dear fellow member of the Communist conspiracy. . . .' We called it an 'Alternative Fantasy.' It worked great.

"What do you mean, it worked great?

"Nobody understood it. . . . It was pure information, pure imagery, which in the end is truth."[56]

This "Yippie" style has been well labeled neo-Dadaist by Herbert Gans.

Belief in the esoteric and the pursuit of understanding through mystery are, of course, persistent elements in human history. But their strength alternates, with waves of mysticism occurring when a society has experienced, as Tiryakian has put it, "a loss of confidence in established symbols and congitive models of reality. . . . Occult practices are appealing, among other reasons, because they are seemingly dramatic opposites of empirical practices of science and of the depersonalization of the industrial order."[57]

Is the resurgence of mysticism a new "failure of nerve," a new retreat into mystery cults and magical solutions brought on by the volatile mixture of promised affluence and persistent crisis? Or is it a wise recognition that human life had been impoverished by excessive dependence upon rationality? Gilbert Murray, in his classic *Five Stages of Greek Religion*, used J. B. Bury's phrase "failure of nerve" to describe the resurgence of mystery cults after the failure of the "Homeric reformation," the loss of faith in the cultural synthesis of the golden age of Pericles, the virtual collapse of the Greek city-states, and the inability of the great ethical philosophers to capture the imaginations of most people in a time of turmoil. Plato believed that there were universal norms of right, which could be discovered by philosophical study, if only a group could be protected from the disruptions of outside influences, of commerce and riches, and could be isolated from the "bitter and corrupting sea." Aristotle was less nostalgic, but he too believed that a life guided by reason and virtue would lead to happiness. In the context of mounting disorder, however, such systems of thought failed to take hold. "When the Olympian gods fell, fate, unpredictable and overwhelming Destiny, came in to take their place."[58]

Are we being faced today with a new failure of nerve, a "retreat from reason into the occult," as Yates put it with reference to earlier times?[59] Or is that judgment based on a narrow rationalist view, whether applied to the Greeks in the third century B.C., the late medieval world, or to our own time? One can agree with Marcuse that there are "fantastic and insane aspects" of rationality. Do we then desert it for the occult? Or run from one to the other? Or seek a blend? Or have we stumbled on the road to reason because it is still so incomplete? Or must all forms of consciousness, as Roszak calls them, ultimately fail, because human problems are so intractable?

Counterculturalists proclaim that they have renewed an essential sense of mystery. Opponents see the retreat from reason as far worse then the disease of excessive rationality for which it is presumably the cure. It is one thing to say that humankind has a need for mystery, but another to applaud that fact, considering the inhumane and exclusive movements that can sweep through a population, powered by mystical beliefs. Supporters of esoterica, however, see such arguments as severly limited. The "failure of nerve" is only in the minds of Western intellectuals, whose views of the human condition are far too narrow.

I have posed the argument in terms much too sharp. Mind may be, as Wells said, at the end of its tether. The two-centuries-long protest against the domination of "cold rationality" may be making some impact. However, we can reject unqualified faith in science— scientism it can be called—without rejecting science. Perhaps the attacks on rational thought, themselves incapable of replacing rationality or dealing effectively with the major issues facing humankind, have at least won for us a little time during which we can find a way more fully to use the powers of mind, blending them with our other powers, to serve larger human purposes.

Notes

1. Karen Horney, *The Neurotic Personality of Our Time*, 1937; Charles S. Johnson, *Patterns of Negro Segregation*, 1943; Ralph Turner and Lewis Killian, *Collective Behavior*, 1957; and Max Weber, *The Sociology of Religion*, 1963.
2. Malcolm Cowley, *Exile's Return: A Narrative of Ideas*, 1934. See also Keith Melville, *Communes in the Counter Culture*, 1972, and Charles Glock and Robert Bellah, *The New Religious Consciousness*, 1976.
3. Charles Reich, *The Greening of America*, 1970, pp. 356-57.
4. R. Serge Denisoff and Mark H. Levine, "Generations and Counter-Culture: A Study in the Ideology of Music," 1970.
5. Peter Clecak, *Radical Paradoxes: Dilemmas of the American Left: 1945-1970*, 1973, and Christopher Lasch, *The Agony of the American Left*, 1969.

6. Jerry Rubin, *Do It*, 1970, p. 116.

7. Abbie Hoffman, *Revolution for the Hell of It*, 1968, p. 61.

8. John Hoyland, "The Long March Through the Bingo Halls," 1973, p. 18.

9. Max Weber, *From Max Weber*, 1946, p. 126.

10. Nathan Adler, *The Underground Stream: New Life Styles and the Antinomian Personality*, 1972, p. 77.

11. Norman Cohn, *The Pursuit of the Millennium*, 1970; Guenter Lewy, *Religion and Revolution*, 1974; and Werner Stark, *The Sociology of Religion*, Vol. 2: *Sectarian Religion*, 1967.

12. See Irving Zaretsky and Mark Leone, *Religious Movements in Contemporary America*, 1974; Thomas Robbins and Dick Anthony, "Getting Straight with Meher Baba," 1972; Ken Kelley, "Blissed Out with the Perfect Master," 1973; J. Stillson Judah, *Hare Krishna and the Counterculture*, 1974; and Glock and Bellah, (note 2 above), 1976.

13. Warren Hinckle, "The Social History of the Hippies," 1967, p. 26.

14. Cowley, 1934 (note 2 above).

15. See Luther Gerlach and Virginia Hine, *Lifeway Leap: The Dynamics of Change in America*, 1973, p. 20.

16. See David Biale, *Gershom Scholem: Kabbalah and Counter-History*, 1979; Norman Brown, "Apocalypse: The Place of Mystery in the Life of the Mind," 1961; and Philip Slater, *The Wayward Gate: Science and the Supernatural*, 1977.

17. Theodore Roszak, *Where the Wasteland Ends: Politics and Transcendence in Postindustrial Society*, 1973, p. xv.

18. Max Heirich, "Cultural Breakthrough," 1976, p. 697.

19. *Christian Century*, January, 20, 1971, p. 75.

20. Reich, 1970 (note 3 above), p. 128.

21. *Ibid*., pp. 260-61. In a later work, Reich wrote that a movement to save America "would rest upon a radical, revolutionary epistemology which declares that our feelings are factual truth." Reich, *The Sorcerer of Bolinas Reef*, 1976, pp. 245-46.

22. David Cooper, *Psychiatry and Anti-Psychiatry*, 1971.

23. Erving Goffman, *Asylums*, 1961; D. L. Rosenhan, "On Being Sane in Insane Places," 1973, Thomas Scheff, editor, *Labeling Madness*, 1975; and Robert Perrucci, *Circle of Madness: On Being Insane and Institutionalized in America*, 1974.

24. See, e.g., in addition to Cooper, 1971, Thomas Szasz, *The Myth of Mental Illness, 1961; idem, Heresies*, 1976; R. D. Laing, *The Politics of Experience*, 1967; and *idem*, *The Facts of Life: An Essay in Feelings, Facts, and Fantasy*, 1976.

25. Gregory Bateson *et al*, "Toward a Theory of Schizophrenia," 1956.

26. Geoffery Pearson, *The Deviant Imagination*, 1975, p. 21.

27. Sigmund Koch, "The Image of Man in Encounter Group Theory," 1971.

28. See Morton Lieberman *et al.*, *Encounter Groups: First Facts*, 1973; Kurt Back, *Beyond Words: The Story of Sensitivity Training and the Encounter Movement*, 1973; Nathan Adler, 1972 (note 10 above), pp. 107-23; Jerome Frank, "The Bewildering World of Psychotherapy," 1972; and Donald Stone in Glock and Bellah, 1976 (note 2 above), pp. 93-115.

29. Regina Holloman, "Ritual Opening and Individual Transformation: Rites of Passage at Esalen," 1974, p. 265.

30. Back, 1973, p. 31.

31. Frank, 1972.

32. See Karl Mannheim, *Ideology and Utopia*, 1936; Robert Merton, *Social Theory and Social Structure* 1968; and Henri Ellenberger, *The Discovery of the Unconscious*, 1970.

33. Vytautas Kavolis, "Post-Modern Man: Psychocultural Responses to Social Trends," 1970a, pp. 438-39.

34. Weber, 1946, pp. 140-41.

35. Donald MacRae, *Weber*, 1974, p. 88.

36. See Kathleen Raine, *Yeats, the Tarot and the Golden Dawn*, 1972.

37. Slater, 1977 (note 16 above), p. 115.

38. *New York Times*, May 5, 1976, p. 15C.

39. Roszak, 1973, p. 341.

40. See William Braden; *The Private Sea: LSD and the Search for God*, 1967; Aldous Huxley, *Doors of Perception and Heaven and Hell*, 1954; Timothy Leary, *High Priest*, 1968; and Alan Watts, "Psychedelics and Religious Experience," in *The Religious Situation: 1969*, Donald Cutler, editor 1969, chap. 25.

41. See Judah, 1974 (note 12 above); Zaretsky and Leone, 1974 (note 12 above); Glock and Bellah, 1976 (note 2 above); Robbins and Anthony, 1972 (note 12 above; Alan Watts, *This Is It, and Other Essays on Zen and Spiritual Experience*, 1967; Roy Wallis, editor, *Sectarianism: Analyses of Religious and Non-Religious Sects*, 1975; and Sara Davidson, "The Rush for Instant Salvation," 1971.

42. Zaretsky and Leone, 1974, p. 460.

43. For a variety of perspectives see, for example, Bruce Johnson, *Marihuana Users and Drug Subcultures*, 1973; Theordore X. Barber, *LSD, Marihuana, Yoga, and Hypnosis*, 1970; Erich Goode, *The Marijuana Smokers*, 1970; Michael Harner, editor, *Hallucinogens and*

Shamanism, 1973; Herbert Hendin, *The Age of Sensation*, 1975, chap. 7; Theodore Roszak, *The Making of a Counter Culture*, 1969, chap. 5; Frank Scarpitti and Susan Datesman, editors, *Drugs and the Youth Culture*, 1980; William Bates and Betty Crowther, *Drugs: Causes, Circumstances, and Effects of Their Use, 1973; Denise Kandel, Longitudinal Research on Drug Use*, 1978; and Vera Rubin and Lambros Comitas, *Ganja in Jamaica: The Effects of Marijuana Use*, 1976.

44. Michael Novak, in Cutler, 1969, 1969, p. 206.

45. Huxley, 1954 p. 40. See also J. Milton Yinger, *The Scientific Study of Religion*, 1970, pp. 163-69.

46. Jacob Needleman, *The New Religions*, 1970, p. 44.

47. *The New York Times*, October 19, 1975, p. 46.

48. Edward Tiryakian, "Toward the Sociology of Esoteric Culture," 1972, 495, citing Philippe Defrance *et al*.

49. Robert Wuthnow, "Astrology and Marginality." 1976a.

50. Martin Marty, "The Occult Establishment," 1970. See also Frederick Lynch "Occult Establishment' or 'Deviant Religion'? The Rise and Fall of a Modern Church of Magic," 1979, and Marcello Truzzi, "The Occult Revival as Popular Culture: Some Random Observations on the Old and Nouveau Witch," 1972.

51. Tiryakian, 1972, p. 502.

52. *Ibid*.; pp. 498-99.

53. *Ibid*. pp. 509-10. See also Frances Yates, *Giordano Bruno and the Hermetic Tradition*, 1964

54. Herbert Marcuse, *One Dimensional Man: Studies in the Ideology of Advance Industrial Societies*, 1964.

55. See Norman Brown, *Love's Body*, 1966; Adam Smith, *Powers of Mind*, 1976; and Roszak, 1973 (note 17 above).

56. Abbie Hoffman, *Revolution for the Hell of It*, 1968, p. 66.

57. Tiryakian, 1972, pp. 510, 494; see also Ernest Gellner, *Contemporary Thought and Politics*, 1974.

58. Yinger, 1970 (note 45 above), pp. 54-55.

59. Yates, 1964, p. 449.

Chapter Five

Goodness, Cultural and Countercultural

Countercultural ethics contradict the values of the dominant society as sharply as countercultural epistemology. Proponents of one, however, are often not proponents of the other. Those who oppose the established ways to truth may be quite conservative in their definitions of the good life; while those who condemn the morality of the establishment may be comfortable with its epistemology. To be sure, the former may claim, as Charles Reich does, that a new consciousness is the slow but peaceful and sure way to revolution. As Wuthnow has recently shown, moreover, some kinds of structural conditions, those found in mass societies, are likely to be characterized by combinations of mysticism and political activism.[1]

The search for a "new head," however, has more often been associated with quietism, introversion, and withdrawal from an evil world than with efforts to change it. These tendencies are not characteristic of those I call ethical counterculturalists. They challenge the world with new visions of the good life. It is important to emphasize that they are not simply aberrant, committing immoral and illegal acts by their own as well as by the dominant standards. They are nonconformists proclaiming the rightness of their views. If they are sent to jail, they are, in their own minds, political prisoners.

"Thou has many baggs of money, and behold I (the Lord) come as a thief in the night, with my sword drawn in my hand, and like a thief as I am—I say deliver your purse, deliver sirrah! deliver or I'l cut thy throat!"[2] This is not a quote from an early edition of Abbie Hoffman's *Steal This Book* or Jerry Rubin's *Do It*, but from George Foster's *The Sounding of the Last Trumpet*, published some three hundred years earlier.

"The Best Things in Life Are Free—If You Steal Them from the Bourgeoisie" read a framed sampler hanging on the wall of an East Village commune.[3] No drawn sword, but a credit card is the weapon of justice. Have Robin Hood and his band returned to rectify the evils of a corporate society based on greed and deceit? Or are such assertions simply "techniques of neutralization" used by law violators or selfish persons to rationalize their actions?

> Ripping off—stealing, to the uninitiated—is rapidly becoming as much a part of the counterculture as drugs and rock music. . . . Stealing from these robber barons, runs the argument, is certainly more moral than working for them . . . it's only a justified redistribution of the wealth. . . . "Paying for a phone call is almost counterrevolutionary". . . . "If we are really serious about destroying the Man, why contribute to his survival by paying?"[4]

The methods, motives, and outcomes of the actions of the Robin Hoods of different times and places differ widely. They share in common, however, the affirmation that goodness requires a reversal of the established way of doing things. The difficulty everywhere is to separate aberrant self-serving, whereby those involved claim justification by reference to the injustices of the dominant order, from nonconformist acts, designed to affirm new standards and to replace the old. "When young radicals steal from corporations that are involved in price-fixing, tax evasion and false advertising," Irving Horowitz asks, "is it a crime or a political statement? Ripping off is essentially a moral outcry. The ambiguity is where morality ends and petty thievery begins."[5]

There is indeed ambiguity. Countercultural ethics raise in an acute way the problems inherent in the assertion that the end justifies the means. This assertion is almost automatically accepted in action in conflict situations. In my judgment it is both acted upon too easily and dismissed as an ethical principle too easily. How can both parts of that statement be true? In action, the principle comes to mean: The end desired is so noble and so important (or so obviously in our self-interest) that we ought not to be too squeamish in selecting the means by which we strive to attain it. He who wills the end, the argument goes, must will the means. Even setting aside the question of whether or not the end is in fact noble, the ready use of this principle in action often disregards the question of effectiveness. Do given means actually achieve the end in view? Is it not true that in most instances the means determine, or powerfully influence, what the ends—the consequences—will be? Drosnin quotes a critic of countercultural rip-off of government and business who judges such activity from a radical perspective: "They're not revolutionaries. . . . We're struggling to get welfare payments increased, and they're giving the government an excuse to put down welfare. They shoplift, so supermarkets raise their prices, and the poor pay more for food. It's a game for middle-class rejects, and it takes the dignity and seriousness out of the real social struggle."[6] Perhaps the principle would be more acceptable if it read: The accomplished end justifies the means.

That modification, however, is insufficient. The sociological imagination should lead us to further refinement: *All* of the consequences, intended and unintended, short-run and long-run, if they are on balance good, justify the means. Since the full range of consequences cannot be known, if ever, until after the means have been selected and used, one makes a leap of faith. Some will go with "accumulated wisdom." Others will see this as a disguise for accumulated privilege and will select deviant means in the effort to attain their nonconformist goals.

The use of countercultural means in an effort to attain what are, at least in some measure, cultural ends can be distinguished from ethical principles that say: The forbidden acts are good in and of themselves. Many acts, of course, have reference to both means and ends. The seventeenth-century English Ranters were not quite in tune with Hoffman's "philosophy of the rip-off" but felt no less hesitation in proclaiming guides to efficient stealing in the search for a better world. To the Ranters, the prevailing moral law was not binding on the true believers. "I know nothing unclean to me," Clarkson wrote, "and therefore what Act soever I do, is acted by that Majesty in me."[7] Do your own thing is a somewhat less elegant way of putting it.

Many Quakers and Ranters went naked through the streets and into churches—no segregated nudist beach for them.[8] Abiezer Coppe and his more effervescent followers were a free speech movement, using obscenity as a weapon; they affirmed the rightness of sex before marriage and attacked the monogamous family; they supported the use of drugs to heighten spiritual vision (though it was alcohol and the new drug tobacco); they dismissed the prevailing doctrines of the church and its structure of authority; they rejected private property in favor of communism.

> The Ranter ethic, as preached by Coppe and Clarkson, involved a real subversion of existing society and its values. The world exists for men,

and all men are equal. There is no after-life; all that matters is here and now. . . . Nothing is evil that does not harm our fellow men. . . . "Swearing i'th (giveth) light, gloriously," and "wanton kisses," may help to liberate us from the repressive ethic which our masters are trying to impose on us.[9]

Much of what the radical sectarians preached and acted out, it should be noted, matched the behavior, if not the expressed values, of more conservative countrymen. To use the phrase of Matza and Sykes, there were subterranean values,[10] particularly among the leisured ruling class, similar to those of the counterculture. The dislike of physical labor, sexual promiscuity, swearing, and emphasis on works rather than on faith were part of the life style if not of the proclaimed culture of the wealthy.[11] They become countercultural when they are openly avowed and become guiding norms, not tolerated nonconformities. Their impact is greater when they are affirmed as new values by persons outside the dominant circles, for this represents a challenge to the social order and not only to the official culture.

A contrasting kind of situation exists when powerful "criminals"[12] who live by an illegal set of norms and values (that is, they are not simply aberrant, but defend, however ambivalently, the justice and wisdom of their actions) are not generally treated as countercultural. Commercial fraud, loan sharking, price rigging, tax evasion, graft, and bribery, for example, if defended as necessary for business as "the only way to run a railroad," or as means to equalize burdens or render a service *are* countercultural acts by our definition. If they are not always so regarded, it may be in part because those who commit such acts are "orthodox" in most other ways. It is also partly due to the fact that they may be too powerful thus to be labeled. They have resources to deflect and neutralize labels. Howard Becker observes that "the questions of what rules are to be enforced, what behavior regarded as deviant and what people labeled as outsiders must also be regarded as political."[13] This is a valuable emphasis on the different levels of probability of being seen as countercultural. Insofar as it implies a thoroughgoing relativism regarding what is countercultural, however, I think it overplays social interaction as a source of emergent standards and underplays the influence of cultural systems as the source of standards that set the context within which interaction occurs. (Seeing interaction as simply the playing out of cultural prescriptions and proscriptions is, of course, no more adequate.)

To the contemporary counterculturalists, what feels good is good. This sometimes collides with another principle: If it is good to the establishment, it is bad for us. Since the establishment takes a somewhat ambiguous middle position with regard, for example, to aggression and sex, countercultural groups have to push away from the center, toward pacifism and celibacy or toward violence and sexual exuberance, meanwhile claiming that the establishment is not in the center, but actually occupies the opposite pole from the one being held up as good.

In a well-known article, Bennett Berger observes that "the moral dimensions of the hippie community are part of a long and honorable tradition." He draws a comparison with bohemian values, as described by Malcolm Cowley thirty-five years earlier.[14] One ought perhaps to note a longer tradition as well, to call attention to the tendency to stereotype those who are seen as moral opponents. Hinckle writes that the songs of the Beatles, Dylan, and the Rolling Stones" reflect LSD values—love, life, getting along with other people."[15] It seems possible to believe that these values were developed in the ethical systems of the world somewhat before the discovery of LSD and that they are widely shared today. Behavior, of course, whether of LSD users or of opponents may not measure up to their values.

Counterculturalists do not escape the common human tendency to make their enemies, as well as their leaders, into what they need them to be—need them in an effort to justify their actions and handle their ambivalences.

Are cultural definitions of the good quite arbitrary, so that countercultural inversions have an open field within which to develop? In Chapter Two I commented on the general question of cultural relativity and expressed the judgment that basic social and individual characteristics set some limits to cultural variation. That may apply more strongly to ethical than to aesthetic and cognitive standards. In fact, it seems probable that there is a genetic component to ethical systems. There is now a substantial body of opinion holding that elements of these systems, the norms of altruism for example, are partly based upon an evolutionary process that has selected for "prosocial" behavior. This is not only a question of maximizing individuals' "inclusive fitness," as sociobiologists argue. A genetically based altruism that prompts one to self-sacrifice, if needed to protect ones relatives, is extended by culture to include much wider circles of persons. A culture of altruism, based, to be sure, on biological potentials, is essential to the maintenance of life among those bound together in mutual dependence.[16] It is thus not by accident that opposition to self-centeredness, expressed in many ways, is deeply embedded in human moral systems.

It is no longer possible to doubt that societies can and do live by enormously variant moral systems. Yet there are humanwide constants that cannot simply be set aside. (This comment *about* moral systems is not itself a moral judgment. One can be dismayed or pleased by the variation or by the constants.) To many counterculturalists, these constants are barriers to the good life.

Criminal Countercultures

In several of the chapters that follow—those dealing with economics, politics, the family, and others—I will be dealing further with issues of "goodness" as seen counterculturally. Some comments here on the normative reversals found in some illegal activities, however, may be of value in the analysis of the conditions under which dominant ethical principles are inverted.

Criminal counterculturalists do not ordinarily proclaim their way of life as a new vision of the good life for all. Their vision is more limited: These are the right standards for me (or for us) under the conditions that I (or we) face. This contrast with more global statements about the good life should not, however, be exaggerated. And the study of the more constricted versions can put the conditions that help to create inverted moral norms into sharp relief. There are times when persons accused of no crime and threatened with no incarceration nevertheless feel that life is a prison or a place empty of meaning, thus reversing the perception of society as a source of satisfactions, safety, and values. That feeling can contribute strongly to the process out of which standard conceptions of the good are inverted.

Most of the difficulties in defining counterculture with some degree of clarity beset any attempt to apply it to criminal activity. One must include only nonconformist, not aberrant, activity; and most criminality is probably aberrant. The nonconformist standards must be anchored in a group. They must be inversions of prevailing norms—technically of legal norms in referring to criminality—not small modifications. None of these is a moral criterion. A nonconformist, group-supported, drastic modification of a legal standard is not intrinsically better or worse than an aberrant, individual, small modification, even though a heroic quality is sometimes associated with the former. Each instance must be judged against specified values.

A widely practiced illegality may become normative, even in the face of a continuing legal proscription. It is difficult, however, to identify such standards confidently. Everyone does it, it may be said. Do they? Observers have reasons for exaggerating as well as for minimizing various rates of deviancy. Do they accept the deviation as right? We may be trapped by pluralistic ignorance—each judging a situation on the basis of what he believes others think or do, while all, or most, are in error in their judgments. Shared misperceptions, of course can have self-fulfulling consequences.[17] If I misperceive that "everyone else" accepts and is acting on the basis of an illegal standard that I mainly reject but am partly attracted to, and if many others see the situation similarly, we may begin to join the fictitious "everyone else," giving them reality. The presumed countercultural or aberrant standard then becomes cultural, even if still illegal. For example, if out of frustration over the rising cost of living, dislike of the way the government spends its (my) money, resentment over the great inequalities in income, or pure cupidity I come to believe, in the first place mistakenly, that everyone, except for you and me, cheats on his income tax, I may succumb to the temptation to join the "majority," helping to bring it into existence.

Once again, this is not moral commentary. Actions based on pluralistic ignorance can conceivably help to destroy not only necessary and preferred standards and practices but abhorrent ones as well, as judged by particular values. Pluralistic ignorance is essential to many acts of collective heroism. I refer to this concept not to evaluate an important social process, but to emphasize the difficulty of setting the boundaries that mark off standards that are not only illegal but countercultural.

In light of these problems of delimitation, I shall define criminal counterculture quite narrowly. It is a set of values and norms that, although they contravene the law, are accepted by a group and proclaimed, in word and action, as their way of life. Usually there are indications of ambivalence in the proclamations.

Although I shall use some forms of delinquency as the chief illustration, a brief reference to countercultures under various conditions of incarceration will permit a sharper demarcation of the issues. They show the process of inversion of values under intense light, whereas a mixture of light and shadow is more often the case. Mitchell describes the emergence of a sexually and aggressively oriented contraculture among a group of boys in a children's ward of a large American psychiatric hospital:

> . . . the Baby Disturbers, convinced that the omniscient adult world had relegated them to the "garbage dump"—which was their name for the hospital—because of their "badness," deprecated the adult culture's

> mores about goodness, especially those pertaining to sexual modesty, by elevating sexual vulgarity, vituperation, and aggressiveness to the level of virtuous behavior. The linguistic and behavioral taboos accepted by the boys' parents, their relatives, and the hospital staff were studiously violated. When reversed, they became the criteria by which a "good" Baby Disturber could be evaluated.[18]

The negative image of an evil and cruel world held by the Baby Disturbers, and scarcely surprising in their case, is matched by the believers in most countercultures. The contrast conceptions are essential to clarify their own style of life and to help in the process of repression of their hidden yet influential sense of involvement in the dominant world.

The normative systems of prisons combine, in varying proportions, the official system of prison authorities, the continuing influence of the culture and subcultures of the outside world, and an emergent counterculture, forged in an effort to create an alternative reality, a way of coping with the frustration and deprivations of prison life. Prison countercultures are most likely to be formed in the "Gulag situation": the packing together of persons already severely alienated or, in Aleksandr Solzhenitsyn's term, "spiritually disarmed." An underground, illegal economy, aggressive and sexual impulses, and deviant political interests are not dealt with simply in random, anarchic fashion. Out of the internal struggle for power, in circumstances where the resources for satisfying one's needs are severely limited, groups are formed, partly around ethnic and racial symbols, and rules emerge, enforced by violence, mutual interest, and rewards.[19]

The informal social structure of prisons does not inevitably support countercultural values. The likelihood of such values' being strongly asserted varies from society to society (it is much higher in the United States than Norway, for example),[20] from prison to prison (it is much higher in prisons where many persons are serving long sentences and have been convicted of serious crimes), and from time to time (it is higher during periods of harsh ethnic and racial antipathy and political turmoil).

Having become adapted to a prison counterculture, some persons seek return after they are released, finding prison preferable to the enormous ambiguities of the outside world.[21] The normative order in opposition to that of the staff and the outside world is strengthened by the fact that prisons release their "successes" and keep their "failures"—the unsocialized, the recalcitrants—who remain behind to indoctrinate newcomers to the prisoner system.[22]

In a comparative study of Polish and American prisons, Adam Podgorecki adds a social-psychological factor to the structural sources of countercultures in prisons. "The establishment of a reverse world (in which reducing others to things becomes a source of gratification by transforming a punitive situation into a rewarding one) can also be seen as a desperate attempt to rescue and reintegrate the self in the face of the cumulative oppression which threatens to disintegrate it."[23]

This same statement might be used to describe the pressures toward normative reversals among some delinquents. Although the experience of "total institutions," of "prisonization," intensifies the pressures, they can be severe in the civilian world as well, as the lives of some delinquents testify.

For a half a century or more, delinquency has been a topic of intensive examination by sociologists, psychologists, and other students of human behavior. Although the literature is rich, both empirically and theoretically, no single paradigm has emerged that commands the support and focuses the research of most criminologists. The intrinsic complexity of the issues involved, problems of access to and validity of the data, ideological inclinations, and the changing nature of delinquency as society changes all combine to slow down the development of consensus. This is not to say that agreement is lacking on the broad categories of variables that require attention in the study of delinquency. Structural, cultural, subcultural, interactional, and personality factors are generally considered.[24] There is less agreement, however, on emphasis and on the ways in which the various factors should be combined under particular sets of conditions.

I will not discuss the extensive and often brilliant literature that deals with delinquency but will simply note some of the critical explanatory factors used, without reference to their various combinations, in order to set the context for a brief commentary on the possible usefulness of countercultural theory as part of any full explanation.

Few concepts have played a more important part in delinquency theory than anomie, which we might define, from its Greek root, as "broken limits." Durkheim thought of it in these terms, adding the connotations of deregulation and normlessness. In the state of anomie, he wrote, "the most reprehensible acts are . . . frequently rendered pure by success. . . . The limits are unknown between the possible and the impossible, what is just and what is unjust, legitimate claims and hopes and those which are immoderate. Consequently there is no restraint upon aspirations."[25] Building on Durkheim's usage, but narrowing it somewhat, Merton notes that industrial societies particularly have opened new opportunities and encouraged their members to strive for new goals. At the same time, less attention is paid to teaching respect for, or furnishing opportunities for, culturally approved means. Anomie exists when there is little agreement on appropriate means to approved goals or when appropriate means are inaccessible to many persons. It is the normless condition, not individual or group responses to it, that constitutes anomie. The responses can vary, as Merton makes clear in his well-known discussion, from conformity, to rebellion against both ends and means, to retreat from both, to ritualistic adherence to approved means despite the consequent sacrifice of goals, to innovation in the use of means—since culturally approved means are unavailable—in an effort to achieve approved goals.[26] Any one of these responses, but particularly rebellion and innovation, can entail delinquency, sometimes, as we shall note, of a countercultural variety.

In sharp contrast with anomie theory, subcultural theory sees delinquency as one natural form of behavior in certain subsocieties, mainly lower-class, where values and norms, not simply opportunities, are different from those in the dominant, and one might add law-writing, society. Putting the issue in overly simple terms: Delinquency is the normal result of socialization to a delinquent subculture. Few students of delinquency would put it that sharply. Such basic early work on delinquency as Shaw's *Delinquency Areas* and Thrasher's *The Gang* gave a great deal of attention to neighborhood differences, but their reference was as much to "social disorganization"—which is conceptually close to anomie—as to variations in custom. Problems of growing up and the influence of collective behavior—emerging from social interaction rather than subculture—are also considered.

Most authors blend several levels of explanation, but primary attention is often given to one level. Those for whom subcultural influences are of major importance stress that many "middle-class values" are given little support in lower-class communities, where the "focal concerns," as Miller calls them, are trouble, toughness, smartness (ability to outsmart), excitement, fate, and autonomy. Concern for the cultivation of skills, ambition, responsibility, the ability to defer gratification, respect for property, and other "achievement" qualities, on the other hand, is attenuated. The dominant motivation of lower-class "corner groups" to engage in delinquent behavior, in Miller's view, is "to achieve states, conditions, or qualities valued within the actor's most significant cultural milieu."[27]

The debate between those who stress *lack* of opportunities and those who stress *presence* of opposing values in explaining delinquency parallels the debate over the usefulness of the concept "culture of poverty." Both arguments need to be incorporated into a larger frame of reference.

I shall not examine the several other factors often cited in studies of delinquency causation. Adolescent striving for adult status and related crises of sex identity, collective behavior, presence or absence of a criminal "opportunity system," and characteristics of a specific situation—including the level of social control and the actions of potential victims—are among th factors that would need to be included in any complete explanation. One additional element, however, does require attention. Because of variation in the tendencies of individuals, a given level of anomie or a given set of subcultural influences will have different effects. Individual factors in deliquency are sometimes neglected by social scientists, partly in response to their exaggeration in some psychological and often in commonsense explanations. Since the degree of delinquency proneness, however, is involved in the shaping of countercultural expressions of delinquency, we need to find a way to incorporate it into our analysis, not to replace explanations based on studies of subcultures or anomie but to complement them.

Undoubtedly the most ambitious attempt to discover delinquency-producing traits is the work of the Gluecks. They are perhaps more sensitive to environmental influences than some of their critics contend, but this is shown more by way of incidental remarks than by systematic research procedures. There is little room either for anomie or for subcultural influences in the belief that tendencies toward delinquent behavior "are deeply anchored in soma and psyche and in the malformations of character during the first few years of life."[28] The Gluecks could not develop an adequate theory of delinquency nor open the possibility of a countercultural factor, because they were looking for "delinquents" and the "traits" that distinguished them from nondelinquents. In my view, delinquents do not exist: Delinquent *behavior* emerges in the continuous transactions between persons with certain tendencies and other persons, social situations, and cultural settings.[29]

When delinquent tendencies are acted upon, the actors are confronted with both internal and external constraints. Internal constraints are felt because many—not all—feel ambivalence and guilt. In his account of "good boy" and "bad boy" factions in a gang, Miller observes that their behavior gives evidence of a fundamental ambivalence:

> . . . the existence of the opposing ideologies and their corresponding factions served important functions both for individual gang members and

> for the group as a whole. Being in the same orbit as the "bad boys" made it possible for the "good boys" to reap some of the rewards of violative behavior without undergoing its risks; the presence of the "good boys" imposed restraints on the "bad" that they themselves desired, and helped protect them from dangerous excesses. The behavior and ideals of the "good boys" satisfied for both factions that component of their basic orientation that said "violation of the law is wrong and should be punished"; the behavior and ideals of the "bad boys" that component that said "one cannot earn manhood without some involvement in criminal activity."[30]

Sykes and Matza note several evidences of feelings of guilt: expression of admiration for some law-abiding persons; drawing a sharp line between those who can and cannot be victimized; the inevitable connections that most persons have with the family, school, law, and other parts of the social order; and the great pains to which they go to rationalize their actions.[31] This last "technique of neutralization" is particularly relevant to our concern, because some of its manifestations have countercultural qualities. Sykes and Matza refer to the denial of responsibility (it was an accident; I could not help myself in such a rotten environment), the denial of injury (he could afford it), the denial of the victim (it was rightful retaliation or punishment; "the delinquent moves himself into the position of avenger and the victim is transformed into a wrongdoer"), the condemnation of the condemners (attention is shifted from one's own deviant acts to the motives and behavior of others—the police are corrupt, brutal, and stupid; teachers play favorites; parents take it out on their children), and the appeal to higher loyalties (interests of the sibling pair, the gang, the clique required neglect of the demands of the larger society). These, say Sykes and Matza, are glancing blows against the dominant normative structure, not an opposing ideology. That is doubtless often the case, but the stronger the ambivalence, the stronger is the need to "neutralize" the appeal and the negative sanctions of the dominant order. And as Cohen and Short observe: "The formation of a subculture is itself probably the most universal and powerful of techniques of neutralization, for nothing is so effective in allaying doubts and providing reassurance against a gnawing superego as the repeated, emphatic, and articulate support and approval of other persons."[32]

Cohen and Short refer to subculture, but the behavior and the values being supported and approved often contain a large countercultural component. In his analysis of delinquency, Cohen makes effective use of the concept of reaction formation. The normative system of lower-class male gangs, he observes, is not learned, accepted, and taught in the same way that one learns what food to eat, what clothes to wear, what language to speak. The very existence of the gang is a sign, in part, of blocked ambition. Because tensions that have been set in motion by this blockage cannot be resolved by achievement of dominant values, such values are repressed, their importance denied, and countervalues affirmed. As Downes has shown, the deprivation that leads to delinquent behavior is not necessarily deprivation of status. In two dockside areas of London, it was inability to attain leisure time goals of excitement and enjoyment that was frustrating. This seems to apply as well to some American street- corner groups.[33] Thwarted in their desires to achieve higher status by the criteria of the dominant society, persons with similar problems of adjustment, in effective communication, evolve standards they can meet. These emerge out of a tentative conversation of words and actions, some of which fit their shared needs. The reaction formation in these responses is shown by the content of some delinquent norms—nonutilitarian, malicious, and negativistic, in Cohen's terms. The negative polarity expresses the need to repress tendencies to accept and strive for dominant cultural standards that, although attractive, are felt to be inaccessible.[34]

This is not an empirical description of "the gang," as the numerous accounts of the diversity of types of gangs make clear.[35] A purely subcultural explanation, emphasizing socialization to a traditional, even if illegal, set of standards, needs also to be taken into account. It too is incomplete, however. Miller criticizes Cohen for calling the behavior of lower-class delinquents negativistic and malicious, seeing it rather as an expression of an established tradition: "The standards of the lower-class culture cannot be seen merely as a reverse function of middle class culture—as middle class standards 'turned upside down.' "[36] I doubt that many persons would disagree with that judgment when it is applied to the prevailing values in stable communities, but it seems poorly aimed as a criticism of Cohen's interpretation of delinquency in disorganized areas. Although he speaks in terms of two levels of culture—an overt and a covert level—Miller himself describes the ambivalence felt by many persons in highly disadvantaged circumstances. If he were prepared to incorporate more psychodymanic elements into his theory, the facts he observed might lead him to add to the emphasis on the traditional and purely cultural aspects of lower-class behavior some reference to emergent norms—norms that develop as efforts to deal with difficult contemporary problems. It is often true that a keen observer sees beyond the constraining influence of his own theory. Miller notes, for example, that the aggressive assertion of autonomy—"I don't need nobody to take care of me"—is not merely a cultural norm. In part it disguises covert dependency needs.

A subcultural explanation, by calling attention to the wide variation in patterns of socialization, is a valuable part of delinquency theory. It leaves several questions unexplored, however: Why do only some of those who are exposed to the delinquent subculture learn it? Why do those who follow the subculture often manifest ambivalence and guilt feelings? Why do many of the same patterns of behavior occur in areas and among groups where the presence of the subculture is much less clear, as in middle- and upper-class delinquency? What is the significance of the fact that some aspects of the delinquent subculture are not only different from, but in fact a reversal of, the values of the dominant culture?[37]

Ambivalence is the key to the appearance of countercultural, not just subcultural, norms. If a boy has a sneaking suspicion that staying in school and trying to stay on the right side of the law are good ideas—because they will lead to better job opportunities, more satisfactory relations with others, and the like—but if, as well, he is not prepared for school, if he lacks facility in the dominant language or dialect, the ability to defer some gratification, home support, and successful models close at hand, then he is torn. For some, failure begins the moment they start school. To avoid feelings of perpetual failure, they repress the sense of identity with the legitimate community. This would be no "solution" at all, however, if the repressed values came constantly back into their awareness. How can they be kept out most successfully?

First, a familiar quality of the human mind comes into play: Do not just deny the values, but reverse them. This is similar to projection, in which one attempts to rid himself of guilt by lodging responsibility for it not simply at random on someone else, but precisely on the victim of the act for which he feels guilty. Second, the reversal of values can be more "successful" in the individual's struggle with ambiavlence if he can get others to share it. I have noted Cohen's interpretation of the way inverted norms emerge out of the tentative and ambiguous steps by which a group of persons sharing similar problems move toward shared definitions. In his systematic review of explanations of delinquency, Johnson found that having delinquent associates and holding delinquent values were the most powerful explanatory variables.[38] Situational vaiables, of course, play an important part in determining whether tendencies will be acted out.[39]

Whether or not the reversals are "successful" in some larger ethical sense cannot be answered in general but only by reference to one's fundamental values. Needless to say, malicious and violent acts of a delinquent gang would not be given high marks by many people, even if they were believed to rescue some persons from utter demoralization. Yet if the values being reversed and the social system in which they are embedded are considered abhorrent, countercultural protests may be seen in a different light. Revolutionary gangs may be regarded, especially in retrospect, as valuable warning signals or even as sources of positive values. I do not intend, by this remark, to support a radical relativism in values, but to emphasize that counterculture is an analytic term. Evaluations must proceed independently.

Notes

1. See Robert Wuthnow, *Experimentation in American Religion*, 1978, chap. 4. See also Max Weber, *The Sociology of Religion*, 1963, p. 55; J. Milton Yinger, *The Scientific Study of Religion*, 1970, pp. 145-51; and Isidor Thorner, "Prophetic and Mystic Experience: Comparison and Consequences," 1965.
2. A. L. Morton, *The World of the Ranters*, 1970, p. 87.
3. Michael Drosnin, "Ripping Off: The New Life Style," 1971, p. 13.
4. *Ibid.*, pp. 13, 47.
5. Quoted by Drosnin in *ibid.*, p. 52.
6. *Ibid.*
7. Quoted in Norman Cohn, *The Pursuit of the Millennium*, 1970, p. 312.
8. Christopher Hill, *The World Turned Upside Down*, 1975, and Cohn, 1970.
9. Hill, 1975, p. 339.
10. David Matza and Gresham Sykes, "Juvenile Delinquency and Subterranean Values," 1961, and David Matza, "Subterranean Traditions of Youth," 1961.
11. Hill, 1975, p. 340.
12. I have put "criminals" in quotation marks to avoid struggling here with the problem of definition. Criminals, some say, are those who have committed illegal acts, however difficult it may be to establish their identi-

ty definitively. Criminals, other say, are those who have been so adjudged in a court of law, however poor a sample of lawbreakers they may be. Still others see criminals as those so labeled by those with the power to define. It would be essential to participate in the struggle over definitions in other contexts.

13. Howard S. Becker, *Outsiders: Studies in the Sociology of Deviance*, 1963, p. 7.

14. Bennett Berger, *Looking for America: Essays on Youth, Suburbia, and Other American Obsessions*, 1971, and Malcolm Cowley, *Exile's Return: A Narrative of Ideas*, 1934.

15. Warren Hinckle, "The Social History of the Hippies," 1967.

16. For a variety of recent works on the sources of ethical behavior, both biological and cultural, see Arthur Caplan, editor, *The Sociobiology Debate: Readings on Ethical and Scientific Issues*, 1978; Stuart Hampshire, editor, *Public and Private Morality*, 1978; John Rawls, *A Theory of Justice*, 1971; Wendell Bell and Robert Robinson, "An Index of Evaluated Equality: Measuring Conceptions of Social Justice in England and the United States," 1978; Wayne Alves and Peter Rossi, "Who Should Get What? Fairness Judgments of the Distribution of Earnings," 1978; R. L. Trivers, "The Evolution of Reciprocal Altruism," 1971; L. G. Wispe, editor, "Positive Forms of Social Behavior," 1972; Donald Campbell, "On the Conflicts Between Biological and Social Evolution and Between Psychology and Moral Tradition," 1975; Ervin Staub, *Positive Social Behavior and Morality*, 2 volumes, 1978.

17. Robert Merton, *Social Theory and Social Structure*, 1968.

18. William Mitchell, "The Baby Disturbers: Sexual Behavior in a Childhood Contraculture," 1966.

19. See, for example, Lee Bowker, *Prisoner Subcultures*, 1977; Joan Moore, *Homeboys: Gangs, Drugs, and Prison in the Barrios of Los Angeles*, 1978; Charles Thomas and Samuel Foster, "Prisonization in the Inmate Contraculture," 1972; John Irwin and Donald Cressey, "Thieves, Convicts, and the Inmate Culture," 1962; Gresham Sykes and Sheldon Messinger, "The Inmate Social System," in *Theoretical Studies in the Social Organization of the Prison*, Richard Cloward *et al.*, editors, 1960; and Stanton Wheeler, "Socialization in Correctional Institutions," 1969. Prison staffs, Gresham Sykes observes, "now face organized activists rather than men 'pulling their own time' or forming a herd of isolated rebels." *The New York Times*, April 21, 1974, p. E5. The inverted standards and conflicting organizations are revealed most dramatically by prison riots. After a disastrous riot in the New Mexico State Penitentiary, inmates declared that the way the prison was run pitted "the prisoners against each other in a tightly controlled pressure cooker that emphasized those elements that are the opposite of civilized society." Frank Clifford, Julie Morris, and Bob Rivard, Honolulu *Star-Bulletin and Advertiser*, February 10, 1980, p. A21.

20. Wheeler, 1969.

21. Bruce Jackson, "Deviance as Success: The Double Inversion of Stigmatized Roles," in *The Reversible World: Symbolic Inversion in Art and Society*, Barbara Babcock, editor, 1978, chap. 10.

22. Stanton Wheeler in *Socialization After Childhood*, Orville G. Brim, Jr., and Stanton Wheeler, editors, 1965, p. 64.

23. Adam Podgórecki, " 'Second Life' and Its Implication," mimeographed, quoted in M. A. K. Halliday, "Anti-Languages," 1976, p. 573.

24. For the most systematic current model of explanation of delinquency, see Richard Johnson, *Juvenile Delinquency and Its Origins: An Integrated Theoretical Approach*, 1979.

25. Emile Durkheim, *Suicide*, 1951, p. 253.

26. Merton, 1968.

27. Walter Miller, "Lower Class Culture as a Generating Milieu of Gang Delinquency," 1958, p. 19. See also William Kvaraceus and Walter Miller, *Delinquent Behavior*, 1959.

28. Sheldon Glueck and Eleanor Glueck, *Unraveling Juvenile Delinquency*, 1950, p. 282. See also their *Predicting Delinquency and Crime*, 1959, and *Family Environment and Delinquency*, 1962; and see Daniel Offer, Richard Marohn, and Eric Ostrov, *The Psychological World of the Juvenile Delinquent*, 1979.

29. See J. Milton Yinger, *Toward a Field Theory of Behavior*, 1965, chap. 10. Several paragraphs in the following pages are adapted from that chapter.

30. Walter Miller, "White Gangs," 1969, p. 23.

31. Gresham Sykes and David Matza, "Techniques of Neutralization: A Theory of Delinquency," 1957. See also M. D. Buffalo and Joseph W. Rodgers, "Behavioral Norms, Moral Norms, and Attachment: Problems of Deviance and Conformity," 1971.

32. Albert Cohen and James Short, Jr., "Research in Delinquent Subcultures," 1958, p. 21. *See also* Moore, 1978 (note 19 above), chap. 2; and Craig A. McEwen, *Designing Correctional Organizations for Youth: Dilemmas of Subcultural Development, 1978.*

33. David Downes, *The Delinquent Solution*, 1966, and Al Larkin and Jerry Taylor, "Drinking, Vandalism, Threats—and Fear," *Boston Globe*, July 9, 1978, pp. 1, 12-13.

34. LaMar Empey and Steven Lubeck, "Conformity and Deviance in the 'Situation of Company'," 1968.

35. See, for example, MIller, 1969; Richard Cloward and Lloyd Ohlin, *Delinquency and Opportunity*, 1960; Cohen and Short, 1958; Fredric Thrasher, *The Gang*, 1936; and Lewis Yablonsky, *The Violent Gang*, 1962.

36. Miller, 1958, p. 19.

37. Solomon Kobrin, "The Conflict of Values in Delinquency Areas," 1951; Alex Inkeles, "Personality and Social Structure," in *Sociology Today*, Robert Merton, Leonard Broom, and Leonard Cottrell, Jr., editors, 1959, p. 254; and Yablonsky, 1962.

38. Johnson, 1979 (note 24 above). See also Dean Dorn, "A Partial Test of the Delinquency Continuum Typology: Countracultures and Subcultures," 1969, and Michael Hindelang, "Moral Evaluations of Illegal Behaviors," 1974.

39. See Howard Erlanger, "The Empirical Status of the Subculture of Violence Thesis," 1974, and Sandra Ball-Rokeach, "Values and Violence: A Test of the Subculture of Violence Thesis," 1973.

Chapter Six

Beauty, Cultural and Countercultural

A culture is as fully defined by its aesthetic standards as by its epistemology and its ethics. Originally meaning perceptible by the senses, "aesthetic" has come largely to mean that which pertains to the appreciation or criticism of the beautiful, as the *Oxford English Dictionary* puts it. And it is in that sense that I shall use the term.

No aspect of recent countercultures has been more visible, more fully a challenge to dominant cultures, than the many drastic changes in the forms of art and the standards of beauty. Art, to be sure, is more than an effort to portray or to elicit an experience of the beautiful—or, in a contrast conception, the ugly. Many people regard art as a major commentary on truth and goodness as well, a view partly expressed in Keats's (and George Herbert's) well-known phrase, Beauty is truth, truth beauty. Fewer would follow the Romantic poet in the remainder of his affirmation: that is all ye know on earth, and all ye need to know. Indeed, he does not always follow himself, for he also wrote that an eagle is not so fine a thing as truth.

I will not try to maintain nice analytic distinctions here, in an effort to isolate the purely aesthetic element in art, but will attempt, instead, to sketch and illustrate briefly the extent to which and the ways in which the values of a society can be challenged by artists of every variety. In making drastic changes in traditional forms and styles, artists often anticipate cultural transformations of a wider sort. (This is not to prejudge the extent to which they may help to cause those transformations and participate in them or, oppositely, alert a society to latent but powerful fractures which, if attended to, could be mended.)

In some ways, artistic opposition is negative, in the sense that artists hold societies and their cultures up to fundamental criticism more than they affirm the values of a counterculture. They join with Dostoevsky in what he described, in *Notes from Underground*, as his battle against "the good and the beautiful"—the beliefs and values of bourgeois society and of the whole humanist tradition. Emphasis on the foibles of the world can set the stage for countercultural values; it may be essential for their creation; but it does not state them directly. And in recent years much of the highly acclaimed art, particularly literature, entails a search for an authentic self more than a search for new values.

When the assumptions, beliefs, and myths that serve to integrate a civilization begin to crumble, often as a result of powerful economic, technical, and demographic changes, artists are among the first to make the process visible, not simply as their individual perceptions, but as a social experience. Edwards saw the desertion of the intellectuals as a major telltale sign of an emerging revolution.[1] We can broaden this to say that the overlapping groups of intellectuals and artists contain a large proportion of those who see the crisis in an old order and begin to clear the ground for a new order, in some instances with images of a counterorder.

In the modern world, the criticism has become especially sharp. Artists and writers have formed a veritable "adversary culture." Rather than (or in addition to) criticism of society for failure to live up to its ideals, the ideals themselves have been opposed, perhaps more strongly than reality.[2]

Among some, the strongest impulse has been to form an *avant-garde*, the front line cultural assault troops. Since the *avant-garde* has to have something to be ahead of, something to push away from, its acceptance or even so much as toleration by the larger society destroys its sense of opposition, requiring still further innovations. When the middle class discovers "that the fiercest attacks on its values can be transposed into pleasing entertainments," as Irving Howe puts it, the *avant-garde* is threatened by its success.[3]

Some oppositional art, by its very creation, defines an aesthetic counterculture, using forms and sounds and ideas that formerly were taboo. It probably remains for our grandchildren, however, to determine whether the critical aspects of contemporary art or the new standards being affirmed are the more important, whether for better or worse, though my eye and ear lead me to guess that the more drastic variations on established artistic themes are more powerful in clearing the ground than in building new styles.

Countercultural Elements in Literature

In describing the standards by which he learned to judge literature, Malcolm Cowley remarked that if writers "were paradoxical—if they turned platitudes upside down, showed the damage wrought by virtue, made heroes of their villains—then they were 'moderns'; they deserved our respect."[4] "The modern" in this sense, one ought to note, is not a chronological concept, limited to recent times. It has occurred at other times. It is opposition to an existing order and seeks to turn its "platitudes," its heroisms upside down. Irving Howe's conception is close to that of Cowley: The modern must be defined by what it is not—it is an "inclusive negative." Modernity consists in a revolt against the prevalent style, "an unyielding rage against the official order."[5]

Lionel Trilling, who was for many years one of the most influential teachers and critics, made a similar point:

> Any historian of the literature of the modern age will take virtually for granted the adversary intention, the actually subversive intention, that characterizes modern writing—he will perceive its clear purpose of detaching the reader from the habits of thought and feeling that the larger culture imposes, of giving him a ground and a vantage point from which to judge and condemn, and perhaps revise, the culture that produced him.[6]

One should not suppose that "detaching the reader" is intended to lead to detachment. In his essay "On the Teaching of Modern Literature," Trilling emphasized that most of the best of modern literature is subversive, filled with "strange and terrible . . . ambivalence toward the life of civilization." I share this appraisal and have no desire to be drummed out of the academy; yet perhaps it should be noted that "best" is largely defined by those who tend to have those ambivalent feelings, which are the frequent if not inevitable accompaniment, and possible result, of the close examination of society and its culture. A popular vote would doubtless give more support to the Henry Wadsworth Longfellows than to the Walt Whitmans. To the general reading public, the literary "adversary culture" is not the dominant one.

Our concern here, however, is not with popularity and general acceptability but with that influential body of literature, going back two centuries or more in the West, that has expressed deep alienation from society, deplored its values, and suggested alternatives. I shall not undertake an explication of even a small part of that literature. A brief reference to illustrative portions, however, can suggest the strength of its cultural opposition. There is no obvious beginning. One might refer to Swift, Richardson, and Blake in English literature, but Blake was strongly influenced by Milton, whose essays (and poems to some degree) had played an important part in the critical thought of the English civil war period more than a century earlier.[7] One can say that by the time the great hopes for social change aroused by the French Revolution had been frustrated, both by the harshness of the revolution and by its collapse, the strength of criticism had mounted. the realization that Newton, who stood as the symbol of rationalism and science, was shaping a new mentality heightened the distress. Among the Romantics, of whom Wordsworth was the central writer, the sense of dismay was profound. They were living in a time, as Keats put it, "where but to think is to be full of sorrow."

On the one side were the dominant beliefs in expansion, progress, and the advance of science, the feelings of optimism, and Adam Smith's "natural harmony"—so happily is the world designed that each person working for himself must inevitably promote the public good. Among the Romantics, however, the ruling perceptions were those of continued violence, societal control, the repression of emotion, and ugliness. And their response to those perceptions was to push away from the established views. "Nineteenth-century Romanticism was strikingly like the contemporary counter culture in its explicit attack on technology, work, pollution, boundaries, authority, the unauthentic, rationality and the family. It had the same interest in altered states of mind, in drugs, in sensuousness and sensuality."[8]

There was a multipronged attack on the dominant order of the nineteenth century, with political and economic radicals joining the artists, although they differed in their responses to the problems they saw. Baudelaire described Paris as "that vast cemetery that is called a great city." In such novels as *Madame Bovary* and *Sentimental Education*, Flaubert attacked middle-class life, its values as well as its practices, although not without pity for its participants. In his writing there is a clearing of the moral ground, perhaps also a clearing of the vision made cloudy by a covetous and acquisitive world. Any counterculture, however, must arise as a contrast conception in the mind of the reader. It is not found in Flaubert. From an economic and political perspective, Marx also condemned domination by machine and acquisitiveness. In addition, however, he developed a utopian counterculture that would, as he saw it, release humanity from its bondage to economic necessity and the modes of production.

By the late nineteenth century, more discernible groups, along with individuals, appeared among the artists. Poets who called themselves the "Decadents" emphasized the primacy of feeling, which, they believed, required a reversal of values. During World War I the Dadaist group was formed, bringing together in uneasy alliance a political and artistic attack on the dominant order. The war, along with all its other effects, had as powerful an impact on art as had the French Revolution. The tragic recognition that the world could fall into such a war, that it could be so utterly destructive, and that its outcome could be so ambiguous, if not futile, shattered the senses. Dada, both as literature and as painting, emerged during the war in Switzerland, an island of peace from which the madness could be observed on all sides. It developed also in the United States and France. As a literary movement its aim was to destroy all existing styles, to create a "salutary chaos." To make a Dadaist poem, Tristan Tzara wrote, one should take a newspaper and a pair of scissors, select an article of the length desired for the poem, cut out each word separately, put them all in a sack and stir gently. Then take the words out one by one and copy them—conscientiously—in the order in which they emerged from the sack. "The poem will resemble you / And you will be a writer of infinite originality and charming sensibility, though misunderstood by the vulgar."[9]

There is an ironic quality to some of the writing that expresses the "adversary function of literature." Tzara and other Dadists, like Rimbaud before them and Henry Miller a little later, went the critics of society one better: Literature itself became an adversary. More than that, "the real Dadaists are against Dada." In *Tropic of Cancer*, Miller wrote: "This is not a book. This is libel, slander, defamation of character . . . this is a prolonged insult, a gob of spit in the face of Art, a kick in the pants to God, Man, Destiny, Time, Love, Beauty . . . what you will."[10]

There was a certain optimism in Dadaism: The world was to be changed by radical art. Among the Bohemians and the "Beats," however, playing it cool, passive resistance, or Secession (the title of a short-lived magazine) was the style. To the dismay with industrial civilization was added the disillusionment that followed the Versailles bickering and the harsh social conflicts. So, disidentify and shape a new kind of life.[11] In the United States these feelings were best expressed, in symbol and reality, by Greenwich Village, which was, as Cowley expressed it, "not only a place, a mood, a way of life: like all Bohemias, it was also a doctrine." He summarized that doctrine, as of

1920, in terms that relate to many preceding movements and also to many that have followed:

> 1. The idea of salvation by the child.—Each of us at birth has special potentialities which are slowly crushed and destroyed by a standardized society and mechanical methods of teaching. . . . 2. The idea of self-expression. . . . 3. The idea of paganism.—The body is a temple in which there is nothing unclean, a shrine to be adorned for the ritual of love. 4. The idea of living for the moment. . . . 5. The idea of liberty.—Every law, convention or rule of art that prevents self-expression or the full enjoyment of the moment should be shattered and abolished. Puritanism is the great enemy. . . . 6. The idea of female equality. . . . 7. The idea of psychological adjustment.—We are unhappy because we are maladjusted, and maladjusted because we are repressed. . . . 8. The idea of changing place.—"They do things better in Europe."[12]

These represent a substantial reversal of dominant views, although I believe Cowley exaggerated in describing all of them as "corrupt ideas" from the standpoint of the prevailing ethic.

One needs to emphasize again that we are not writing about all literature, or all contemporary literature, or even the largest part of it. Surely the adversary culture is large and, in educated circles, influential. But among the best as well as among the less substantial writers different themes are also prominent. Saul Bellow, through Moses Herzog, takes a more detached or analytic, yet sympathetic, view as he puzzles over the reversals of the day:

> The whole feeling-and-sensation market has shot up—shock, scandal priced out of range for the average man. You have to do more than take a little gas, or slash the wrists. Pot? Zero! Daisy chains? Nothing! Debauchery? A museum word for prelibidinous times! The day is fast approaching—Herzog in his editorial state—when only proof that you are despairing will entitle you to the vote, instead of the means test, the poll tax, the literacy exam. You must be forlorn. Former vices now health measures.[13]

For particular audiences, of course, the critical and adversary literature has the greatest appeal. With the development of the mass media, those audiences can be very large. Bob Dylan is sometimes called the first poet of the juke box. He speaks powerfully to the longings, the fears, the angers, of many of the young and not-so-young.[14] We should note, however, that mixed with his themes of rejection of dominant values (or to some degree a caricature of dominant values) are some old-fashioned views ("for all people laugh in the same tongue and cry in the same tongue") that a conservative minister could readily use to supplement his quotations from the Bible and Shakespeare. It is one thing to criticize the failure of a society to live up to its values; it is something else to propound an inversion of those values. Dylan has done both and to these themes has added lyrics of loneliness and love—a Rorschach mixture of wide appeal. Recently he has become a Christian, which may not be so long a step as those who have emphasized only his countercultural themes might imagine.

Many novels and plays in the "theater of the absurd," using that term in a broad sense, are countercultural comments on the world. Esslin[15] has a more restricted usage, and others would restrict it even more. I will follow Kierkegaard, however, in thinking of absurdity as a central aspect of human experience. Even this absurdity that we portray, I hear the dramas saying, makes sense by comparison with our sorry state. It is fascinating to compare, let us say, Carl Mayer's and Hans Janowitz's *The Cabinet of Dr. Calgari*, Ken Kesey's *One Flew Over the Cuckoo's Nest*, Philippe de Broca's *King of Hearts*, and Jean Giraudoux's *The Madwoman of Chaillot*. Despite their differences they share the view that the truly mad are those in power. To understand the world, we shall have to turn our usual preceptions upsidedown. In quite different ways, both *The Cabinet of Dr. Caligari*, and *One Flew over the Cuckoo's Nest* picture attempts to deal with "insane" authority, in one instance cruel, in the other inept. In *King of Hearts*, only persons from the mental hospital made any sense in a battle over a French village during World War I. With a wonderfully comic touch, Giraudoux, in *The Madwoman of Chaillot*, holds the rich, the power hungry, the presumably successful up to ridicule. The industrialist, the general, the broker, the Southern fundamentalist minister, and the commissar are seen as truly mad. They are about to destroy Paris and the world as they seek to get the oil they believe is under the city, while the "madwoman" with her eccentric friends recognize the absurdity in the powerful and try to stop them.

It is easy in the contemporary world to identify with the madwoman, but I shall try to retain an analytic stance, reserving declarations of preference for other occasions.

Among the most powerful expressions of a counterculture will be its literary expressions. These will abound when confidence in the integrity of a society's culture has been shaken; they will expose what the authors believe to be the inauthenticity, the cruelty, the emptiness of life, the weaknesses and absurdities of prevailing values; and at least by inference they will propose a sharply different set of values.

Much of the influential literary work of recent decades expresses the impact of the century-long existential experience—the sense that life is problematic, that a civilization has lost its way, that alienation is the common, even essential stance. Thus Sartre has Roquetin, in *La Nausee*, express the hope, out of his despair, that he can write a story "beautiful and hard as steel and make people ashamed of their existence."[16] Out of such a context countercultures grow.

Countercultural Painting

The same story of cultural upheaval found in literature can be told about painting and other visual forms of art. In commenting briefly on these cultural reversals, one needs to continue to think of counterculture as a variable, lightly touching some segments of life and deeply changing others. That full range is illustrated, during the late medieval and early modern periods, by the remarkably widespread use of the ancient art or craft of the broadsheet, that artistic "comic strip" and social commentary.

As the medieval system of order gave way, through generations of controversy, to the modern world, one theme became especially prominent in the broadsheet sketches: the World Upside Down (WUD) or, to follow David Kunzle in emphasizing the widespread use of the theme: Mundus Perversus, Mondo alla Rovescia, Monde à l'envers, Mundo al Revès, Verkehrte Welt, Verkeerde Wereld.[17] Perhaps contemporary equivalents are some of the comic strips ("Doonesbury"), *Mad* magazine, or those animated TV broadsheets *M*A*S*H** and "Laugh-in." The WUD sketches pictured inversions of human relationships (a peasant riding while the king walks, a wife going to war while the husband spins), of human to animal relationships (sheep shearing the shepherd), of animal-to-animal relationships (chicken eating a fox), and other themes.

As religious and political controversies intensified, the criticism implicit in the broadsheets became harsher, matching the attack of Luther against the papacy. In the *Passional Christi und Anti-christi*, Luther drew a series of parallel word images that pictured the Pope as the inversion of Christ: "the Pope is arrogant, corrupt, and greedy, lives in selfish luxury, and wages war. Jesus was humble, pure, and selfless, lived in poverty, and brought a message of peace. Christ was crowned with a crown of thorns, the Pope with a triple gold tiara. Christ washed his disciples' feet, the Pope's 'disciples' kiss the Pope's foot. Christ protected his flock, the Pope attacks his by force of arms."[18] (To complete this story one should note that when peasants took Luther's revolt to apply to profane as well as to sacred activities, Luther repudiated them; the broadsheets are one indication of the peasants' continuing opposition to the secular as well as the religious state of affairs.)

To some readers, the broadsheets were doubtless sheer frivolity; to others, as Kunzle observes, a mockery of the ideas about changes in the social order (contemporary America has had "Little Orphan Annie" as well as *Mad*). But to some, the World Upside Down sketches were scathing comments on the social order and promises of something better.

The often anonymous creators of the broadsheet sketches were matched in their depictions of incongruity and inversions of status, and sometimes influenced, by various painters. The weird pictures of animal-human reversals in the painting of Hieronymus Bosch influenced the style and the subject matter of the Reformation and post-Reformation cartoonists. Several generations later, Jan Steen painted scenes of dissolution and inverted conventions, pictures of complex and ambiguous meaning. Is Steen's "Dissolute Household," Simon Schama asks:

> . . . a saturnalia or a sermon? At first sight the question might seem perverse. The comic turmoil unleashed in Steen's domestic burlesques, awash with drink and allied mischiefs, surely proclaims him to be Lord of Misrule among Dutch artists, the great orchestrator of licentious havoc. . . . But just as conceivably, it may have been his intention to infer the elements of a moral order through the vision of its disintegration; so that a hedonistic tableau might simultaneously imply both a moral regimen and the rituals of its parody, without dictating which has the upper hand.[19]

These comments may serve to illustrate the fact that our modern experience of elements in the visual arts used to attack the social order, to picture its absurdities and cruelties, and to seek to transform it has been prefigured. At no time, however, have their countercultural qualities been more pervasive than during the twentieth century. A succession of visual art movements has sought to turn our accustomed ways of seeing the world upside down, sometimes in the hope of inverting the political and social world as well. Expressionism, Hilton Kramer remarks, "was the first of the 20th-century counter-cultures—spawned, like the counter-cultures closer to our own historical experience, in the resentments and frustrations of youthful dropouts from the middle class, and intent upon shattering the conventions of middle-class society in the hope of displacing it with a utopian order, or disorder, believed to be freer and more life-enhancing than any to be found in the advanced industrial world just then approaching a new pinnacle of development."[20]

A little later, Dada, in painting as in literature and the dance, was important in setting dramatic changes in motion. It was an effort to bring about a total revolution in art, to create an anti-art.[21] Both as a literary style dedicated to the overthrow of existing forms of expression and as a visual art, the Dada movement sought through radical art to change what its participants experienced as an absurd world. It lasted for scarcely a decade; but during that brief period it demonstrated again that if the world within which art is created is experienced as chaotic and purposeless, faith in prevailing artistic standards will be lost. As a cult of the irrational, Dada sought to expose the irrationality of World War I and the world that made it. Rejecting all prevailing standards of beauty and conceptions of the noble, it insisted on negative action: Destroy and demoralize first. Or, as some thought, since everything had already been torn down, Dadaism could only be an inventory of the ruins, a declaration of the death of a civilization.[22] Since opposition was total, it followed that one should accept no prohibitions. (This sentiment was later expressed by French students during the May 1968 protests in their famous—and paradoxical—slogan: "Il est interdit d'interdere'—Prohibition is prohibited.) After the ground is cleared, build the new society.[23]

Dada was more powerful in attacking what were seen as outworn traditions than in building new standards—which, indeed, by its anarchic quality it was ill equipped to do. Its larger effects come from Surrealism, Pop Art, and other movements that it influenced, even when, as in the case of Surrealism, they broke sharply with Dadaism. As a revolutionary movement (for a time its "official" publication was *Surrealism in Service of the Revolution*), Surrealism was especially sharply torn by the contradiction in its opposition to rationalism, its subjectivism, its belief that the world could be transformed by radical art, on one hand, and its political interests, which required some attention to the structures of power, on the other. It sought to bring together two approaches to what its adherents saw as the same revolution—that of Marx and that of Rimbaud. Surrealism sought new human beings, with transformed images of the world, more than new institutions.[24] These new images could be discovered, as Andre Breton believed, in a half-dream state out of which truths normally hidden could be released in words or artistic compositions. Echoes of these views could be heard in the revolutionary movement in France in 1968 and even in Charles Reich's description of "Consciousness III," seen as a peaceful revolution produced not by struggle but by a reordering of the mind.

It is not on such more or less conscious efforts to blend artistic and political transformations, however, that the importance of Surrealism rests. In the end, Breton and others chose Rimbaud over Marx, asceticism over revolution. At first, as Camus noted, it "was rash enough to say— and this is the statement that André Breton must have regretted ever since 1933—that the simplest surrealist act consisted in going out into the street, revolver in hand, and shooting at random into the crowd."[25] Its lasting impact, however, came through what it created, not its nihilism. It used chaos to jolt the viewer into new perceptions. Picasso, who is more than Surrealist to most of us, has made us experience the mechanization of people, the cruelty and atomism of modern life. "Guernica" is not only a Spanish town bombed almost into oblivion in a cruel war, but a picture of human fragmentation and despair that forces us into its experience by denying us the comforts (and blinders) of accustomed artistic forms.

Some contemporary art, as Rubert de Ventós observes, seeks to compel us to invert our familiar visual experience, to see a typewriter, with Claes Oldenburg, for example, not as hard and metallic, but as soft and flexible. This is part of a process of displacing familiar usages and experiences (which in any event are not intrinsic to the nature of things, but are substantially a result of past interpretations) thus to open to us the opportunity for entering a new visual world.

Art participates in an experience much larger than itself—the experience that life is more contingent and interpretations more historically relative than we had supposed; "and art couldn't help but intervene in this promising project of prolonging, displacing, mixing, or inverting the established sensual 'order'; in forcing, above all, the imagination and the reason to the point where both break with intuition and good sense."[26]

Of course, some efforts to force an inverted sensual, visual, or tactile experience upon us fail. They are not compelling artistically, or they cannot pull us away from our accustomed ways of seeing things. Or they succeed only to compound our sense of contingency, our feelings of alienation from a world within which we must learn to live in spite of a flood of disasters and stupidities.

I suspect that the time may be approaching, after decades during which artists have helped us to see the chaos within which we are engulfed and persuaded us to invert our usual ways of looking at things, that more will turn to the parallel task of helping us to see a promise, however frail, of a humane community. This may equally require a "break with intuition and good sense," in Rubert's phrase, an inversion of our now compelling sense of utter disorder. It is no less essential, however, as part of the difficult human enterprise of living with one another on this crowded earth.

Countercultural Music

> *. . . any musical innovation is full of danger to the whole State, and ought to be prohibited . . . at first sight it appears harmless . . . and there is no harm; were it not that little by little this spirit of licence, finding a home, imperceptibly penetrates into manners and customs; whence, issuing with greater force, it invades contracts between man and man, and from contracts goes on to laws and constitutions, in utter recklessness, ending at last . . . by an overthrow of all rights, private as well as public.*
>
> Plato, Republic IV, 424[27]

I shall only point to some of the other forms of aesthetic counterculture—those drastic efforts to redefine the beautiful, to break away from old standards that seem not only to inhibit the imagination but to confirm the whole culture within which they are embedded. Some of these innovations, by their artistic merit and the timeliness of their appearance, change the culture and become part of new aesthetic traditions, whether classical or popular. Other innovations fade rapidly, particularly if they are to an important degree a vehicle for carrying other kinds of protest than the aesthetic one.

Most great musicians push back the boundaries of the received tradition and are sometimes regarded as countercultural by defenders of the prevailing classicism. Though counterpoint has long been regarded simply as one aspect of harmony, when it first appeared in the late medieval period, with its polyphonic styles, independent rhythms, and distinctive sets of sounds, it was an affront to those who knew how music "should" sound. Even generations later some of Bach's contrapuntal forms—experimentally, perhaps playfully, turning a melody upside down or running it backward—seemed bizarre to some of his contemporaries. It is difficult today to understand how, a little later, a Mozart quartet could have been labeled "the Dissonant." But it was inevitable—if I can offer a sweeping and quite unsupported hypothesis in the sociology of music—that the growing complexity of society should be expressed in the growing complexity of music.

To leap into our own century, Schönberg and Stravinsky and many others turned against the Romantic tradition, as many of their literary contemporaries did, to explore the farthest possibilities of dissonance—one is tempted to say, in a world filled with crashing sounds and disharmonies. The centuries-long rationalization of Western music opened great possibilities for the development of complex harmonic themes; but in another sense it imposed a constraining cultural frame.[28] For that very reason, contrasting musical forms had a clear tradition from which to push away.

Happy New Ears

John Cage

To some composers today, music includes the entire world of sound—or the absence of sound. Rather than elaborating the complex possiblilities of harmony, Cage sees his own musical contribution as the elimination of harmony, the training of our "new ears" to experience music in the full range of the sounds of our everyday lives.

Seen against the history of music, it comes as no surprise that popular as well as classical forms can drastically challenge prevailing standards. The contemporary counterculture in music, to be sure, seems to bring a much more powerful dissent, both in the sharpness of its reversal of standards and in the breadth of its influence. The enormous power of the electronic media to give voice to new sounds, the economic resources to produce them and listen to to them, the depth of the disenchantment, and its expression in so many other ways all support the musical protest of our time.

The *avant-garde*, in music as in other forms of art, must of necessity keep running ahead of the troops. Yesterday's new form is stretched to its limits today. In part, this reflects the emergence of a new "generation," shaped by common and shared experiences in late adolescence and early adulthood that are significantly different from those of their prececessors, even those just a few years older. The traditionalist, the merely progressive, becomes the "square."

In his well-known writings, Howard Becker describes the way the square is defined and regarded by jazz musicians: "The term refers to the kind of person who is the opposite of all the musician is, or should be, and a way of thinking, feeling, and behaving (with its expression in material objects) which is the opposite of that valued by musicians," among whom "behavior which flouts conventional social norms is greatly admired."[29]

Becker referred less to the sounds of jazz than to the life style of the musicians he was describing. The music itself, however, and the context of its performance, can also be contranormative, as in "free jazz." Archie Shepp, for example, often playing before sympathetic white audiences, has sought to provoke, frustrate, even alienate his listeners. "He often produces, without interruption, a particularly exacerbated sound, pointing his saxaphone aggressively at the hall—the instrument being, as he says, many things, notably a Freudian symbol and a machine-gun . . . he never acknowledges applause—inverted Uncle Tomism."[30]

During the last quarter of a century, it is undoubtedly rock music that has been most powerfully counterculture. For some, of course, rock is entertainment, fad, and declaration of independence. Or it is a source of great profit, a billion dollar industry that lives "through the propagation of transient tastes and meaningless crazes."[31] For others, however, it is the chief ritual of a new life; it is community; it is religion. The whole culture complex—the music, lyrics, volume, artifacts, audience, set, and setting—facilitates, as Harmon puts it, "an unprecedented questioning of basic cultural values and institutions."[32] The "acid rock" groups have given coverage and confirmation to the use of drugs; the lyrics define a new morality ("All the things they said were wrong are what I want to be"); the festivals bring together a community that supports the new values; the music itself declares that the old harmonic and well-modulated sounds of the past are the sounds of a repressive society. "For a large minority [presumably of those under twenty-five] rock is the *only* possible grid through which to filter all other data of 'reality'."[33]

In the words of one faithful participant in the culture of rock (faithful because he has commented on the way some rock musicians have become rich and have exploited their followers, yet thinks this irrelevant to judging its significance): "In the final analysis it is, as Eldridge Cleaver put it, a generation of white kids getting into their bodies for the first time in centuries, and that is the major contribution of rock and roll as a force for change in society."[34] Neither the history nor the inference of that sentence stands up well. Contemporary cultural protesters are the descendants of bohemian and beat generations, who themselves had many predecessors; and all may be more symbolic than causal in social change. Yet there is little doubt that a larger proportion of young people have been involved, and perhaps to a greater degree, than in earlier periods. Moreover, the uninhibited sexual energy and in some instances the violence express deep conflicts with dominant values.

Counterculturalists may well agree with Plato's observations on the impact of muscial innovation, although of course they reverse his evaluations. Some now worry not that "this spirit of licence" is full of danger but that it has faded or has been co-opted. With commercial success and artistic acclaim for some, with the end of the Vietnam War, with disillusionment over the absence of revolution by flower power, love, and an amplified guitar, with the *rite de passage* into the thirties for those who lived by rock in the 1960s, some expressions of rock have been moderated and absorbed. New currents, however, have continued to flow through the fields of popular music: acid rock, progressive rock, new rock, the blended sounds of disco, and—when the fire seemed to be cooling—funk and punk rock of many varieties have appeared. Big brother can begin to look and sound like part of the establishment if the musical styles he acclaims are heard in major concert halls and supported by corporate TV advertisers. Yesterday's rock seems bland, especially to younger listeners. In a familiar process, we see inflation in the demands for sharper and sharper contrasts with the dominant order. Critics in the press and, from an opposite perspective, the eager audiences agree: punk rock is gross, disgusting, outrageous.

Punk rockers don't want music made for them by multimillionaires over thirty. To them, the Rolling Stones produce cabaret music.[35] It is not the music of punk rock that is most countercultural, although the steel-hammer drums and electric guitars are played with an ear-shattering intensity. The music is part of an experience that turns the world upside down: Obscenity, vomiting and spitting at the audience; the mocking of style by the use of nails and razor blades for jewelry and safetypins through the ears; and lyrics that do their best to shock ("Groove with me in the gutter, girl").

Conclusion

It would take another volume to examine in any detail the full range of art forms that express countercultural themes. Many films, for example, share the adversarial cultural perspective so important in literature and the theater. Although much that was considered beyond the bounds in portraying violence or sexually explicit material only a decade or so ago has now become a cultural alternative, some films go beyond even this greatly enlarged range. There is less disagreement on the extent to which they invert dominant values than on the degree to which that inversion is socially constructive or destructive or aesthetically enriching. They may be regarded as "realistic and honest representation of contemporary youth"[36] or, as Susan Sontag says of Jack Smith's *Flaming Creatures*: "What I am urging is that there is not only moral space, by whose laws *Flaming Creatures* would indeed come off badly; there is also aesthetic space, the space of pleasure. Here Smith's film moves and has its being."[37] Others, however, take a sharply different view: "Certainly, what we have today is the mass distribution of films which are brilliantly effective, perhaps beautiful, glamorous—and yet which make an assault on our deepest meanings, or urge a total reversal of all values, or urge those who see them toward the impulse to harm."[38]

Whatever the consequences of aesthetic reversals, we are beginning to see that the pace of deviation cannot be continuously accelerated. The *avant-garde* has to slow down to catch its breath. Or, to change the figure, countercultural inflation has finite limits.

Some of the innovations are adapted and absorbed, becoming part—perhaps a large part—of a new, multifaceted, and modified set of standards. Some older elements, however, have been maintained and others are brought back into the cultural mix. The appeal to chaos and dissonance and the overwhelming of the senses correspond with and comment powerfully upon many experiences of our time; but when that point has been made, we may begin (I think we are now beginning) to demand of our artists that they help us find—help us experience—some new sense of order and consonance.

If this occurs, it will not necessarily be an entirely fortunate development. Harmful literature, Evgeni Zamyatin writes, "is more useful than useful literature because it is anti-entropic, it militates against calcification, sclerosis, encrustedness, moss, peace. It is utopian and ridiculous."[39] Morse Peckham speaks of an aesthetic negative as "variability training," a kind of rehersal for real situations wherein flexibility will be required. "After so many centuries of praising order, I think it is time to praise disorder a little," and with that praise to recognize the artist, whose task it is, in his view, to offer disorder. He believes that human beings have a primary drive for order. We are trained to bring to each situation a perspective, an orientation, that filters out data not deemed relevant. Much of the suppressed information, however, may be relevant to new circumstances. "Thus arises the paradox of human behavior: the very drive to order which qualifies man to deal successfully with his environment disqualifies him when it is to his interest to correct his orientation."[40] We need an activity that breaks up orientations, that can "weaken and frustrate the tyrannous drive to order." He wants art to be, and virtually defines it as, such an activity.

We need not accept his definitional limits to recognize the importance of the point he is making. We continually rehearse our various roles; we are trained to participate in a predictable social world. "But we also must rehearse the power to perceive the failure, the necessary failure, of all those patterns of behavior."[41] This too severely limits art, in my judgment; it too easily leads to the view that the "aesthetic negative," however well or crudely expressed, is *ipso facto* art; it minimizes art's constructive role. It is difficult to doubt, however, that the norm-smashing impact, the "rage for chaos" of the aesthetic negative acts powerfully to reorient us, making it almost impossible to fall back into accustomed roles and perspectives. Whether this means that art makes it difficult to restore a treasured culture or makes it difficult to perpetuate a hated culture each must decide. Most persons doubtless design a blend.

The aesthetic negative may be expressed in a self-consciously ugly form, not just to highlight the beautiful of a given tradition by use of a contrast conception but thoroughly to reverse it—a countercultural beauty. Junk, garbage, rags, noise, verbal chaos—these are the stuff of some art. Their use grows, as Adams suggest, "from a feeling, too widespread to be an affectation, that the world *is* essentially ugly, that to show it as anything else is to falsify it intolerably."[42] In the vision drawn for us by Allen Ginsberg, life is a junkyard, "a collection of battered and rusted forms." "Moloch! Solitude! Filth! Ugliness! Ashcans and unobtainable dollars! Boys sobbing in armies! Old men weeping in the parks!"[43]

We are more aware of the ugly because human hopes for its reduction, in all of its forms, were so raised by technical advances, because those very advances have, along with the gains, created ugliness (affluence = effluence?), because the incredible ugliness of war continues to pollute the earth, and because age-old problems have rapidly become more visible and more overwhelming, as the "dump-dwellers" of the world, living in a sea of trash, expand into mega-populations. It is not possible to measure whether the world actually is more ugly, but that many sensitive people believe so has powerfully affected the standards of art. In such a context, the products of inverted aesthetic norms fascinate us.[44] They are not simply a challenge to artistic styles; they expose and comment on the values of the social order generally.

Although it may be stretching a point to say that in their sometimes scruffy appearance many youths are making an artistic statement, they can claim precedents in the use of rags and scraps by writers from Jonathan Swift to James Joyce, and many more. Or perhaps a closer comparison is with the hermits and monks who have expressed their loathing of the world by living in tatters. Whether or not these comparisons are appropriate, it is clear that an aesthetic negative, expressed by contrasts of style, is readily available, easily perceived by friend and opponent alike, and widely responded to as a countercultural statement. Cromwell's "Roundheads" cut their hair short and wore dark clothing to set themselves apart from the effete supporters, as they saw them, of the Stuart kings. More than three centuries later, Britain's "skinheads" and "rockers," largely working-class youths, have set themselves apart from conventional society by their shaven heads and "outrageous" clothing as well as by their street fighting and vandalism. They also separate themselves from the well-groomed "mods," who, in turn, oppose the "rockers" as well as adult society.[45]

Clothing and hair "revolts" do not signal a decisive revolutionary break with the establishment. Part of their attractiveness is that they are inexpensive, quickly reversed, and permit—even require if they are to be effective—continuing contact with the supporters of the old order. They are, however, more than fashion. Sapir, in a brilliant article on fashion, defines it as "custom in the guise of departure from custom."[46] It is the pursuit of individual attention, but in a spirit of "adventurous safety," since many are being adventurous together. More extreme fashion changes may be intended as, and be responded to as, tentative countercultural gestures; but the main intent is to gain prominence in a group, not to break with it. A style rebellion is, however, as Klapp calls it, a protest against the social order and a statement about new values.[47] Some traditional groups respond negatively even to the "low dosage" countercultural expressions of fashion change, while others applaud them; but all dominant groups react against a style rebellion, an aesthetic negative that is a continual reminder of the clash of values.

Earlier I suggested that we tend to ask of art that it help us experience, because it is not art as argument but art as experience that more strongly carries the countercultural (or the cultural) impact. "The world doesn't fear a new idea," D. H. Lawrence wrote. "It can pigeonhole any idea. But it can't pigeonhole a new experience.".[48] Or as John Lennon said of rock 'n' roll, it doesn't need to go through the brain—it gets right to you. In a society whose major values are intact, the artistic experience, though filled with turmoil and agony, becomes in the last analysis an affirmation of those values. In a society torn by doubt, much of the art—often including some of the best—will take us into a different world. The pilgrim in Dante's *Divine Comedy* moved from low to high, into a kind of rebirth. Samuel Beckett has his heroes, if that is the word, still *Waiting for Godot* as the curtain falls. The protagonist of Kafka's fable is no nearer *The Castle* at the end of his journey than at the beginning.[49]

Susan Sontag raises into a value and a principle of criticism the fact that artistic experience, not analysis or argument, carries the major impact: The experience should not be tampered with by analysis; "interpretation is the revenge of the intellect upon art. Even more. It is the revenge of the intellect upon the world. To interpret is to impoverish, to deplete the world—in order to set up a shadow world of 'meanings'."[50] Paradoxically she thus, in *Against Interpretation*, brilliantly interprets the need to avoid interpretation. For my part, I prefer a continuing dialectic between art as experience and art as a commentary on experience. One can readily agree with Sontag that art in the service of a cause is denatured, as for example in "socialist realism." But art that fails to touch our lives as co-members of the human community is "precious."

Notes

1. Lyford P. Edwards, *The Natural History of Revolution*, 1927.
2. See Lionel Trilling, *Beyond Culture: Essays on Literature and Learning*, 1966, and Irving Kristol in *The Third Century: America as a Post-Industrial Society*, Seymour M. Lipset, editor, 1979, pp. 328-43.
3. Irving Howe, editor, *The Idea of the Modern in Literature and the Arts*, 1967, p. 24. See also James Ackerman, "The Demise of the *Avant Garde*: Notes on the Sociology of Recent American Art," 1969; Christopher Butler, *After the Wake: An Essay on the Contemporary Avant-Garde*, 1980; and Hilton Kramer, *The Age of The Avant-Garde: An Art Chronicle of 1956-1972*, 1973.
4. Malcolm Cowley, *Exile's Return: A Narrative of Ideas*, 1934, p. 22. The countercultural aspects of literature can appropriately be discussed as challenges to prevailing standards of truth and goodness, as well as of beauty. All three challenges will receive some attention here.
5. Howe, 1967, p. 13.
6. Trilling, 1966, pp. xii-xiii.
7. See Christopher Hill, *Milton and the English Revolution*, 1977.

8. Frank Musgrove, *Ecstasy and Holiness: Counter Culture and the Open Society*, 1974, p. 65.

9. Quoted by Pierre Gallissaires in Alfred Willener, *The Action-Image of Society*, 1970, p. 206.

10. Henry Miller, *Tropic of Cancer*, 1961, pp. 1-2.

11. Allen Ginsberg, *Howl and Other Poems*, 1956; Jack Kerouac, *On the Road*, 1957; and Richard Miller, *Bohemia: The Protoculture Then and Now*, 1977.

12. Cowley, 1934, pp. 69-71.

13. Saul Bellow, *Herzog*, 1965, p. 187.

14. See Ralph Gleason in *Conversations with the New Reality: Readings in the Cultural Revolution*, by *Ramparts* editors, 1971, pp. 71-82.

15. Martin Esslin, *The Theatre of the Absurd*, 1973.

16. Jean Paul Sartre, *Nausea*, 1964, p. 237.

17. David Kunzle, in *The Reversible World: Symbolic Inversion in Art and Society*, Barbara Babcock, editor, 1978, chap. 1.

18. *Ibid.*, p. 62.

19. Simon Schama, "The Unruly Realm: Appetite and Restraint in Seventeenth Century Holland," 1979, pp. 3-5.

20. Hilton Kramer, *New York Times*, November 9, 1980, section 2, p. 1.

21. See Hans Richter, *Dada: Art and Anti-Art*, 1965; Dickran Tashjian, *Skyscraper Primitives: Dada and the American Avant-Garde, 1910-1925*. 1975; and Cowley, 1934, pp. 146-180.

22. Marcel Raymond, in Howe, 1967 (note 3 above), p. 203.

23. See Pierre Gallissaires in Willener, 1970 (note 9 above), pp. 200-203.

24. *Ibid.*, p. 224; see also Gaetan Picon, *Surrealists and Surrealism 1919-1939*, 1977.

25. Albert Camus, *The Rebel: An Essay on Man in Revolt*, 1956, p. 93.

26. Xavier Rubert de Ventós, *Heresies of Modern Art*, 1980, p. 120.

27. Plato, *Dialogues*, B. Jowett translation, 1937, Vol. 1: 686-87.

28. See Max Weber, *The Rational and Social Foundations of Music*, 1958.

29. Howard S. Becker, *Outsiders: Studies in the Sociology of Deviance*, 1963, pp. 84, 87.

30. Willener, 1970, pp. 243-44.

31. Jonathan Eisen, *The Age of Rock: Sounds of the American Cultural Revolution*, 1969, p. xiii. See also R. Serge Denisoff, *Solid Gold: The Popular Record Industry*, 1975.

32. James Harmon, "The New Music and Counter-Cultural Values," 1972, p. 81.

33. Andrew Weiner, "Political Rock," 1972, p. 187. See also Morris Dickstein, *Gates of Eden: American Culture in the Sixties*, 1977, and

Jeff Greenfield, "They Changed Rock, Which Changed the Culture, Which Changed Us," 1975.

34. Mick Farren, a letter on "Political Rock" by Andrew Weiner, in *New Society*, February 10, 1972, pp. 306-17.

35. See Paul Hendrickson, "The Music They Call Punk Rock," *National Observer*, June 27, 1977, pp. 1, 16, and Jeremy Bugler, "How Punk Rock Became a Four-Letter Word," *The Observer*, December 5, 1976, p. 3.

36. Charles Winnick, "From Deviant to Normative: Changes in the Social Acceptability of Sexually Explicit Material," in *Deviance and Social Change*, Edward Sagarin, editor, 1977, pp. 219-46.

37. Susan Sontag, *Against Interpretation and other Essays*, 1966, p. 231.

38. David Holbrook, *London Times*, October 4, 1976, p. 6.

39. Evgeni Zamyatin in Howe, 1967 (note 3 above), p. 175.

40. Morse Peckham, *Man's Rage for Chaos: Biology, Behavior, and the Arts*, 1965, pp. 40, xi.

41. *Ibid.*, p. 314.

42. Robert Adams, *Bad Mouth: Fugitive Papers on the Dark Side*, 1977, p. 96.

43. Ginsberg, 1956 (note 11 above), p. 17.

44. Adams, 1977. Inverted aesthetic norms also affect our perceptions of the good. It can be shown experimentally that what is perceived to be good is also more likely to be seen as beautiful, and vice versa. (See Alan E. Gross and Christine Crofton, "What is Good is Beautiful," 1977). Inverted aesthetic norms, by the same token, influence moral judgments.

45. See Mike Brake, "The Skinheads: An English Working Class Subculture," 1974.

46. Edward Sapir, "Fashion," 1931, pp. 139-44.

47. Orrin Klapp, *Collective Search for Identity*, 1969, pp. 84-95.

48. Quoted by Trilling, 1966 (note 2 above), p. xvii.

49. See Nathan Scott in *Society and Self*, Bartlett Stoodley, editor, 1962, pp. 615-16.

50. Sontag, 1966 (note 37 above), p. 7.

Chapter Seven

Symbolic Countercultures

"The things of this world can be truly perceived only by looking at them backwards." This statement from a seventeenth-century Spanish novel refers to Proteus, "minister to a king who reigns over an inverted city where nothing is as it seems. . . . Proteus . . . so dissimulates that he can be seen only if one turns one's back and uses a mirror."[1] Such sentiments are expressed, in one way or another, in most societies. Things are seen, imaginatively, upside down, reversed, or in distorted form, whether to perceive them better, to oppose them, or to reaffirm their validity. These symbolic reversals can take the form of rituals, festivals, art, or literature, but they share in common the capacity to place the dominant cultural and social world in a new light.

No clear line can be drawn between symbolic inversions and more direct acting-out of countercultural standards. Every act has a symbolic content; and a symbol, to be perceived, must be acted upon in some way. It is useful, however, to think of a continuum ranging from actions that are direct expressions of oppositional values (life in a commune, for example) to symbolic actions that imply rather than state the opposition directly (through the use of metaphor, irony, satire, or ritualized role reversals, for example).

The *continuing* influence of countercultures is shown more strongly in symbolic inversions than in the development of new groups whose members act out norms and values contrary to those most widely accepted. The latter reversals are more episodic; they draw on the steady stream of symbolic inversions embedded in language.[2]

In her excellent introduction to *The Reversible World*, Babcock defines symbolic inversion as "any act of expressive behavior which inverts, contradicts, abrogates, or in some fashion presents an alternative to commonly held cultural codes, values, and norms be they linguistic, literary or artistic, religious, or social and political."[3] By examining various symbolic inversions we can get some sense of their importance as a continuous part of cultural life.

Rituals of Opposition as Countercultures

If countercultures are rooted in characterological and social constants, one should find them, in one form or another, in all societies. Their strength can be expected to vary widely, along with their specific or precipitating causes, but they should be found everywhere in incipient or highly developed form. This argument is put to its most severe test in its application to small, tribal societies relatively isolated from contact with other societies. Perhaps our perceptions of such societies need to be altered by further study of their conflicts and internal cultural variations[4] and by further examination of the importance of the inversions and reversals built into their classification system.[5] Our interest here is in the role reversals and the rituals of rebellion and opposition that are not only permitted but sometimes required of persons occupying certain positions. Related to them are the saturnalia, the feasts of fools, the charivaris that come down to us from at least the days of classic Greece and Rome.

From *The Golden Bough*, Fraser's great compendium of custom and folklore, to Gennep's *Rites of Passage*, to Gluckman, Victor Turner, Goody, Norbeck, Peter Rigby, Beidelman[6] and many others we have had a steady flow of ethnographic description and a variety of interpretations of rituals of opposition and of role reversals. Many American Indian tribes had burlesque ceremonies during which tricksters did, often hilariously, everything the culture forbade. Clowns "parodied serious rituals, introduced obscenity into sacred places . . . and showed open disrespect for the gods themselves."[7] During periods of threat among the Gogo, women are permitted to dress like men, to carry out male tasks, to carry spears and knives that normally are limited to men, to behave aggressively and sing lewd songs.[8] A striking feature of the organization of the Zulu "is the way in which they openly express social tensions: women have to assert license and dominance as against their formal subordination to men, princes have to behave as if they covet the throne, and subjects openly state their resentment of authority."[9]

Such activities can be matched in the medieval and contemporary worlds.[10] During designated periods "the social hierarchy and the social decencies could be turned upside down."[11] By the late fifteenth century All Fools Days were banned by the cathedrals, but they were picked up by laymen, by families, craft guilds or "societés joyeuses" who planned ribald festivals, Abbeys of Misrule. Lyon had a Judge of Misrule and a Bench of Bad Advice; Rouen's Abbot had serving him the Prince of Improvidence, the Cardinal of Bad Measure, Bishop Flatpurse, Duke Kickass, and the Grand Patriarch of Syphilitics.[12]

The mocking of traditional moral precepts is particularly startling during a religious ceremony, a practice that is still found in some religious contexts. Pruess describes a procession bringing wooden support beams to prop up a sacred Bo tree in a Theravada Buddhist merit-making ceremony in northern Thailand: "Hilarity and disorder were the chief features of the parade. . . . There was much raucous laughter, frenetic dancing, bawdy singing, excited drumming, mutual pummeling, staggering, and falling down." In addition, most of the carts and beams were adorned with posters scarcely designed to win merit. "Examples included (a) a standing rear-view female nude, a young man and woman (also nude) embracing each other, with the caption (in English) 'FREE LOVE'; (b) a young man with a whiskey bottle warding off the advances of an amply endowed young woman, with the caption (in Thai) 'I don't want love, intoxicating drink is better' . . .; and (c) a map of Thailand, before which a soldier fired his rifle at the visage of Mao Tse-Tung and several fierce-looking members of the People's Liberation Army."[13] The ribald behavior continued even after the procession had reached the sacred zone of the shrine.

Pruess sees these displays or intimations of three impure themes in the moral system of the group involved (intoxication, violent aggression, and unrestrained sex) as "sanctioned expression of disorder, chaos, unpredictability, potentiality—forces that threaten the image of a stable ideal society and hence must be neutralized and structured within the moral framework of the social order."[14] This counterpoint reflects the tension between order and disorder that is dealt with by all religions seeking to develop an image of a cosmos, for such an image must take account of and deal with the reality of disordering experiences.[15]

The disordered experiences are not simply possibilities; they are part of everyday life. The inversions in the rites of reversal are antitheses not of what Linton called "real culture"—the daily acting-out of the values and norms of society—but of "ideal culture." Carnival or festival behavior, by exaggerating and caricaturing common deviations, calls attention not only to this cultural blueprint but also to the frequency with which it is disregarded. Describing festivals in St. Vincent, West Indies, and the La Have Islands, Nova Scotia, Abrahams and Bauman observe that the obvious inversions (men dressing as animals or supernaturals, transvestitism, sexual license) should not cause us to forget that order was scarcely universal at other times. And those who engage in the license during the festivals were those who "are the community agents of disorder during the remainder of the year."[16]

Rituals of reversal, some of them mainly playful (although not for that reason unimportant),[17] but others more serious, are not uncommon in contemporary Western societies. We have Halloween, football weekends, Mardi Gras, New Year's Eve, and twenty-four-hour rock concerts, all tolerated and to some degree protected by the agents of the official culture.

Less obviously, but perhaps more powerfully, some teaching, particularly in the humanities and the social sciences, can be seen as a ritual of opposition attacking the established order and describing, or implying, an alternative cultural world.[18] To some degree to analyze a society is to weaken the mythic hold of its culture. I do not argue against this—indeed at this moment I am engaged in such analysis—because the alternative, a kind of rigid ignorance, is more risky. Yet we need continually to remind ourselves that "a little learning is a dangerous thing."

From Blake and Wordsworth to Nietzsche, Baudelaire, Conrad, Lawrence, Gide, Yeats, and Joyce (make out your own list) runs a "bitter line of hostility" toward the dominant culture. By the time students have read Nietzsche's *The Birth of Tragedy*, Conrad's *Heart of Darkness*, and Dostoevsky's *Notes from Underground*, "a work which made all subsequent subversion seem like affirmation, so radical and so brilliant was its negation of our traditional pieties and its affirmation of our new pieties," students seemed ready, as Trilling put it, to engage in "socialization of the antisocial, or the acculturation of the anti-cultural, or the legitimation of the subversive."[19]

Such study—and the exams on the material—is a kind of ritual of rebellion, allowing strongly countercultural feelings and ideas to be expressed, but within a culturally permitted and ritualized frame of reference—the classroom. It is not by chance that students and the young generally are those granted this license. To some degree they see themselves and are seen as in a liminal phase, to use Gennep's term, surrounded by cultural ambiguities as they move from one social position to another.

How can we account for these sanctioned, even sponsored, deviations from the established cultures, these culturally circumscribed countercultures? They are most commonly seen as cultural inventions that serve, whatever their origins, as lightening rods. Gluckman described rituals of rebellion that blatantly subverted the usual moral and sexual norms as cathartic release mechanisms that lowered anger and resentment.[20] It seems paradoxical, Wallace notes, that some people should be permitted, even required, to do the "wrong" thing, the culturally forbidden. "The paradox, however, is only a seeming one, for the ultimate goal is still the same: the maintenance of order and stability in society. Rituals of rebellion are intended to contribute to this order by venting the impulses that are chronically frustrated in the day-to-day course of doing what is required."[21] Gluckman developed the distinction, formulated earlier by Aristotle (or if you prefer, by Weber), between rebellion and revolution, and argued that only rebellion against rulers, not against the system, could develop in tribal societies, because they could envisage no alternatives. Such rebellions, he argued, were culturally contained and ritualized even as they permitted drastic counternormative symbolic behavior.[22]

A similar argument is frequently made with reference to the effects of religious sects, whose doctrines often contain themes of status reversal and embody values that conflict sharply with those of the dominant society. In her discussion of "Spirit-Possession Belief and Trance Behavior in Two Fundamentalist Groups in St. Vincent," Henney comments on "the opportunities for ritualistic ventilation and releasing of tensions that pose no threat to the established order, but, on the contrary, contribute to its maintenance."[23] In his study of the Shango cult in Trinidad, George E. Simpson noted that the energy, time, and resources spent on Shango could not be spent on activities designed to bring about social and economic change.[24] In addition, the emotional release attained by participation in the ceremonies of Shango deflected fervor away from political activity. In a similar vein some contemporary political radicals believe that drug-oriented countercultural protests block drastic social change. From this point of view, such protests can be seen as encapsulated rituals of rebellion.

These explanations seem to me true but incomplete. Even in the most isolated societies persons who feel abused can imagine alternative norms and values in the form of contrast conceptions to those that prevail. Rites of opposition express a contradiction in society. They do not resolve that contradiction but give voice to strongly ambivalent feelings. They often contain sharp criticisms of the social order, allowing some persons to express values that stand as potential reversals of the dominant standards. This keeps such values alive while not compelling the participants to see themselves wholly in terms of them. Such rituals also allow the orthodox, the "straight," to see and hear and sense the force behind alternative ways, perhaps breaking their cultural isolation and rigidity. As Victor Turner puts it, describing the contemporary "rock" experience: "The structure-dissolving quality of liminality is clearly present." He then goes on to note that the "rock" experience is ancient, arguing against those who suppose that contemporary rock music, with its accompanying group experiences and multiple stimuli, is unique:

> Anthropologists the world over have participated in tribal "scenes" not dissimilar to the rock "scene" . . . "synnaesthesia," the union of visual, auditory, tactile, spatial, visceral, and other modes of perception . . ., is found in tribal ritual and in the services of many modern religious movements. Arthur Rimbaud, one of the folk heroes of the counter-culture, would have approved of this as "*un deréglement ordonné de tous les sens*," "a systematic derangement of the senses."[25]

As a writer for the *Oracle* put it: "imagine *tasting* G-minor."

Elsewhere Turner observes that the destablizing effects of rituals of opposition are found mainly in complex, industrial societies. In *The Ritual Process* he "stressed the potentially subversive character of liminality in tribal initiations, when, in the betwixt-and-between states, social-structure categories are forced to relax their grip on thought and behavior, but this potentiality never did have any hope of realization outside a ritual sphere hedged in by strong taboos."[26] He suggests that one speak of "liminoid" rather than "liminal" contexts when referring to the charivaris, art, literature, and other forms of symbolic inversion in industrial societies. These may have revolutionary impact, he believes.

Although Turner may draw too sharp a distinction, there seems to be little doubt that the symbolic inversions of complex and rapidly changing societies are less likely to serve as catharsis and more likely to stimulate culture change than the inversions of tribal societies. Dominant members of a society may not, however, recognize the potential for turning the world upside down. "It is sometimes expedient to allow the people to play the fool and make merry, lest by holding them in with too great a rigour, we put them in despair," wrote the French lawyer Claude de Rubys at the end of the sixteenth century.[27] But Natalie Davis wisely observes that this traditional view tells more about magistrates than the real consequences of the festivals of "misrule." The king might be attacked under his very nose, as in Paris when a festival group "put on a farse demonstrating that Mére Sotte reigned at court and that she was taxing, pillaging and stealing everything."[28] At times mobs grew out of the festivals, giving expression to their oppositional views, not supporting the social order.

Although some Marxists have regarded folk festivals as "safety valves" that hindered the development of revolutionary consciousness, Marx saw them more positively as steps toward such consciousness. "The occurrence of many actual rebellions, especially in the slave communities of the New World, during the Christmas and carnival seasons would seem to confirm Marx's insight and challenge Gluckman's thesis."[29]

Of course, we lack the kind of controlled study that would allow us to speak with confidence about the countercultural aspects of rituals of rebellion or more contemporary forms of sanctioned deviation. What we do have is the experience of seeing such rituals being developed before our eyes, in the form, for example, of rock festivals licensed by city officials and aided by the police—even as many of the norms and values of the dominant society are disregarded. By careful study through time we may be able to determine to what degree such rites promote cultural integration (or rigidity) by serving as safety valves and the degree to which they promote cultural change and conflict by keeping alternatives alive.

Many societies have what the outsider or unbeliever sees as mythical countercultures—conceptions of some social order of another time and place that is based on sharply contrasting values. When the images are positive—a heaven, the Garden of Eden, nirvana, utopia, or the land of Rousseau's "noble savages"—they do not so much reverse the prevailing values as symbolize them in pure form: This is the way existence will be, or could be, if we were to attain our highest cultural level; or, this is the way life was "before the fall." Yet a sharp critique of the operating, if not of the established, values is also implicit in such conceptions.

Negative images of symbolic societies are more clearly countercultural. The Karavarans of New Guinea contrast their society with an antisociety they call *momboto*, which they imagine to have existed in earlier days. "During the time of the *momboto*, men looked like wild animals and behaved as such. They did not shave nor did they cut their hair; they had red eyes 'like wild pigs'; they ate human flesh, even the flesh of those who would now be considered their kinsmen. There was no kinship or regulation of sex."[30] This vision of an antisociety makes clear the Karavaran belief that basic human nature is filled with greed, violence, and unqualified self-interest. The constraining power of a stable social order is needed to hold an essentially anarchic human nature in check. Hobbes would be proud of them.

Their contemporary order, in sharp contrast with *momboto*, was formed generations ago on the arrival of a missionary; and a new, more promising order can be attained with equal speed by embracing the Cargo movement, blending traditional ritual with strenuous efforts to learn European ways of doing business.

Middleton describes a similar symbolic counterculture among the Lugbara in what is now Uganda. "Inverted beings" of several sorts are believed by the Lugbara to exist or to have existed before their society was formed. The earlier mythical beings represent a presocial period, a period of disorder and chaos. These "inverted beings" behaved in ways "the opposite of the ways expected of normal socialized persons in Lugbara society today."[31]

The threat of disaster held before the Karavarans and the Lugbara in these images of life governed by inverted values is primarily a social threat. If our social order decays or is not adjusted to new circumstances, these images imply, we can fall back into chaos. Conceptions of hell, which is not necessarily seen as a past antisociety, are more likely to suggest an individual threat: Those individuals who violate fundamental social standards are doomed to exist in an antisociety governed by inverted values.

Modern societies, perhaps no less in need of images of "inverted beings," create them out of "witches" and other deviants who are seen as living by inverted values. In the late medieval and early modern period a purely negative image of witches emerged. Witchcraft was no longer seen simply as a supernatural technology, now malevolent, now beneficial, for dealing with day-by-day problems. Profound changes in the social order—expressed both in expanding opportunities and in a declining sense of a coherent moral universe—left both the leaders and the populace at large with great anxiety. Witchcraft came to be seen, as Ben-Yehuda observes, as an independent "antireligion," a blend of sorcery and heresy. In Europe by the fifteenth century, "The stories and myth of the witches can be regarded as the exact qualitative opposite of the conception of Christ, and witchcraft as the exact opposite of what was supposed to be the true faith, Christianity."[32]

However much the image of witches distorts reality, it can operate as a powerful symbol of feared and hated forces loose in an uncertain world. Contemporary malevolent witches, if I can stretch the meaning of the term somewhat, are not generally seen as possessed of supernatural power; but they are seen as inverted beings of enormous and mysterious influence, dedicated to the overthrow of the social order. The "witchcraft trials" promoted by Senator Joseph McCarthy, for example, developed a powerful symbolism of a threatening counterculture. The United States was entering a bewildering time. In possession of weapons of incredible destructiveness, it faced the fact that a cultural adversary (as much as or more than a geopolitical adversary) had also created such weapons. The world was changing in many ways at unprecedented speed. Scarcely able to draw the line against such massive and impersonal changes as were occurring, some felt the need to personalize them, to lodge their source in individuals whom one might hope to constrain.

Some literary genres create inverted beings for us, but from an ironic perspective intended more as a commentary on society than on the actions of the antiheroes in the narratives. The writer of picaresque novels, Barbara Babcock notes, seeks to speak the truth about society "through dramatic inversions of social, moral, and literary orders; . . . rather than talking of truths he must speak in double negatives of not untruths." Criticism of the picaro, the prankster, who violates social norms becomes at the same time criticism of "absolute convention in general." This is shown particularly in the satire of religion, from the earliest picaresque novels down to the present. In *Easy Rider*, for example, "a meal in New Orleans during Mardi Gras becomes a mass; a church becomes a brothel; a whore, Mary; LSD, the sacred host; and a cemetary, the place of conversion—'turning on.' "[33]

Counter-Languages

Countercultural groups are almost always characterized by language practices that are used to oppose, confuse, offend, or separate themselves from the dominant society. An antisociety, to use the term employed by Halliday, "is a society that is set up within another society as a conscious alternative to it. . . . An anti-language is not only parallel to an anti-society; it is in fact generated by it."[34] Employing a similar concept in *Bad Mouth: Fugitive Papers on the Dark Side*, Adams describes what he calls a counter-language, used not to communicate directly but to hurt others, to deliberately violate standards of decency and truth. This restricts the meaning of counter-language more narrowly than I want to do—indeed more than Adams does in his development of the theme. Dominant language can also hurt people and violate standards of decency and truth ("We had to destroy that village in order to save it"). The general concept is a neutral one, however much we may make moral judgments in particular cases. We need here to emphasize that the concept of anti- or counter-language refers not to a dialect or to class variations in vocabulary and grammar but to language practices that result directly from intrasocietal conflict. (I will use the two terms as approximate synonyms, although counter-language seems the better term. Anti-language could seem to connote opposition to language as such, rather than opposition to a dominant language and the social order within which it is embedded.)

Halliday describes the "pelting speech" of the "counterculture of vagabonds" in Elizabethan England, the argot of the Calcutta underworld, and the anti-language used in Polish prisons. Wherever a counterculture persists for any length of time, it is likely to develop a language component, especially the substitution of new words for old, in the process of creating an alternative reality.

There are many illustrations of the counter-language process. In a 1567 pamphlet, Thomas Harmon describes the "pelting speech" referred to by Halliday:

> Here I set before the good reader the lewd, lousy language of these loitering lusks and lazy lorels, wherewith they buy and sell the common people as they pass through the country; which language they term pedlars' French, an unknown tongue only but to these bold, beastly, bawdy beggars and vain vagabonds, being half mingled with English when it is familiarly talked.[35]

A little later in English history many Ranters, faced with persecution, "seem to have adopted a secret language and to have carried on a wary and clandestine propaganda, exactly like the heretical Beghards and Beguines before them."[36]

Writers may create antilanguage styles in an effort to convey some new sense of reality, to force readers into new ways of perceiving, or to express criticism of the social order. To unravel the meaning of James Joyce, as Cowley observed, the reader needs to master several languages, the mythology of all peoples, and the geography of Dublin. Gertrude Stein seemed to carry obscurity, as opposed to clarity, even further. "She seemed, indeed, to be writing pure nonsense, and yet it was not quite pure; one felt uneasily that much of it could be deciphered if only one had the key. But in reading a Dada poem it was often useless to search for clues: even the poet himself might not possess them. The door of meaning was closed and double-locked; the key was thrown away."[37] If one applies the usual linguistic conventions while reading or seeing Beckett's *Waiting for Godot*, he will miss the comments on the absurd while experiencing only absurdity. In some cases, as Erich Kahler put it, we have seen "the gradual decomposition of language into its components . . . to the final evaporation in silence and the void."[38] Literary antilanguages are not necessarily countercultural. They may more strongly criticize the social order than affirm a new one. Not being tied to a linguistic group, readers can interpret them in various ways.

In the special sense that Halliday uses the term, ghetto English vernacular has counter-language qualities. It affirms a social identity in opposition to the one profferred by the larger society. The power structure of the dominant society is revealed and supported by its language, so a counter-language is used by the oppressed to construct a new reality.

Since the significance of the ghetto vernacular for black-white relations is a matter of some controversy, several comments on the use of the term counter-language in reference to it seem desirable: (1) Counter-language is not a pejorative term. If the reality to which it is opposed is repugnant, one assesses the value of a counter-language by seeking to discover the degree to which it is successful in changing that reality or protecting members of the antisociety from its injustices. (This is, to be sure, a difficult task—one that I shall not undertake here.) (2) Counter-language is not a synonym for nonlanguage. It is probably no longer necessary to emphasize that nonstandard modes of speech are full and complex languages.[39] (3) Empirically, counter-languages are often mixed with subcultural dialects, and the protest elements are difficult to separate from the traditional elements. A subcultural dialect is "somebody's mother tongue." "An anti-language, however, is nobody's 'mother tongue'; it exists solely in the context of resocialization, and the reality it creates is inherently an alternate reality . . . a *counter*-reality, set up in *opposition* to some established norm."[40] The black English vernacular is composed of elements of standard speech, of a traditional dialect forged on the plantation and in the city, and of counter-language. This last ingredient indicates the effort to create a counter-reality, freed from the inevitable entanglement of the dominant reality—within which they suffer—with dominant language usages.

Labov's discussion of sounding or playing the dozens, the trading of ritual insults, in some black communities shows clearly that their language practices cannot be fully understood unless relationships with the dominant society are taken into account:

> Obscenity does not play as large a part as one would expect from the character of the original dozens. Many sounds *are* obscene in the full sense of the world. The speaker uses as many "bad" words and images as possible—that is, subject to taboo and moral reprimand in adult middle-

> class society. . . . the meaning of the sound and the activity would be entirely lost without reference to these middle-class norms. Many sounds are "good" because they are "bad"—because the speakers know that they would arouse disgust and revulsion among those committed to the "good" standards of middle-class society . . . sounds derive their meaning from the opposition between two major sets of values: their ways of being "good" and our way of being "bad."[41]

Language usages that separate a group from the dominant society, in some measure protecting them and expressing their opposition, characterize deviant groups as well as minorities. Lerman found that knowledge of a deviant argot correlated highly with the likelihood of participation in an illegal "youth culture."[42]

Language change or the development of distinctive usages is not synonymus, of course, with counter-language.[43] Change occurs continuously as a result of lingual drift and of shifts in social circumstances. Even when clear signs of a counter-language are lacking, however, the student of countercultures can find hints of important trends by monitoring changes in vocabulary, grammar, or syntax that do not, by themselves, directly express counter values. Such a possibility is well illustrated by Thomas Middleton in his comments on the use of "me" when "myself" would formerly have been deemed appropriate:

> "Jane, how could you just pack up and leave Jerry and the children?"
> "I did it for Me."
>
> That's a perfect case where *myself* is called for, but you'd never hear "I did it for myself" these days, any more than you'd hear, "I have to be myself." It's "I gotta be Me." "I just thought it was time I thought about Me for a change."
>
> It's as though *myself* were somehow less of the essence than *me*. And the *Me* is always said with a capital M. God, the Holy Grail, the Eternal Verities, and Me. . . .
>
> "I want to make something of myself" has a rather pleasant ring to it—a ring of determination to do something worthwhile. "I want to make something of Me," on the other hand, carries overtones of narcissism involving batteries of techniques for making that special Me into something complete and content, with little need or care for anyone else.[44]

Lest we press this argument too far, we should recall the sentiment expressed in Walt Whitman's "Song of Myself," which manages to use both "me" and "myself" to sing his self-regard: "I dote on myself; there is a lot of me and all so luscious." Whether or not one shares Middleton's interpretations and preferences, one can agree that language shifts of the kind he described are valuable clues to changes in value.

Obscenity and Pornography. Some comfortable or could-be-comfortable persons, as well as the disadvantaged, proclaim their opposition to dominant values by attacking standard speech. Their counter-language is used, like others, to oppose, confuse, and offend the dominant society and to separate the counterculturalists from it. They hold, as David Martin puts it, "that ordered, elegant speech is treason against the existential vagaries of genuine emotion."[45] Perhaps the clearest illustration is the use of obscenity. Although not limited to language or to the higher strata, obscenity is similar, in its social meaning, to the counter-language forms to which we have referred. It too can be partly understood as symbolic counterculture, used to expose the absurdity and cruelty believed to characterize the dominant culture and to help construct a new reality (although like much counterculture, it is more successful in doing the former than the latter).

Not all obscenity is countercultural. Some of it simply reflects a person's socialization to a deviant, or not so deviant, subculture. In some cases it is an individual "art form," helping one draw the picture of the world as he sees it or giving one a stage. Often obscenity allows one to express, in a fit of anger perhaps, how perversely the world operates. Such individual and subcultural forms shade off into countercultural uses, wherein obscenity is employed more or less deliberately to mount an attack on the dominant values, as in the writings of the Marquis de Sade or Henry Miller.

Whether individual or countercultural, obscenity requires a taboo, a verbal barrier to be breached. The stronger the taboo, the more powerfully the obscenity is experienced. It is, as Adams puts it, "a shock rupture of ingrained social codes controlling verbal or physical action."[46] Obscenity deals not with social conventions but with moral codes related to basic human activities—sex, excretion, food, treatment of the dead. When social conflict etches social divisions more sharply, the taboos are experienced on all sides as more significant. Their violation is seen as more odious or, to the violator, as more clearly a sign of contempt for the culture they protect.

What is obscene varies greatly from place to place and from time to time. The French counterpoint the clarity of their normal speech by the rich profusion of their obscenities. A Spaniard, renowned for pride in family, may express his ultimate obscenity by a curt "*Tu madre* . . .

a particularly devious and deadly form of obscenity, since it forces the victim to contaminate his own mind, to call up the expression that the speaker does not even deign to voice."[47]

After much use, an obscenity loses its ability to shock, without which it is no longer obscene. For many American males—and a growing number of females—to say that something is a God-damned fuckin' shame is to say scarcely more than "too bad." The law of diminishing returns sharply reduces the power of a counterculture to express its opposition to established values lingually.

In the United States in the last few decades verbal inflation has so reduced the power of obscenity that much more has to be "spent" to achieve the same effect. But in the context of a "stinking war," the "fouling of the environment," and other harsh social conflicts, the motive to spend has also increased. Polite language is the true obscenity, said participants in the Berkeley Free Speech movement; the deceitful rhetoric of the powerful merely hides or disguises an evil society. They drew on a long tradition, one that goes back in American literature to Whitman, Twain, and beyond. "The scent of these arm-pits is aroma finer than prayer," Whitman wrote in *Leaves of Grass*. This is modest obscenity by contemporary standards, but like some current writing it is an effort, to use Norman Mailer's words, "to restore the hard edge of proportion to the overblown values" of society. The "overblown values" to which Mailer was referring were those of military life, "viz: being forced to salute an overconscientious officer with your back stiffened into an exaggerated posture. 'That Lieutenant is chickenshit,' would be the platoon verdict, and a blow had somehow been struck for democracy and the sanity of good temper."[48] The language of the vernacular and the vulgar is used to suggest an alternative set of values to those embodied in polite speech or to carry on "a kind of class struggle . . . dirty words against the pretentious vocabulary of domination."[49]

Thus obscenity in a counterculture is used not as something intrinsically important but as a weapon to expose the hypocrisy of the dominant society, as seen by the speaker or writer, and to suggest a contrary set of values. "Through the obscene one declares one's independence of the rotten genteel tradition, and achieves the instant, universal *bona fides* of moral authenticity."[50] Of course there is the possibility of fraud, as Adams notes; and of course the tradition may not be rotten. In addition, one must ask: After obscenity, what follows? Is it more than verbal trashing and vandalism? Leo Marx, who asks this question, believes that it is more, or can be. We are a long ways from knowing, however, the conditions under which, and among whom, the counter-language of obscenity goes beyond symbolic opposition.

In recent years pornography—literally, or originally, that which pertains to the life and manners of prostitutes—has become in many usages almost a synonym for obscenity. It is the representation of obscene things in art or literature, as the dictionary puts it. It is fantasy designed to remedy what are experienced as sexual deficiencies in reality. To determine the countercultural aspects of obscenity and pornography, one needs to distinguish the argument that they are good in themselves—because they help destroy repressive codes, for example—from the argument that says, whatever harm they may bring is less than the harm that comes from censorship. The latter defense is scarcely countercultural.

A substantial proportion of Americans (along with British, West Europeans, Japanese, and others) accept the availability of explicit sexual material in films and in writing. In one American sample, from 15 to 59 per cent, depending on the nature of the material and the degree of privacy—with men being more accepting than women—expressed favorable attitudes.[51] One cannot tell from the data, however, the basis of the acceptance. Some may support the material as a positive good, perhaps because they see it as a way of lifting sexual repression. Others may believe that pornography cheapens and mechanizes sex, agreeing with Jules Feiffer that "*Screw* and its like are basically narcississtic, anti-woman, and about as pro-sex as the clap."[52] Yet they may "accept" its availability as a price to be paid for freedom of speech. Others doubt that the recent change of standards for obscenity and pornography has enhanced a larger freedom. "Government permissiveness," Adler writes, ". . . offers nakedness and circuses and permits erotic liberties so long as these do not lead to presumptions against property or challenges against the established order."[53] Certainly one would not find many recruits for a revolution of a late evening in the Soho district, along the Ginza, in Times Square, or in a Playboy club. Many, probably most, radicals have been quite ascetic, believing that efforts to secure freedom from the powerful and freedom for workers, peasants, minorities, women—the list varies—are deflected by movements that manage, somehow, to trivialize the erotic while making it the hoped-for engine of social change.

In principle one can distinguish betwen pornography, concerned only with sexual arousal, and art with sexual themes, designed to help us experience and understand the subtleties of human relationships. Many works of art are both, leading to endless controversy. Even when agreement is reached on what works are pornographic, it remains arguable whether or not they are countercultural: Are they not protected to a substantial degree by law? (Or is it, in the United States for example, the First Amendment that is protected, with pornography hiding under its shelter?) Are such works not widely seen and accepted, thus best regarded as cultural alternatives, not as countercultural behavior? To some degree, the answer to each of these questions, I believe, is yes, indicating that only part of pornography can be subsumed under a countercultural label. There remains, however, a "hard core" proclaimed by some as a right and acclaimed as a value, although opposed to dominant values, that is a significant part of the symbolic counterculture of the day.

We are a long way from knowing the larger social and cultural consequences of obscenity and pornography, despite continuous study.[54] I believe that there are good grounds for the claim that there is a negative correlation between emphasis on the erotic and revolutionary fervor, but the causal connection is not clear. Those for whom the release of inhibitions is the major goal may be poor candidates for a movement that emphasizes relief from institutions. I agree with Cynthia Epstein that "we can work out a way to differentiate between the pornography that is bad for our culture, ourselves and our families, and that which is a frolic into the world of sensuality or even a tolerable vulgarity."[55] It is not clear to me, however, what a democratic society can do, once that distinction is made, to discourage the one and allow the other. Zoning ordinances that "restrict public encounters," as proposed by Hausknecht and others, seem unlikely to be effective. A paperback book is less easily sequestered than a glue factory, to use Hausknecht's example.

The full range of consequences of ready access to pornography, now so widely distributed in the name of profit and freedom, will not emerge for a generation or more. The task of students of countercultures is to enlarge our understanding as the consequences increase. Meanwhile, our views are governed by assumptions and feelings to a large degree. Mine are close to those of Irving Howe:

> My response to pornography is not so much to be socially alarmed as imaginatively disheartened. I don't know what damage, if any, it does to society or the future generations. I don't know if it encourages rape or stimulates perversion. I don't know if it threatens the family. But when I

walk along 42nd Street in New York City and pass the peep-hole joints, the hard-core movie houses, the shabby bookstores, I find myself growing depressed. Is *this* what humanity, or even a portion of it, has come to in the late years of the 20th century?[56]

Countercultural Courtesy and Humor. There are several other symbolic forms in which countercultural values can be stated. A brief reference to two of these forms may suggest further the diversity of oppositional symbols in countercultures.

Patterns of courtesy symbolize and reinforce various norms, particularly the status arrangements. Courtesy is "graceful politeness," as the dictionary puts it. The first meaning in French is even more favorable. Courtesy is the spirit of chivalry; it is the ideal, the ethical. A second meaning, however, is perjorative: Courtesy is cold and conventional politeness—just the connotation given the word by those who see it as a way to gloss over shabby values. If courtesy to some is the lubricating oil of the social machine, countercultural courtesy is sand thrown in by those who don't like what the machine is producing by way of self-images, social interactions, and status arrangements. When the control system for protecting dominant values and statuses is powerful, it can command proper deferential behavior, although it cannot so successfully command belief in the values and status patterns it supports.[57] When the control system becomes shaky, however, and when submerged groups begin to see opportunities to affirm new values more directly, "common courtesy" is replaced by countercourtesy. "Good manners" become a negative symbol of despised practices and values.

The power of courtesy as a symbol is shown by the intensity of feeling aroused among members of established society when standards are violated. There is no clearer sign that one is "going to the dogs" than open discourtesy. Therefore, no better sign can be found for declaring ones allegiance to counter-values (as well as one's independence).

Early Quakers refused "hat honor," as some Blacks have done in the United States in recent years, to emphasize their unwillingness to accept an inferior social status. "When the Lord sent me into the world He forbade me to put off my hat to any, high or low; and I was required to 'thee' and 'thou' all men and women, without any respect to rich or poor, great or small."[58] The gesture of protest and the affirmation of egalitarian values were directed not only toward society at large. They were also "a refusal of deference from the young to the old, from sons to fathers,"[59] a countercultural statement, we should remember, not limited to the contemporary world.

Humor can be used to affirm values in a way quite distinct from the reversal of etiquette, which is usually quite a serious affair. Most conflict situations produce humor. It can be used as a means of control, as catharsis, as protest against discrimination, or as a statement about universal dilemmas. But it can also be used to devalue one set of standards in favor of another.

Inversions of roles or social situations is basic to humor, whether one is referring to high jinks and "merry pranks" or to more symbolic comedy. For this reason, one person's humor may be another's tasteless, disgusting nonsense—an indication of the clash of values.

Henri Bergson saw humor and laughter, that frequent if not inevitable accompaniment of humor, as the enemies of the rigid, repetitive, and mechanical. Their chief characteristic is the symbolic reversal of the usual social order. Life is essentially an *élan vital* to Bergson; it is not to be understood simply by reason. Paradoxically, laughter is in many ways highly intellectual; it requires a temporary suspension of feeling, of love or pity; it involves "something like a momentary anesthesia of the heart"—thereby casting an overly mechanical existence in a new light. An M.P., questioning the Home Secretary after a terrible murder, which had taken place in a railroad carriage, is told: "The assassin, after dispatching his victim, must have got out the wrong side of the train, thereby infringing the Company's rules."[60]

Rigid, mechanical, bureaucratic responses are fair game, but the impulse "to correct our neighbor" that Bergson finds in laughter is as readily directed against deviation as against the standard values and ways of behaving. It is a mistake to forget that laughter inhibits and censors as well as exposes.

Freud also saw laughter as an attack on the system of control,[61] although the attacks he described are more on individuals than on a disliked culture: "Vanity is one of his four Achilles' heels." We sat down for a "tête-a-bête."

It is in black and gallows humor and in the humor of minority groups that we find dominant values most powerfully satirized, the foibles, foolishness, and cruelty of the prevailing culture held up to scorn. The jabs range from the severe to the subtle, from "get your bloody gut from around my knife," to advice on how a black person can get a cab in New York (from Godfrey Cambridge I believe): I stand there with a broad smile on my face, remove my sunglasses so they'll not think I'm a drug addict, and try to show them I'm a white Negro: I carry an attache case—hail them with it—they think I'm an executive.

Humor can express conflict with other groups and with a repressive culture. It can also serve as a powerful social control within a group, helping recruit support for opposition to the opposed culture, but also acting as a lightning rod by making a deplorable situation less important, more bearable. It is more powerful as criticism than as a source of countercultural alternatives, except by implication. Its main countercultural effect may be its contribution to the maintenance of the morale of a group that believes itself caught in a deplorable cultural situation, thereby sustaining the strength of opposition to that situation. In the last analysis, Bergson did not find it a powerful social force. Laughter is like froth on a wave, "a slight revolt on the surface of social life . . . like froth, it sparkles. It is gaiety itself. But the philosopher who gathers a handful to taste may find that the substance is scanty, and the aftertaste bitter,"[62] For those concerned with social change, this may seem an overly pessimistic appraisal. It may be a necessary reminder, however, that dominant values and institutions are not easily replaced.

The question of influence is relevant to the whole range of symbolic countercultures, not only to humor. For some persons, symbolic reversals may be used precisely as a disguise that makes a more conservative way of life psychologically more acceptable: You see, we have not accepted the ways of a despised orthodoxy. Insofar as the protest is only symbolic, there is the possibility of seeming to have it both ways, thereby assisting them in handling the ambivalent feelings so characteristic of those involved in countercultures. The impact on dominant values is likely to be small. Under other circumstances, however, symbolic countercultures serve as rallying cries of opposition, keeping protest alive. Whichever is the larger effect, the moral question remains: Protest against what; a rallying cry for what?

Notes

1. I am indebted to Barbara Babcock, *The Reversible World*, 1978, p. 13, for this illustration.
2. See Kenneth Burke, *Language as Symbolic Action*, 1968.
3. Babcock, 1978, p. 14.

4. See George Balandier, *Political Anthropology,* 1970; Elizabeth Bott, "Psychoanalysis and Ceremony", 1972; Victoria Bricker, editor, "Intra-Cultural Variation," 1975; and Geroge DeVos and Lola Romanucci-Ross, editors, *Ethnic Identity,* 1975.

5. See Emile Durkheim and Marcel Mauss, *Primitive Classification,* 1963.

6. Max Gluckman, *Rituals of Rebellion in South-East Africa,* 1954; *idem, Order and Rebellion in Tribal Africa,* 1963; Victor Turner, *The Ritual Process: Structure and Anti-Structure,* 1969; *idem, Dramas, Fields, and Metaphors,* 1974; Jack Goody, *Death, Property, and the Ancestors,* 1963; Edward Norbeck, "African Rituals of Conflict," 1963; Emile Durkheim, *The Elementary forms of the Religious Life,* 1965, pp. 245-50; Peter Rigby, "Some Gogo Rituals of 'Purifiction,'" 1968; and T. O. Beidelman, "Swazi Royal Ritual," 1966.

7. Anthony Wallace, *Religion: An Anthropological View,* 1966, p. 136. See also Elsie C. Parsons and R. L. Beals, "The Sacred Clowns of the Pueblo and Mayo-Yaqui Indians," 1934, and Paul Radin, *The Trickster,* 1956.

8. Rigby, 1968.

9. Gluckman, 1963, p. 112.

10. See, for example, Babcock, 1978; Harvey Cox, *The Feast of Fools,* 1970; Emmanuel Ladurie, *Carnival in Romans,* 1979; Herbert Rubin and Irene Rubin, "The Function of Liminal Events in the Succession to a Position of Power," 1975; Frank E. Manning, "Celebrating Cricket: The Symbolic Construction of Caribbean Politics," 1981; and Enid Wilsford, *The Fool,* 1935.

11. Christopher Hill, *The World Turned Upside Down,* 1975, pp. 16-17.

12. Natalie Davis, "The Reasons of Misrule," 1971, pp. 41-44.

13. James Pruess, "Merit and Misconduct," 1979, p. 263.

14. *Ibid.*, p. 270.

15. *Ibid.*, p. 271. See also Clifford Geertz, "Religion as a Cultural System," 1966.

16. Roger Abrahams and Richard Bauman, "Ranges of Festival Behavior," in Babcock, 1978, p. 195.

17. See Gregory Bateson, *Steps to an Ecology of Mind,* 1972, pp. 177-93, and Clifford Geertz, "Deep Play: Notes on the Balinese Cockfight," 1972.

18. Particular circumstances make a given discipline "a fulcrum for the rejection of established social arrangements." E. C. Ladd, Jr., and S. M. Lipset, *The Divided Academy,* 1975, p. 73. During earlier periods the physical sciences were also a source of radical challenge.

19. Lionel Trilling, *Beyond Culture,* 1966, p. 25.

20. Gluckman, 1954 (note 6 above).

21. Wallace, 1966 (note 7 above), p. 135.

22. Gluckman, 1963 (note 6 above).

23. In Felicitas D. Goodman, Jeannette H. Henney, and Esther Pressel, *Trance, Healing, and Hallucination*, 1974, p. 4.

24. George E. Simpson, *The Shango Cult in Trinidad*, 1965.

25. Turner, 1974 (note 6 above), p. 264.

26. Victor Turner in Babcock, 1978 (note 1 above), p. 281.

27. Quoted in Davis, 1971 (note 12 above), p. 41.

28. *Ibid.*, p. 68.

29. Babcock, 1978, p. 23.

30. Frederick Errington, "Indigenous Ideas of Order, Time, and Transition in a New Guinea Cargo Movement," 1974, p. 256.

31. John Middleton in Rodney Needham, editor, *Right and Left*, 1973, p. 372.

32. Nachman Ben-Yehuda, "The European Witch Craze of the 14th to 17th Centuries: A Sociologist's Perspective," 1980, p. 5.

33. Babcock, 1978, pp. 95, 104.

34. M. A. K. Halliday, "Anti-Languages," 1976, p. 570.

35. Thomas Harmon in Gãmini Salgãdo, editor, *Cony-Catchers and Bawdy Baskets*, 1972, p. 146.

36. Norman Cohn, *The Pursuit of the Millennium*, 1970, p. 296.

37. Malcolm Cowley, *Exile's Return*, 1943, pp. 157-58.

38. Quoted from Kahler's *The Disintegration of Form in the Arts*, by Vytautas Kavolis, "Post-Modern Man," 1970a, p. 473.

39. William Labov, *Language in the Inner City*, 1972; and Geneva Smitherman in Leonard Michaels and Christopher Ricks, editors, *The State of the Language*, 1980, pp. 158-68.

40. Halliday, 1976, p. 575.

41. Labov, 1972, p. 324. See also Thomas Kochman, " 'Rapping' in the Black Ghetto," in *Deviant Life Styles*, James Henslin, editor, 1977, pp. 39-58.

42. Paul Lerman, "Gangs, Networks, and Subcultural Delinquency," 1976. See also David Maurer, "The Argot of the Dice Gambler," 1950.

43. See Gary Schwartz and Don Merten, "The Language of Adolescence," 1967.

44. Thomas Middleton, "Light Refractions: Me, Myself, and I," 1978, p. 56.

45. David Martin, *The Dilemmas of Contemporary Religion*, 1978, p. 68.

46. Robert Adams, *Bad Mouth, 1977, p. 67.*

47. *Ibid.*, 1977, p. 73.

48. Norman Mailer, *The Armies of the Night*, 1968, p. 47.

49. Leo Marx, "The Uncivil Response of American Writers to Civil Religion in America," 1974, p. 223.

50. Adams, 1977, p. 87.

51. W. Cody Wilson and Herbert I. Abelson, "Experience with and Attitudes Toward Explicit Sexual Materials," 1973.

52. Quoted by Sandra Levinson, in *Ramparts* editors, *Conversations with the New Reality*, 1971, p. 139.

53. Nathan Adler, *The Underground Stream*, 1972, p. 75.

54. See United States Commission on Obscenity and Pornography, *Report*, 1970; W. Cody Wilson and Michael J. Goldstein, "Pornography," 1973; Murray Hausknecht *et al.*, "The Problem of Pornography," 1978; and Susan Sontag, *Styles of Radical Will*, 1969, pp. 35-73.

55. Cynthia Epstein in Hausknecht *et al.*, 1978, p. 204.

56. Irving Howe in Hausknecht *et al.*, 1978, p. 204.

57. See Bertram Doyle, *The Etiquette of Race Relations in The South*, 1937.

58. From George Fox's *Journal*, quoted by E. Digby Baltzell, "Epilogue: To Be a Phoenix—Reflections on Two Noisy Ages of Prose," 1972, p. 211.

59. Hill, 1975 (note 11 above), p. 189.

60. Henri Bergson, "Laughter," in Wylie Sypher, *Comedy*, 1956, p. 90.

61. Sigmund Freud, "Wit and Its Relation to the Unconscious," 1938, Book IV.

62. Bergson, 1956, p. 190.

Chapter Eight

Countercultures Among the Disadvantaged

It is often observed, sometimes with surprise, that most recruits to countercultures come from privileged classes. At first thought, one might suppose that those at the bottom of the status ladder would be most attracted to a movement that condemns the established order and seeks to replace it. It also seems probable, however, that those who have enjoyed unusual opportunities and received many benefits from society might feel even more opposition, if for some reason the expected satisfactions turn out to be tasteless, meaningless, "ashes in the mouth." Privilged individuals cannot readily condemn the power structure or the distribution of opportunities for their lack of satisfactions. Their hostility is more likely to be turned against the culture: We were promised the moon, but when we arrived we found it a barren land.

Expectations and aspirations can be raised more easily than satisfactions. Having discussed the principle of relative deprivation in Chapter Three, I need only to recall it to our minds here, especially with reference to one of its crucial manifestations, hedonic relativism. Ten toys, or their adult equivalents, do not necessarily bring greater pleasure than one toy. We quickly adjust our satisfaction levels to keep up with a rising standard of living. It is true that among some groups the belief that one is rich to the degree that his wants are few can be not only a source of contentment but also an "opiate of the people." Among other groups, however, the *lack* of such belief can be not only a source of creative energy but also the "speed of the people"—driving them to seek ever higher levels of enjoyment and excitement, only to lead to a more frantic life without greater satisfactions.

It is to be expected, then, that circumstances that greatly heighten expectations without embedding them in responsibilities, a sense of community, and a knowledge that wants—as contrasted with needs—are infinite, can create strong anticulture feelings, They can lead first to a caricature of some dominant values—a drive for experience beyond the usual bounds (an uptight society inhibits our pursuit)—and then, for some, to an opposite kind of counterculture: The pleasure kick is a fraud; discipline, sacrifice, ritual, poverty are the road to happiness (a materialistic society pursues the wrong goals).

The first thought, however, is also true: In some circumstances the most disprivileged seek to turn the world upside down. The last shall be first. It is not often believed that this will occur simply as a result of a shift in power. A new way of life must be followed, one that demands sacrifice and discipline. No easy way can seem adequate to those whose lot is desperately hard. In the first and second centuries A.D., it was the lower classes who were most likely to embrace Christianity, surely seen as a counterculture both by those who continued to embrace emperor worship and by converts. In India, most converts from Hinduism to Buddhism or Christianity come from the lower castes. Most members of the Black Muslims, (now the American Muslim Mission) have been drawn, particularly in the earlier years of the movement, from the most disprivileged.

Thus the common tendency to associate countercultures only with the middle and upper classes fails to see that they are often a two-pronged attack on the established culture, expressing different kinds of stress. On one side we get the countercultures of the privileged who say, in effect: Here are values we can respect, that give us a sense of meaning. On the other side are the countercultures of the deprived who say: Here are values we can attain that give us a sense of control.

Usually only a small proportion of the disadvantaged are countercultural, even during periods of sharp protest against their circumstances. With reference to the United States in recent years, for example, some have said: We want *in*; we want to be accepted as individuals; America is not living up to its own values. Others have said: We want *out*; we want to be separate; American culture is shoddy and cruel. And still others have said: We want over; we want to prevail, to dominate where we have always been dominated; white people are evil, their laws a sham. These three statements, put here in overly simple terms, are connected with progressively stronger countercultural tendencies.

In Chapter Two I noted that a distinction has to be drawn between oppositional cultural movements among a group that is in a society but not of it and those among persons who are, or could be, fully integrated. The variable implied by that statement is difficult to measure. In a political and legal sense, black South Africans are in the society but scarcely of it. The complicated patterns of interpendence that have developed between them and the South Africans of European background, however, have produced elements of a shared culture. In the light of the comparative strength of these two identities, one can say that revolutionary values and norms in South Africa substantially reflect intersocietal conflict; yet to some degree they are intrasocietal, and therefore countercultural. In his study of South Africa's "New Black Puritans" Uys describes "a cultural revolution of quite extraordinary character . . . an almost ritualistic destruction of the hierarchical social order in their segregated townships—the order which has tolerated apartheid all these years."[1] Self-denial is a dominant theme of the new puritans. The girls must stop wearing cosmetics, wigs, and slacks. Parties, levity, and dancing are over. Dozens of illicit "liquor dens," places where Blacks have fought verbal battles against apartheid while drowning their sorrows but in fact have drunk together to forget about apartheid, have been destroyed. Their owners are seen as Uncle Toms. Most black, coloured, and Indian leaders, whatever their personal views, owe their positions to apartheid, say the young radicals. The values that these arrangements express and the system in which they are embedded, including both the accommodative norms of the oppressed and the coercive norms of the oppressors, must be replaced.

These developments in South Africa are similar to some aspects of the Black Power movement in the United States, using that term in the broadest sense. Black Americans, however, are more thoroughly participants in a shared culture, to which they have contributed richly both out of their African heritage and out of the cultural products of their often traumatic American experiences. Their movements of cultural reversal, therefore, fit the countercultural pattern quite closely. They involve high levels of ambivalence (internal conflict) as well as high levels of anger and hostility (external conflict).

Before discussing a few of the countercultural tendencies among black Americans let me note that some minority countercultures in the middle range of the variable suggested above are fighting a two-front war: They confront and invert many of the values of the dominant culture, but they also attack some of the culture of the minority itself, seeing it as regressive or accommodative. I have observed that South

African cultural conflict can partly be characterized in this way. Even the Ghost Dance, which swept across many Plains Indian tribes in the 1870s and 1890s, had some of this quality, despite the sense that Indians were quite separate from "American society." Its dominant message was mainly attractive in those tribes which had been most disrupted by white contact. It was blatantly antiwhite: All the dead Indians will be brought back to life by the dance, white people will disappear forever, and Indians will return to "a life of aboriginal happiness, forever free from death, disease, and misery."[2] The power structure and the values by which it is governed will be turned upside down. This dominant message of reversal was mixed with some criticisms of Indian life, especially during the later waves of the dance: The Ghost Dance forbade war; some of its missionaries stressed the need for Indians to live in peace with one another and with Whites, to avoid lying and stealing, and to stop self-mutilation, the killing of horses, and other aboriginal practices. On the whole, however, it sought restoration of a strong and integral culture, a culture that was still a living memory despite the accelerated loss of land and of the buffalo herds after the Civil War. The Ghost Dance was a renaissance of Indian culture to the Pawnee, "the very flame of new hope to the Sioux." In Lesser's vivid words:

> Into this situation of cultural decay and gradual darkness, the Ghost Dance doctrine shown like a bright light. Indian ways were not gone, never to be recovered. Indian ways were coming back. . . . Dance, dance, dance. The white man would be destroyed by a great wind. The Indian would be left with the buffalo, with his ancestors, with his old friends and his old enemies. Cast aside the white man's ways like an old garment; put on the clothes of the Indian again. Get ready for the new day and the old times.[3]

Cultural movements among Indians who had experienced more powerful and long-lasting intrusions of white society than had the Plains Indians were less revivalistic or restorative in aim and more designed to deal with the cultural conflicts and individual dilemmas created by dual "citizenship." I will not discuss such movements as Handsome Lake's Great Message to the Iroquois, Peyotism, or Shakerism,[4] but each of them develops themes that contradict some of the values both of the dominant society and of the aboriginal cultures. They are at the same time doubly countercultural and doubly affirmative in the development of what Voget has called "reformative nativism."[5]

Countercultures Among Black Americans

America's black population has created a wide variety of countercultural themes in religious, political, literary, and other forms. In most instances cultural, subcultural, and countercultural elements are mixed together, making it difficult to sort out the inversions. If we seek to understand the deep impact of discrimination, the dismay felt by many Blacks over the shabby "white" culture, and the ambivalence the love-hate relationship with which they approach American society, however, it is imperative that we examine the range of countercultures among black Americans and the circumstances that produce them.

Some of the most directly countercultural themes among black Americans are expressed in religious terms—theological, doctrinal, and organizational. If, as I have argued, countercultures grow most profusely when fundamental values have lost credibility, it is not surprising that new religious movements arise, alongside other efforts, to establish new values. Countercultural theologies that challenge the prevailing assumptions are likely to develop in such contexts. It is not only minority groups that are affected, of course. Crises that drastically disorganize life are usually accompanied by a body of religious thought designed to bring the new experiences into a framework of systematic religious interpretations. "Among minority-group members, theology often interprets disprivilege as a peculiar sign of God's grace, of the special mission of the group, of its unique insight based on its unique experiences."[6] The theology cuts two ways: In an integrative form, the persecuted group is seen as the "suffering servant" chosen to bring a message to all humankind. As a group treated unjustly, however, the minority may hear from some of its religious spokesmen that fundamental conceptions of the prevailing faith of the majority are in error, indeed the reverse of the truth, and that they are destined to prevail in a holy war.

"Black Theology is revolutionary in its perspective," James Cone writes. It "affirms that the church of the Oppressed One must be a black church, a community that is totally identified with the goal of all oppressed people as symbolized in the condition of black people. There can be no *white* churches because the white reality is the work of him who seeks to destroy humanity by enslaving men to false ideologies regarding race. The church of Christ must be black."[7] Or, in the words of Albert Cleage, Jr., when Jesus said walk a second mile, "he meant only with your brother."[8] "We must stop worshiping a cute white baby and recognize the adult, black revolutionary that Christ was."[9]

Such ideas reverberated through liberal theological circles, white and black, during the late 1960's but most of those who might have found them congenial were more likely to be involved in secular than in religious protests. More influential reversals of religious perspectives occurred among persons of lower status. Perhaps the Black Muslims, the Nation of Islam, can best illustrate the way in which countercultural norms are expressed religiously by some minority-group members.

Founded in the 1930s, the Black Muslims attracted little public attention until the late 1950s. By that time they had begun to win some grudging respect for their success in converting prisoners and for the stern asceticism that marked their individual and business behavior, an asceticism that required drastic changes in customary activity.[10] At the same time they were feared as a violent group seeking "black supremacy." There is little evidence of actual physical violence, but their rhetoric was violent. Instead of love and cooperation, they talked of hate whenever they referred to white people. *Time*, with unconscious irony, referred to Elijah Muhammad as a purveyor of "cold black [*sic*] hate."[11] Instead of integration or pluralism they talked of a separate nation. Christianity is evil. All science stems from the discoveries of twenty-four black scientists, thousands of years ago. Blacks, not Whites, are good, right, and powerful—or they can be by following the tenets of the faith.

Because Christianity is labeled "the white man's religion," its repudiation is an act of aggression as well as a drastic change in values. "The true believer who becomes a Muslim casts off at last his old self and takes on a new identity. He changes his name, his religion, his homeland, his 'natural' language, his moral and cultural values, his very purpose in living. He is no longer a Negro, so long despised by the white man that he has come almost to despise himself. Now he is a Black Man—divine, ruler of the universe, different only in degree from Allah Himself."[12]

The Black Muslims have changed significantly over the nearly half-century of their existence, a fact reflected in their changes of name, first to Nation of Islam, then to World Community of Al-Islam in the West, and now to American Muslim Mission. Two major schisms underline the tensions inherent in most sectarian groups. When Malcolm X returned from a trip to Mecca in 1964, he began to call for a more moderate approach, with reduced opposition to racial integration, more cooperation among the several groups working for improvement in the status of black Americans, and elimination of the "hate whitey" theme. He had been removed from his leadership role a year earlier by Elijah Muhammad, not for such views—for he had been speaking of the need for sharper protests and perhaps violence before his trip to Mecca—but out of fear that he was becoming the dominant figure in the movement. In 1965 he was murdered by unknown assailants, leaving problematic the strength of his ideological challenge to the leadership of the Black Muslim movement.

The second schism began with the succession of Wallace Muhammad to the post of Supreme Minister of the Nation of Islam after the death of his father, Elijah Muhammad, in 1975. The harshly antiwhite tone had begun slowly to change earlier, partly because of the continuing, even growing influence of Malcolm X, who was even larger in death than in life. Now it was actively shifted, as were other doctrines and practices. Wallace Muhammad changed the name to the World Community of Al-Islam in the West, to dissociate the group from the more black nationalist "Nation of Islam." He disbanded the quasimilitary Fruit of Islam group, sold many of the businesses and farms, liberalized dress and behavioral codes, abandoned the doctrine that "blue-eyed devils" were the cause of the world's misery, and even opened the sect to white membership. Opposition to these changes mounted as the economic and political gains of the 1960s came to a halt. Louis Farrakhan, long the leader of the Harlem mosque but transferred to Chicago in 1978, has been the chief opponent. The separatist policies should be reaffirmed, Farrakhan believes. White concessions have been minimal, and many of those are being lost because of the mistaken allegiance to integration.

At this writing, one cannot say whether the denominational trend will continue in the American Muslim Mission or whether the separatist and more countercultural themes will prevail. This depends mainly on major social trends. Recession, high rates of unemployment among Blacks, high crime rates in black communities, and a pervading sense that nothing effective is being done to reduce these hardships will make reversal themes more persuasive.

There is little doubt that during the first decades many of the values and norms of the dominant society were inverted. In my judgment there is also little doubt about the deep ambivalence felt by Black Muslims. On the surface they seemed blatantly antiwhite and opposed to the dominant culture, but at a deeper level they were also attacking the lack of self-respect. As Keil observes, "the Muslim program is based on a complete, harsh, and puritanical negation of the Negro lower-class stereotype."[13] In *White Man Listen*, Richard Wright noted that ambivalence, hate combined with love, was always a part of the experience of looking from below upward.

Although the themes of protest and to some degree of separation have been widely supported among black Americans, the Black Muslims have not been the most representative in their approach to discrimination. Unless one considers the very fact of challenging white supremacy countercultural, most of the religious and many of the secular branches of the civil rights movement have appealed to the American creed, calling for its application and renewal, not its reversal. There are some countercultural elements in the Black Power segments of the civil rights movement, however, that should be noted. Perhaps the most influential statement of the black power position was that made by Carmichael and Hamilton. They opposed not only the distribution of power and rewards in American society but also the values of the dominant middle class:

> The goal of black people must *not* be to assimilate into middle-class America, for the class—as a whole—is without a viable conscience as regards humanity. The values of the middle class permit the perpetuation of the ravages of the black community. The values of that class are based on material aggrandizement, not the expansion of humanity. The values of that class ultimately support cloistered little closed societies tucked away neatly in tree-lined suburbia. The values of that class *do not* lead to the creation of an open society.[14]

The statement of the perspective of black power by Carmichael and Hamilton—independence and separation for Blacks and condemnation of the ruling values of Whites—is relatively moderate. Conflict was emphasized and the likelihood of illegal acts and violence recognized, but their call "to reject the racist institutions and values of this society" was reasoned—one would say academic if the word had not acquired negative connotations for many people. Despite their attack on values in the quotation above, their main concern is with justice—with the failure of America to live up to its values and the need for disadvantaged groups to close ranks before they "can enter the open society." Thus counterculture is mixed with social criticism.

The same mixture is found in the writings and activities of the Black Panthers, even during the period of their most vigorous protests against racial discrimination, 1968-70. Although their rhetoric was harsh and they defended violence, court trials demonstrated that police action and public perception greatly exaggerated the actual use of violence.[15] Their demands for jobs, education, and the end of police brutality against Blacks were scarcely countercultural. The attacks on American institutions, however, and the calls for guerrilla warfare and revolution—to achieve fundamental change in values—did envisage drastic reversals.[16]

There is a literary dimension to the Black Power movement that emphasizes additional reversals of the perspectives of the dominant white society. Some literature develops the theme of black nationalism or revolution that we have already mentioned. One of the most prolific writers, Amiri Baraka (LeRoi Jones), has moved from nonconformist beatnik (he dedicated some of his early poems to Allen Ginsberg and other *avant-garde* white writers), to angry, strident black nationalist (in the mid-1960s he denounced white liberals and integrated efforts to achieve civil rights), and on to Marxist (for example, by turning away from Maulana Karenga's black nationalism, which he had supported earlier). Although these changes involve drastic shifts in point of attack, they are similar in their unrelenting opposition to the dominant culture.[17]

Before about 1950 much of the work of black writers dealt with the struggle for justice and for identity in the face of cruelty and oppression, a theme well represented by Richard Wright's *Native Son*. In a context of black power, however, and of economic and political protest, other themes appear: Black is beautiful, black is powerful, black is all the sexual force white people fear it to be.[18] Cecil Brown criticizes Richard Wright for not making the chief character in *Native Son*, Bigger Thomas, a sufficiently potent figure sexually. Brown's own hero, in *The Life and Loves of Mr. Jiveass Nigger*, George Washington, suffers no such weakness. His jive is to con almost everyone he meets, especially white women. As Dickstein remarks, Brown's own jive may have been to write a sex novel, to put on the public and the publishers.[19] Eldridge Cleaver and Calvin Hernton make the same criticism of Wright, but indirectly, and with an opposite approach. They sexualize "Bigger Thomas into a walking phallus."[20] Through much of this literature describing the power, the violence, and the sexuality of the black man there runs the reciprocal theme of the weaknesses of the white man. Both descriptions frequently border on, indeed fall into, caricature, to their detriment as literature and as social criticism. (White authors, of course, are seldom more skillful in avoiding caricatures of Blacks.) Gross exaggeration often covers uncertainty and ambivalence. The counter-society symbolized in the work of some black authors may release anger, reduce self-doubts, support self-respect, and even alert a few Whites to the cruelty of prevailing race relations (while confirming more in their stereotypes of Blacks), but it does little to change the underlying conditions. We all might be wise to explore our latent ambivalence to see what new, but not necessarily counter, values and practices might lead to creative reduction in the harshness of intergroup and interpersonal relations.

The "Culture of Poverty": Traditional Way of Life or Counterculture?

Poor naked wretches, where so e'er you are
That bide the pelting of this pitiless storm,
How shall your houseless heads and unfed sides,
Your loop'd and window'd raggedness, defend you
From seasons such as these?

King Lear to the Fool, III, iv

How indeed? How do the poor defend themselves from seasons such as these, which is to say, from all seasons? Do they fight the distribution of power? Do they wrap the cloak of shared values around themselves, seeking the protection of the dominant culture itself? Do they invent new values, perhaps reversing the established order of things to affirm that the last shall be first or the possible shall be good? All of these things, I believe, occur in complicated mixtures. Our concern here is to comment on the conditions under which countercultural values appear among the responses made by the poor to their disadvantaged circumstances.

The paragraphs on religious countercultures among black Americans were primarily ethnographic. I want now to examine a related set of issues more analytically, seeking to define the system of causes within which countercultures of the disadvantaged evolve. The focus of attention will be on poverty as a basic factor in that system. For at least a generation there has been an outpouring of works that examine the extent to which and the ways in which social classes differ in culture and behavior.[21] Although perspectives vary greatly, almost all of those who have written on this topic emphasize that the seriously disadvantaged do have different life styles from the standard. Some interpret the differences sympathetically, others unsympathetically. In numerous works, Oscar Lewis described a "culture of poverty" that he believed should be examined as a dignified life style, or at least regarded with anthropological objectivity.[22] Eric Hoffer, on the other hand, referring to black Americans, remarked that they "seem to lack the will and the gumption to build and create something impressive. . . . They expect Whitey to feed and house them, housebreak and educate their children, and supply them with stores, adequately stocked with liquor and television sets for periodic looting."[23] The point of view is not often put that brusquely, but many middle- and upper-class Americans share Hoffer's view, showing in words and actions that they resent the "welfare chiselers," the lack of ambition, the inability to plan ahead or to defer gratification, the use of a quasi-legal or illegal hustle that they see as characteristic of the values of the lower class.[24] One could use almost the same words to describe the dominant view of the hippies in the 1960s, the succession of new immigrants in the nineteenth century, or the cony catchers in Elizabethan England.

Whatever ones moral sensitivities, for purposes in hand we need to ask: To what degree are behavioral differences among the classes indications of cultural differences; and to what degree are such cultural aspects as may exist among the disadvantaged reversals of dominant values and norms? The structuralist will argue, with good evidence, that poverty and behavior related to it are primarily products of discrimination, of inadequate opportunities for training and jobs, of poor arrangements for income maintenance during periods of individual or family crisis, of self-perpetuating inequalities in a rigid class system. They are not, in any significant way, signs of cultural differences.[25] Those who think in terms of a "culture of poverty," however, believe that a traditional style of life validates and reinforces the poor in their status. Lewis uses this concept to describe "in positive terms a subculture of Western society with its own structure and rationale, a way of life handed on from generation to generation along family lines. The culture of poverty is not just a matter of deprivation or disorganization, a term signifying the absence of something. It is a culture in the traditional anthropological sense in that it provides human beings with a design for living, with a ready-made set of solutions for human problems, and so serves a significant adaptive function."[26] Putting these various interpretations together, one comes to a multilevel or field explanation: "Low opportunity leads to values adapted to poverty that prevent recognition or pursuit of available opportunities."[27]

Neither lack of opportunity nor socialization to a traditional subculture that rewards getting by as best one can, rather than getting ahead, is an adequate explanation of poverty. The two have to be combined. Moreover, the normative component contains values in sharp conflict with those of the dominant society. It is not simply part of "a distinctive tradition many centuries old with an integrity of its own," to use Walter Miller's comment on "lower class culture."[28] In the context of persistent low opportunity mixed with tantalizingly visible affluence, that tradition is built upon, stretched, and in some ways reversed in the effort to survive and to protect the sense of ones own worth. The result of what Hyman Rodman has called a "value stretch"[29] is a normative system that combines some of the values of the dominant society, some elements from a traditional subculture of poverty, and some new cultural adaptations.

Malcolm X observed, with calculated exaggeration, that everyone in Harlem needed some kind of hustle to survive and some way to stay high to try to forget what they needed to do to survive. In his *Autobiography* he does not, however, interpret these as normative. They are painful adaptations. In a similar way, Valentine's description of *Hustling and Other Hard Work: Life Styles in the Ghetto* emphasizes that most people in the community she studied were raised in families that share the popular negative views of welfare recipients, of hustling, of stealing. Many abide by the dominant norms; those who do not explain their actions by reference to other norms, those related to family obligations, for example. Liebow also doubts that the continuity in contranormative behavior among the men around *Tally's Corner* is the result of cultural transmission. It results instead "from the fact that the son goes out and independently experiences the same failures, in the same areas, and for much the same reasons as his father."[30]

Undoubtedly the structure of opportunities, which is the primary explanatory variable in such studies, is a major factor in the behavior of those in poverty. The point is made decisively by Dostoevsky in his novel *Poor Folk*. He describes with great clarity the contrast between the life of poverty and the life of wealth. When Makar receives a gift of 100 rubles, his life, behavior, self-image, and treatment by others change drastically. He had not been living out a culture of poverty, but a life style coerced by poverty.

Persuasive as the structural argument is, I find it incomplete. It is part of a movement of protest against "blaming poverty on the victim," a movement I support on both moral and analytic grounds. Not much is to be gained, however, simply by shifting the blame to "society." When we can rid ourselves of the vocabulary of praise and blame altogether we will be better able to investigate the interactions in complicated systems. Persistent poverty in a visibly affluent society (it is a different experience to be poor in a society where almost everyone else shares the same fate) is not simply borne. There is resentment and resistance. Some means of protest work better than others and emerge as part of the life style of the affected groups. This does not mean that the protests necessarily work very well; they may not reduce the fact of poverty very much, but they allow survival. They furnish a set of standards that one can reasonably hope to attain and thus protect ones personhood. If "the man" won't give me a job, I'll design a hustle—an antijob routine, a denial of the obligation to work, a racket, a source of income by the easiest possible means. I'll organize my life around the search for kicks—any acts tabooed by squares—and thus show my disdain for the dominant values.[31]

A counterculture, let me reemphasize, is not an independent culture. It develops out of conflict with the dominant tradition. Those who embrace it have been socialized to the dominant tradition and feel ambivalent about the normative reversals they now accept. The intensity of the opposition to established values can be explained in many instances by the need to repress the attractiveness of those values, while at the same time they are seen as repugnant or unobtainable. Rodman and Liebow do not use the term counterculture, but their concepts of value stretch and shadow system of culture seem harmonious with it, particularly when applied to the seriously disadvantaged. Liebow describes the shadow system as "the cultural model of the larger society as seen through the prism of repeated failure."[32] It is a thinner, less weighty system, linked inevitably to the dominant culture, which, however, is significantly inverted in the norms of those who find it unjust and inaccessible. The adaptations of the shadow system may also be picked up by more advantaged persons who are experiencing stressful change. Thus the counterculture of the poor and the hip may serve as cultural leads or "mutations."[33]

Rohrer and Edmonson describe what they call the "male culture" of the gang among lower-class Blacks in New Orleans. It fits the countercultural model closely in its opposition to the normative system that surrounds the gang members, in its reversals of many of the dominant values, and in the ambivalence with which the contradictory values are held. Participation in the gang can be seen as a mutually invented initiation rite whereby the young men seek to escape a world, as they see it, dominated by women and by inaccessible and coercive institutions. Independence becomes the key value. Women are victimized. Occupational and educational achievement, religion, and responsibility to any group except the gang are scorned. "Acceptance by the gang provides almost the only source of security for its members, but such acceptance is conditional upon continual proof that it is merited, and proof can only be furnished through physical aggressiveness, a restless demonstration of sexual prowess, and a symbolic execution of those illegal deeds that a 'sissy' would not perform."[34] Conformity to the gang's standards is severely enforced by physical violence, by a code of secrecy, and by "playing the dozens"—verbally probing and exploiting a person's greatest sensitivities.

This is not a subculture, expressing normal socialization from birth to a subsociety, but a counterculture that develops among boys and young men in harsh conflict with both the larger society and the subsociety of which they are a part. The radical rejection of the white world's and the stable black community's definition of their "place" reflects the impact of severely limited opportunities and the discriminatory culture on the most seriously deprived. In another time and place expanding opportunities and even more rapidly expanding aspirations can lead to a protest more cultural than countercultural: We want in. In still other contexts the poor, of whatever race, who are sustained by hope even if their worldly aspirations are modest, may embrace a fundamentalist religion and emphasize an ascetic life. They substitute religious status for social status, in Liston Pope's phrase, and condemn the life style of the affluent.

The *fact* of poverty, in my judgment, is first of all an effect of the system of opportunities. The *value system* of those in poverty in affluent societies combines, in various proportions in different settings, elements of the dominant culture, a fairly traditional subculture of poverty—a mode of adaptation that is passed along from parent to child, as Oscar Lewis has so well described—and a value-reversing counterculture that expresses resentment against deprivation and represents an adaptation to a system seen as unjust and not deserving of support.

In a cybernetic process, these cultural effects of deprivation sometimes feed back into the system that produced them, reinforcing their own causes. This leads some observers to attribute poverty primarily to the distinctive counterculture and the individual beliefs and actions that express it.[35] This is a very thin explanation. Criticizing or trying to change such effects-turned-into-secondary-causes is of little value if the primary causes remain unchanged. Those forbidden to go near the water find it difficult to learn to swim. Opportunity is the first requisite.

Notes

1. Stanley Uys, "South Africa's New Black Puritans," 1976, p. 702.

2. James Mooney, *The Ghost-Dance Religion and The Sioux Outbreak of 1890*, 1965.

3. Alexander Lesser, "Cultural Significance of the Ghost Dance," 1933. In addition to Mooney and Lesser, see Weston LaBarre, *The Ghost Dance*, 1972; W. W. Howells, *The Heathens*, 1948; and David Aberle, "The Prophet Dance and Reactions to White Contact," 1959.

4. See Anthony Wallace. *The Death and Rebirth of the Seneca*, 1970; J.S. Slotkin, *The Peyote Religion*, 1956; David Aberle, *The Peyote Religion Among the Navaho, 1966; and Homer Barnett, Indian Shakers*, 1957.

5. Fred Voget, "The American Indian in Transition: Reformation and Accommodation," 1956.

6. George E. Simpson and J. Milton Yinger, *Racial and Cultural Minorities*, 1972, p. 524.

7. James Cone, "Black Consciousness and the Black Church: A Historical-Theological Interpretation," 1970, p. 53.

8. Albert B. Cleage, Jr., *Black Messiah*, 1968.

9. Albert B. Cleage, Jr., quoted in *The New York Times*, November 9, 1970, p. 30.

10. Lawrence Tyler, "The Protestant Ethic Among the Black Muslims," 1966.

11. *Time*, August 10, 1959, p. 25.

12. C. Eric Lincoln, *The Black Muslims in America*, 1961, pp. 108-109. See also E. U. Essien-Udom, *Black Nationalism*, 1962.

13. Charles Keil, *Urban Blues*, 1966, p. 185. See also Essien-Udom, p. 337.

14. Stokely Carmichael and Charles Hamilton, *Black Power*, 1967, p. 40.

15. *The New York Times*, March 2, 1971, p. 7, and May 14, 1971, pp. 1, 20.

16. For representative works, see Eldridge Cleaver, *Soul on Ice*, 1968; Bobby Seale, *Seize the Time*, 1970; and Huey Newton in August Meier, Elliott Rudwick, and Frances Broderick, editors, *Black Protest Thought in the Twentieth Century*, 1971, pp. 491-515.

17. Two recent collections only partially represent the range of the work of Amiri Baraka: *Selected Poetry of Amiri Baraka/LeRoi Jones*, 1979a, and *Selected Plays and Prose of Amiri Baraka/LeRoi Jones*, 1979b. See also Le Roi Jones, *Black Magic: Collected Poetry, 1961-1967*, 1969.

18. Simpson and Yinger, 1972 (note 6 above), pp. 615-26.

19. Morris Dickstein, *Gates of Eden*, 1977, p. 179.

20. Cleaver, 1968, pp. 97-111, and Calvin Hernton, "Blood of the Lamb: The Ordeal of James Baldwin," 1970. See also Dickstein, 1977, Chap. 6.

21. For a useful summary based on a life cycle approach, see Irving Krauss, *Stratification, Class and Conflict*, 1976, pp. 105-90. See also Albert Cohen and Harold Hodges, Jr., "Characteristics of the Lower-Blue-Collar Class," 1963; John Hewitt, *Social Stratification and Deviant Behavior*, 1970; John Rohrer, Munro Edmonson, *et al.*, *The Eighth Generation*, 1960; and Lee Rainwater, "The Problem of Lower Class Culture," 1970.

22. Oscar Lewis. *The Children of Sanchez*, 1961; "The Culture of Poverty," 1966a; *Five Families: Mexican Case Studies in the Culture of Poverty*, 1959; and *La Vida: A Puerto Rican Family in the Culture of Poverty*, 1966b.

23. Honolulu *Star-Bulletin*, September 16, 1968, p. A-22.

24. For valuable discussions of the facts and the debates concerning inequality and welfare programs, see the chapters by Harold Wilensky, Joan Huber, and Harold Watts in *Major Social Issues*, J. Milton Yinger and Stephen J. Cutler, editors, 1978, pp. 87-140.

25. See Sydel Silverman, "Agricultural Organization, Social Structure, and Values in Italy: Amoral Familism Reconsidered," 1968, pp. 1-20.

26. Lewis, 1966a, p. 19. For a variety of views on the concept of the culture of poverty, see Troy Abell and Larry Lyon, "Do the Differences Make a Difference? An Empirical Evaluation of the Culture of Poverty in the United States," 1979; Richard L. Della Fave, "The Culture of Poverty Revisited: Strategy for Research," 1974; Seymour Parker and Robert Kleiner, "The Culture of Poverty: An Adjustive Dimension," 1970; Jack Roach and Orville Gursslin, "An Evaluation of the Concept 'Culture of Poverty', 1967; and Charles Valentine, *Culture and Poverty*, 1968.

27. Simpson and Yinger, 1972 (note 6 above), p. 176.

28. Walter B. Miller, "Lower Class Culture as a Generating Milieu of Gang Delinquency," 1958, p. 18.

29. Hyman Rodman, "The Lower-Class Value Stretch," 1963.

30. Elliot Liebow, *Tally's Corner: A Study of Negro Streetcorner Men*, 1967, p. 223.

31. Harold Finestone, "Cats, Kicks, and Color," 1957.

32. Liebow, 1967, p. 221.

33. Louis A. Zurcher, Jr., "The Poor and the Hip: Some Manifestations of Cultural Lead," 1972.

34. Rohrer, Edmonson, *et al.* 1960, (note 21 above), p. 160.

35. See particularly Edward Banfield, *The Unheavenly City*, 1968. He does not, it should be noted, use the term counterculture.

Chapter Nine

Countercultural Institutions: Politics

We have to realize that no other generation will ever experience what we have experienced. In this sense we must recognize that we have no descendants, as our children have no forebears.

Margaret Mead, *Culture and Commitment*

All societies have patterned ways of producing and distributing scarce goods and services; dealing with conflict and power; reproducing the next generation and protecting and socializing its members, with related norms dealing with sexual behavior; preserving, communicating, and extending its accumulated knowledge; and coping with the fact that life is filled with hazards and mysteries and—beyond the reach of all their efforts—with death. In the vocabulary of contemporary social science, that complex sentence states that all societies have economic, political, familial, educational, and religious institutions.

Put in such an unqualified form, the statement poses a number of problems. In light of the range of beliefs and behaviors in each one of these areas, particularly in modern societies, it becomes problematic how patterned, how structured and predictable, the activities are. In the news media, in our private conversations and gossip, and in some scholarly work, there is a tendency to emphasize deviation, the weakness of norms, and the variation in beliefs. Certainly that emphasis has factual support. Although one can scarcely speak precisely on the issue, these are anomic times, beyond the usual in human experience. Deviation is common. Those who want to stress the extent of deviation, however, not simply to assess it, are often those who want also to stress the rigidity and power of established institutions. The two points are not necessarily incompatible, but unless they are seen together one is tempted to emphasize first one and then the other, rather than examining their mutual limitations. The farther we are, in space or time, from a social situation, the more pattern we are likely to see, the more life seems to flow along institutional lines. At close range, we see individual deviation.

Granted the wide variations in levels of anomie and of deviation, the structural and cultural influences of institutions are nevertheless generally strong in social life. To those opposing a society and wishing to change it, the established institutions are likely to be seen as major barriers. I have said structural and cultural, because institutions link a set of norms and values with a set of positions and of continuing interactions among persons that are guided by those norms and values. Thus political institutions are defined by standards that describe how power should be allocated, administered, and limited, and how disputes should be settled. They are also defined by a set of relationships and of groups involved in the effort to fulfill those standards. Political institutions in the United States combine a cultural element—the constitution, laws, precedents, and customs—with a structural element—the legislatures, courts, administrations, parties, and other groups.

Separate institutions can be readily described for modern societies, even if the extent of cultural standardization of activity related to their functions is not so well agreed upon. The situation is less clear in tribal societies, and that raises a second question related to my sweeping statement that all societies are institutionalized. Do acephalous societies have political institutions? Can one say that societies without schools have educational institutions? I will not go into that issue here, except to note that the recent tendency has been to see at least rudimentary, and sometimes quite complex, institutions where they had not been seen before,[1] and to emphasize that the activities with which institutions are involved are found everywhere, even if not in separate structures. The degree of separation is an issue, of course, even in contemporary societies. One can stir up a sharp debate by asking to what degree, in the United States, church and state are separate or to what extent "free enterprise" is independent of government. Although we can make clear analytic distinctions, institutional connections are often as important as their separations, and as much the target of countercultural opposition. Some of the strongest opponents of current educational practices, for example, are especially unhappy about the extent of governmental and business domination of education.

In the discussion of institutions, therefore, we shall need to keep in mind that, although it is easy enough to distinguish among a church, a school, a courthouse, a factory, and a house, the institutions of a society are laced together in many ways. We separate them in the effort to achieve analytic clarity.

A third question refers to the list of five institutions. Is that a definitive list? Ought one not to include structures, activities, and norms related to art, leisure, social stratification, health care, the military, and others? The five institutions that I will be discussing, at varying lengths, certainly do not exhaust the list of social institutions. Some of the others have already been examined in different contexts. My aim is not to explore all the ways in which cultural reversals can be understood by seeing them as counter-institutions but to emphasize, by examining a few is some detail, that countercultural standards are not simply isolated inversions.

Berke puts the negative issue sharply, although he does little to define alternatives:

> Institutions—schools, hospitals, courts—not only do not do what they have been set up to do, but the opposite. They have become the ghouls, vampires, werewolves of our culture, the Frankensteins of our way of life. We now have the extraordinary situation where schools and universities keep students stupid; hospitals perpetuate the suffering they are supposed to alleviate; radio, TV, newspapers and magazines prevent the communication they are supposed to facilitate; the factories produce goods designed to destroy themselves, and/or the people who use them (e.g., automobiles) as well as the environment (the water, the land, the air) in which they are supposed to work. We have a transport system which impedes transportation, courts which produce criminals and a political system whose manipulators haven't the foggiest idea of what is going on, but mostly use it to work out their hate fantasies toward themselves against us and others.

It is scarcely surprising that Berke concludes this statement with the sentence: "In short, I am describing a world, our world gone mad."[2]

The study of counter-institutions reveals two levels of opposition. On one level the criticism of the dominant institutions is unrelenting. The very process of institutionalization, not just the existing forms of it are condemned. To use the word in its broadest sense, anarchy is the preferred arrangement.

On another level, the proposed counter-institutions are more critical of prevailing means than of ends or, in a related distinction, seek to reverse the governing norms more than to replace the dominant values.

Utopias and Communes as Countercultures

The most sweeping criticisms of dominant institutions may take the form of imagined utopian societies within which, it is believed, all institutions would be transformed. Or it may take the form of communes, designed to show that vastly different institutional patterns can form the basis of viable communities.

Although utopias and communes are often discussed together and the words are sometimes used as synonyms, various distinctions are helpful. In coining the term "utopia" ("not a place"), Thomas More was suggesting that the ideal society was nowhere. Perhaps it was a secularized Eden, an imaginary heaven-on-earth. In the nearly five centuries since he wrote, utopian ideas have more and more been influenced by ideas of progress, by optimistic views of human nature, and yet also by opposition to the prevailing order. Utopians "invent the future." Their inventions, however, "are more than blueprints or dreams of the future; they are significant as *revitalizing myths*, ones that proclaim and hallow a radical departure; a society at once distinctively different from and better than the old one."[3] With Tom Paine they believe that "we have it in our power to begin all over again." Utopias should not, Lewis Mumford thought, be set over against the world. The cities and mansions that we dream of are those in which we will finally live.

Oppositely, George Orwell and Aldous Huxley hoped that the utopias—or dystopias—that we have nightmares about might be those that we could learn to avoid. Perhaps we should think of *Nineteen Eighty-Four* and *Brave New World* as doubly countercultural utopias. They turn our fantasy worlds upside down. If we define a utopia, with Ruth Levitas, as "that state of society ultimately aspired to by an individual or group," Orwell's and Huxley's now classic dystopias describe that state of society ultimately to be rejected—the very epitome of all that is to be condemned among the trends in industrial societies.

Karl Mannheim adopted the prevailing modern view by his distinction between utopias, which, if they are effective at all, tend to shatter the social order, and other incongruous states of mind, such as visions of celestial paradises, which can be integrated within the social order. Utopias are myths that mobilize action. Their relationship to society is dialectical: Arising out of the needs of an age, utopias "become the explosive material for bursting the limits of the existing order."[4]

If Mannheim's point of view is adopted, the utopian quality of many current communes is less than that of earlier intentional communities. In Rosabeth Kanter's words, they express "fewer visions of social reconstruction"; they are more designed to promote "internal discovery" and personal growth. We need to recognize, however, that "the content, form, location and social role of utopia vary with the material conditions in which people live."[5] At one time utopia may be a wish-fantasy, at another a form of social criticism, and may shift again to begin a catalyst of social change. Such a process depends upon a belief in progress, a picture of society as malleable. Levitas believes that contemporary utopias, developing in a more fatalistic time, have reverted to wish-fantasy, becoming more utopian in the original sense.

Contemporary communes, as well as those of the past, vary along a range, from those strongly influenced by a utopian dream to those that are more reactive. Some participants, one might say, are immigrants into the promised land; others are refugees from a society experienced as coercive or dreary. They all share to some degree, however, the vision of a dramatically new social order. One institution or another—the economic system, for example, or the polity, or the family—may be the focal point of opposition to the dominant society. A line of thought running from Rousseau to Pestalozzi to Robert Owen down to the present emphasizes the relationship between communalism and education. The most effective and long-lived are often built around sectarian religious values. Alternative standards, however, are often proposed for all institutions.[6]

Communitarians, unlike revolutionaries, "picture a society in which the means for ushering in a new age are readily at hand," demanding only a stirring of the heart, not a violent struggle for power. What is needed is a new vision.[7] It is a rare time when it is not said, at least by a few: Surely there are better ways to live than those dictated by our present institutions. In the United States alone, since 1965, five to ten thousand—perhaps even more—communes have been founded. Most have been small and short-lived; but their very founding proclaims the appeal of new visions of society. Many people who do not join are attracted to the communal idea—an attraction expressed in the large body of literature dealing with it. For most, however, the feelings are ambivalent. "It is as though we wanted at one and the same time to convince ourselves that our most licentious fantasies could really happen and to stigmatise those who suggest, however modestly, that social life might be possible on terms other than those of our own tightly constrained system."[8]

This ambivalence is carried into the communes as well; it is expressed in the origanizational problems and dilemmas they face. Communes survive, as Kanter has so well argued, only if they maintain among their members commitment to the community's work, to its values, and to each other. This requires the development of effective ways of dealing with several complex questions:

How to get the work done, but without coercion
How to ensure that decisions are made, but to everyone's satisfaction
How to build close, fulfilling relationships, but without exclusiveness
How to choose and socialize new members
How to include a degree of autonomy, individual uniqueness, and even deviance
How to ensure agreement and shared perception around community functioning and values[9]

It is scarcely surprising that visions of a new social reality are difficult to bring to life. "The ecstasy and the transcendence, the mini-apocalypse of the counter-cultural myth," Abrams and McCulloch observe, after their study of several score contemporary communes, emerged only "as fleeting moments in a catalogue of strangely domestic excitements (Sunday dinner), problems (keeping warm) and aggravations (cleaning up)."[10]

In spite of such problems and dilemmas and the prosaic way in which on the whole they are dealt with, whether in communes or in the more institutionally specific countercultures to which we now turn our attention, we need continuously to ask ourselves: What if such visions, such efforts were quite lacking? Do they help us to see the structure and values of the dominant world in clearer perspective? Do they test ingredients that can be used in different contexts? Are there among them early models of social arrangements that, in due course, will be modified and enlarged to become essential parts of the prevailing culture? If we are all "equally immigrants into the new era," as Margaret Mead remarked, we cannot afford to assume that the familiar culture is an adequate model.

Political Institutions

Because many of the goals for which people strive—most notably power, prestige, and income—are in scarce supply, every society has the potential for or is faced with the fact of disruptive tensions.[11] If all were permitted to pursue these goals by means of their own choosing, an organized society would be impossible. Yet if no room is left for the play of self-interest, not just for the few but generally, a coercive and inegalitarian society is inevitable. In relatively stable societies, or in all societies during relatively stable periods, certain means are generally approved as the right ways to maintain or to secure a share of the scarce goals. Political institutions are the norms—and the organizations expressive of those norms—that designate how the collective power of the group shall be used, and by whom, to enforce the approved ways of achieving life's goals. Legitimacy means a high level of agreement on the assignment of that power: These are the ways our leaders shall be chosen; these are their rightful powers; and these are the limits on their powers.

There are political processes in small groups and private associations—for example, in university faculties, churches, labor unions, or business clubs. We are concerned here, however, only with politics on a societal scale. It is distinguished, as Weber noted, by claims to a monoply of legitimate coercive power, even to the extreme of the administration of death. Indeed, Weber regarded this appeal to the legitimacy of violence as essential to the very definition of a "political association," but he seems to be thinking primarily of the state.[12]

The existence of a political system does not solve the problem of order. It does not guarantee that the approved means for achieving scarce values will be employed. If the norms are not substantially self-enforcing, as a result of the socialization of the members of the society to the prevailing definition of legitimacy and their perceptions of valued reciprocities, the level of coercion has to be high, with resulting disruption. The political authorities themselves, those who have the culturally established right to use coercive power, may violate the approved means to their own advantage. The norms may be designed to protect privileged access to scarce values enjoyed by only a few. They may be poorly adapted to changed social circumstances. These conditions are particularly important in the modern world, where continuous shifts in the claims and aspirations of many persons and groups affect not only the allocation of political power but the degree of acceptance of the legitimacy of the political systems themselves.

Those in power and those who feel well represented by those in power are inclined to regard the political system as sacrosanct. As Eisenstadt puts it in his important comparative study: "In all societies studied here, the rulers attempted to portray themselves and the political systems they established as the bearers of special cultural symbols and missions."[13] For a variety of motives—fear of chaos, awe, hope, respect that comes from socialization—those not in power and not well represented may also regard the established political system as sacrosanct. Moreover, because they are often the ones who have been called upon to make the largest sacrifices, even of life itself, for the state, they cannot afford to believe that the system is evil. The blood of the martyrs is the seed of the church; and the blood of the soldiers, Kenneth Boulding observes, is the seed of the state.[14] Revolutionary and countercultural groups, of course, also employ the psychology of sacrifice: If hesitant participants are drawn into activities utterly in opposition to established ways and drastically different from some of their own tendencies, they are more likely to become dedicated, even fanatical, supporters of the inverted norms. Their actions cut them off from contact with those who accept the dominant standards. More important, those actions create the need for justification, for beliefs that will aid the repression of their own former standards.

Countercultural politics develops among those who do not accept the belief that the rulers and the established political systems are "the bearers of special cultural symbols and missions," to repeat Eisenstadt's phrase. The opposite is believed to be the case. It is not only that the rulers or leaders are considered to be incompetent or evil. The political institution itself is repudiated, its values denied, and its means rejected.

If policies regarding nuclear weapons or nuclear power or environmental protection seem abhorrent, direct actions to prevent their being carried out are undertaken, despite the law. Principled and acknowledged refusal to pay taxes (not to be confused with covert evasion of taxes) to support war or increased defense spending denies the legitimacy of the government and the validity of its decisions. From the right, discontent with the direction of politics may lead, as McDonald says of contemporary France, to a group that "wants to reject the very core of Occidental thinking."[15]

It may be helpful to distinguish between an extreme version of a political counterculture, which attacks the very value of or the need for any established political process, and a more restrained view. The latter opposes existing politics because it is believed to be based on false values and because the institutionalized means are thought to be preventing rather than promoting the attainment of fundamental political goals. It does not, however, attack the idea of politics. This distinction is not easily drawn in practice, of course, and we will be wise to think of it as a way of designating a range rather than as an indication of two separate types of political countercultures.

The no-politics or antipolitics ethic affirms the value of anarchy. Just leave us alone. We do not need an organized system of conflict resolution. Efforts to establish such systems create more conflict than they resolve. Individual improvisation is better.

Ask not what your country can do for you,
Ask what your country is doing to you.

Graffito on an American university campus

Most Americans, and in varying degrees persons in most societies, have a touch of anarchy in their beliefs and actions.[16] In his essay on "Civil Disobedience," Thoreau advised: "Let your life be a counter friction to stop the machine." The picture of government as unfeeling machine remains strong. Although this point of view is often associated with leftist politics, it is not uncommon on the right. Senator Paul Laxalt, for example, has expressed what he saw as a fundamental belief among many of those who supported President Reagan for election in these terms: We want nothing from government except to be left alone. (Were he to act on that principle, he would soon be an ex-Senator.) Objections to excessive authority, however, and to the acceptance of rules for rules' sake can be distinguished from a world view that attacks the very idea of an organized society. It is with this ideological anarchism that we are concerned.

It is easy to caricature the anarchic position. How are we to get two million people daily in and out of Sao Paulo, Tokyo, or Manhattan without some agreed upon procedures? How can we deal with the fact that my freedom to "do my own thing" may entail your subjugation?

Such caricatures, however, can prevent one from examining the rigidity, the unfairness, and the overload of regulation that help to provoke the anarchic response. They may deprive the dominant members of a society of the insight that "those wise restraints that make men free" can turn into straitjackets.

Anarchists struggle to live by that insight. Faced with a paradox—anarchism is a normative defense of a nonnormative situation, a declaration that there *should be* no norms—they often turn to small social systems, formed *de noveau*, where they seek to live with a minimum of outside constraints. The governance systems of some communes are, in fact, quite constricting and hierarchical, as many participants as well as students have found.[17] For a time, however, rules that one has had a direct hand in making and personalized conflict resolution in small-scale communities can seem, in contrast with the larger society, like utter freedom.

Communes are not, of course, simply an expression of anarchic beliefs. They combine, in varying proportions, opposition to the authority structure of the larger society with beliefs and actions designed to create new structures. Their opposition to coercive authority is directed especially at the state, hence many participants feel no contradiction in attempting to create or participate in organized communities based on anarchic principles. Just as Marx believed that with a change of productive relations, the state would wither away—almost by definition, the state being, in his view, the instrument of the ruling class—so many anarchists believe that with the removal of "external" domination, selfishness will wither away. It was from such a perspective that some of the nineteenth-century communes drew their inspiration. Insofar as they were religious in orientation, they generally expressed an ultra-Protestantism—the priesthood of all believers—that quite readily combined with political anarchism: Neither church nor state shall rule over men.[18]

Intentional communities typically design, or live by, cultural systems sharply at odds with the whole range of dominant institutions, not simply with the system of governance. A more purely political expression of anarchism actively attacks the structure of power rather than withdrawing into separate communities protected, in some measure, from that power.

Contemporary expressions of anarchism vary quite widely from society to society. If continental European countries have developed few parallels to the countercultures of Anglo-Saxon countries, Otto Klineberg observes, "we find nevertheless a whole anarchist current converging on the same objectives as the counterculture." The "situationists" in France, "Kommune I" in Germany, the "Provos" in the Netherlands, and many other movements reject both socialist and capitalist societies, focusing "on the freedom of the individual and their refusal of all centralized authority and organization." In their view, as a French situationist put it, the purpose is no longer to acquire power "but to put an end to it once and for all."[19]

The protest movement in France that culminated in the events of May 1968 was strongly anarchic. Statements from Proudhon were written on many walls in Paris: "To be governed is to be watched, inspected, spied on, directed, legislated, regimented, penned, indoctrinated." No ready-made solutions are required before one can oppose the existing order; what is needed is "an opening onto hitherto unknown possibilities." Activism, not political debate over programs that can divide a movement, is the common denominator. And the basis of this activism is spontaneity. Rather than a revolutionary process "too easily associated with the idea of the conquest of central power and the establishment of a new order," activism seeks the establishment of permanent change, a "moving itinerary." "I'm only a loudspeaker, not a leader," Cohn-Bendit declared, thus expressing the view that "the revolutionary movement can tolerate neither prophets nor guides."[20]

The appeal to action rather than to program draws heavily, if incompletely, on Marx. It is not enough to criticize the impersonal force of modern society, epitomized by the "cash nexus," and to lament the resulting alienation. The truth of one's thinking, Marx insisted, must be proved in action. In the often-quoted sentence from his *Theses on Feuerback*: "The philosophers have only *interpreted* the world differently, the point is, to *change* it."[21]

The Constitutional Left and Right. By what criteria can one determine that a political movement is countercultural? These include not only the declaration that the major goals of the polity are repugnant but also a refusal to accept the rules of the game, seeing in them only a recipe for perpetual defeat. The refusal can come from either the left or the right, that is, from what has been called the radical, as opposed to the constitutional, left or right. Those on the left want to push ahead to an imagined new world. Although the lives of some have been difficult, others have prospered, yet advantages and achievements seem meaningless, tasteless, costly.

Those on the far right want to go back to a previous world, real or imagined, where they and those with whom they identify were better off and less threatened by competing groups—or so they believe. In the world they see emerging or already upon them, they feel handicapped by a new set of requirements. Their skills are downgraded in an increasingly technical and bureaucratic world. They see their values and their conceptions of the good life disappearing, and they can find no way within the system to restore them.

Behind the feeling of being a member of a permanent minority within the prevailing political system is a more widespread sense of inefficacy that has had a powerful effect on politics. A 1964 issue of *Daedalus* entitled "A New Europe?" contained many optimistic statements about the way economic growth, affluence, and expanded educational opportunities were weakening radical movements of both left and right by drying up the discontents. Fifteen years later, however, Suzanne Berger, referring to that issue, noted drastic changes. Her emphasis was on the fact that "a loss of faith in the evolutionary/developmental view of industrial societies underlies the uncertainty about the future of politics." The changes were often expressed in protest movements preceding the economic crisis that began in the early 1970s. Thus they reflected rejection of a society and state "perceived as affluent and expansive . . . not reactions against new deprivation and insecurity." In all of the countries of Western Europe, Berger notes, "what seems to have been at stake was an explosion of doubt about the quality and direction of life in advanced industrial societies, about the kinds of human relationships that develop in mass consumer societies, about the irreconcilability of the kinds of organization required to run an industrial society with the values and personal relationships that are necessary for the satisfaction of deep human needs. This was a protest not against the failure of state and society to provide for economic growth and material prosperity, but against their all-too-considerable success in having done so, and against the price of this success."[22]

The same doubts play an important part in recent radical thought in the United States, where they combine, as in Europe, with other causes of political protests. Confronted with the embarrassment that the more established communist societies are as dominated by bureaucracy and technocracy as they believe capitalist societies to be (which Weber, more than sixty years ago, thought inevitable), some radicals turn to China or Cuba, where they believe these problems to be much less severe. Others, however, place their emphasis on spontaneity and individual freedom. Thus the "new left" has attacked not only the existing order but also its "old left" critics, the latter for being too thoroughly routinized and too unconcerned with ways to release human creativity and enjoyment. In an "Appeal from the Sorbonne," June 13-14, 1968, we read: "The bourgeois revolution was judicial; the proletarian revolution was economic. Ours will be social and cultural so that man can become himself."[23]

Although influenced by the powerful attack on prevailing institutions made by the "critical theory" of the period after World War II (Max Horkheimer expressed it well: "Though everything changes, nothing moves"), the "new left" does not share the deep pessimism of critical theory. It seeks to combine politics with self-fulfillment, institutional change with the release of emotions. As a counterculture, its politics, as Geoffrey Pearson puts it, is shocking and libidinal. Among this predominantly affluent group, "fuck your way to freedom" is a much more congenial slogan than "workers of the world, unite!" They fear boredom more than powerlessness, routine more than poverty; "in exchange for the guarantee of not dying of hunger," Vaneigem wrote, our world "offers only the prospect of dying of boredom."[24] A sociology of boredom has yet to be written; but in societies that mix continuous sensual stimulation with leisure and affluence, boredom becomes a powerful force, not only in politics but in the full range of institutions.

The emphasis of the "new left" on self-fulfillment more than on institutional reconstruction has long been seen by the "old left" not as countercultural but as counterrevolutionary. "Dissoluteness is bourgeois," as Lenin put it, in a not uncommon caricature, the reciprocal of caricatures of the old left as life-hating. When Lipset, in a recent symposium, noted the dismay over the "nihilism" of revolutionary students expressed by several nineteenth-century radicals, Friedenberg disagreed sharply: "I wouldn't have expected that what I would regard as uptight effective revolutionary left wingers or whatever to dig at all the kind of trip I have been trying to get into." There are costs, he said, to the struggle for individual liberation from social constraints, and he didn't want to conceal those costs. "I wanted to add them in and take responsibility for paying them, and that if insisting on the kind of freedom that did indeed grow out of privileged middle class life was going to be a drag on the revolutionary tendencies of the world, I would still do it."[25] To those of the left for whom governmental threats to the Bill of Rights, inegalitarian tax provisions, the dominance of military considerations, weakness in environmental protection laws, racial discrimination, and the like are major issues, the values of the new left seem as threatening as those of the establishment.

In many countries today persons on the right as well as on the left feel a great loss of confidence in the state and seek to narrow its scope, although military and police functions are not generally included by the right in the list of excessive state functions. The reasons for this loss of confidence are not entirely consistent: The state can no longer govern—yet it governs too well, denying opportunity for individual choice.[26]

In democratic societies, most critics from the right, as from the left, seek to make their case by the use of accepted political means and within the frame of the dominant political values. From the Nouveau Philosophes of France to the Glistrup party in Denmark, to the neoconservatives of the United States, to mention a few examples, a kind of political "smaller is beautiful" theme is propounded within the context of political competition and philosophical debate.

On the far right, however, as on the far left, political competition and philosophical debate are seen as recipes for failure. Countercultural right-wing groups have little hope of establishing, or reestablishing, by constitutional means, their views on such topics as white supremacy, ultra-nationalism, or opposition to religious pluralism. Although such groups as the Ku Klux Klan, the John Birch Society, and the neo-Nazi groups in the United States vary widely in several respects, they have in common the view that their values can be served only by working outside the normal political process. Within that process, they see only continuing destruction of their familiar world.

Terrorism. In the mid-1960s there was a shift among some counterculturalists toward violence, although more in rhetoric than in fact for most. Frantz Fanon's *The Wretched of the Earth*, with its view of violence as a "cleansing force," received wide attention, its view given added credence in Jean-Paul Sartre's preface to the book. This irrepressible violence, Sartre wrote, "is neither sound nor fury, nor the resurrection of savage instincts, nor even the effect of resentment; it is man recreating himself."[27] The Weathermen, Charles Manson's "family," and the Symbionese Liberation Army were extreme cases, but many more sought, as Michael Lerner put it, to get back in touch with their own capacity to hit, shout, face physical danger, and feel. The task of integrating the acceptance of violence into one's life becomes, somehow, a "sacred task."[28] It is perhaps inevitable that a movement that fears and disdains "cold rationality" should find, among its various expressions, strong support for hot pursuit.

Violence and terrorism are the most visible expressions of some forms of anarchism. Such actions repudiate the dominant view that society needs, through its political institutions, to monopolize the use of "legitimate" violence and to have the power to contain illegitimate violence. To anarchists, it is exactly that monopoly that entrenches evil. Some seek to withdraw from its circle of influence, others to confound and oppose it. The latter, in contrast with William Morris and other "philosophical" anarchists, whose political, economic, and familial goals may be countercultural, are characterized primarily by countercultural means, including violence. Their goals are open-ended, to be improvised as situations unfold. A goal or plan implies the very idea of order that is being opposed. Even revolutionary ideas and cultural products get co-opted by the dominant society, anarchists believe, but violence cannot thus be contained. Borrowing an argument that had been used in reference to Surrealism, activists of the 1968 protests in France wrote in *Bulletin du Mouvement du 22 Mars:* "We know that there is no gesture so radical that ideology will not try to absorb it. . . . The contestation of culture must be done in such a way that culture cannot absorb the contestation and use it as a new form for its lies. . . . Violence cannot be absorbed by the established order because violence is the negation of order."[29]

Even among groups strongly supportive of radical change, it should be emphasized, violence is usually condemned by the large majority. In their comparative study of university students in eleven countries, Otto Klineberg and his associates found that more than two-thirds of their respondents condemned violence as a political technique.[30]

Despite this opposition, violence has been a factor in the politics of many societies. In recent years terrorism has been the most visible form of violence. It denies and seeks to subvert the right of the established order to monopolize coercive power. In the substantial literature on terrorism one can find dozens of definitions, none of them entirely satisfactory for our purposes.[31] The very word is pejorative, although many people can find some terrorist campaign, as they can find some revolution, that is praiseworthy—if it is far enough in the past. Terrorism is the use of violence as a political weapon. It seems reasonable to include, as well, the robbery and ransom demands used to finance the campaign of violence. Terrorism occurs in circumstances in which a group is powerfully motivated to destroy the existing political system or remove the rulers but sees no way of doing it through the accepted political processes. It is not at all of recent origin. In some societies it has been taken for granted that it was justifiable to kill a political opponent. Cicero remarked that tyrants had always come to a violent end; Romans usually acclaimed those who killed them. It is necessary to distinguish between the killing of a person believed to be a tyrant and a violent campaign to overturn a system. This does not imply, however, that one or the other is less repugnant. The former act ought perhaps to be excluded from the meaning of the word, as in the definition given by Chalmers Johnson, from a statement made at a conference on terrorism: "Terrorism is political, goal-oriented action, involving the use or threat of extraordinary violence, performed for psychological rather than material effects, and the victims of which are symbolic rather than instrumental."[32]

Not all terrorism should be seen as countercultural. Although the distinction is not easy to make in practice, the use of violence in a nationalist-separatist cause is not countercultural, or it is marginally countercultural by our definition, since it implies intercultural rather than intracultural conflict. The terrorism employed by the Palestine Liberation Organization or, less clearly, the Irish Republican Army, is different in this respect from that of the Red Army Faction in Germany, the Red Brigade in Italy, or the Weathermen in the United States. (That does not mean, of course, that PLO or IRA violence is more justified, or less justified, than it would be if it were countercultural.) The violence, moreover, must be nonconformist, not aberrant, to be countercultural; it must be proclaimed by a group as an act in the name of new values.

Such proclamations are commonly made by terrorists, whether of the left or the right; the values sought are acclaimed as new and superior. The arguments used by terrorists to justify their actions sometimes remind one of "just war" doctrines stemming from St. Augustine, but more often they are the harsher statements of the "holy war" advocates. They see themselves as freedom fighters, driven to overturn institutions based on false values. They are seen by outsiders, however, as frustrated participants in a stalled movement. Their violence seems aimed as much at their own problems of commitment as at the establishment.[33]

Such justification is aided by the difficulty in drawing a clear line between the violence attributed to the "establishment" and that of "terrorists." This difficulty is sharply etched by the differing views of Jean-Paul Sartre in *Critique of Dialectical Reason* and Raymond Aron in *History and the Dialectic of Violence*. Sartre argued that all human relationships have a potential for violence and that revolutionary violence cannot be judged without reference to the institutionalized and official violence of governments. Aron sees this as an attempt to justify the attacks of a self-selected minority on imperfect but relatively democratic governments, with the outcome likely to be totalitarianism and more violence. In my judgment, we have yet to find our contemporary St. Augustine to examine this issue in its broadest context, separate from contemporary political conflicts. Sartre has the better of it on grounds of general, philosophical argument; Aron has the better of it when one looks at actual terrorist events in our time and their consequences.

Take away the humanistic quality of Sartre's development of the theme and one finds an argument similar to that of Leon Trotsky, who wrote scathingly of

> . . . those moralists who, on the occasion of every terrorist attempt, pontificate triumphantly about the "absolute value" of human life. They are the same people who in other circumstances, in the name of other absolute values, for example, the honor of the nation or the prestige of the monarchy, are ready to push millions of people into the hell of war. Today their hero is the minister who gives orders to shoot unarmed workers in the name of the most sacred right of property. Tomorrow, when the hand of the desperate unemployed clenches into a fist or takes up a weapon, they will mouth empty words about the inadmissibility of violence.[34]

Those for whom the reduction of violence is the desirable goal are caught by their own and others' tendencies to overlook the cruelty of established regimes and to exaggerate both the amount and the effectiveness of terrorist attacks on those regimes. Because it is so newsworthy and cameraworthy, terrorism is given a great deal of attention. It is not, of course, simply a media event. Ten thousand killed over the last decade[35] is a tragic fact; it is not, however, a sign of great power. Terrorism can cause a great deal of human suffering, but it is far more likely to strengthen than to weaken the will to power of the dominant groups. Moreover, "terrorists have found it far easier to overthrow semi-democratic governments than to survive the authoritarian backlash."[36]

It is not clear to me that one must adopt either of the two extreme positions regarding terrorism. On one side there is the declaration that governments and the privileged people they serve are violent, therefore violence against them is justified. On the other side are declarations that terrorists are indiscriminate killers, using a social vehicle for personal anger, weakening representative much more than they weaken autocratic governments, the former, for all their weaknesses, being the best we have, and that, therefore, terrorist claims are utterly without merit. It is violence itself that is most to be lamented, its reduction most to be sought. Somewhere we must find space between indifference to or acceptance of the violence of the powerful and support for the violence of the alientated or desperate.

Notes

1. See, for example, Georges Balandier, *Political Anthropology*, 1970, and M. H. Fried, *The Evolution of Political Society*, 1967.

2. Joseph Berke, editor, *Counter-Culture: The Creation of an Alternative Society*, 1969, Preface.

3. Joseph Gusfield, *Utopian Myths and Movements in Modern Societies*, 1973, p. 7. See also Frank Manuel and Fritzie Manuel, *Utopian Thought in the Western World*, 1979; Karl Mannheim, *Ideology and Utopia*, 1936; Lewis Mumford, *The Story of Utopias*, 1922; and Ruth Levitas, "Sociology and Utopia," 1979.

4. Mannheim, 1936, p. 199, and see the whole of chap. 4.

5. Levitas, 1979, p. 19.

6. For a sampling of writings on communes, see A. E. Bestor, Jr., *Backwoods Utopias*, 1950; W. H. G. Armytage, *Heavens Below: Uto-*

pian Experiments in England, 1560-1960, 1961; Hugh Gardner, *The Children of Prosperity: Thirteen Modern American Communes*, 1978; Philip Abrams and Andrew McCulloch, *Communes, Sociology and Society*, 1976; John Hostetler, *Hutterite Society*, 1974; Charles Nordhoff, *Communistic Societies of the United States*, 1965; Laurence Veysey, *The Communal Experience*, 1973; Keith Melville, *Communes in the Counter Culture: Origins, Theories, Styles of Life*, 1972; Andrew Rigby, *Communes in Britain*, 1974b; Benjamin Zablocki, *Alienation and Charisma: A Study of Contemporary American Communes*, 1980; *idem*, *The Joyful Community*, 1971; and Rosabeth M. Kanter, *Commitment and Community: Communes and Utopias in Sociological Perspective*, 1972. Although I have not yet had a chance to read it, Bennett Berger's *The Survival of a Counterculture* has appeared as this goes to press.

7. Zablocki, 1971, p. 21.

8. Abrams and McCulloch, 1976, p. 3.

9. Kanter, 1972, p. 64. See also Veysey, 1973, pp. 409-80.

10. Abrams and McCulloch, 1976, p. 20.

11. Several sentences in the following paragraphs are adapted from J. Milton Yinger, *The Scientific Study of Religion*, 1970, chap. 18.

12. Max Weber, *From Max Weber*, 1946, p. 334.

13. S. N. Eisenstadt, *The Political Systems of Empires*, 1963, p. 141.

14. See *New Republic*, October 7, 1967, p. 7.

15. Marci McDonald, "Le Nouveau Nazism: A Rightest Fashion from France," 1980.

16. See, for example, David DeLeon, *The American as Anarchist*, 1979; Richard Sennett, *The Uses of Disorder*, 1970; *idem*, *Authority*, 1980; Terry M. Perlin, editor, *Contemporary Anarchism*, 1979; Michael Lerner, "Anarchism and the American Counter-Culture," 1970; and James Martin, *Men Against the State: The Expositors of Individualist Anarchism in America, 1827-1908*, 1953.

17. Zablocki, 1980 (note 6 above).

18. See DeLeon, 1979; Martin, 1953; and Bestor, 1950 (note 6 above).

19. Otto Klineberg *et al.*, *Students, Values, and Policies: A Crosscultural Comparison*, 1979, p. 12.

20. This paragraph is based on Alfred Willener's excellent *The Action-Image of Society*, 1970. See also Bernard Brown, *The French Revolt: May, 1968*, 1970.

21. Murray Kempton adds a rich interpretation to Marx's statement by noting that, like all great statements, it "has the germ of untruth." We have come to see that unexplained things have changed the world "and the task now is to describe them." (*New York Review of Books*, September 24, 1981, p. 28.)

22. Suzanne Berger, "Politics and Antipolitics in Western Europe in the Seventies," 1979, pp. 27, 32.

23. Quoted by Morris Dickstein, *Gates of Eden: American Culture in the Sixties*, 1977, p. 267. See also Armand Mauss, editor, "The New Left and the Old," 1971.

24. Willener, 1970, p. 147.

25. For the Lipset and Friedenberg observations, see Charles Thrall and Jerold Starr, editors, *Technology, Power, and Social Change*, 1972, pp. 86-87, 101.

26. See Berger, 1979.

27. Jean-Paul Sartre in Frantz Fanon, *The Wretched of the Earth*, 1963, p. 21. See also S. R. Lichter, "Young Rebels: A Psychopolitical Study of West German Male Radical Students," 1979, and Albert Ellis and Linda Eckstein, "The Psychology of Political Deviance," In *Deviance and Social Change*. Edward Sagarin, editor, 1977, pp. 195-218.

28. Lerner, 1970 (note 16 above), p. 439.

29. Quoted by Willener, 1970, p. 142.

30. Klineberg *et al.*, 1979 (note 19 above), pp. 218-22.

31. See Walter Lacquer, *Terrorism*, 1977; *idem*, editor, *The Terrorism Reader*, 1978; Kenneth Minogue, "The Doctrine of Violence," a review essay, 1975; and Raymond Aron, *History and the Dialectic of Violence*, 1975.

32. In Lacquer, 1978, p. 268.

33. See Michael Walzer, *Just and Unjust Wars*, 1977, pp. 197-206; Yinger, 1970 (note 11 above), pp. 459-66; and several of the selections in Lacquer, 1978. For a conservative interpretation of terrorism, see Claire Sterling, *The Terror Network*, 1981; and for a contrasting view, Thomas Sheehan, "Italy: Terror on the Right," 1981.

34. Lacquer, 1978, p. 222.

35. *Ibid.*, p. 260.

36. *Ibid.*, p. 1.

Chapter Ten

Countercultural Economic Institutions

Thus much of this will make black, white; foul, fair;
Wrong, right; base, noble; old, young; coward, valiant.

Shakespeare's *Timon of Athens*, on money.

Some of the things that human beings desire are in scarce supply. Since demand exceeds supply, some way has to be found to determine how the goods and services will be distributed among persons desiring them. The scarcity of resources requires, in addition, decisions about how they will be allocated for the production of competing goods and services—that is, for determining their comparative values. The economic institutions of a society say, in effect: Here are the standard ways these problems should be solved. They also include standards of final use—the group within which and the manner in which the goods and services are consumed. The patterned interactions among employers and employees, buyers and sellers, family members, governments and their citizens, and the like relative to those standards are the visible expression of the economic institutions.

Much of the time the members of a society take its economic standards for granted, although they struggle over the outcomes. For example, persons in tribal societies organized primarily around kinship groups sometimes will go along for generations, often in opposition to the different standards of an invading imperial power, knowing how resources should be distributed among its members; the right division of labor between men and women, young and old; the persons or groups with whom land and other property is identified; and the priorities among competing uses of scarce resources. This does not indicate simply "blind conservatism" as the standard economic response to change among tribal peoples—an interpretation refuted by recent anthropological studies.[1] It is, rather, a form of adaptation to the existing conditions. When these cultural "oughts" collide with economic realities, often in the form of change imposed by outside powers, the whole social system is affected.

Although modern societies generate continuous disputes over the operations of economic institutions, many values and norms are accepted by the majority. They are not fully aware of their underlying assumptions about the right way to carry on economic activities, the appropriate goals, the nature of ownership, and the meaning of work until those assumptions are severly challenged, as they have been in the industrial and the industrializing world for several generations. The challenges began, of course, much earlier. In Europe the development of commerce, urbanization, and the concentration of economic power (in the hands of nobles and the church) was matched, at least as early as the fourteenth century, by a continuing series of protests—often in religious form—against the dominant economic standards, along with opposition to the familial, religious, and political institutions. I shall not examine that fascinating story here, except to note the thread of egalitarianism and communism that runs from Wyclif to Hus to Müntzer to the left wing of the Anabaptist movement to the English Ranters, Diggers, and Levellers. There is variation among these groups, of course, with some propounding more radical economic views than others. Contemporary claims that one has the right to "rip off" large corporations were anticipated by fifteenth-century Taborites, who accepted no human authority and claimed the right to rob. Two centuries later, some of the Ranters, in contrast with the Puritan emphasis on the sin of idleness, believed that a man ought not to weary his body in labor, again anticipating a current view.[2]

Gerrard Winstanley, in *The Law of Freedom* and other writings and in his actions, developed one of the fullest programs of drastic economic change, based on redistribution of the land, which was to be held communally, and equalization of wealth. The civil disobedience campaign that he and others carried out was not a teach-in or a love-in, after the fashion in America in the 1960s—although there was a little of both—but a dig-in, in an effort to restore ownership of the commons to the people. "True religion and undefiled is this, to make restitution of the Earth which hath been taken and held from the common people. . . . You jeer at the name Leveller. I tell you Jesus Christ is the head Leveller."[3]

Against such a background we can better understand more recent expressions of countercultural economics. The protests became more widespread as a money economy, commerce, industrialism, and—paradoxically—improved economic conditions became the norm. Developments that seemed to promise more wellbeing brought also more misery, both relative and absolute.

Karl Marx quoted with approval the attributes that Shakespeare, through *Timon*, gave to money. It is, Marx wrote, "the visible deity, the transformation of all human and natural qualities into their opposites, the universal confusion and inversion of things . . . ; it is the universal whore.[4] In his classic *Die Philosophie des Geldes*, Georg Simmel richly explored the way a money economy depersonalizes economic transactions, removing community restraints from the powerful and detaching exchange from the network of responsibilities.

It is not only money itself, of course, nor the love of it that is "the root of all evil" and the focus of opposition. It is also what money symbolizes about economic arrangements that has called forth criticism. Although the list could be extended, I shall mention four themes that seem to me to dominate recent—and many earlier—attacks on economic institutions: The concentration of economic power through control by a few of the major means of production; great inequality in the distribution of income; materialism—overemphasis on the human value of possessions; and technocracy, which I define not just as rule by the managers of the industrial apparatus but as rule by the machine itself, which has become a cruel master.

Needless to say, these themes are closely related. As the basis for criticisms of the economic order, however, they are combined in various ways, because each can be a separate focus of attention. Marxism in its fullest sense, from the young and the old Marx, contains all four themes. But it is difficult to hold them together. If inequality looms as the major evil in existing economic arrangements, it is difficult to maintain steady opposition to technocracy and materialism. If technology is believed to be the primary villain, attention to inequality tends to fade. On the whole, in societies with low per capita productivity, countercultural opposition focuses on inequality and control of the economy by the few. That is particularly true if those who have propounded inverted values have come to power, overthrowing oligarchic and inegalitarian regimes. That part of the Marxian tradition that is antimaterialist and critical of technology has little influence in the Soviet Union today, except among some of the critics of the critics-turned-rulers. (Indeed, it is problematic whether those parts of the Marxian tradition emphasizing egalitarianism and opposition to the concentration of economic power have remained vital in the Soviet Union. But that is another story.)

The situation in China, whose revolution occurred a generation later than the Soviet Union's, is fluid. There are those who hope, and others who fear, that large-scale technology will rapidly augment (displace) small-scale, local, communal, labor-intensive production units. In some measure, recent policy struggles in China have demonstrated the different sets of priorities seen elsewhere, with some persons emphasizing the reduction of inequality and concentrated power, others emphasizing the need to oppose materialism and domination by the machine. Differences in culture, history, population, and resources, and the visible evidence of the effects of technology elsewhere, make it unlikely that China will closely match the Soviet transition. Yet some aspects of the process of industrialization may be inexorable.

In societies with high per capita productivity, countercultural economic values tend to emphasize materialism and technocracy as the major evils.[5] Thoreau more than Marx is the guide; self-realization more than social transformation is the goal.

There are many exceptions to these generalizations, of course. The more philosophically inclined opponents of established economic institutions seek ways to reverse all four themes. Among deprived groups in an affluent society, moreover, and among alienated persons during times of economic crisis, the inequality and concentrated power themes gain salience. During the Depression of the 1930s the Communist Party in the United States grew to some fifty thousand members, mainly from the middle and upper classes, and to higher proportions of the electorates in the countries of Western Europe. Since there was a rapid turnover of membership, the total number of persons who participated in the party before 1950, by which time membership had begun to decline rapidly in the United States, was many more than fifty thousand. Many of its policies were countercultural: collective ownership of the means of production, worker management, redistribution of wealth, and equalization of income were goals sharply in contrast with dominant economic values. They were defended with religious zeal, and when faith in them was lost, as it was for many, the loss was experienced as "the God that failed." Arthur Koestler vividly describes the intensity of belief:

> By the time I had finished with *Feuerbach* and *State and Revolution*, something had clicked in my brain which shook me like a mental explosion. To say that one had seen the light is a poor description of the mental rapture which only the convert knows (regardless of what faith he has been converted to). The new light seems to pour from all directions across the skull; the whole universe falls into pattern like the stray pieces of a jigsaw puzzle assembled by magic at one stroke. There is now an answer to every question, doubts and conflicts are a matter of the tortured past—a past already remote, when one had lived in dismal ignorance in the tasteless, colorless world of those who don't know.[6]

By the 1960s the concentrated power—inequality protest was substantially replaced, among the prosperous counterculturalists, by the materialism-technocracy protest. This has resulted in dramatic changes in the nature of the criticism of economic institutions. The values and programs required to attain economic salvation from the meaninglessness of work are different from those required to attain salvation from the powerlessness of poverty. My statement, to be sure, is not entirely adequate, since opposition to the overwhelming emphasis on technology and the failure to incorporate it smoothly into the ongoing process of production imply opposition to the industrial giants that manage the technology. It is a deflected opposition, however, not a direct attack on their power and the institutional structure that sustains it.

There is also concern for inequality and poverty among the "new" economic counterculturalists; yet the gains are seen to be attainable only if technology is "humanized" and materialism restrained, not simply by economic growth and redistribution. This may be a sound judgment. It is not likely to seem so, however, to those whose jobs are on the line or those who live in poverty. They, as well as the prosperous who see the economy as essentially sound (if the critics can be restrained and a pro-environment technology—not just environmental protection through nonuse—can be advanced), may be more likely to agree with Herman Kahn, who sees the future as "incredibly bright." Kahn has observed that two centuries ago, with 750 million people on earth, the gross world product was $150 billion and per capita income $200 a year. By the mid-1970s, with 4.1 billion people and a gross world product of $5.5 trillion, per capita income was $1,300 a year. A century from now, he envisions a population of 15 billion and a gross world product of $300 trillion. Per capita income will have risen to $20,000 in 1975 dollars.[7]

The opposing view is well stated by Roszak. He recognizes that shifting attention to the inner self seems unappealing, even threatening, to a "vast public consensus" that sees technological advance as the best hope for achieving freedom and decency. A full life, from this perspective, requires a "dependable abundance" that can replace poverty and oppression. What is lacking in this view, Roszak states, is a recognition of "the ecological reciprocities" surrounding industrialism. "Only now do we begin to see that the very forces which have produced the astonishing middle-class affluence of the Western world—unrestrained economic growth, the unfettered ingenuity of technicians and entrepreneurs—can overshoot their promise and bring down upon us a new dark age of privation and barbarism more devastating than anything mankind has yet experienced."[8]

The self-discovery theme leads to drastic changes in attitudes toward work. In the absence of experience that makes work an utter necessity, the weakening of the sense of work as a calling, and the near destruction by technology of work as craftsmanship, work comes to be seen as antilife, as routine, bureaucratized, and—in Marx's term—external to the worker. The economic system is seen to be filled with jobs that are inherently worthless if not actually harmful.

Even the "successes" of the industrial economy prove to have heavy costs attached. The "green revolution," which has certainly increased the supply of food, has also encouraged the development of large "industrial" farms, weakened the position of those engaged in small-scale farming, increased dependency on energy and commercial fertilizers, and even promoted the production of food for export from countries whose populations are undernourished.[9] There has been some humanizing of work settings by a number of changes: more worker control over the rhythms of a job, restoration of a group dimension in places where isolation—by noise if nothing else—had become the rule, and the reduction of health hazards, along with a reduction in the hours of work and, seen over a long-time period, an increase in income. These gains, however, have been adopted primarily as techniques to increase productivity, not as ways of giving more meaning to work. To use a phrase of C. Wright Mills, which he used in a somewhat different connection in *White Collar*, they are efforts "to conquer work alienation within the bounds of work alienation."

Two kinds of response to this economic and occupational situation have developed, one quite thoroughly countercultural, the other less so and perhaps on the way to becoming an acceptable, if minority, view in a pluralistic debate over economic alternatives in industrial societies.

The first response we can call the no-work or the antiwork ethic. In some persons it takes the form not of sabotage (presumably those who threw their wooden shoes into the machinery wanted to work, but not with an iron monster and for an iron-willed employer) but of high rates of absenteeism, poor workmanship, and frequent withdrawal from the labor force. In other persons not working becomes a way of life, a calling one might say, for they take their not working very seriously and often work very hard at it. I am not referring, of course, to the permanently unemployed who are propelled into poverty by personal tragedy or societal failure, although there are countercultural elements in the lives of some hoboes, tramps, and beggars. I am referring to those for whom not working is a cultural statement, "who believe in a no-work ethic," to use a headline from *The New York Times*,[10] and have learned how to take advantage of the various support systems of an affluent society to avoid falling into dire poverty. They are countercultural, we ought perhaps to reemphasize, only if they proclaim their nonwork as right and good, not hiding it or apologizing for their aberrancy. So long as jobs are so dehumanizing, some say, we shall take a permanent coffee break.

A less intense version of this view is sometimes taken by persons who stay within the occupational system but resent what they see as its unfairness. One used to speak of "soldiering" on the job. We need, however, to identify the numerous occupational structures that produce such actions and be aware of the group support for them that can develop. Rosabeth Moss Kanter, Tom Burns, and others have examined the antisuccess peer solidarity that develops among persons who are shut out of opportunity for advancement. They need not believe themselves to be failures if they collectively create new criteria of success and at the same time flout the authority of the "bosses."[11]

While in the United States the no-work point of view seeems not to involve strong political ideologies, in Western Europe it is one of the expressions of radical thought, as in the writings of Antonio Negri. Radicalism today must somehow come to terms with the fact that communism, which has attained power only in relatively undeveloped industrial or in peasant societies, has not led to the extinction of the state and the abolition of alienated labor, as Marx believed it would. It "has in fact spawned regimes that enforce both state and labor much more repressively than under capitalism."[12] Student participants in the French protest movement in 1968 saw themselves becoming mere cogs in a wheel, whether they worked in a society characterized by centralized capitalism or state capitalism of the Russian type. To be a cog is to be mutilated, crushed, castrated, blinded—to use terms found in pamphlets of the movement.[13]

If, as it is put in a well-known quip, capitalism is the exploitation of man by man whereas socialism is the exact opposite, radicals in the West are confronted with a dilemma. In his excellent analysis of several of Negri's books, Sheehan observes that Negri deals with this dilemma by emphasizing what he sees as the Marxian no-labor view. In Negri's words: "The liberation *of* labor is liberation *from* labor. There is no question of exaggerating. Marx himself says this tens and hundreds of times."[14]

I read Marx to say liberation from labor but not from employment, from alienating jobs but not from constructive and self-fulfilling work. However that may be, one can agree with Sheehan's judgment on the appeal of Negri's interpretation to young people who resent and reject the work ethic. It may be, moreover, that on a subliminal level, as

Lyman suggests, many of us are tempted by similar views. Torn by semisecret ambivalence, the working person publicly condemns but secretly envies the bohemian and hippie whom he sees "indulging in sensual perversions and promiscuity and basking in an unearned indolence."[15]

Parallel with the rise of public support systems designed to maintain at least a minimum income during periods when unemployment, illness, substandard wages, or other problems threaten an individual's or a family's welfare has been a welfare "backlash."[16] The belief that many persons on welfare are "freeloaders" and "welfare cheats" is based on the conviction that those receiving public support are living by a different set of values, not responding to economic necessity. This is substantially in error. Those to whom it does apply are more likely to be occupational dropouts from the middle and upper classes. To assess their role in the economic system we need to ask a Durkheimian question: Does their deviation help a society reaffirm its occupational values; and, perhaps more important, does it help a society reassess its occupational values in light of major but neglected forces for change?

I do not know the answer to this question but suspect that the correct answer to the latter part—the reassessment part—is no. Whatever the implications of the no-work ethic for the individuals involved, the societal response seems to be less a thoughtful appraisal of its sources and meaning than resentment against it. This is quite understandable, but perhaps an opportunity is being lost to examine the social, and not just the individual, sources of this counter-ethic.

A second response to the drastically changed economic situation in industrial societies, a more widely accepted and less thoroughly inverted set of values and actions, may be contributing to important economic changes. It shares with the no-work ethic the belief that many jobs are meaningless but adds a sharp criticism of economic imperialism and the emphasis on bigness. To some degree it can be described as a "demodernizing consciousness," expressed by opposition to rational control over the material universe, social relations and the self. "Instead of dominating reality, one should 'dig' it. Instead of manipulating others, one should 'encounter' them. Feeling ('sensitivity,' 'sensibility') is given priority over rational thought. Indeed, the youth culture has a generalized hostility to all planning, calculation and systematic projects. These are categorized as 'uptight,' . . . as against the free-flowing, unconfined spontaneity of 'natural' living."[17]

In such a view one finds support for the ecology movement, for mystical religion and the nonrational world of the occult, for emphasis on wholeness in opposition to the analytic procedures of modernism, and a stress on now rather than on planning and waiting. "This reversal of values is not only a repudiation of the achievement ethos that has served as a key motivation for individual action in modern society, it is inimical to the very notion of life-planning and to the experience of time that life-planning is based upon. In other words, the youth culture is not only 'anti-bourgeois' but, more deeply, demodernizing."[18] In oppositon to the whole range of institutional structures and ones roles within them, the real self becomes the impulse self, in Turner's words.

A different pattern of cultural-countercultural conflict appears when one looks at economic development not in a society that is experiencing a demodernizing movement or has entered a "post-modern" period, but in a society that is undergoing very rapid economic development. The traditional sectors of such a society, including many of its leaders, may be strongly attracted to modernization even while, in dismay at its tradition-destroying powers, they regard development as countercultural. Thus the war aims of Japan during World War II, as Bellah observes, were described as "overcoming the modern" and the protection of the "Japanese spirit." In a similar way, numerous movements in Germany during the Hitlerian period equated "modern" with alien, Jewish, Western, polluted—as opposed to the life of the traditional German folk.[19] Rather than a fairly long period of industrialization, during which liberal views and a substantial middle class had time to grow, Japan and Germany grafted industry onto societies that still contained many feudal qualities. The result was harsh cultural disharmony.

A certain romanticism characterizes the responses to modernization in both the "overdeveloped" societies and in those that are rapidly developing. Exaltation of a folk tradition in the latter scarcely disguises the fact of continuing rapid industrialization: and the former "demodernization" scarcely disguises belief that the still further industrialization will shift most hard work over to cybernetic systems, the efficiency of which will permit the free-flowing life deemed most desirable by counterculturalists.

Some expressions of the demodernization theme involve another romantic idea with a lineage that includes Rousseau (pull down the corrupting influence of society; human nature is good and pure if allowed to develop free from the corroding influence of institutions), some elements of the *gemeinschaft-gesellschaft* tradition (urban and industrial life is unnatural; it destroys the moral fabric of community life), and of some earlier anthropological studies (tribal and peasant peoples live contentedly in their small-scale societies and communties). Needless to say, all of these points of view have been challenged in recent years. They live on, however, or are revived in the economic and political beliefs and actions of those who oppose what they see as a rampaging industrialization.

To say that these ideas are romantic is not to condemn them. In Irving Babbitt's phrase, I think of something as romantic when it is wonderful rather than probable. Few of us live without such supporting mythologies. Certainly Herman Kahn's projections of the economic future are no less romantic. The critical question is the effect of our beliefs on our appraisals of the human situation and on our actions. Here we see sharp contrasts: While the dominant view in industrial societies has been to think of the world's resources as infinite and the waste products of industry as finite and easily disposed of, the countercultural critics have literally inverted both ideas. We are waging economic war against our own grandchildren by consuming a vast proportion of the world's irreplaceable resources and leaving them, in place of those resources, a legacy of garbage, junk, chemical pollutants, and radioactive waste, some of it with a half-life of 32,000 years, that we have barely begun to learn how to contain.

In the 1980s it is scarcely countercultural (although probably still not common) to say that the supply of oil is limited, that we must learn to bring the protection and repair of the environment into our costing processes, or that concern for worker morale is a necessary part of doing business. Major industrialists, politicians, and scientists have endorsed and work for ecological causes. Legal restraints are beginning to reverse the pollution of water and air. The cost of materials, if not environmental considerations, is increasing the amount of recycling.

The countercultural critique of industrial economies, however, goes beyond these developments to challenge the assumption that growth is desirable, even if possible, that the large corporate structure, even if domesticated, is the way to do business. Half a century ago Lord Keynes speculated, a little more cautiously than Kahn, that the day might come—perhaps in a hundred years—when everybody would be rich, a condition within which, he believed, humankind will "once more value ends above means and prefer the good to the useful."[20] Today, economic critics doubt both the probability that everybody will, within a few generations, be rich and the likelihood, if that were somehow to happen, that we would value ends over means and the good over the useful. Only a few countries have entered the ranks of the affluent during the last several decades. There have been small gains in absolute levels of income but losses relative to the wealthy nations. Suppose that situation were to change and the fuel consumption, to use that as an index, of the two-thirds of the world least well off matched that of the richest one-third. The demand for fuel would treble. More realistically, if per capita consumption of fuel during the last third of the century were to increase by 2 1/4 per cent per year in the wealthy countries and 4 1/2 per cent per year in the poorer countries, while population grew annually by 1 1/4 per cent in the former and 2 1/2 per cent in the latter, total demand would increase, by Schumacher's calculations, 4 1/2 times; and 2/3 of the increase would be due to the wealthy countries.[21]

Such estimates are hazardous, of course. Technical advances may change the situation regarding fuel and other resources. Countries now far behind may begin to catch up without a drastic depletion of resources. Would this confirm the dominant economic values that growth is good and wealth brings happiness? Not at all, say the counterculturalists. Rapid economic growth almost certainly implies bigness, with the concentrated power and impersonality it entails. It accentuates the sense of relative deprivation, rather than alleviating it, since desires and visions of the possible run ahead of attainments. Technology's very successes magnify our problems: Supertankers mean super oil spills; superhighways mean super smog banks; supersonic planes mean noise pollution and threats to the ozone layer. The pursuit of economic growth makes likely the continuing loss of meaningfulness of work. Schumacher, in his sweeping indictment, expressed doubt that universal prosperity could lay the foundations of peace, "because such prosperity, if attainable at all, is attainable only by cultivating such drives of human nature as greed and envy, which destroy intelligence, happiness, serenity, and thereby the peacefulness of man. It could well be that rich people treasure peace more than poor people, but only if they feel utterly secure—and this is a contradiction in terms. Their wealth depends on making inordinately large demands on limited world resources and thus puts them on an unavoidable collision course—not primarily with the poor (who are weak and defenseless) but with other rich people."[22] The great need, Schumacher declared, is for a technology that is inexpensive, suitable for small-scale application, and supportive of the creativity of the user. Such a technology is appropriate to an "economics of permanence," a "Buddhist economics" that lives within the resources available in a framework of meaningful labor.

Some of the possiblilities for such a technology are illustrated in Stewart Brand's *The Next Whole Earth Catalog* and discussed by Stavrianos in *The Promise of the Coming Dark Age*. Small-scale and environmentally sensitive experiments are receiving extensive support, much of it from the public and private establishment. Stavrianos wonders, however, whether the industrialized world will be prevented by its "retarding lead" from pressing ahead with these experiments. The values and institutions that were developed during industrialization now stand as obstacles. The lead turns into a handicap if it prevents a society from adapting to new conditons. New values and new methods are required.

The changes called for by Schumacher, Stavrianos, Roszak, Commoner, and other environmentalists have a much greater potential for altering the prevailing economic values than an antiwork ethic or the barter, free stores, and "head shops" designed not so much to work for new societywide economic patterns as to serve a nonconformist clientele.[23] The environmentalists, using this term in its broadest sense, have something in common with Thoreau's view that people are rich in proportion to the number of things they can afford to do without. But they place less emphasis than Thoreau on withdrawal, more on change of economic institutions. They would shift priorities from production, profit, increase in wealth, and the maximum use of technology to meaningful work, production in harmony with the environment (don't do that which cannot be sustained on a permanent basis), technology within human scale, and a measure of profit based on long-run societal interests (which would mean, for example, that recycling would not wait for the time it was profitable in the current budget of individual firms but would be judged by its effects on the long-run societal budget).

There is the possibility, as I have already mentioned, that such changes in priority would entail costs borne predominantly by the poor. The well-to-do, some persons argue, can afford to be concerned with the meaningfulness of work and the quality of the environment that will be part of the inheritance of their grandchildren. The poor worry more about the availability of work and the quantity of food available to their children. In my judgment, that poses the dilemma too sharply. A polluted environment sickens and kills the poor much more often than the wealthy, because the poor live and work in the most polluted parts of the environment. Profit decisions that pay no attention to the uselessness, danger, or built-in obsolescence of products have no great impact on the rich, but "the poor pay more." The least well-off, moreover, have the most to gain by increases in the meaningfulness of work, the availability of small-scale self-help projects, and the reduction of an emphasis on wealth as the measure of success and the good life.

It would be foolish, nevertheless, to overlook the possible class-based aspects of the economic counterculture and to forget the potential dilemmas involved in some of the choices.

Paradoxes and unintended consequences abound when the world is turned upside down. John Wesley observed that the virtues accompanying sectarian fervor helped one to climb the economic ladder, that piety led to riches, which endangered piety. In *The Cultural Contradictions of Capitalism*, Daniel Bell argues that capitalism's successes have encouraged values opposed to the value of rational calculation on which the successes were built. The value of work, saving, and restraint produced, ironically, the possibility of an emphasis on the value of consumption and enjoyment. We now have "countercultural capitalists" who attend schools for "entrepreneurs." They are the "Castaneda-like warriors of the marketplace," a "*Whole Earth Catalogue* chamber of commerce." The approach at Robert Schwartz's executive conference center

> . . . appeals to proponents of the counterculture who have outgrown the other worldly spiritualtiy of imported gurus and domestic prophets. They want to bring the spirituality of the monastery into the marketplace—to apply what has been learned from drugs, meditation, encounter workshops or other "human potential" experiences to what Saul Wilmet, a peppy 24-year old proprietor of a New York City granola factory, called "the business of life." It is impossible to predict which will change most—the spirituality or the marketplace.[24]

John Wesley, I believe, would not have hesitated to predict. "I fear, wherever riches have increased," he wrote, "the essence of religion has decreased in the same proportion. . . As riches increase, so will pride, anger, and love of the world in all its branches. . . . So, although the form of religion remains, the spirit is swiftly vanishing away."[25]

Is it possible that where the Methodists were seen by their founder to be doomed to riches and religious decay, "spiritually" inclined economic counterculturalists can maintain both? Or was Schumacher right in believing that drastic changes in economic values are required?

Notes

1. See Roy A. Rappaport, "Nature, Culture, and Ecological Anthropology," in *Man, Culture, and Society*, Harry Shapiro, editor, 1971 pp. 237-68, and Sutti Ortiz, "The Structure of Decision-Making Among Indians in Colombia," in *Themes in Economic Anthropology*, Raymond

Firth, editor, 1967, pp. 191-228. For a wide variety of perspectives on economic anthropology, see Richard Fox, editor, "Political Economy," 1978; J. R. Clammer, editor, *The New Economic Anthropology*, 1976; George Dalton, editor, *Studies in Economic Anthropology*, 1971; idem, editor, *Tribal and Peasant Economies*, 1967; Raymond Firth, editor, *Themes in Economic Anthropology*, 1967; and E. E. LeClair and H. K. Schneider, editors, *Economic Anthropology: Readings in Theory and Analysis*, 1968.

2. See Eduard Bernstein, *Cromwell and Communism: Socialism and Democracy in the Great English Revolution*, 1963; Lewis Berens, *The Digger Movement in the Days of the Commonwealth as Revealed in the Writings of Gerrard Winstanley, the Digger*, 1961; Norman Cohn, *The Pursuit of the Millennium*, 1970; Cristopher Hill, *The World Turned Upside Down*, 1975; A. L. Morton, *The World of the Ranters*, 1970; David Petegorsky, *Left-Wing Democracy in the English Civil War*, 1940; and G. P. Gooch, *English Democratic Ideas in the Seventeenth Century*, 1927.

3. From Gerrard Winstanley, "A New Year's Gift for the Parliament and Army," In *Law of Freedom and Other Essays*, 1973, pp. 159-210. See Berens, 1961, pp. 132-45, and Gooch, 1927, p. 187.

4. Karl Marx, *Selected Writings in Sociology and Social Philosophy*, 1964, p. 192.

5. Ronald Inglehart, *The Silent Revolution*, 1977.

6. Arthur Koestler in Richard Crossman, *The God That Failed*, 1949, p. 23.

7. From an interview with Kahn by Andreas de Rhoda in *The Christian Science Monitor*, July 28, 1976. See also Herman Kahn, William Brown, and Leon Martel, *The Next 200 Years*, 1976.

8. Theodore Roszak, *Person/Planet: The Creative Disintegration of Industrial Society*, 1978. See also William R. Catton, Jr., "Carrying Capacity, Overshoot, and the Quality of Life," in J. Milton Yinger and Stephen J. Cutler, editors, *Major Social Issues*, 1978, chap. 20.

9. See Frances Lappe and Joseph Collins, *Food First: Beyond the Myth of Scarcity*, 1977, chap. 17.

10. *The New York Times*, June 1, 1975, p. 45.

11. See Bernard Lefkowitz, *Breaktime: Living Without Work in a Nine to Five World*, 1979; Rosabeth Moss Kanter, *Men and Women of the Corporation*, 1977, pp. 149-152; Tom Burns, "The Reference of Conduct in Small Groups: Cliques and Cabals in Occupational Milieu," 1955.

12. Thomas Sheehan, "Italy: Behind the Ski Mask," 1979, p. 24.

13. Alfred Willener, *The Action-Image of Society*, 1970, p. 136.

14. Antonio Negri, quoted by Sheehan, 1979, p. 24. What Marxist *societies* say, by their policies and actions, is skillfully examined by Gerhard Lenski, "Marxist Experiments in Destratification: An Appraisal," 1978.

15. Stanford Lyman, *The Seven Deadly Sins*, 1978, p. 37.

16. See Joan Huber, "The Politics of Public Assistance: Western Europe and the United States," in Yinger and Cutler, 1978, chap. 9, and Harold L. Wilensky, *The Welfare State and Equality*, 1975.

17. Peter Berger, Brigette Berger, and Hansfried Kellner, *The Homeless Mind*, 1973, p. 202.

18. *Ibid.*, p. 208.

19. Robert Bellah, *Beyond Belief*, 1970, chap. 4.

20. Cited by E. F. Schumacher, *Small Is Beautiful*, 1973, p. 32.

21. *Ibid.*, pp. 23-25. See also The Club of Rome, *The Limits to Growth*, 1974, and Barry Commoner, *The Closing Circle*, 1971.

22. Schumacher, 1973, p. 30.

23. See George H. Lewis, "Capitalism, Contra-Culture, and the Head Shop: Explorations in Structural Change," 1972, and *idem*, "The Structure of Support in Social Movements: An Analysis of Organization and Resource Mobilization in the Youth Contra-Culture," 1976.

24. Mark Gerzon, "Counterculture Capitalists," *The New York Times*, June 5, 1977, Section 3, p. 1.

25. Quoted by Max Weber, *The Protestant Ethic and the Spirit of Capitalism*, 1930, p. 175.

Chapter Eleven

Countercultural Religion

But the culture of a margin, especially of a margin under pressure, may need to defend its own stability and tradition, even against choice. . . . Monasteries become wealthy bastions of the system they attack; free churches become stagnant pools of tradition. Therefore countercultures have to be followed by different countercultures: a dialectic within the dialectic.

David Martin, *The Dilemmas of Contemporary Religion*, p. 3

A set of values that changes life drastically, that threatens not simply opposition but persecution, that is entangled with deeply ambivalent feelings about oneself and others is not adopted casually. For many persons it demands a powerful revelation to a charismatic leader or a deep-going mystical encounter or the support of a select community of believers or an image of the devil and his institutional embodiment—or all of these—if it is to be experienced as a viable new way of life.

This is not a list of the causes of countercultures—see Chapter Three—but an indication of the kinds of sponsorship that can develop when those causes are operating strongly. The same influences can reinforce traditional values. Religion can sanctify existing institutions, as Marx, joining a long list of critics, declared; but it can also be the engine of changes, both intended and unintended.[1] Powerful leaders claiming a sacred mission are often involved. Under some circumstances, to be sure, a charismatic leader seeks to protect and repair an endangered moral order. The idea of charisma—a "gift of grace"—came from early Christianity, and in the view of Rudolph Sohm, who brought the term into modern discussions, charisma was a conservative force.

In different contexts, however, charisma not only expresses opposition to the sense of an excessive rationalization and bureaucratization of life but also proclaims that an established moral order must be broken.

"It is written . . ., but I say unto you. . ."

That is the sense in which Weber used the term. Although his examples were frequently drawn from the Judaic-Christian tradition, he extended its meaning beyond religion."Charismatic authority . . . is sharply opposed to rational, and particularly bureaucratic, authority, and to traditional authority. . . . Within the sphere of its claims, charismatic authority repudiates the past, and is in this sense a specifically revolutionary force."[2]

If one sought, for purposes of emphasis, to select one theme for the study of the cultural-countercultural dialectic, religion would be, in my judgment, the wisest choice. Why new religious beliefs and practices appear, why some people accept them and others reject them, and how those ideas evolve, in interaction with the surrounding environment, are questions vital to the study of cultural reversals. However they are answered in specific cases, their examination reveals the intensity of emotion, the transformative potential, and the legitimating power of a religious movement—forces that give "direction to practical conduct," in Weber's words.

Cultures contain systems of meaning, socially constructed mental universes, in Peter Berger's terms, without which individuals face the "ultimate danger"—meaninglessness, "anomic terror." We are all heirs of belief in some system of fundamental order, the cosmos, which is thought to characterize the universe. "Religion is the human enterprise by which a sacred cosmos is established."[3] It is the ultimate shield against chaos.

One ought perhaps to qualify this statement. Powerful systems of meaning do not let the urge toward order obscure the tragic sense of the reality of chaos. Some persons, in fact, find the experience of chaos less threatening than the constraints they feel in a received tradition. They adopt the gnostic position that order is most to be feared. Many, however, respond to the threat of chaos by seeking new ways to avoid "anomic terror." Berger's point is reinforced by the flowering of new systems of meaning when "the sacred canopy" is cracked or broken. Some of those who think it cannot or should not be repaired drift away, seeking individual shelters. Others design or embrace a new cosmos, a sectarian alternative that cuts itself off from what has come to be seen as a flawed view of the universe.

During periods of major countercultural protest, religious movements are among the most vigorous opponents of the established order. The opposition can be expressed in many different ways. Werner Stark has stated that "the sect is typically a countraculture."[4] Although this is based on a more limited definition of sect than I find appropriate—for Stark, a sect is "a conflict society" that can last for only one generation—he is certainly right in emphasizing dissent and "nay"-saying as important characteristics. Stark noted that sects deviate from the prevailing social order in three basic polarities: They can emphasize a glorious past, to be rediscovered and revitalized, or a glorious future, expressed in millenarian or utopian hopes (the present is repudiated). They can adopt an ascetic or a licentious, antinomian morality (moderation is repudiated). And they can deal with the dominant society passively or violently (cooperation and negotiation are repudiated). Each of these contrasting ways of pushing away from the dominant world is represented among contemporary sects. In view of the great proliferation of "new religions" since World War II, we readily see that a Durkheimian history and theory of the unity of society and religion, of the conservative tendency of churches and their secular power, is seriously incomplete without a matching history and theory of religious attacks on the social order.

Perhaps on this topic I need particularly to emphasize that the presence of countercultural religions is not intrinsically good or bad. As in times past, for every person who supports one of the new religions today, there are probably ten who oppose them, along with the even larger number who are indifferent. Although I have my own preferences, which doubtless will be visible, I want here only to illustrate the importance of religious countercultures, not to applaud or attack them.

In his monumental study of *The Social Teaching of the Christian Churches* with its detailed description of the churches' complex structures and formal organization, Troeltsch also noted that there was something in Christianity that defied institutionalization. We can extend this remark to cover other religions, including such "secular religions" as communism, because none escapes the tendency to schism and sectarian protest. The depth of the adversarial perspective of much of modern literature has been widely observed. We need also to emphasize that religion, with its inherently ambivalent relationship to "the world," carries the continuous potential for the same adversarial approach.

An enormous literature examines Christianity as a counterculture—although the term is not used—and, for the years after Chrisitanity became the dominant religion of the West, as a target for its own countercultures.[5] We can better understand the contemporary situation by examining some of the charges—and claims—of heresy, sedition, gnosticism, and antinomianism.

Christianity was, at first, countercultural mainly to Judaism, from which most of its early converts as well as many of its beliefs—and much of its opposition—came. In a few generations, however, it was more drastically at odds with the Roman Empire. It was probably a member of the synagogue in Thessalonica who protested, as reported in *Acts*, that "these men who have turned the world upside down have come here also"; but "here" soon became many other places as well. As Christians became more numerous and Roman rulers less confident of the unity of their empire, the refusal of members of the early church to grant primary allegiance to the Emperor, their exaltation of the poor and weak, their substitution of faith and millenarian hopes for Graeco-Roman belief in reason, and their attacks on the civic religion led to their persecution.

The opposition to Christianity, most intense under regimes that history would record as among the more just, such as that of Marcus Aurelius, reflected the growing strength and the more open challenges of Christian groups. Caricatures of Christians as cannibals engaged in ritual murder and incestuous orgies reflected "the absolute incompatibility of primitive Christianity with the religion of the Roman state."[6] The gods of Rome were its guardians; the imperial cult bound the various regions of the Empire together. To the Christians, however, Rome was thoroughly evil, the realm of the Antichrist.

Near the end of the second century, Tertullian summed up the charges that Romans made against his fellow Christians: "You don't worship the gods, and you don't offer sacrifices for the emperors." To this one can add the penchant some had for "voluntary martyrdom," for going beyond what the churches required as demonstrations of faith, provoking the public, smashing things, and then giving themselves over to the authorities.[7]

In his "true account" of early Christians, Celsus, an Epicurean of temperate and cultivated mind, complained that they would neither reason nor listen to reason. "The world's wisdom is evil, and the world's foolishness is insight." He objected to their beliefs and rites, their ignorance of the ways of the world, their refusal to support the governing authorities. Nearly a century later, Origen, one of the fathers of the early church, was chosen to reply to Celsus' argument, indicating its continuing influence. He answered in the language of faith. Had reason, he asked, alleviated the miseries of mankind, miseries often fostered by the depravity of the educated? Is not compassion for the weak to be preferred to their neglect or persecution? The philosophers and rulers of Rome could not reach the "enthusiasm of emotion which would choose a better life for its own sake, independent of motive," an observation that challenges rationalists of every age, who wonder whether "enthusiasm of emotion" is not equally or more often associated with poor choices. Froude, to whom we owe this thoughtful account of the "debate" between Celsus and Origen, makes clear the sharp contrast in their views of the world.[8]

Christianity, Augustine noted, turned all previous values around. It was not simply the Roman setting that promoted its countercultural qualities, as seen from the perspective of the dominant values. Those qualities are intrinsic to its beliefs, as they are to all universalistic religions. Tensions with the political order arose when the brotherly ethic of salvation religions challenged the barriers of locality, tribe, and polity with conceptions of "a unified God of the entire world," to use Weber's words. The belief in a "Kingdom of God set over against principalities and powers," although it often succumbs to the unitary pull of the nation-state, "creates counter-cultures above and below the unity of the natural society; it initiates breaks in the natural community of tradition and generation."[9]

Other sources join with universalism to support early Christian and later countercultural movements. Gnostics kept the term cosmos—order, symmetry, wholeness, discipline—which was the critical concept for the Greeks, but they reversed its value loading. Order was what they deprecated, because it is tyrannical law; it is fate; it is rigid and alien to individual purposes. Thus the term "cosmos" could pass over into gnostic use and, "with its value-sign reversed, become as symbolic as it had been in the Greek tradition."[10] Although it preceded Christiantiy, its inversion of the dominant tradition continued when Christianity became established. As a Christian heresy, Gnosticism was identified as a claim for salvation by esoteric knowledge that was substituted for the Gospel. Its principle of inner independence, the "divinity of the Absolute Self," became associated with nihilism and libertinism (but also with asceticism: freedom by non-use as well as by ab-use). Jonas emphasized that allegiance to the law, "part of the great design upon our freedom," was repudiated.

The theological idea of sin is inverted by the extreme versions of Gnosticism: Sin is the road to salvation. In elevating Cain to an honored position, opting for "the traditionally infamous," the "prototype of the outcast," the Cainites, a Gnostic sect, affirmed that they were bringing out the real truth in the story of Cain and Abel, "by turning the intended meaning upside down." "In the construction of a complete series of such countertypes, stretching through the ages, a rebels' view of history as a whole is consciously opposed to the official one."[11]

It is probably not so much the preservation, translation, and circulation of gnostic works that account for the frequent reappearances of their views, as in medieval and contemporary Satanism or as symbolized in the Faustian myth developed by Goethe and others. The roots lie much deeper, in the sociological and psychological conditions that make the reversal of dominant values seem, to some, to be desirable—even essential. In his Introduction to the Nag Hammadi library of Gnostic texts, James Robinson states that "Jesus called for a full reversal of values," taking a stand quite at odds with the authorities of his time, who soon eliminated him. When many of his followers adopted a more conventional life, the radical impulse was not quelled. It reappeared in many ways—in monasteries, in sects, and in Gnostic beliefs. As Christianity became established, Gnostics were excluded as heretics; but the rejection was mutual.[12]

Contemporary Religious Countercultures

". . . if a person smite you on your left cheek SMASH him on the other."

Anton LaVey, *The Satanic Bible*, p.33

Religious countercultures range from those that almost literally turn the spiritual world upside down to those that invert traditional beliefs, conversion practices, and rites while affirming some sense of kinship with other religions. Some of the Gnostic sects, the more impatient chiliastic groups, eager to speed the inevitable disaster that must precede the perfect new order, extreme advocates of the doctrine of the Free Spirit, and Satanist groups of many different periods illustrate the reversals.

From the point of view of influence and the number of persons involved, the drastic reversals of religious traditions are probably less important than the partial inversions. Because they mark the outer edge of deviation, however, the drastic reversals highlight the cultural-countercultural contrast, as in Satanism, which has been revived in recent years. Satan, the adversary, is invoked to legitimate the opposite of traditional standards. Satanists "systematically supplant what is holy in a society with the blasphemous."[13] Contemporary versions have moved in the magical direction of the religiomagical system—that is, they are concerned primarily with efforts to satisfy, by nonempirical means, immediate and pressing needs, to deal with great anxieties.

> The crashing music stops and in the sudden silence the air seems to throb and pulse. Then a candle flickers into life, and then another, and another. In their flickering light dark and shadowy figures can be seen, their shadows dancing grotesquely on the wall of the ritual chamber.

From above, the Goat God gazes down upon the motionless tableau. Then a black-robed figure steps forward to the stone altar beneath the Baphomet and, as the gong is struck, lifts the gleaming sword high above the naked and motionless body of the young girl stretched supine upon the altar before him.[14]

Moody has not drawn this exotic scene from medieval Europe or tribal Africa; the setting is the First Church of the Trapezoid, the Church of Satan, San Francisco, in the early 1970s. All the participants were deviant in some aspects of their social behavior—not so much disturbed, Moody notes, as disturbing to others. Their childhoods had been marked by pain and strife. They had often been cut off from normal social interaction and forced into contact with other marginal or abnormal persons. Their first steps into magic were efforts to make the world "predictable and therefore less anxiety-provoking." Their troubling lack of self-esteem is kept under control by the belief that it is not simply personal shortcomings, but "great and mysterious powers, the power of evil, for example, before which *all* are relatively helpless," that account for their failures and distress.[15]

The shift from Christian to Satanist is difficult, since the "deadly sins" of Christianity are depicted as virtues. In *The Satanic Bible* we read that Satan represents indulgence; kindness to those who deserve it, instead of love wasted on ingrates; vengeance, instead of turning the other cheek; all of the so-called sins, as they all lead to physical, mental, or emotional gratification.[16] The Black Mass is designed to blaspheme Christian rituals in a way that will replace anxiety over the reversals with disgust, anger, or laughter. Moody noted, for example, the cross hung upside down, the Lord's Prayer recited backward, obscene phrases chanted in Latin, urine used for communion wine, and a naked female used for the altar.

Satanic cults seek to create the image of a formidable and dangerous group to arouse the emotions of their members and to stir up public opposition, which they also need. They speak and write in harsh rhetoric. In *The Gods of War* written by one of the leaders of "The Power," a pseudonym used by Bainbridge to refer to such a cult, the "Lord Satan" advises:

Release the Fiend that lies dormant within you, for he is strong and ruthless, and his power is far beyond the bounds of human frailty.

Come forth in your savage might, rampant with the lust of battle, tense and quivering with the urge to strike, to smash, to split asunder all that seek to detain you. . . .

Rape with the crushing force of your virility; kill with the devastating precision of your sword arm; maim with the ruthless ingenuity of your

> pitiless cruelty; destroy with the overpowering fury of your bestial strength; lay waste with the all-encompassing majesty of your power.[17]

No members of the group that he knew, Bainbridge notes, took these words as commandments requiring action. Various accounts in the media, however, used the words as indications of a violent cult. Some noted that Charles Manson, who did act out such words, was acquainted with the group and had written a short article for its magazine.[18]

Such groups as the Church of Satan and "The Power" would disappear rapidly, it can be argued, if their beliefs and rituals did not "work"—did not bring some feeling of relief from pervading anxieties, some increase in life's satisfactions. Moody believes that the magic worked not only for the individuals involved, as in the case of the young man whose self-confidence was promoted and sexual inhibitions overcome, but also for society: Deviance was confined to a specific social context; the participants were resocialized, in many ways, to prevailing norms; the terrible price demanded by the "gods" of progress, science, and technology was made more apparent; and, in a more traditional argument, members of the dominant society had a vivid illustration of the "anticultural" for their use to explain the world's misfortunes and to mark off the imprecise and fading lines of the dominant culture.

It is well to be reminded of the latent consequences of deviation. Before one agrees, however, with Moody's assessment that "marginal religions such as the Church of the Trapezoid should be encouraged," one ought to inquire about still further consequences: the growth of intolerance and rigidity in the larger population; possible injury to persons who tried the inverted rites and beliefs only to be driven into still further distress; the appearance of charlatans who play on others' anxieties to their own benefit; and the development of secularized versions that give distraught individuals ideological support for acting out their deepest hostilities. This last is illustrated by the Charles Manson family, with its plan for provoking race conflict and its claim to justification for murder. In light of his harsh childhood, one can sympathize with Manson's plight without finding social gains in his anguished struggles. He spent twenty-two of his first thirty-five years in prison. "Let me tell you something," he remarked in 1980. "I been in prison all my life." Combine his desolate childhood—filled with rejection—with a social climate favorable to defense-by-cultural-invention and one gets, in his case, a satanic group capable of enormous cruelty.[19]

We are greatly in need of further study of the consequences of countercultures for different persons in a variety of situations.

The "*New Religions.*" Fully countercultural cults are less common than religious groups that are closer to established goals although still highly deviant in rites and beliefs. Some of these groups claim a historical kinship to a major religious tradition even as they proclaim their deviations from it. Others embrace an "alien" tradition, using it as a standard against which the religion in their own backgrounds can be criticized and reversed. The imported religions—Buddhism and Hinduism in the United States, for example—are typically changed and domesticated by the converts.

Religious countercultures are seldom lacking in complex societies where one of the "world religions" predominates. They are especially abundant, however, during periods when several forces promoting deviation converge. During such times the dominant religious groups become weaker and a wave of new religions sweeps over a land.[20]

The number of participants, it should be noted, as contrasted with the number of groups, is often greatly exaggerated, both by spokesmen for the groups and by the general public. When I have asked relatively well-informed persons (but nonspecialists) to estimate the number of American members of Sun Myung Moon's Unification Church, for example, the figures range from 10,000 to "there must be well over a million Moonies." The group claims 30,000; Lofland's estimate, based on long study, is 2,000.[21] Precise information on religious memberships is notoriously difficult to obtain. The difficulty is compounded with reference to new, highly publicized, and deviant groups. Many persons participate for a little while, so that ex-members are often more numerous than members, complicating the problem of estimation. One can say quite confidently that the conservative churches are gaining members. Some of the more marginal groups—the Jesus Movement and the Catholic and Protestant charismatic and neo-Pentecostal groups, for example, are also quite large. The most deviant groups, however, including the quasi-religious therapeutic groups, such as Scientology and *est*, tend to be smaller.[22] I would estimate the total number of active participants to be a few hundred thousand (a vague number, to match my uncertainty). Those who have had some brief contact with one of the groups would be several times more numerous.

These comments on the size of the more deviant religious groups are made not to minimize their importance but to emphasize that their importance rests on the nature of their cultural challenge, not their memberships. One could draw illustrations of that challenge from many different societies. I shall refer primarily to the United States, where the variety and number of new religions is enormous. Brief references to Japan and Melanesia, however, can prevent us from believing that these developments are found exclusively in the West and can help us identify the conditions that make the religious challenges moderate or drastic.

In Japan the tight control over all religions maintained by a 1939 law, which reinforced the prevailing practices, was completely removed by a directive from Douglas MacArthur in 1945. The established religions had been seriously weakened by their association with the defeated empire. Millions of people found themselves culturally and physically uprooted by the war, by rapid urbanization, and by contact with the West, particularly with Americans. In this context, dozens of new religious groups appeared or began to develop rapidly from earlier beginnings. Some attained memberships of several million. The largest, Sōka Gakkai, draws a sharp line between its members and the unregenerate; its conversion methods tend toward the coercive; and it empahsizes individual success more than social or national welfare. "Through this supreme religion," one reads in an offical publication, "a person can escape poverty and live a prosperous life, if only he works in earnest; a man troubled with domestic discord will find his home serene and happy; and a man suffering from disease will completely recover his health and be able to resume his former job. By the power of the Gohonzon [object of worship], a mother worried with her delinquent son will see him reform."[23] Such a "happiness-manufacturing machine," as one of its leaders called it, departs rather widely from the Buddhist Nichiren Shoshu tradition with which it identifies.[24]

"New religions," however, are not synonymous with countercultural religions. The developments in Japan, while containing some tendencies toward the reversal of dominant religious themes, are not so thoroughly at odds with traditional beliefs and practices as are many of those in the United States. For the most part they are serving as bridges to a drastically changed world, by blending the old and the new. Despite the stresses and changes of the last several decades, some of the critical sources of countercultures that I have discussed earlier have been less powerful in Japan than in the West. There has been no period of rapid increase in the proportion of youths in the population. The birth rate was cut in half between 1947 and 1957 and has remained low. (It declined in the United States also after 1947, but at a slow rate until 1960.) Intimate social circles, the family and larger kin structures and even communities, despite migration to cities, have shown less disruption than in other industrial societies. Aspiration levels have been more nearly matched by actual increases of income and status or have risen at a less rapid pace, so that the sense of relative deprivation, a powerful force in many societies, pushes less strongly against the Japanese system.[25]

It remains to be seen whether these conditions are intrinsic to Japanese society and culture or whether they reflect the relative recentness of its full industrialization. I would expect both to be true, suggesting that some increase in countercultural protests, including those of a religious nature, will appear in the years ahead. Along with the "new religions" there have been political and economic protests, some of them quite violent; but a relatively small part of the population has been involved. Perhaps the strongest protests have been on university campuses, among persons most sensitive to national and economic changes.[26] They may be forerunners of more widespread movements seeking social and cultural transformations.

The islands of Melanesia, although affected by events vastly different from those of Japan, have shared the influence of culture contact, conflict, and social change. They too have experienced a wave of religious and religiopolitical movements, most notably the millenarian Cargo Cults, by which the islanders have sought to deal with the social disorganization and personal frustration produced by European domination of their lands. These movements are millenarian in the sense that they envisage a dramatic and rapid transformation of a frustrating and deprived state into a rewarding and glorious state by religious means.

The traditional societies have been seriously disrupted by a succession of culture shocks, by the labor methods of plantation and mine overseers, by racial antipathies, and by military invasion. The contrast between the values taught by the missionaries and those practiced by the men who dominated the lives of the inhabitiants only added to the confusion. In these conditions the native resident could not go back—the white man had not only disrupted his societies but had also given him new wants and new values—nor could he go ahead, for his pay was minimal, his opportunities few, his command of the white man's ways marginal at best. The stage was set, as Peter Worsley observed, for the appearance of independent native movements that cast social and economic aspirations in religious form.[27]

At first the movements tended to be nativistic and revivalistic. Like the Ghost Dance among several American Indian tribes in the West, they affirmed that the old order would be reestablished and the invader driven from the land. At that stage there was little countercultural about the Cargo Cults. The order that they sought to reverse was that of the Europeans. The doctrine of "resistance and hope" envisaged the return of the ancestors, the winning of independence, and, for the faithful, a prosperous and happy life.

Even in the early versions of the Cargo Cult, however, there were expressions of new needs and values. They were conservative and restorative in many ways, but innovative cults were common even in traditional religion. It was to be expected that those appearing after extensive contact with Europeans and Americans would contain the seeds of radical change, including a revolutionary nationalism that gave separate tribal groups, as Peter Lawrence emphasized, a sense of common fate and purpose. Many versions of the movement developed the theme of "stolen cargo." From the point of view of the native inhabitants of the island, the white men in their midst were receiving vast supplies of goods by steamer and plane from unknown sources—goods which they had not manufactured and for which they merely sent back slips of paper. It was not difficult for the natives to believe that the goods had been made by their own ancestors and stolen from them by the Whites, who had control over some secret. Work was obviously not the secret. Prophets appeared to reveal the way to secure the cargoes and to reestablish native supremacy.

If the beliefs and rites, the destruction of goods and refusal of work seem, to the prosaic eye, to be impossible ways to defeat the white man and gain mastery of his secret for obtaining the vast cargoes, we should remind ourselves of the extent to which the aboriginal cultures had been weakened and new, attractive—yet hated—ways made visible. The islanders could not simply adopt the ways of white people. Self-respect would not permit that, even if partial socialization and the policies of the authorities had opened the way. Nor could they simply forget the new ways. With their economy disrupted, their hopes raised, their contacts with other styles of life broadened, their dependence upon European goods established, any protest movement that could hold their allegiance had to help carry them over to new ground, *through anomie* to a new order.[28]

The situation is thus filled with both individual and cultural ambivalences, which help to account for the extremism of many of the Cargo Cults. "The severing of old ties and the rejection of old norms demand an enormous effort and engender a deep sense of guilt, hence much of the hysteria and the aggression. Many of the antinomian manifestations are a deliberate overthrow of the accepted norms, not in order to throw overboard all morality but in order to create a new brotherhood and a new morality."[29]

Cargo cults are by no means unalloyed countercultures. They vary too much among themselves and are too complex to be thus classified. Along with the "deliberate overthrow of the accepted norms" that Talmon refers to are efforts to rehabilitate the traditional cultures, programs of reform (increasingly taking a political form), some Chrisitan elements, and antiwhite sentiments mixed with a desire for goods introduced by white people. Insofar as outside cultures are the focus of their opposition, Cargo Cults are not, by my definition, countercultural; but those parts of their belief systems and rituals that invert the values and norms to which the participants have been socialized are. The empirical world does not shape itself nicely to our categories. We can learn a great deal, however, from the study of the various mixtures.

The religious situation of the United States is equally complex, with groups ranging from the traditional and orthodox to such thoroughly countercultural beliefs and practices as those of the Satanic groups we have discussed. Most readers of this book would probably agree that the following charcteristics of a religious group are wise adaptations to a pluralistic, modern, and rapidly changing society: It is reasonable in its relationship to the larger society and receptive to outside criticism; it is democratic in internal affairs; it will work with other groups in efforts to meet human needs; it is not dogmatic and obsessed with "cultic purity"; it is interested in interfaith dialogue and ecumenism. These are the characteristics of churches that are declining. Those that are growing, whether they be conservative and fundamentalist Christian churches or "new religions" from other traditions, do not fit that pattern. Referring to the former, Kelley noted that they "often refuse to recognize the validity of other churches' teaching, ordinations, sacraments." They observe unusual rituals and dietary customs. They persist in such "irrational behavior" as refusal to accept the ministrations of modern medicine—blood transfusions, for example. "They try to impose uniformity of belief and practice among members by censorship, heresy trials, and the like."[30]

One can scarcely call such beliefs and practices countercultural in democratic societies with freedom of religion. It may be a mistake to think of them even as alternatives. They may simply indicate the range of religious views in a pluralistic society—a range wide enough, ironically, to include intolerate assertion of ones own perspective and authoritarian control over religious organizations. They do have some countercultural quality, however, expressed by their opposition to the drift of the dominant American culture toward what they see as an utter lack of standards and moral anarchy (but seen by proponents as the expansion of freedom).

Insofar as the Supreme Court can be seen as speaking for the dominant culture, the range of religious alternatives has recently been widened. In the early 1960s the Court began a series of decisions that reinterpreted the legal status of various religious practices. The main tendency has been to shift them from illegal and countercultural to the category of acceptable alternatives, although not without continuing ambiguity.

As late as 1931, in *U.S.* v. *MacIntoch*, the Court stated, "We are a Christian people." In 1940 the expulsion from school of Jehovah's Witnesses children for refusal to take part in a ceremony of saluting and pledging allegiance to the flag was upheld (*Minersville School District*). Hundreds of attacks on Jehovah's Witnesses, it should be noted, occurred during the next few years. Three years later, however, the Court began to reverse itself. In 1963 it held that denial of unemployment compensation benefits to a Seventh Day Adventist who refused to work on Saturday, but who otherwise was eligible was unconstitutional (*Sherbert v. Verner*). Shortly thereafter religious conscientious objection to military service was upheld even if it was not based on belief in a supreme being (*U.S. v. Seeger*, 1965). In 1964 the California Supreme Court granted immunity against arrest for possession of peyote to Navajo Indian members of the Native American Church (*People v. Woody*).[31]

Despite these changes, the line between the legally acceptable and the religiously countercultural continues to be difficult to draw. Timothy Leary, who was convicted in 1966 for the illegal possession of marijuana, founded the League for Spiritual Discovery.[32] He was not successful, however, in getting the protection granted to the established religious community of Navajos, in the Woody case, extended to himself and his League. Leary's conviction was upheld by the Fifth Circuit Court. Although some serious legal criticisms were raised by this decision,[33] traditional Indian religious groups continue to be the exception to the general public and legal opposition to "psychedelic churches."

Joseph Damrell's study of the "Church of the Cosmic Liberty" makes clear the difficulty in American society (and undoubtedly in the West generally and in other societies) of bringing drug use into the framework of acceptable religious practices. He describes a small group of hippies who shared interest in drugs, the occult, and Hindu mysticism as they evolved from a unity built mainly around secular drug use and dealing into one built around meditation and "sacralized" drug use. At first, the "church," even after it had won official tax-exempt status, was largely a front for their drug activities, which they kept hidden. Gradually their sense of identity with Hindu belief and practice became dominant, until the founders "had come to see all psychedelic drugs, particularly marihuana, as a link to the divine, and themselves, as dispensers of these drugs, as sacred emissaries whom God had instructed to 'turn on' the world."[34] After a few years, however, the group gave up the definition of themselves as a church. Some of the new members, attracted by the hope of a church- protected drug scene, had little interest in the religious beliefs and practices; some of the founders were ambivalent, and their drug dealing and use continued to be illegal. Whether or not under the banner of the Church of the Cosmic Liberty, they remained countercultural.

Drug use is only one of the tensions between the principle of religious freedom and various beliefs and practices of the "new religions." As so often in the past,[35] deviant religions have, in several societies in recent years, experienced legal pressure and public attack. Roszak observes that the opposition comes from several different directions: "For the Christian establishment, much of this is whoring after alien antinomian gods. For conventional humanism, it is an affront to reason and a contemptible failure of nerve. For left-wing ideologues, it is a betrayal of social conscience, if not a sign of downright bourgeois decadence. For the mass media, it is a faintly sensational fad. For the majority of middle Americans, it is a shocking offense to good manners and common sense."[36] Roszak once shared these views but believes now that the new groups deserve and require a more sympathetic hearing.[37] This requires, however, a sense of the reasons for the opposition, an account of the practices and beliefs that are seen as particularly objectionable by the groups whom Roszak chides.

Undoubtedly the events in Jonestown, Guyana, in November 1978 have made it more difficult to examine this issue with reasonable objectivity. The murder of a Congressman, three newsmen, and a member of the People's Temple attempting to escape, followed by the suicide (and in some instances murder) of more than 900 members of the cult, sent a shock wave of dismay and bafflement throughout America.[38] The fact that similar events have happened before, in several different places, scarcely lessened the impact. Many people were already involved in an anticult movement—as either supporters or opponents—based on conflicting charges of brainwashing, indoctrination, kidnapping, and violations of religious freedom. Hence the Jonestown tragedy came into an already polarized scene.

In what various ways are the new religions countercultural? If some use drugs in search of enlightenment, others, such as the Meher Baba movement, Hare Krishna, and Maharaj Ji's Divine Light Mission tend to be ascetic. They illustrate well the dialectic within a dialectic that David Martin referred to. Most of the devotees of Hare Krishna, for example, having abandoned the religion of their families for hippiedom, have made another abrupt change. In place of hippie hedonism and the hang-loose ethic, they have accepted an ascetic life style; they also accept beliefs and practices significantly different from those of their parental religions. Not only drugs and alcohol, but tea, coffee, meat, and fish are prohibited. Sex is illicit except for procreation. Each member is expected to chant privately for sixteen rounds of his 107 prayer beads daily. They shave their heads and paint their faces and eleven places on their bodies with wet clay. Seeking a transcendental spiritual solution to their problems, they reject material success, the established educational institutions, and all authorities who seem involved in the materialistic society.[39]

Some of the leaders of new religions have been accused, and a few convicted, of fraud, of deceiving their members and the general public for private gain. Such actions, however, insofar as they occur, are not countercultural: They are hidden and aberrant, not carried out in the name of inverted values. I have not seen any comparisons of the rates of such illegalities and immoralities with the rates among businessmen, politicians, or other groups. Granted the lack of adequate information, the guesses we tend to make about the rates could make an interesting Rorschach test.

Claims or strong suggestions of Messiahship (for example by L. Ron Hubbard, Sun Myung Moon, and Moses Berg) contradict the religious beliefs of most people. Some do not accept the idea of a messiah; some believe that he appeared long ago; and others that he is still to come. Now, as at other times, those who claim their own messiahship contradict these beliefs.

Among the most important countercultural qualities of several of the new religions are their epistemological and cosmological beliefs. Scientology calls itself the science of knowing how to know. Rather than the "maybes" of fields generally called sciences, Scientology is "the science of certainty." "Scientology confronts the conventional world with a deviant reality of massive proportions."[40]

Don't just do something. Sit there!

Those Eastern religions that emphasize the attainment of enlightenment through silence, meditation, and yoga also challenge the prevailing Western beliefs about the ways to attain insight and knowledge. Perhaps more powerfully, the Buddhist-derived groups in particular contradict the prevailing Western conceptions of happiness and selfhood. The satisfaction of desire is not happiness; the goal is to transform desire, not to satisfy it. This belief is tied closely to conceptions of the self. The Buddha taught "that the principal cause of all human suffering and desolation is the deeply ingrained belief that there is such a thing as a self, or ego, that persists through time and change."[41] In the Western versions, the potential countercultural quality of these beliefs is muted. They are more neo than Oriental; the self is not pushed back, but affirmed.[42]

Several of the new religions are thought to be particularly countercultural in their methods of recruitment. Some people see these methods as raising questions of "who gets caught" rather than "who is converted," believing that sects and cults have powers of indoctrination sufficient to persuade almost anyone to participate and share their beliefs. "Barely a soul is immune to the pleas and promises of the 'new' religions," Stoner and Parke write, although I should add that they do not hold consistently to this view. Various studies have compared the conversion process in some of the new religions with the thought-control methods of the Chinese during the Korean War, using the work of Robert Lifton in *Thought Reform and the Psychology of Totalism*. Parallels between the Chinese indoctrination process and the activities of the Unification Church and Hare Krishna, for example, are not difficult to find, nor with the Jesus movement.[43] What is not often observed is that many of the same activities characterize fundamentalist churches generally, and to some degree all religious groups involved in conversion and revitalization, although usually with less intensity and self-consciousness. With a few changes of emphasis, one could take Lifton's conditions for thought control—such as milieu control, mystical manipulation, demand for purity, cult of confession, aura of sacred science, loading the language, dispensing of existence—and apply them to a wide variety of religious services.[44]

Opposed to the view that the power of recruitment and conversion techniques is most important is the argument that personality change in the new religions is due primarily to individuals' predispositions, their underlying anxieties and immaturity. Others emphasize the social context—the rapidity of social change, cultural vacuums, and harsh conflicts over public issues.

A field theoretical approach that combines the several influences seems to me essential. In a well-known model, Lofland and Stark describe a seven-step process that they apply to conversion to "an obscure millenarian perspective"—in fact, an early segment of the Unification Church:

"For conversion a person must:

1. Experience enduring, acutely felt tensions

2. Within a religious problem-solving perspective,

3. Which leads him to define himself as a religious seeker;
4. Encountering the [group] at a turning point in his life,
5. Wherein an affective bond is formed (or pre-exists) with one or more converts;
6. Where extra-cult attachments are absent or neutralized;
7. And, where, if he is to become a deployable agent, he is exposed to intensive interaction."[45]

The Lofland-Stark model is a valuable description of the personality and interactional factors involved. It leaves out, except by implication, the wider social and cultural context within which the interaction occurs. For our purposes, a simpler model can serve as a framework for an examination of the often harsh debate over the methods of conversion and retention used by some of the new religions. These factors interact in the process of conversion to a deviant religious perspective:

Social soil *x* individual propensity *x*
contact (opportunity) at a strategic time

This is a multiplicative, not an additive model, since absence of any one of the variables would prevent the activity from occurring. We must take the social context into account, because new religions are much more likely to develop at certain times than at others. Since some persons join and others do not, individual tendencies are involved. Those who have no contact with one of the new groups cannot participate, even if they are so inclined; nor are they likely to participate if contact comes at a time when they are closely tied to opposing networks.

It is easier to disregard this whole field of forces in favor of the view that "cults" (which has become something of a swear word) have great independent power. In recent years criticism of several of the new religions for their methods of recruitment, the extent to which they insulate their members from outside contacts, and the harshness with which they try to prevent apostasy has become especially strong. This reflects the extensive media coverage of the charges and countercharges and the belief, in a pluralistic setting, that some measure of tolerance is expected, not only for deviant religious groups but by them. Persons whose religious convictions and identities have become somewhat bland are often shocked at the severity of the belief, held in many sects and cults, that their way is the one true way. Those same persons may be deeply worried about the fuzziness of the cultural boundaries of their society, a worry that prompts them to use deviant groups as contrast conceptions.

Thus we have some who are saying: We are bringing faith back into the world; we have found the way and we take it seriously; we are willing to sacrifice for it, to be ostracized, to be misunderstood. If we draw a sharp line between ourselves and the unregenerate, it is partly to create a community within which we can practice our faith and partly to protect ourselves against persecution.

From the opponents, of course, we hear quite a different story: Children and young adults are deceived, seduced, and brainwashed into joining groups that invert the standards of their upbringing. Once inside, they are isolated and exploited, their individual identities nearly eliminated. The will to walk away from the group is often destroyed, but where it is not, they are prevented from leaving by physical coercion and fear. Ted Patrick, a professional "deprogrammer," is a well-known exponent of this view: "The cult movement is increasing by the day. . . . the worst disaster of all this is the takeover of the minds of our youth. All I can say is 'wake up, America.' "[46] "Jonestown may be a picnic," Jim Siegelman and Flo Conway have stated, compared with what might happen in other cult groups.[47] Several other works, some of them autobiographical, have dramatically described a process of enticement, conversion, alienation from family, desperate—and finally successful—parental efforts to liberate them from the cult, first physically and then by "deprogramming." Christopher Edward's *Crazy for God* illustrates well the personal accounts. He makes himself seem, whether or not by intent, to be quite naive and dependent. After several months in the Unification Church, he came to see the "sinister indoctrination process" that transformed him into a "subservient disciple."[48]

I have seen a film, produced by a fundamentalist church, that dramatizes similar material. It carried the message—a bit ironically to this somewhat jaded observer—that the cults were intolerant and authoritarian and ought to be exposed and constrained.

In addition to these two perspectives—those of the participants in nonconformist new religions and their anticult opponents—a third perspective is brought by those who neither condemn nor support the new groups, but wonder about the implications of the controversy for religious freedom and civil liberties. Harvey Cox puts the issue well:

> It is frightening to me to see people who are otherwise alert guardians of the First Amendment's guarantee of freedom of religious expression condoning the deprogrammers when we are all aware that such methods could also be used—and have been used—on Catholics, members of Christian sects and followers of other religious movements. . . . One wonders what these zealous defenders of psychological orthodoxy would have done wtih Jesus—whose parents considered him demented—or with . . . St. Thomas Aquinas, whose parents tried every device they knew to get him to renounce his religious vows.[49]

After the tragic events in Jonestown, a number of religious leaders expressed the fear, as Dean Kelley put it, that it would become "open season on the so-called cults." Shortly after the news came out of Guyana, "a television newscaster went to the Hare Krishna Temple in Manhattan and asked Romapada Das, the president of the temple: 'Do you hold suicide drills?' The follow-up question was: 'Well, if you did, how often would you practice them?' "[50]

Thomas Robbins and Dick Anthony, who are among the most active students of the cults and of the anticult movement, have skillfully stated the sociological perspective on the sources of opposition to countercultural religious groups. They interpret both the growth of deviant cults and the growth of opposition to them as part of a larger structural and normative crisis in America (and elsewhere, one might add). The cults act as surrogate extended families; they provide novel therapeutic and spiritual mystiques, giving meaning to social processes and experiences that traditional ideologies can no longer explain. "In so doing, however, they exploit the weaknesses of existing institutions (churches, nuclear families, psychiatry) and perhaps pose a threat to these institutions." The threat is neutralized and conventional views and institutions reaffirmed by allegations of brainwashing. "Counter-subversive campaigns defend and redefine Americanism."[51]

Such campaigns against deviant groups also reflect a "moral panic" brought on by status anxiety as well as by conflict of values.[52] From the perspective of those experiencing such distress, we have a new variety of witches among us. Exorcism reappears in an effort to allay anxiety and to reinforce the moral boundaries of society, but "men who fear witches soon find themselves surrounded by them."[53] And the fear, with its attached labels and persecution, helps to increase the very thing that is feared, as Erikson goes on to say. Some deviate more, when attacked as deviants, acting out the profferred role partly because their convictions are reinforced, but partly out of resentment, partly because it makes them more attractive to other alienated persons, and partly because their options have been narrowed by the designation.

Sociological analysis may seem irrelevant or foolish to those who have suffered personal distress as a result of cult activities. Harm does occur. The psychological pressure to join and remain in a group is sometimes severe when brought to bear on vulnerable persons. Physical coercion is not entirely absent, and many people have died. Charlatans, exploiters, and the mentally unstable are not entirely absent from among the cult leaders. Lewis and Rose Coser have described Jonestown as a "perverse utopia," a "greedy institution" that was isolated, tightly controlled, and total. The leader boasted that he dominated the group by his sexual power.[54] Power corrupts in religion as well as in politics, and the second phrase of Lord Acton's famous aphorism may be even more applicable to religion: Absolute power corrupts absolutely.

Yes, there are dangers, which require careful study. We need also to remember, however, that charges are not facts, that indictments are not convictions, and that convictions are of individuals, not of groups and movements. More importanty, the *absence* of deviant religious groups is also dangerous. In contexts with strong instigations toward deviance, with unimaginative churches, with parents who are indifferent, confused, or overwhelmed with their own problems, many varieties of countercultures will arise, most of them with serious risks involved. How does a society deal with those risks effectively? Not by frontal attack. That tends to be categorical, condemning all for the actions of a few. In recent months I have seen several such sweeping judgments of religious groups even from persons strongly opposed, on most matters, to prejudice. Frontal attack also promotes deviance amplification rather than a removal of the undesired behavior.

Rapidly changing societies that try to seal off their value confusion by creating witches succeed only in blinding themselves to the need for adaptations. We need some mix of defense of religious liberty, prosecution of criminal acts, and increase in our knowledge so that we will know better how to begin to reduce the destructive elements of a religious deviation.

Our knowledge is quite incomplete if we rely on apostates from the cults and their parents. Their accounts are essential but unrepresentative. The biographical materials tend to be sketchy, covering only selective slices of time, and the temptation of self-justification is not entirely avoided. In an earlier period, some enterprising individuals made a lucrative profession of being ex-communists. Perhaps a society welcomes back its prodigals and lets them eat of the fatted calf because their accounts help the rest of us to deal with our own confusion.

We have little information about those who stay in the groups willingly and the large number who have dropped out willingly and freely. Nor do we have much information that permits pre-membership comparisons with those who do not join. Many of the converts are seekers, looking for ways to deal with the pain of an unsatisfactory childhood seen against a (not unreasonable) picture of a confused and unjust society and a threatenting future. If those are among the causes of vulnerability to the destructive elements in the new religions (and other countercultures), is it not better to try to reduce them than to condemn their consequences? Better to light a candle, Eleanor Roosevelt was wont to say, than to curse the dark.

The consequences of the new religions for society are diverse. Some interpret their effects in a way similar to a common interpretation of "rituals of opposition": They are safety valves. "They translate the individual's enthusiasm for change into a kind of change that will be tolerated. . . . They are conservative, although often in radical guise."[55] In a related way, some see them as alternatives to radical politics or as routes out of drug-oriented groups. They are sufficiently radical and countercultural on the symbolic level to fill the need for protest against the dominant society, this argument goes, and to allow escape from violent political movements or "bummed-out" drug scenes without the feeling that one was simply falling back into the dull old grooves and capitulating to the power of a messed-up society. This is true not only of the groups that draw their themes from Oriental religions,[56] but also of the Jesus movement. In *Right On*, the newspaper of the Christian World Liberation Front, the following notice appeared:

> REWARD
>
> Jesus. Alias: The Messiah, Son of God, King of Kings, Lord of Lords, Prince of Peace, etc.
>
> Notorious Leader of a world-wide liberation movement.
>
> Wanted for the following charges:
>
> Practicing medicine and distributing food without a license.
>
> Interfering with businessmen in the Temple.
>
> Associating with known criminals, radicals, subversives, prostitutes, and street people.
>
> Claiming to have authority to make people God's children.
>
> Appearance: Unknown. Rumored to have no regard for conventional dress standards. . . .
>
> Beware—This man is extremely dangerous. His insidiously inflammatory message is particularly effective with young people who haven't been taught to ignore him yet. He changes men and sets them free.
>
> WARNING: HE IS STILL AT LARGE![57]

Streiker sees the Jesus Freaks as a "counter-counterculture"—a parody, not an example, of the youth movement. In many ways this is true, but the range is wide. The sharp criticism of society and of the established churches, the symbolism of hippie appearance, of "surfers for Jesus," and of "Karate for Jesus" invert many traditional standards.

Most of the new religious groups are small and fragile. This is particularly true of those that depart most widely from the traditional values and symbols of a society. Many of them fade away after a few years or when the leader dies. Others "denominationalize"; they reduce their isolation and the harshness of their opposition to the larger society. They begin, as Scientology has done, to get involved in programs of social reform.[58] They send some of their leaders-in-training to established schools of theology, as the Unification Church is doing.[59] The denominationalizing process can stop after a few changes; it can be reversed; or it can proceed to the point that the group loses most or all of its deviant quality and label.

Other groups evolve in the opposite direction. They become more isolated and more countercultural. Their deviance is amplified by a mixture of several forces: increased societal pressure, a growing hunger for power on the part of leaders, and selectivity of members, with the less alienated dropping out and the more alienated and distressed joining or remaining.

For a time, at least, a group may seem to be moving in both directions at once, with one branch adapting in some measure to the world around it while another pushes strongly against the dominant norms. That may be the case today, for example, among the Rastafarians in Jamaica. The subject of specialized study for decades, they have recently become a topic of public discussion and controversy. "From the beginning," George E. Simpson writes in his definitive work, "the normative system of Rastafarians has constituted a contraculture."[60] Based on the belief that Haile Selassie was a messiah, the movement spread first among the most deprived of Jamaica's population. In a less deviant form, however, Ras Tafari has begun to win converts among the more privileged.

One may be tempted to believe that it is the most deviant and extreme religious groups of the sorts we have been discussing, that will fade away. The temptation should be resisted, both on evidential and on evaluative grounds. Prior questions have to be answered: Is the culture they seek to reverse so monstrous that only a world turned upside down is worth pursuing? Are the accommodating groups becoming a part of the very establishment they sought to criticize and change?

Notes

1. See Guenter Lewy, *Religion and Revolution*, 1974, and J. Milton Yinger, *The Scientific Study of Religion*, 1970, chaps. 22-23.
2. Max Weber, *The Theory of Social and Economic Organization*, 1947, pp. 361-63. See also Rudolph Sohm, *Kirchenrecht*, 1892, pp. 26-28;

Bryan Wilson, *The Noble Savages*, 1975; Peter Berger, "Charisma and Religious Innovation: The Social Location of Israelite Prophecy," 1963; Edward Shils, "Charisma, Order, and Status," 1965; Guenther Roth, "Socio-Historical Model and Developmental Theory: Charismatic Community, Charisma of Reason, and the Counterculture," 1975; and Max Weber, *The Sociology of Religion*, 1963.

3. Peter Berger, *The Sacred Canopy*, 1967, p. 25. See also Clifford Geertz, "Religion as a Cultural System," 1966, pp. 1-46, and Mircea Eliade, *Cosmos and History,*, 1959.

4. Werner Stark, *The Sociology of Religion*, Vol. 2: *Sectarian Religion*, 1967, p. 129.

5. See W. H. C. Frend, *Martyrdom and Persecution in the Early Church*, 1965; T. R. Glover, *The Conflict of Religions in the Early Roman Empire*, 1932; Hans Lietzmann, *A History of the Early Church*, 1961; Eduard Meyer, *Ursprung und Anfange des Christentums*, 1962; and G. E. M. de Ste. Croix, "Why Were the Early Chrisians Persecuted?" 1963.

6. Norman Cohn, *Europe's Inner Demons: An Enquiry Inspired by the Great Witch-Hunt*, 1975, p. 12.

7. Ste. Croix, 1963, pp. 10, 21-24.

8. James A. Froude, *Short Studies on Great Subjects*, Vol. 4, 1917, pp. 361-431.

9. David Martin, *The Dilemmas of Contemporary Religion*, 1978, pp. 1, 12.

10. Hans Jonas, *The Gnostic Religion*, 1958, p. 250.

11. *Ibid.*, p. 95; see also Elaine Pagels, *The Gnostic Gospels*, 1979.

12. See James M. Robinson, *The Nag Hammadi Library in English*, 1977.

13. Y. Michael Bodeman, "Mystical, Satanic, and Chiliastic Forces in Countercultural Movements: Changing the World—or Reconciling It," 1974, p. 441. See also Randall Alfred, "The Church of Satan," in *The New Religious Consciousness*, Charles Glock and Robert Bellah, editors, 1976, pp. 180-202.

14. Edward Moody, "Magical Therapy: An Anthropological Investigation of Contemporary Satanism," in *Religious Movements in Contemporary America*, Irving Zaretsky and Mark Leone, editors, 1974, p. 355.

15. *Ibid.*, p. 362.

16. Anton LaVey, *The Satanic Bible*, 1969, p. 25.

17. Quoted by William Bainbridge, *Satan's Power*, 1978, p. 121.

18. *Ibid.*, pp. 119-24.

19. See Peter Berger, *Facing Up to Modernity*, 1977, pp. 83-94; David Felton, editor, *Mindfuckers: A Source Book on the Rise of Acid Fascism in America*, 1972; R. C. Zaener, *Our Savage God: The Perverse Use of*

Eastern Thought, 1975; and Kenneth Wooden, *Weeping in the Playtime of Others*, 1976, chapter 4.

20. See J. Gordon Melton, *The Encyclopedia of American Religions*, 1978.

21. John Lofland, *Doomsday Cult*, 1977, pp. 315, 320.

22. See Robert Wuthnow and Glen Mellinger, "Religious Loyalty, Defection, and Experimentation: A Longitudinal Analysis of University Men," 1978, and Robert Wuthnow in Glock and Bellah, 1976, pp. 267-93.

23. Seikyo Press, *Sōka Gakkai*, 1960.

24. See H. Neill McFarland, *The Rush Hour of the Gods: A Study of the New Religions in Japan*, 1967; Kiyomi Morioka and William Newell, *The Sociology of Japanese Religion*, 1968, chap. 6; Kiyomi Morioka, *Religion in Changing Japanese Society*, 1975; Ichiro Hori, *Folk Religion in Japan*, 1968; and Earl Babbie, "The Third Civilization: An Examination of Sokagakkai," 1966. For the influence of these religions in the United States, see Robert Ellwood, *The Eagle and the Rising Sun: Americans and the New Religions of Japan*, 1977.

25. See Edwin O. Reischauer, *The Japanese*, 1977; Ezra Vogel, *Japan as Number One*, 1979; Chie Nakane, *Japanese Society*, 1972; Kazuko Tsurumi, *Social Change and the Individual: Japan Before and After Defeat in World War II*, 1970; and Takie Lebra, *Japanese Patterns of Behavior*, 1976.

26. See William Cummings, "The Aftermath of the University Crisis," 1976.

27. Peter Worsley, *The Trumpet Shall Sound*, 1957. For other studies and interpretations of Cargo Cults, see Andrew Strathern, "The Red Box Money-Cult in Mount Hagen 1968-71," 1979 and 1980; Peter Lawrence, *Road Belong Cargo*, 1964; Yonina Talmon, "Pursuit of the Millennium: The Relationship Between Religious Change and Social Change," 1962; Lucy Mair, "Independent Religious Movements in Three Continents," 1959; Kenelm Burridge, *Mambu: A Melanesian Millennium*, 1960; Bryan Wilson, *Magic and the Millennium*, 1973, chap. 10; Vittorio Lanternari, *The Religions of the Oppressed: A Study of Modern Messianic Cults*, 1963, chap. 5; and Wilhelm Mühlmann *et al.*, *Chiliasmus und Nativismus*, 1961, pp. 165-89.

28. Yinger, 1970 (note 1 above), pp. 317-19.

29. Talmon, 1962, p. 141.

30. Dean Kelley, *Why Conservative Churches are Growing*, 1972, p. 26. See also W. Clark Roof, *Community and Commitment: Religious Plausibility in a Liberal Protestant Church*, 1977, and Martin Marty, *A Nation of Behavers*, 1976.

31. See Leo Pfeffer, "The Legitimation of Marginal Religions in the United States," in Zaretsky and Leone, 1974 (note 14 above), pp. 9-26. See also his *God, Caesar, and the Constitution: The Court as a Referee of*

Church State Confrontation, 1974, and John Burkholder, "The Law Knows No Heresy'," in Zaretsky and Leone, 1974, pp. 27-50.

32. Timothy Leary, *High Priest*, 1968. See also William Braden, *The Private Sea: LSD and the Search for God*, 1967, and Walter Clark, *Chemical Ecstasy: Psychedelic Drugs and Religion*, 1969.

33. Milton Konvitz, *Religious Liberty and Conscience*, 1968.

34. Joseph Damrell, *Search for Identity: Youth, Religion and Culture*, 1978, p. 76.

35. See David B. Davis, "Some Themes of Counter-Subversion: An Analysis of Anti-Masonic, Anti-Catholic, and Anti-Morman Literature," 1960. See also Sydney Ahlstrom in *Understanding the New Religions*, Jacob Needleman and George Baker, editors, 1978, pp. 3-22.

36. Theodore Roszak, *Where the Wasteland Ends: Politics and Transcendence in Postindustrial Society*, 1973, pp. xvi-xvii.

37. For a sampling of the literature on the "new religions," see Glock and Bellah, 1976 (note 13 above); Needleman and Baker, 1978; Lofland, 1977 (note 21 above); Zaretsky and Leone, 1974; Jacob Needleman, *The New Religions*, 1970; Robert Wuthnow, *Experimentation in American Religion*, 1978; Harvey Cox, *Turning East: The Promise and Peril of the New Orientalism*, 1977; Roy Wallis, *The Road to Total Freedom: A Sociological Analysis of Scientology*, 1977; James Richardson, editor, *Conversion Careers: In and Out of the New Religions*, 1978; William Bainbridge, *Satan's Power: A Deviant Psychotherapy Cult*, 1978; J. Stillson Judah, *Hare Krishna and the Counterculture*, 1974; Dick Anthony and Thomas Robbins, *In Gods We Trust: New Patterns in American Religious Pluralism*, 1980; Gini G. Scott, *Cult and Countercult*, 1980; David G. Bromley and Anson D. Shupe, Jr., "Financing the New Religions: A Resource Mobilization Approach," 1980; and Eileen Barker, "Living the Divine Principle: Inside the Reverend Sun Myung Moon's Unification Church in Britain," 1978.

38. See Marshall Kilduff and Ron Javers, *The Suicide Cult: The Inside Story of the Peoples Temple Sect and the Massacre in Guyana*, 1978; Charles Krause, *Guyana Massacre: The Eyewitness Account*, 1978; James Reston, Jr., *Our Father Who Art in Hell*, 1981; Ethan Feinsod, *Awake in a Nightmare*, 1981; and James T. Richardson, "People's Temple and Jonestown: A Corrective Interpretation and Critique," 1980.

39. See Judah, 1974; Francine Daner in Roy Wallis, editor, *Sectarianism*, 1975, pp. 53-69; Thomas Pilarzyk, "The Origin, Development, and Decline of a Youth Culture Religion," 1978; Thomas Robbins and Dick Anthony, "Getting Straight with Meher Baba," 1972; and Ken Kelley, "Blissed Out with the Perfect Master," 1973.

40. Wallis, 1977, p. 212.

41. Needleman, 1970, p. 26.

42. Cox, 1977. See also Emma Layman, *Buddhism in America,* 1976.

43. Carroll Stoner and Jo Anne Parke, *All Gods Children: The Cult Experience—Salvation or Slavery?*, 1977, pp. 118, 236-69. See also James Richardson, Mary Harder, and Robert Simmonds, "Thought Reform and the Jesus Movement," 1972.

44. See Robert J. Lifton, *Thought Reform and the Psychology of Totalism: A Study of "Brainwashing" in China,* 1961, pp. 419-37. See also James Beckford, "Through the Looking-Glass and Out the Other Side: Withdrawal from Reverend Moon's Unification Church," 1978.

45. John Lofland and Rodney Stark, "Becoming a World-Saver: A Theory of Conversion to a Deviant Perspective," 1965, pp. 874-75. For other valuable discussions, see Max Heirich, "Change of Heart: A Test of Some Widely Held Theories About Religious Conversion," 1977; Wuthnow, 1978, p. 18; and James Richardson and Mary Stewart in Richardson, 1978, pp. 24-42.

46. From an ad for *All God's Children*, by Stoner and Parke, 1977. See also Ted Patrick and Tom Dulack, *Let Our Children Go!* 1976.

47. Quoted in *Cleveland Plain Dealer*, May 10, 1979, p. 10A. See Flo Conway and Jim Siegelman, *Snapping: America's Epidemic of Sudden Personality Change*, 1979.

48. Christopher Edwards, *Crazy for God*, 1979. See also Barbara and Betty Underwood, *Hostage to Heaven*, 1979.

49. Cox, 1977, pp. 141-42.

50. *The New York Times*, December 3, 1978, p. 31.

51. Thomas Robbins and Dick Anthony, "Cults, Brainwashing, and Counter-Subversion, 1979, pp. 88-89. See also Anthony and Robbins, 1980 (note 37 above); and Thomas Robbins, "Even a Moonie Has Civil Rights," 1977.

52. See Stanley Cohen, *Folk Devils and Moral Panics*, 1972, and Anson Shupe, Jr., Roger Spielman, and Sam Stigall in Richardson, 1978, pp. 145-60.

53. Kai Erikson, *Wayward Puritans: A Study in the Sociology of Deviance*, 1966, p. 22. See also J. Milton Yinger, "Salvation and Witches in a 'Secular' Age," 1980.

54. Rose Laub Coser and Lewis Coser, "Jonestown as a Perverse Utopia," 1979.

55. Zaretsky and Leone, 1974 (note 14 above); p. xxxv.

56. Thomas Robbins, "Eastern Mysticism and Resocialization of Drug Users: The Meher Baba Cult," 1969, and Kelley, 1973 (note 39 above).

57. Quoted by Donald Heinz in Glock and Bellah, 1976 (note 13 above), pp. 153-54. See also Jack Balswick, "The Jesus People Movement: A Generational Interpretation," 1974; Robert Simonds in Richardson,

1978 (note 37 above), pp. 113-28; Donald Peterson and Armand Mauss in Charles Glock, editor, *Religion in Sociological Perspective*, 1973, pp. 261-79; Andrew Kopkind, "Mystic Politics: Refugees from the New Left," 1973; Lowell Streiker, *The Jesus Trip: Advent of the Jesus Freaks*, 1971; and Bodeman, 1974 (note 13 above).

58. Wallis, 1977 (note 37 above), pp. 254-55.

59. *The New York Times*, November 4, 1979, p. 28.

60. George E. Simpson, *Religious Cults in the Caribbean: Trinidad, Jamaica, and Haiti*, 1970, p. 227. For comments on similar movements, see Roy S. Bryce-Laporte, "Crisis, Contraculture, and Religion Among West Indians in the Panama Canal Zone," 1970.

Chapter Twelve

Countercultural Families and Sex Norms

". . . the irrevocable thing has happened . . . : The male-female collaboration to keep history mad . . . has become impossible to sustain."

Dorothy Dinnerstein, *The Mermaid and the Minotaur*, p. 276.

On no topic has the cultural debate of the last few decades been sharper than on issues dealing with the family and sex. The issues, of course, and the debate are ancient. They relate to the most fundamental requirements, problems, and dilemmas of human life—those dealing with sex and affection, the reproduction, protection, and socialization of children, and their placement in society. It is noteworthy, considering the inventiveness of the human species in cultural matters, that these basic elements of human experience are almost everywhere bound together. There is substantial evidence to support Murdock's contention, based on extensive cross-cultural study, that the family is universal. Even the nuclear family, he believed, was found everywhere, although often—and perhaps usually—as part of a larger kin structure.[1]

Spiro wondered whether the Israeli kibbutz might not be an important exception to the rule of the "universality of the family." He concluded that the kibbutz viewed structurally did constitute an exception, but viewed functionally and psychologically it did not. In the absence of the usual family structure, Spiro noted, "it has become necessary for the entire society to become a large extended family. But only in a society whose members perceive each other psychologically as kin can it function as a family."[2] In later years, he and others have observed, more traditional family structures have reappeared within kibbutzim. Whereas a near-identity of roles had, at first, been thought necessary to the attainment of sexual equality, Spiro found that a "counterrevolution" had occurred by the mid-1970s. Equality has come to be defined by both men and women more as equivalence: Equality exists so long as any differences of role are held to be equally valuable. Basic social, psychological, and biological parameters of existence had, in his judgment, determined the change. "As a cultural determinist, my aim in studying personality development in Kiryat Yedidim in 1951 was to observe the influence of culture on human nature or, more accurately, to discover how a new culture produces a new human nature. In 1975 I found (against my own intentions) that I was observing the influence of human nature on culture; alternatively, I was observing the resurgence of the old culture (in modern garb) as a function of those elements in human nature that the new culture was unable to change."[3]

Changes in practices in kibbutzim are scarcely a pure "experiment" that allows us to speak definitively. Spiro's studies do seem to indicate that social choices regarding family structures and male and female roles are affected by precultural conditions.

Whether or not the family is universal, however, is partly a matter of definition. What is a matter of observation, and not simply of definition, is the cultural linkage of sex, affection, reproduction, socialization, and the placement of children in society. The combination is not exclusive, of course. All of these activities are found outside the family. The issue being tested in many societies today, with little explicit recognition that we are testing it, is the degree to which they can be formally separated from the family. Is the family one of the great social inventions, within which a wide variety of needs are optimally satisfied? (Interdependent and partially conflicting values are seldom maximally satisfied.) Or is it outmoded, whatever its earlier value—a constrictive and inegalitarian relationship that blocks our full development? In between these two extreme questions are others that inquire about the changing circumstances to which families must adapt.

In some societies the traditional linkage of activities within the family remains strong. Deviation occurs, of course, but there is little *cultural* ambiguity; the values and norms are clear. In other societies, including most modern urban societies, the situation is more complicated. Alternative arrangements—in the anthropological sense of permitted, although not preferred, patterns—have become more common. Some of these alternatives may once have been countercultural, that is, to have been seen by the large majority not simply as different from but inversions of "true values." For example, divorce, with its frequent accompaniment of "serial monogamy" (which with equal validity might be called "serial polygamy"), has become widely accepted as an alternative in law, custom, and the codes of many religious groups. Other familial and sexual practices continue to be countercultural. They are proclaimed as right and good by proponents, although not without ambivalence and not without ambiguity in public discussion. In recent commentaries, the tendency has been to assume, without investigation, that changes in sexual and family practices have become acceptable alternatives or norms that are counterculturally supported.[4] Clear distinctions are seldom drawn among alternatives, countercultural practices, and aberrancy. Since these vary, however, in causes and consequences, such distinctions are essential.

The possibility and the desirability of the unlinking of the several functions of the family have been on the public agenda since the industrial revolution, with each generation facing a "crisis in the family." At first the crisis mainly reflected the continuing removal of economic, educational, and religious functions from the family. More recently questions related to sex, affection, reproduction, and child care have become more persistent. While the traditional family and sex ethic continues to be widely upheld (although less often in actions than in words), countercultural values are now being given increased support (perhaps also less often in actions than in words, particularly if one includes the words of those who profit by the belief in a sexual revolution and those of others who, from an opposite perspective, enjoy a delicious anger at the thought of such a revolution).

As in other institutions, countercultural values pertaining to the family and sex vary over a wide range. There are persons who, while envisaging drastic alternatives to the family, still emphasize the complexity, importance, and interdependence of its functions, for society as well as for individuals. The more thoroughly countercultural have a narrower focus: They see sexual "repression"—any inhibition on sexuality—as the fundamental barrier to human happiness, or they see the traditional family as the chief agent of coercion.

Those who hold the more extreme countercultural views do not necessarily agree among themselves. Indeed, they can be as sharply at odds with each other as they are with the dominant culture. Attacks on the family as a system of power[5] may contain little direct reference to the inversion of sexual norms, although radical feminist versions that make male domination the basic form of coercion and men "implacable enemies" carry the implication for some that autosexuality, lesbianism, or celibacy, not heterosexuality, is preferred. In a fascinating variation on the sex-and-politics connection (against which Lenin spoke so sharply), some feminists have expressed an antisex, antifamily connection with politics which also, I expect, would have made Lenin distraught. Certainly the theme of a "revolutionary in every bedroom," rather than in every boardroom, makes some contemporary radicals distraught. Jean Elshtain sees it as a "politics of displacement, which erodes personal life even as it vitiates the emergence of a genuine public life."[6] The inversions of authority structures and values that she seeks include those based on sexuality and the family, but not to the disregard of those in economics and politics, and not at the cost of disregarding female-male mutualities. Dorothy Dinnerstein also emphasizes the mutuality, with reference to both negative and positive outcomes. Her reference to "male-female collaboration to keep history mad," quoted above, is connected with a sharp critique of the predominant family and sexual values. She implicates female-dominated childhoods with male rule of the world and all of its unhappy consequences. She sees only further madness, however, in the removal of permanent adult commitments to childhood and attacks on the humanizing effects of "stable, longstanding, generation-spanning primary groups."[7]

Those for whom inversions of sexual norms and values are of primary interest may or may not be concerned with the family as an institution needing drastic reorganization. It is the repression of sex, not the repression of the creativity and influence of females (or of everyone), that they see as the more onerous. The release of female sexuality may be acclaimed, but male sexism is also a prominent if usually unrecognized theme. Although marriage is not regarded as a permanent and exclusive bond, it is sometimes argued that "swinging sex" and more open marriages can improve the quality of the relationship.

Thus many groups, for rather widely differing reasons, are trying to turn the familial, marital, and sexual world upside down. The model of the nuclear family is not only under attack, it is difficult to attain even among those who accept it, for a variety of structural and cultural reasons. In a period of rapid social change it is a less successful socializer, at least by traditional means. As Margaret Mead so often said, parents cannot effectively prefigure the adult lives of their children if circumstances continually shift.[8] Indeed, children may postfigure the lives of their parents, with the result that there is imitation down the age ladder as well as up. When parental models are brought into question by the speed of change, the more experimental attitudes of youth take on added strength. This influence was accentuated in the United States and many other societies during the 1965-80 period by the unusually large cohorts of youth.

The extent of the shift from prefiguring to postfiguring has been exaggerated in my judgment. Powerful continuities in values, interests, and motives still flow along the family stream.[9] Nor is the de-authorization of older persons, in Lewis Feuer's term, a new phenomenon. Nevertheless, this is one of the periods during which discontinuities in socialization are of great importance.

Family institutions have also been strongly affected by the social movements seeking to build more egalitarian societies. No institutions have escaped the influence of the numerous democratic, socialist, and civil rights movements. Attacks on male dominance, on sexual inequality, and on authoritarian control over children have become part of these movements, although belatedly. Insofar as the dominant family culture is still patriarchal, the attacks are carried on in the name of countercultural standards.

What, then, are some of the consequences of such developments for familial and sexual values and norms? We need to be aware that what is often called a sexual "revolution"—a centuries-long process that has moved, now rapidly, now slowly[10]—has extensively changed the dominant values against which countercultural values must be measured. The evolutionary changes have been more extensive than today's "sexual radicals" are willing to admit (they need the picture of a highly restrictive, repressive society) and more basic than traditionalists are willing to grant. Nevertheless, the modal view still strongly influenced by religion, law, and custom remains in sharp contrast with the sexual standards proclaimed by a long succession of counterculturalists. William Blake's "startling inversions of the erotic tradition"[11] are as startling today as they were two hundred years ago. "Sooner murder an infant in its cradle than nurse unacted desires," he wrote, with poetic license, in *The Marriage of Heaven and Hell*. It is reason, not desire, that leads to human ruin. "The road of excess leads to the palace of wisdom."

I will not trace the long story of reversals of prevailing sexual ethics, a story that goes back in the West at least to medieval and early modern religious sects (although the accounts of their nonconformity did not suffer from understatement from the pens of their opponents or the imaginations of their contemporaries).[12] Nearly two centuries ago, Blake was part of a Romantic movement that challenged prevailing views of sex and marriage. Its influence continues to the present.

Several of the nineteenth-century communes were more countercultural in their view of the family and sex than in most other ways. Perhaps the celibacy that was the preferred pattern among the Shakers, Rappites, and others can better be regarded as an alternative than as a countercultural norm. The "Complex marriage" of the Oneida community, Mormon polygyny, and the "free love" of Joseph Warren's Modern Times community, however, were clear reversals of the dominant sexual and family ethic. Robert Owen was more pluralistic in his attitudes, but like many other founders of communes he associated the established family pattern with other insitutions that he saw as coercive. In a Fourth of July oration in 1826, he spoke of "a Trinity of most monstrous evils that could be combined to inflict mental and physical evil, . . . private, or individual property—absurd and irrational systems of religion—and marriage, founded on individual property combined with some one of these irrational systems of religion."[13]

This list of reversals could be greatly extended, of course. Challenges to the dominant family institutions and sexual patterns have become most intense, however, in the twentieth century, influenced by, although often drastically modifying, Freud's perspectives.

Interpretations of Freud vary enormously. Those whose theories and values have been significantly influenced by his work (which means most of us), would agree that he emphasized the decisive role of sex not only in the lives of individuals but in society as well. How that emphasis is interpreted and its effects spelled out, however, and how it is valued—whether it is used to support the established culture or to shape a counterculture—differ greatly from person to person. Some see Freud as essentially a conservative who argued, perhaps with tears in his eyes, that only by the repression of sexual energy and its sublimation can the creative tasks of civilization be carried forward. Others see Freud as a liberal individualist who emphasized the cost of that repression as well as its necessity. He was on the side, Philip Rieff argues, neither of a domineering superego nor of an irrational id. He sought ways to protect some small space between them, a space within which ego, the governing self, could develop, using the resources of both superego and id, but not being controlled by them.[14]

Neo-Freudians, of whom Karen Horney and Erich Fromm have been the most influential, modified Freud by holding that it was not society as such, politics as such, but certain kinds of society that are repressive. By identifying and learning to reduce the sources of *The Neurotic Personality of Our Time* we can begin to build a *Sane Society*, to use two of their titles.

Other students and critics of Freud find this modification inadequate. Geza Roheim, Wilhelm Reich, and, most influentially among recent counterculturalists, Herbert Marcuse go further: Not only is sexual repression unnecessary, it is destructive of civilization.[15] Marcuse and Reich see it as a principal mechanism of political domination, thus seeking to link Freud and Marx. In *Eros and Civilization*, Marcuse developed the concept of "surplus repression," matching Marx's concept of "surplus value." He thus implied that some repression may be needed but that society vastly overdoes it. These members of the "Freudian left," as Robinson calls them,[16] joined with D. H. Lawrence and other authors to emphasize sexual pleasure as the ultimate pleasure, repression the ultimate disaster. This point of view is vividly expressed by Philip Slater:

> The idea of placing restrictions on sexuality was a stunning cultural invention. . . . In it man found a source of energy which was limitless and unflagging—one which enabled him to build his empires on earth. By the weird device of making his most plentiful resource scarce he managed, after many millennia, to make most of his scarce ones plentiful. On the negative side, however, men have achieved this miracle by making themselves into donkeys, pursuing an inaccessible carrot.[17]

Suppose, after building our "empires on earth" at great sacrifice, we find them abhorrent, their achievements empty? Suppose, in response to those feelings, some no longer want a society of do-ers, but one of be-ers, not one of conquerers, but one of experiencers? Such a belief involves a sharp reversal of values, including—if the Freudian view of sublimation is accepted—those related to sex.

In this context the Judaic-Christian tradition, which has been the basic source of the culture of family and sex in the West, undergoes still more pressure for change. To the primordial difficulty in containing sexuality according to some cultural standard, add such influences as the following: the belief that sexual controls are part of the repression characteristic of the whole institutional structure; the development of reliable contraceptation; the reduction of the power of personal social controls generally in a mobile and less personalized urban world; a rise in the expectation of pleasure; and a general shift toward greater tolerance and cultural pluralism.

Influences such as these, some of them generations old, have had numerous cultural, and not simply behavioral, consequences. The legal and religio-moral taboos on homosexuality have been significantly modified, so that in more urbane circles at least it can perhaps best be characterized as an alternative. Even where that has not occurred, for some persons it has become countercultural—that is, defended normatively against the dominant values—rather than being experienced by homosexuals themselves and being regarded by others as aberrant. On a much smaller scale the number of polygynists in the United States has grown, claiming religious support despite the illegality of their marriages, to twenty or thirty thousand.[18] To the larger society they are clearly countercultural. Nevertheless they are widely tolerated, except when intersect violence occurs. (It is unlikely that polyandry would be equally tolerated, an indication that countercultures often have some implicit cultural support—male supremacy in the case of polygyny.) On an even smaller scale, the incest taboo, so nearly universally regarded as fundamental to human societies, is occasionally opposed, its inflexibility lamented.[19]

By far the most widespread challenges to traditional sexual standards, however, are those involving the norms and values governing premarital and extramarital sexual activity. In an effort to invert what they see as the prevailing sexual values, counterculturalists regard the problem as one of eliminating repression. The release of an energy that is creative, life-giving, bonding, and pleasurable is important not only in its own terms but also as a "wedge for reorienting all human relations."[20] Sex becomes the road to salvation. When faith in other roads leading to some promised land is shaken, "the search for an orgasm more apocalyptic than the one which preceded it," as Norman Mailer put it, may take on credibility and salience. This is especially true among youth who are fearful of their own and society's repression of their sexuality, to which they have been alerted not only by their own feelings but also by the great wave of public attention. It is true also among older persons who are fearful, beyond all need, of their bodies' repression. What better news than that sex is not only pleasurable and permitted but the very road to salvation and the good society?

Perhaps the amazing thing is not that this message gets a great deal of attention; makes heroes; sells books, magazines and theater tickets; and finds expression in a few clubs, communes, and commerical enterprises, but that it has not brought about a sexual revolution. In the United States, at least, the changes that have occurred, and they have been substantial, have been mainly within the personalized frame. A few years ago headlines stated that the number of unwed couples had doubled since 1970. The stories beneath the headlines carried the more prosaic information that the new, larger number constituted less than 2 percent of all households and that a significant proportion of couples confirmed the arrangement later by marriage. In some college settings, to be sure, perhaps as many as one-third have, by the time of graduation, participated in a temporary arrangement.[21] Among a national American sample of more than two thousand twenty to thirty year-old males, 18 per cent said that they had cohabited for six months or more. The rate among college students was 15 per cent. Two-thirds of the total (12 per cent) had had only one nonmarital relationship.[22]

This practice of what one might call "going steadier" is part of the more extensive increase in premarital sexual activity that began decades ago, with rapid change in the 1920s and thereafter. Sex-with-affection has been a guiding principle for many persons, indicating that the increase has been strongly influenced by prevailing values.[23] Depersonalized sex has also increased but is much less often defended as right. It is more likely to be regarded as aberrant than nonconformist. That may not be true of what Jurich and Jurich call "nonexploitative permissiveness without affection," which is accepted as a standard by some of their respondents.[24] In an imprecise estimate, I would regard it as countercultural, in many instances, by the criteria we have discussed. Until the last few decades that was also true of "permissiveness with affection"—one of the four standards of premarital sex discussed by Reiss. That now seems more nearly an alternative, as I have used that term. The double standard, on the other hand, has moved in the opposite direction, although behavior has probably changed less than the standard. Support for greater latitude in sexual behavior for men has not, traditionally, been given full cultural approval, but it has been a cultural alternative. In recent years, however, there is some evidence that the dual system is being challenged.[25] The double standard has become or is becoming countercultural; those who defend it contradict the prevailing view.

George Bernard Shaw once remarked that marriage was so popular because it combined the maximum of temptation with the maximum of opportunity. Although the advantages in the combination have been reduced in recent years (nonmarital temptation and opportunity have both gained), marriage retains its popularity. Divorce rates have increased; one-third of American couples will divorce, if present rates continue. Two-thirds will not, however, and a majority of persons remarry. In a nationwide sample of men, three-fourths cite marriage as "the ideal sex life."[26] Extramarital sex tends to be carried on secretively with only a small proportion acclaiming it in the name of countercultural values or regarding "mate-swapping" as acceptable.[27]

By the mid-1970s, some headlines were suggesting that events were "reversing the sex revolution." If Henry Miller had sold millions of copies of his books, Barbara Cartland had sold tens of millions of her romantic novels, with their stories of virtuous heroines protecting their honor. When one cannot "be more nude than nude," she remarked, "the 'fig-leaf' becomes attractive and virtue replaces evil."[28]

There may not, in fact, have been much of a pendulum swing back toward a more conservative sexual ethic. It is difficult to separate behavior and value changes from change in media attention. Having examined and to some degree created the picture of a sexual revolution, the media may have reduced its newsworthiness. Innocence now may make good copy, but evolutionary change seems the more likely reality.

Some counterculturalists of sex see no alternative to the (partially imaginary) uptight, rigid, repressive sexual ethic that they see as dominant but complete freedom. If this point of view has been adopted and acted upon more frequently in recent decades, it is not because society has become more sexually repressive. In fact, the reduction of repression has raised expectations of fulfillment through sex even while we are learning, yet once again in human experience, how closely entwined sexual fulfillment is with other values.

By one figure of speech or another, most societies teach that it does little good to back away from the claws of a tiger only to fall into the jaws of a crocodile. Do the development of new family structures and the release of sexual inhibitions solve our problems or only bring new ones to the fore? By stating a few questions, I may suggest the complexity and importance of this issue:

If sex is a value unto itself, how do we avoid self-centered pursuit of pleasure? How do we avoid exploitation and the sexism so prominent, for example, in the work of Mailer and Miller? How do we deal with feelings of abandonment and jealousy? One cannot humanize and personalize sex more fully without facing the reality of these emotions. How do we escape the trap of hedonic relativism—equal pleasure for the sexually sophisticated requiring ever stronger or more exotic stimuli? When the level of pleasurable input increases, to repeat Donald Campbell's comment, do we simply shift our criterion level upward "so that once again experience is scored as one-third pleasure, one-third pain, and one-third blah"?[29] In a similar vein Durkheim discussed the "morbid desire for the infinite" which he saw associated with anomie—normlessness—in sexual as in other matters. In the absence of the "salutary discipline" of culture, "new hopes constantly awake only to be deceived, leaving a trail of weariness and disillusionment behind them."[30]

What is the relationship between sex and aggression—between the release of sex from cultural inhibitions and the decrease or increase of tendencies toward aggression? Freud is not without ambiguities on this question, sometimes linking the two, as when he argued that on the unconscious level there is an aggressive element in sexual behavior, and somtimes seeing them as competitors for "instinctual energy."[30] Harold Lasswell, following a line of argument from Plato, emphasized the link, seeing it as the result not of some basic human nature but of specific social conditions. Excessive attention to the value of wealth leads, in the younger generations, to self-indulgence and powerful demands for immediate enjoyment. Extremes of sexual and aggressive impulse are released in the absence of an ego ideal and a strong superego.[31]

Those who have made the release of sex from social restrictions the very measure of progress take the opposite point of view. In *Eros and Civilization* Marcuse declared that the release of erotic energies meant the reduction of aggression. He also observed, however, that aggressiveness was "rampant throughout contemporary industrial society,"[32] leading inevitably, from his point of view, to the conclusion that the contemporary relaxation of sexual mores was spurious.

It is not clear to me how one would determine that relaxation was genuine, rather than spurious, in a way so definitive that one could avoid Marcuse's circular reasoning. He would argue that a true release of human sexuality implies also a transformation of the libido, "from sexuality constrained under genital supremacy to erotization of the entire personality,"[33] This has not been accomplished, in his view, by the "partial and localized sexuality" now more permissively granted, hence aggression is not reduced.

There is a mystical and utopian appeal to the idea of "the erotization of the entire personality" and to the way Marcuse connected it with his Marxian views—"to make the human body an instrument of pleasure rather than labor"—and to his critique of international aggression. The less philosophically inclined, however, do not follow his nice distinctions. Those distinctions are partly caught up in "make love, not war," perhaps the most insightful and inciteful slogan of the 1960s. At the farthest extreme, however, the countercultural message that the oppressive and repressive sexual ethic must be turned upside down to create a new world is interpreted in a quite old-fashioned way. Some of the communards with whom Rigby talked, for example, used the language of protest, "rejecting the repressive morality of the straight society," but also indicated that they were in a commune "because it was the one place where you could be guaranteed an easy lay every night."[34]

Laboratory study of the links between sex and aggression suffers from lack of "realism" but its results confirm what we see in the headlines: The links are both close and complicated.[35] Under some conditions the release of sexual inhibitions increases the likelihood of aggressive behavior; under other conditions it decreases that likelihood. We will be wise to avoid proclamations that they are inevitably inversely related or that they are positiviely related. These are violent times, even as they are times when sexual inhibitions have been significantly released. Whether humankind is capable of the sexual exuberance envisaged by the counterculturalists while also moving toward other values and avoiding aggression has yet to be determined.

Only slowly has one of the most important questions emerged: What is the meaning of changing sexual attitudes and practices and of countercultural family structures for any children affected?[36] Roszak speaks of the "spontaneous and unconditional loyalty" at the core of the kinship system—a loyalty that he believes is "welded into the biological continuity of life."[37] He realizes, of course, that the loyalty may be lacking or may be misdirected. Parenting can narrow the choices of children at a time when drastic social changes are requiring flexibility. Thus he sees the need for an "open childhood" that leaves children free to weave "an original fabric." It is not clear just what this means. I doubt that he would think the *Children of the Counterculture* described by Rothchild and Wolf are free, although they are being raised in the name of freedom. Freedom from constraints is not synonymous with freedom to strive effectively for either self-selected or community goals.

There is substantial evidence that the blending of love and discipline is a vital process in the development of self-loving, other-loving persons.[38] In some ways, however, this is more difficult within the bonds of small and socially isolated conjugal families. Some of the impetus to the development of new family patterns comes from the desire to break the "dependency hang-up," as Beatrice Whiting calls it, the resting of so much emotional weight on a few persons. New support systems are sought. "In some cases they seek to break the exclusive dyadic intimacy of the marital bond by encouraging the exchange of sexual partners. They all wish to embed the nuclear family in a larger household unit than the nuclear family or to organize some type of microcommunity." This requires, however, Whiting goes on to say, new habits and values that are not easily acquired; "living in a viable microcommunity requires some of the traits valued by traditional Kikuyu—an ability to share, to cooperate with people beyond the confines of the nuclear household, to feel responsible for others, to value interdependence rather than independence."[39]

The experiences of children raised in countercultural environments are as diverse as those of adults, but the comments of Rothchild and Wolf on the effects of a "free school" describe one common pattern—what might be called "ambivalent neglect." The "educational vision of the free school began and ended with what was once called recess. There were no courses of any kind, no schedule, no grades, no permanent records, and no material to cover. The children spent the day milling around doing what they felt like doing—setting fires with large magnifying glasses, chasing each other on tricycles, building forts out of lawn chairs, trying (and mostly failing) to read comic books. The fear of stifling the children, of 'laying a trip on them' was so great that education became the absence of teaching." The parents' ambivalence, however, was great: "They valued their children's freedom now more than their chance to get into Harvard later. An exact reversal of the sputnik age." Yet most of the parents were trying to get the children to cram for traditional studies at night, wanting them to spend their days "in the new culture and still get into Harvard." This "fantasy of anarchy" could be abandoned at the first sign of trouble; the "flirtation with freedom for their children" was given up after a year.[40]

In the raising of children as in other countercultural activities, persons spend a great deal of energy. In the effort to develop a coherent life style, they repress motives and values that contradict their dominant ones. This is done by exalting interests that express their dominant values, despite hidden doubts, and by caricaturing the weaknesses of the values they are trying to repress, despite hidden acceptance. Collective support for the countercultural values aids in the repression; but if the hidden values are also shared, they press for recognition. Countercultural parents face a complicated situation: Insofar as they are ambivalent, they cannot wholeheartedly train their children for the new values (so insist on homework at night). Even when they are quite certain what their values are, they can train their children to accept them only by becoming quite traditional parents, denying the open childhood. (This is a dilemma similar to that of religious sects. Many become churches with a training apparatus complicated enough to teach the next generation that individual free choice, not churchly doctrine and ritual, is the road to salvation.)

Today, greater emotional weight is placed on the family at the same time that community supports have declined. "All we have done is to resign ourselves to our domestic isolation and call it 'privacy.' "[41] Renewed interest in communes and other alternatives involving families partly expresses a refusal to accept that resignation. In them one sees the intent to resolve a great dilemma: The family is experienced as constricting, yet the lack of an emotionally supporting group is equally distressing. Hendin describes a student who dreamed of being forced to eat an apple pie as big as a house. His fantasy of a happy world was one where he could feel hungry. Persons who believe that they are only agents of their parents' interests—how to look, what to do—rebel by not looking or acting by parental standards. They do not thus escape the need for emotional support. Writing from his clinical experience, Hendin observes that people "who have experienced such despair in their families that they feel required to eliminate their family from their emotional lives are forever tied to their parents by the love they never got, by numbness, depression, and inability to feel pleasure and love for a person, a cause, a career."[42]

What better way to try to resolve the dilemma of feeling both emotionally surrounded and emotionally alone than to join an antifamily family that is at the same time a small community and quasi-family. Some communes and other groups are "antifamily" in the sense of variously opposing such traditional standards as those regarding the place of children, monogamy, and the balance of emphasis on achievement or acceptance. Yet attacks on the family are strongly connected with longing for a family.[43]

The family is no more immune from the stresses and strains of civilizational change than are other institutions. It is difficult to doubt the need for new thoughts and practices, whether designed to protect traditional families against those stresses and strains or to create new forms. We now have new forms in abundance—unintended "experiments" with the limits and possibilities in primary groups and intimate experiences. Because participants are self-selected, however, it is difficult to assess the long-run implications of communes, group marriages, and other countercultural variations on traditional family and marriage models. Some of the groups may work well because those drawn in are motivated by strong religious views or by unusually thoughtful concern for the contemporary difficulties in matters related to sexuality, families, and the raising of children. Other groups may work poorly because members are retreating from or rebelling against painful experiences more than they are attracted to new standards. Clayton and Voss found, for example, that among the young males in their national sample, those who were or had been involved in a nonmarital liason were more likely than others to have used illegal drugs.[44] Lyness, Lipetz, and Davis found that men living with their women friends had less trust and respect for them than had men for women with whom they were "going steady."[45]

It is well known that "experiments" that seem to work at first prove ineffective when less dedicated, less highly motivated persons become involved. We need also to note, however, that experiments that seem to fail may simply be showing that the self-selection process drew in persons for reasons extraneous to the experiments' aims. Persons less burdened with anger or self-doubt or ambivalence might make them work.

One additional question can serve as a summary of these comments on possible consequences of inverting the dominant sexual standards. Are such issues as I have suggested, in connection with the degree and kind of social control of sex, swept away when sexual experience becomes part of a religious view? Religious sexuality is part of many ancient creeds. It appears today, with or without theological interpretations, as the center of a belief in the apocalyptic transformation of the human condition by freeing the body from repressions. Based on tantric sources, a sect with Hindu and Buddhist elements, led by Rajneesh Chandra Mohan expresses that belief in more mystical terms than are common in the West. Through Tantra, says Swami Anand Alok, a Rajneesh disciple, one attains the "transformation of sexual energy to a sense of communion with the world." The role of the partner is not one of dependence or permanence "but that of a temporary avenue to a higher consciousness, ideally reaching a 'oneness' with the universe, or 'cosmic orgasm.' "[46]

Twenty-five hundred years ago, Jeremiah protested the worship of Astarte—the cult of sacred sexuality—not so much, or at all, Peter Berger observes, because of the sex, but because making a religion of "voluptuous ecstasy" meant moral betrayal. "Those who offer cakes to the queen of heaven are the same ones who oppress the weak and who shed the blood of the innocent . . .; there is not much voluptuousness in taking care of widows and orphans."[47]

Today's "sacred sexuality" takes many forms, from Brown's overtly religious celebration to more secularized versions in various therapeutic groups, from those of Wilhelm Reich to some varieties of "sensitivity training." Berger is no Jeremiah; "there are worse things in our time that Astarte Rediviva." It is *sacred* sexualtiy that troubles him: sex as salvation. "In a world of mass murder and mass starvation, of unprecendented terror, odious tyrannies, and the threat of nuclear holocausts, there is something obscene about an order of priorities that starts off with bigger and better orgasms."[48]

The continuing preoccupation with the crisis in family institutions and with sex in industrial societies lends weight to Focault's judgment that trends in recent years have not so much lifted sexual repression (which in any event has been exaggerated) as lifted repression from talk about and study of sex. These have had the ironic effect of leading to a rationalization of emotional life, contributing to mechanization, compulsion, and the concern for technique.[49] The total effect has scarcely been liberating.

Notes

1. George Murdock, *Social Structure*, 1949.
2. Melford Spiro, "Is the Family Universal?" 1954, p. 846. See also his *Kibbutz: Venture in Utopia*, 1955 (1971), and *Children of the Kibbutz*, 1958 (1975).
3. Melford Spiro, *Gender and Culture: Kibbutz Women Revisited*, 1979, p. 106. In an important paper, Alice Rossi describes a shift somewhat similar to Spiro's in her own thinking. She laments the tendency to confuse equality with identity and diversity with inequality— "where age and sex are concerned, diversity is a biological fact, while equality is a political, ethical, and social precept." Alice Rossi, "A Biosocial Perspective on parenting," 1977, p. 2.
4. See Gay Talese, *Thy Neighbor's Wife*, 1980, and Sam Keen, "A Voyeur in Plato's Cave," 1980. There is little evidence, from these reports, of the extent to which the sexual practices they describe are countercultural or aberrant.
5. See Shulamith Firestone, *The Dialectic of Sex: The Case for Feminist Revolution*, 1971.
6. Jean B. Elshtain, "Feminists Against the Family," 1979, p. 497.
7. Dorothy Dinnerstein, *The Mermaid and the Minotaur*, 1976.
8. Margaret Mead, *Culture and Commitment*, 1978. See also David Riesman, *The Lonely Crowd*, 1961.
9. For a sampling of relevant studies, see Bruce Biddle, Barbara Bank, and Marjorie Marlin, "Parental and Peer Influence on Adolescents," 1980; Denise Kandel and Gerald Lesser, *Youth in Two Worlds*, 1972; Otto Klineberg *et al.*, *Students, Values, and Policies: A Crosscultural Comparison*, 1979, chap. 6; William Westley and Nathan Epstein, *The Silent Majority*, 1969; Philip Converse and Howard Schuman, "Silent Majorities and the Viet Nam War," 1970; and Joseph Adelson, "What Generation Gap," 1970.
10. See Michel Focault, *The History of Sexuality*, Vol. 1, 1977, and Carl Degler, *At Odds: Woman and the Family in America from the Revolution to the Present*, 1980.
11. Diane Christian in *The Reversible World*, Barbara Babcock, editor, 1978, p. 117.
12. For a variety of views, see Robert Lerner, *The Heresy of the Free Spirit in the Later Middle Ages*, 1972; Norman Cohn, *The Pursuit of the Mil-*

lennium, 1970; and Jeffrey Russell in *On the Margin of the Visible: Sociology, the Esoteric, and the Occult*, Edward Tiryakian, editor, 1974, pp. 179-89.

13. Quoted by Arthur E. Bestor, Jr., *Backwoods Utopias*, 1950, p. 222. See also Raymond Muncy, *Sex and Marriage in Utopian Communities: Nineteenth Century America*, 1974; Rosabeth Kanter, *Commitment and Community: Communes and Utopias in Sociological Perspective*, 1976; Andrew Rigby, *Alternative Realities*, 1974a; and Benajamin Zablocki, *The Joyful Community*, 1971.

14. Philip Rieff, *Freud: The Mind of the Moralist*, 1959.

15. Géza Roheim, *Psychoanalysis and Anthropology*, 1950; Wilhelm Reich, *The Sexual Revolution*, 1945; and Herbert Marcuse, *Eros and Civilization*, 1966.

16. Paul Robinson, *The Freudian Left: Wilhelm Reich, Géza Roheim and Herbert Marcuse*, 1969.

17. Philip Slater, *The Pursuit of Loneliness*, 1971, p. 84.

18. *The New York Times*, October 9, 1977, pp. 1, 80.

19. Benjamin DeMott, "The Pro-Incest Lobby," 1980. See also the letters in reference to his papers in *Psychology Today*, June 1980, p. 7.

20. Morris Dickstein, *Gates of Eden: American Culture in the Sixties*, 1977, p. 81. Dickstein is discussing Norman Brown, Norman Mailer, and Paul Goodman. In a somewhat similar vein, Tom Wolfe, referring to the publisher of *Suck*, observed, "Whatever it had been for him once, sex had now become a religion, and he had developed a Theology in which the orgasm had become a form of spiritual ecstasy." Tom Wolfe, "The 'Me' Decade and the Third Great Awakening," 1976, p. 38.

21. Eleanor Macklin, "Heterosexual Cohabitation Among Unmarried College Students," 1972.

22. Richard Clayton and Harwin Voss, "Shacking Up: Cohabitation in the 1970s," 1977.

23. See Ira Reiss, *The Social Context of Premarital Sexual Permissiveness*, 1967.

24. A. P. Jurich and J.A. Jurich, "The Effect of Cognitive Moral Development upon the Selection of Premarital Sexual Standards," 1974.

25. Mirra Komarovsky, *Dilemmas of Masculinity: A Study of College Youth*, 1976.

26. Anthony Pietropinto and Jacqueline Simenaur, *Beyond the Male Myth*, 1977. Matching this is the finding that in 1973 and again in 1975, 75 per cent of a random sample of Americans expressed a "very great deal" or a "great deal" of satisfaction with family life. United States Department of Commerce, Bureau of the Census, *American Families and Living Arrangements*, 1980, p. 1.

27. Morton Hunt, *Sexual Behavior in the 1970s*, 1975.

28. Quoted in the *San Francisco Chronicle*, May 17, 1977, p. 35.

29. Donald Campbell, "On the Conflicts Between Biological and Social Evolution and Between Psychology and Moral Tradition," 1975, p1121.

30. Emile Durkheim, *Suicide*, 1951, p. 271. See pp. 259-76.

31. Sigmund Freud, "Three Contributions to the Theory of Sex," in *Basic Writings*, 1938; and Harold Lasswell, "The Garrison State Hypothesis Today," in *Changing Patterns of Military Politics*, Samuel Huntington, editor, 1962.

32. Herbert Marcuse, *One Dimensional Man*, 1964, p. 78.

33. Marcuse, 1966 (note 15 above), p. 201. See also Norman Brown, *Life Against Death*, 1959.

34. Andrew Rigby, *Communes in Britain*, 1974b, p. 77.

35. See Seymour Feshbach and Neal Malamuth, "Sex and Aggression: Proving the Link," 1978, and Neal Malamuth, Seymour Feshbach, and Yoram Jaffee, "Sexual Arousal and Aggression: Recent Experiments and Theoretical Issues," 1977. At the least we need to be aware of the possibility that when, in the media, "violence is fused with sex, we have a potentially dangerous form of alchemy." Seymour Fesbach, "Mixing Sex with Violence," *The New York Times*, August 3, 1980, p. D-29.

36. As Bernice Eiduson and Jannette Alexander observe, alternative life styles are usually expressive of the desires of parents, not efforts to provide their children with different roles or rights. "The Role of children in Alternative Family Styles," 1978. See also Norma Feshbach and Seymour Feshbach, editors, "The Changing Status of Children." 1978; Jerome Kagan, "The Child in the Family," 1977; J. Milton Yinger and Stephen Cutler, editors, *Major Social Issues*, 1978, Part IV; Rossi, 1977 (note 3 above); and Rosabeth Kanter, D. Jaffe, and D. K. Weisberg, "Coupling, Parenting and the Presence of Others: Intimate Relationships in Communal Households," 1975.

37. Theodore Roszak, *Person/Planet: The Creative Disintegration of Industrial Society*, 1978, p. 163.

38. Eleanor Maccoby, "The Choice of Variables in the Study of Socialization," 1961; Christopher Lasch, *Haven in a Heartless World*, 1979, pp. xiv-xv, and Ralph White and Ronald Lippitt, *Autocracy and Democracy: An Experimental Inquiry*, 1960.

39. Beatrice Whiting in Yinger and Cutler, 1978, p. 225.

40. John Rothchild and Susan Berns Wolf, *The Children of the Counter-Culture*, 1976, pp. 13-14. "Free schools" vary widely of course. Some are quite successful in teaching a paradoxical mixture of autonomy and group skills, although less successful in teaching academic skills. See Ann Swidler, "What Free Schools Teach," 1976.

41. Roszak, 1978, p. 146.

42. Herbert Hendin, *The Age of Sensation*, 1975, p. 339.

43. See Abrams and McCulloch, 1976 (note 13 above), chap. 5.

44. Clayton and Voss, 1977 (note 22 above).

45. Judith Lyness, Milton Lipetz, and Keith Davis, "Living Together: An Alternative to Marriage," 1972.

46. *Honolulu Advertiser*, February 16, 1980, p. C-2.

47. Peter Berger, *Facing Up to Modernity*, 1977, p. 201.

48. *Ibid.*, p. 206.

49. Focault, 1977 (note 10 above).

Chapter Thirteen

Countercultural Education

Select your courses for next semester from the following: Anti-cultures, Anti-environments, Anti-poetry, Anti-families, Counter-institutions.

The first prospectus of London's Anti-University (1968)[1] illustrates clearly that educational institutions were not immune to countercultural protests in the 1960s, nor have they been in earlier times. The Taborites denounced the masters of Prague University in the fifteenth century. When one reads: "The enemy was the close if invisible link which bound the ideologists produced by the universities to the values of the society in which they functioned,"[2] the time and place of reference are not readily apparent. Though the statement refers to Oxford and Cambridge more than three hundred years ago, it matches criticisms of universities in Russia after 1860, and in Western Europe, China, Japan, Latin America, and the United States in recent decades.

During periods when countercultural challenges are strong, we should expect to find that the established roads to truth, the keepers of evidence, persons with accrediting power, and their institutions are attacked or disregarded. Stewards of "the truth" are not necessarily in educational institutions as we think of them today. In England during the period preceeding the Civil War, when universities were indissolubly linked with the churches, sectarians called for discussions after sermons (a practice adopted for a brief period in Boston). Itinerant interrupters, professionally skilled hecklers, moved among the churches and, despite legal difficulties, denounced the self-righteousness of the pastors and their greed in taking tithes.[3] Truth, they declared, was not the monopoly of the clergy, but could be given to anyone through an inner light. It would require little shifting of terms to use this set of activities and claims to describe recent countercultural criticism of universities and the rationale for "free universities."

Student particpation in revolutionary and countercultural movements concerned with economics, politics, family and sex, and religion is well known.[4] That is not our direct concern in these comments on educational institutions, however. Schools are not only the locale for protests and the development of countercultural programs for other institutions; they are themselves targets. From the student point of view, to be sure, the distinction between educational settings as staging areas for general protest movements and as themselves in need of drastic change is not easily drawn. This is especially true on college and university campuses. Having something of the quality of a "total institution," a college can be experienced by students not only as an educational institution but also as a major part of government, dealing with policy issues critical in their lives; as an economic institution, requiring a major share of their resources and shaping their economic futures; as a church or, more accurately for most, a cluster of competing "churches" propounding diverse roads to salvation; and as a temporary family, despite opposition to any official parental quality, furnishing intimacy and emotional support. Faculty, administration, alumni, parents, and the general public, for whom other institutions are more available (or at least more utilized) to serve most of these functions, are sometimes amazed, and dismayed, at the strength of student criticism of educational institutions. If protests are seen as partly against the educational process, partly against the noneducational aspects of schools that I have mentioned, and partly as deflected ways to oppose other institutions, they may seem less baffling, even if no more to be supported or opposed.

Countercultures and Secondary Education

Although I will refer mainly to higher education, it would be a mistake to overlook the inversion of standard values by some younger students. There are those for whom schooling has been a torment from the beginning. Poorly prepared lingually or by the range of their experiences for the process of formal learning, their first regular contacts with the world beyond the family are marked by failure, and they fall continuously farther behind. In a loud voice, the schools say: You are no good. Some students come to believe that, and they join with others hearing the same message to design an inverted culture where they *are* good, where they have a chance to be somebody. Insofar as possible, those who don't share that culture are assigned to a category of persons who don't count. The fact that values are reversed, however, in the effort to repress lingering hopes and ambitions, is an indication of persistent ambivalence.

Standard high school subcultures, with their emphasis on sports, fun, and a modicum of learning,[5] are quite different in sociological meaning from groups oriented to truancy, petty theft, masculine hyperaggressiveness, and gang combat. The "fun" subcultures are, in some measure, accepted and supported by the adult community. To a substantial degree they can be blended with the dominant values and beliefs of the schools and of the nonschool world, at least as acceptable alternatives. On the basis of their study of English schools, Murdock and Phelps disagree with the argument "that adolescents are caught between two fundamentally opposed cultures; the culture of the school based on deferred gratification, cognitive skill, individual achievement and deference to authority, and the out-of-school 'youth culture' based on immediate gratification, physical skill, group solidarity and the equality of group members. Hence they are forced to choose either one or the other."[6]

Many students find it unnecessary to make a choice between the "official" culture of the school and some of the "peer" cultures. There are countercultural groups, however, whose inverted norms do represent such a choice. If the dominant society says that it is good to go to school, work hard, and respect your teachers, a countercultural group, caught in circumstances that seem to deny access to values so tantalizingly displayed, may evolve among themselves a set of values that say: Skip school as often as possible and withdraw at the earliest possible age, work at minimum speed while disrupting the work of others, flout the authority of the teachers, smash the windows of the school—that symbol of your "death at an early age."

Not all secondary school students who reverse the prevailing educational values come from deprived backgrounds. Some are seeking to deal with the anomie of affluence.[7] They turn away from education (show "lack of motivation," drop out, disrupt the school, turn to drugs) as a result of the highly volatile mixture of fear of failure (how can I hope to come up to the level of my well-trained, disciplined parents?) and fear of success (why should I try to come up to their level when the process of training is so dull and the outcome so deadening and meaningless?).

Those who lament the outcomes of this mixture—the countercultural values that are invented being inadequate to deal with either the individuals' distress or society's great needs—face a delicate task: Efforts to reduce the fear of failure (increased counseling, removal of grades and exams, automatic promotion, a student-selected curriculum) may only increase the fear of success, while at the same time they are perceived by students as fraudulent—that is, not actually relevant to their needs.

Efforts to reduce the fear of success are not easily made in the context of schools. That fear rests on the experience in and the perception of families driven to attain goals that seem cheap and inauthentic to children brought up in affluence. It also rests on youths' picture of wealthy societies fighting and scrambling for power, oblivious to their interdependence and apparently unconcerned with the sources of day-by-day happiness. Not that many eleventh-grade drug freaks have become moral philosophers. It takes little imagination, however, to see and hear that although affluent societies have reduced many problems, the costs have been great, and new difficulties have rushed in to take their places.

In the United States at least, no institution has been more thoroughly criticized than the school, not just by the actions and assertions of some students, but by teachers and social commentators. One person after another has declared that it is inegalitarian, fails to teach even the basics, let alone creativity, and is trapped in an unthinking, self-serving bureaucracy. I shall not examine that criticism here. Despite its vigor, most of it is not strongly countercultural and is thus not directly germane to our concerns. The basic value of formal education, its importance for societies at all levels of development and for individuals, is not usually denied. Methods and quality of teaching, the sources of financing and of decision-making, and the effects on the system of opportunity available to children from different classes and races are almost continuously, and in my judgment wisely, under review.

Some of the criticism, however, does challenge the very premises upon which systems of education are built. In *Compulsory Mis-Education*, Paul Goodman remarked that American schools are not geared to middle-class values. "The schools less and less represent *any* human values, but simply adjustment to a mechanical system." He wondered, not entirely facetiously, whether the failure to teach children how to read is such a bad idea, considering how poor most of the reading material is, how reading it regiments people and blocks a vital folk culture. Why, he inquired, should we promote being "swamped by trash, lies, and bland verbiage"? Perhaps his criticism can be summed up in the statement that schools are effectively flouting "independence, initiative, scrupulous honesty, earnestness, utility, respect for thorough scholarship."[8]

Where Goodman seems ready to try to reform the schools (although his proposals, following such a sweeping condemnation, are scarcely visible), Ivan Illich, in his influencial *Deschooling Society*, believes that compulsory education should be abolished, that it only serves to link education with the occupational system and to reinforce the patterns of inequality. The great faith in education, especially in developing societies, is misplaced, in his view. Its major lessons are unintended: The poor are taught about their inferiority; a personal success ethic predominates; and in the developing lands where only a minority can hope, for the foreseeable future, to get more than minimal education, the emphasis on schooling shuts the door on the great majority. Even for those who manage to obtain a substantial amount of education, "imagination is 'schooled' to accept service in place of value. Medical treatment is mistaken for health care, social work for the improvement of community life, police protection for safety, military poise for national security, the rat race for productive work."[9]

I find it difficult to disagree with Illich about the prevalence of these beliefs. He seems much less successful, however, in demonstrating their origins in the school. His appraisal, as Hurn remarks, "stands the liberal conventional wisdom about the effects of schooling on its head," seeing schools as a source of increased inequalities between nations and between individuals. Illich's judgment rests on the premise that schools are somehow very effective "in transmitting ideas and values he dislikes and very ineffective in transmitting ideas and values of which he approves."[10] When the interdependence of education with other institutions is emphasized, those who believe that the governing values of schools ought to be drastically changed direct their criticism at a larger target.

That is the approach of Bowles and Gintis in their study of *Schooling in Capitalist America*. The educational system doesn't fail, they argue, but succeeds in carrying out its hidden agenda—to produce the values and the personalities needed for a capitalist society. (Noncapitalist societies seem scarcely to avoid this linkage of education and economic values.) To this end, different schools train different kinds of individuals, depending on their destination in the larger society. Some are trained for obedience and efficiency, a few for authority and imagination. Like Goodman and Illich, Bowles and Gintis see little by way of a contribution to a more egalitarian and democratic society.

The countercultural element in the kind of criticism represented by Goodman, Illich, Bowles, and Gintis is the inversion of faith in schooling. There are different reasons for the loss of faith, of which two are fundamental: The educational system is designed to perpetuate the advantages of elites (although probably not consciously for the most part), and it crushes spontaneity and creativity. There is substantial evidence for both of these statements.[11] It is an important achievement of recent critics to have kept the issues before us. They have been less successful, however, in designing new procedures. Although small-scale projects have tested ways of reducing the problems, large-scale alternatives have eluded societies around the world.

Commenting only on the United States, I see a dilemma faced by those who attempt to reduce the two problems at the base of most criticism: Those changes that might reduce inequality are likely to bring still more pressure against spontaneity and creativity. Oppositely, most extensive school reforms seem to work well for the upper-middle-class and upper-class students for a time but seldom help, and often harm, the less well prepared. Even were financial support increased and bureaucratic control reduced, that dilemma remains. In his criticism of Goodman, Michael Katz seems to put the issue too strongly, leaving too little room for differences within classes and for common interests across class lines. However, he makes the dilemma clear when he writes: "In fact, I suspect that what the poor want for their children is affluence, status, and a house in the suburbs rather than community, a guitar, and soul. They may prefer schools that teach their children to read and write and cipher rather than to feel and to be. If this is the case, then an uncomfortable piece of reality must be confronted: Educational radicalism is itself a species of class activity."[12]

Countercultures and Higher Education

The fervor, the religious quality, of student movements is often remarked. Leaders of the "free university" in London announced that it would be distinguished from other universities by the fact that "teachers would be *totally committed* to what they taught, and students *totally committed* to what they learnt." What could this mean, Ernest Gellner asks, and suggests that it implies that tentative exploration of ideas to explore their soundness is out. "Sexual experimentation is perfectly permissible—but intellectual experimentation, exploration, tentativeness, anything short of 'commitment,' are viewed with a neo-Victorian prudery. Propositions at least may only be embraced with total love."[13]

Michael Rossman, one of the leaders of the Free Speech Movement in Berkeley looking back on it after ten years, also emphasizes commitment, but without Gellner's light humor or heavy sarcasm, as you prefer. Rossman observes that out of the months of struggle

> . . . there was born among us a new vision of community, and of culture, to make whole the vision of social justice that had moved us to action in the New Left. Emboldened to risk and dare only by each other's presence, we were out there on the existential edge, where what we know dropped off into the unknown, toward a vision of a different reality. Everything was torn loose for a time. Our careers cast off, our lives at times in jeopardy, our very conceptions of who we were and how to be a person among persons were shaken and revised as profoundly, though differently, as in any current transcendental conversion."[14]

This statement called to mind a comment of Ortega y Gasset: "Conversion is man's change not from one idea to another, but from one definite point of view to its exact opposite: life suddenly seems to us turned upside down and inside out."[15]

If one sees efforts to change universities drastically as a "religious" movement, not as a rational task of designing a new curriculum or system of governance, then the emphasis on "total commitment" is no longer puzzling, however much one laments or applauds its appearance.

Like other efforts to transform an institution or society, radical educational movements face a difficult strategic dilemma. If they press for drastic change, support is lost and repression is intensified. If they moderate their goals, the movement may be co-opted by the dominant forces of society, who are ready to grant liberalizing changes within the system. Those who want radical changes, however, brand these as tokens, and escalate their demands. They see liberalizing changes as a fresh coat of paint on a building with a crumbling foundation, merely hiding its fundamental weakness.[16]

The importance of this dilemma is emphasized by its impact on social change in many parts of the social structure, not simply in education. In economics, politics, and religion, we are continually having to navigate between the rocks and the whirlpool, with those who see the dangers lurking in one often oblivious to the dangers in the other. Jacques Maritain was discussing Thomas Aquinas, but the words need little change to refer to recent educational controversies: Recognizing the dilemma of all social action, St. Thomas fought "against two eternal and opposite inclinations to error: on the one hand, against the *accumulative inertia* of a backward scholasticism which clung to the accidental and passing elements of the Christian tradition; and on the other, against an instinct of *spendthrift disassociation*."[17]

Several recent writers have seen those characterized by "spendthrift disassociation" in their demands for radical educational change as nihilists, as extreme personality types, quite different from the "attractively portrayed, ego-integrated 'Young Radicals' of Keniston's admiring—and probably romanticizing—study," as Endleman puts it.[18] It is difficult not to fall into stereotyping in trying to draw the line between fervent idealism and ego-alien nihilism. Perhaps those characterized by the latter can be most readily identified by their repudiation of tolerance, not only for their opponents but for those in a different faction of the same movement. "This is the dogmatism of religious fanaticism; it is not the political language of conflict, but the religious one of heresy."[19]

While recognizing the presence of apocalyptic views among some of those who would remake the universities, I differ from Liebert, Hendin, Feuer, and others in noting that extreme personality types, under some circumstances, can be a dynamic element in precipitating changes that seem to be utterly blocked in their absence. Until humankind has developed a dependable system of step-by-step evolutionary change, we may have to pay the costs of movements seeking explosive change. Such movements can be regarded as mutants, as I will argue later, most of which are harmful to social wellbeing. Yet now and again a countercultural institution will be advocated, perhaps by persons badly adapted to the world around them, that is more nearly in harmony with a rapidly changing world than the institution it challenges.

To understand countercultural movements, moreover, requires attention to the structural sources of extreme personality types, who can be seen from one perspective as the carriers of sociocultural disharmonies rather than as original causes. Remarking the perpetual conflict of Mao Zedong with his father, Feuer sees "the family civil war" as the "prototype for the political civil war of later years." Mao Zedong's views were "molded in the politics of the student movement," which brought together many persons caught in the same kind of family conflict.[20] I find such psychohistory not so much false as thin. The interpersonal tensions of families had not just appeared. What made them critical for the process of social change in China in mid-twentieth century? Why did they seem to push some young people toward revolutionary views, but not others? What was the structural setting that gave scope to the working out of personal dramas on a public stage?

Criticisms of contemporary higher education have been much more powerful than proposals for counterculture alternatives. Perhaps the strongest and most widespread inversion of values has been in epistemology, not in curriculum or governance. Having discussed the challenges to the scientific and rational world view in Chapter Four and elsewhere, I will not examine that issue here. The emphasis on knowledge through mystical insight, meditation, yoga, affective education, and the like is not so much opposed to the institutionalization of education (indeed, new institutions are formed) as to its rationalism. Roszak wonders if we ought not to include in our "visions of education" Carlos Castaneda's adventures with the shamanic initiation rites of the sort he experienced with the Yaqui sorcerer Don Juan (whether imaginery or real? we might ask). Ought we not go beyond worrying over the fact that Johnny cannot read, Roszak wonders.

> Why do we not worry that Johnny's body is gripped by thwarted anger and desire, that his metabolism is tormented by a diet of junk foods and nervous tension, that his dream life is barren, his imagination moribund, his social conscience darkened by competitive egotism? Why not worry that Johnny can't dance, can't paint, can't breathe, can't meditate, can't relax, can't cope with anxiety, aggression, envy, can't express trust and tenderness?[21]

I am uncertain just what Roszak's statement means. Putting on my rationalistic hard hat, I wonder: Was ist das Evidenz? Have these problems become more serious? If so, are schools primarily at fault? (The quotation is from a chapter entitled "School: Letting Go, Letting Grow.") If we assume—we can scarcely know—that the answer to these questions is yes, what do we do to mitigate the problems? Lamentations abound; they may be salutory; but one looks almost in vain for thought about alternatives that show awareness of the range of values—in some measure contradictory—which most of us strive to attain.

Other criticisms of colleges and universities, usually accompanied by countercultural values only by implication, are well known. To some degree they have come from the "right": Campuses are "alien" territories within which radical thoughts and radical life styles grow; or they are ivory towers wherein abstruse and arcane subjects, irrelevant to the needs and interests of the real world, are explored at tedious length.

In recent years, however, in many parts of the world the criticism has come from the "left." I need only list some of the major themes: Higher education is so closely tied to the political, economic, and military power structure that it cannot well serve its own autonomous functions, such as the preservation, communication, and extension of knowledge; the development of ethical and aesthetic sensibilities; and the encouragement of creativity. One does not need to look far to find an account of a major political figure, fresh from a political or military victory, being given an honorary degree, proclaiming the importance of the university to the state and promising further financial support. Although this is a paraphrase of an account of Oliver Cromwell at Oxford, in 1649,[22] a similar story can be told for many times and places. (Needless to say, the belief that colleges and universities are adjuncts of economic and political, or religious, powers is partly true.)

Opponents who see higher education as scarcely more than agents of the "military-industrial complex" are not certain whom to challenge. The university itself is not an autonomous political unit, because "outside" groups—trustees, regents, donors, legislatures—have decisive voices in making policy. Since the campus is their home ground, however, and since, on most issues, career-minded administrators, faculty, and students are comfortable with the association between education and the "outside world," opponents of the values and policies of universities most often make their protests on the campus. In *The Radical Probe*, as Michael Miles calls it, they seek to break apart uncertain coalitions and to provoke administrators into actions (perhaps the use of force) that will expose their "true identities" as agents of a coercive society.

Internal governance is attacked for the imposition of a double tyranny, that of an unfeeling bureaucracy and of remote professors, interested only in their own research or in courses that support it. A century ago, Leo Tolstoy argued that no one has the right to educate, because those who educate will do so in their own interests; yet all persons have a right to be educated.[23] One can respond to this dilemma by *focused* opposition to the courses and methods of schools or by general attacks. The latter kind of opposition is less likely to create a countercultural alternative or to reform education than to furnish an opportunity, as Joseph Schwab put it, for "kicking their surrogate fathers in the teeth."[24] Or one can try to create "experimental colleges" or "free universities" that broaden the curriculum and challenge the process of granting credentials that is seen as highly inaccurate and unjust. In the most countercultural of these schools, experts, as defined by society, are replaced by a process of self-teaching, self-discovery, and peer interaction. The curriculum is transformed to include some courses that the faculty is likely to believe belong in summer camp or a vocational high school and to include other courses—"counter-institutions," for example, or "anti-poetry"—that turn the established curriculum upside down. One of the courses at the Free University of Berkeley was described by its teacher as a way of overcoming alienation and isolation by communitarian sexuality, by participation in "sheer, undiluted orgy" without guilt or shame.[25]

During the Cultural Revolution in China, in 1966 and for several years thereafter, "bourgeois education" was a prime target of attack. With only a tiny fraction of those desiring higher education able to be admitted and with traditional standards of testing, admission, and teaching continuing in many ways, the opposition was severe. Grades and examinations, utterly unable to reflect the degree of revolutionary fervor, were denounced. Teachers suspected of bourgeois attitudes became janitors and gardeners. In the last few years, however, political credentials have come to be seen as insufficient for studying mathematics, building a bridge, or—more tentatively so far—becoming a social scientist.

Tolstoy's dilemma remains, in China and in the rest of the world. Perhaps countercultural educational movements should be judged by the degree to which they disturb a system in which those who educate do so in their own interests, and by the degree to which their new values increase the right to be educated. By this test, I see little by way of creative countercultural education. Perhaps a Freedom School that seeks to reverse the white-imposed self-image of its black students by challenging a highly inegalitarian educational system meets the standard.[26] Some protests have been sensitive to the dilemma and have not simply succeeded in hardening the established system. By their opposition they have helped to focus public attention on serious educational problems, thereby increasing the right to be educated while decreasing the impact of self-interest among those involved in education. I see little chance, or reason, for making schools themselves into countercultural institutions. There is a much larger chance for them to be major participants in the examination of alternative visions of what society might be, with some opportunity to get involved in a corner of a changing pattern, thus helping to prepare all of their participants for continuing change.

Notes

1. See Roberta Elzey in *Counter-Culture: The Creation of an Alternative Society*, Joseph Berke, editor, 1969, pp. 229-48, and Theodore Roszak, *The Making of a Counter Culture*, 1969, p. 45.
2. Christopher Hill, *Change and Continuity in Seventeenth-Century England*, 1974, p. 133.

3. Christopher Hill, *The World Turned Upside Down*, 1975, pp. 105-6.

4. See S. M. Lipset, *Rebellion in the University*, 1971; Immanuel Wallerstein and Paul Starr, editors, *The University Crisis Reader*, 1971; Lewis Feuer, *The Conflict of Generations: The Character and Significance of Student Movements*, 1969; and Richard Flacks, *Youth and Social Change*, 1971.

5. See Burton Clark, *Educating the Expert Society*, 1962, and James S. Coleman, *The Adolescent Society*, 1961.

6. Graham Murdock and Guy Phelps, "Youth Culture and the School Revisited," 1972, p. 78. See also Shirley Jessor and Richard Jessor, "Maternal Ideology and Adolescent Nonconformity," 1973; Elise Boulding in *Social Forces and Schooling: An Anthropological and Sociological Perspective*, N. B. Shimahara and Adam Scrupski, editors, 1975, pp. 187-220; and Ralph H. Turner, *The Social Context of Ambition*, 1964.

7. William Simon and John Gagnon, "The Anomie of Affluence: A Post-Mertonian Conception," 1976, pp. 356-78, and Robert K. Merton, *Social Theory and Social Structure*, 1968.

8. Paul Goodman, *Compulsory Mis-Education*, 1964, pp. 26-27. See also John Holt, *Instead of Education*, 1976.

9. Ivan Illich, *Deschooling Society*, 1971, p. 1. See also Paulo Freire, *Pedagogy of the Oppressed*, 1970, and *idem*, *Education for Critical Consciousness*, 1973.

10. See Christopher Hurn, *The Limits and Possibilities of Schooling*, 1978.

11. For a variety of evidences, see Raymond Boudon, *Education, Opportunity and Social Inequality: Changing Prospects in Western Society*, 1974; Christopher Jencks, *Inequality: A Reassessment of the Effect of Family and Schooling in America*, 1972; William Sewell and Robert Hauser, *Education, Occupation and Earnings*, 1975; David Featherman and Robert Hauser *Opportunity and Change*, 1978; and Nelson Ashline, T. R. Pezzullo and C. I. Norris, editors, *Education, Inequality, and National Policy*, 1976. There is little evidence that "free schools" reduce these problems as they teach "a set of norms nearly the inverse of those traditional schools teach." Ann Swidler, "What Free Schools Teach," 1976, p. 214.

12. Michael Katz, *Class, Bureaucracy, and Schools*, 1971, p. 139.

13. Ernest Gellner, *Contemporary Thought and Politics*, 1974, p. 8.

14. Qutoed by Robert Bellah in *The New Religious Consciousness*, Charles Glock and Robert Bellah, editors, 1976, p. 80. Gerald Grant and David Riesman also emphasize the sense of mission or commitment characteristic of the few colleges that, in their judgment, have sought drastically to redefine the goals of higher education. See their *The Perpetual Dream: Reform and Experimentation in the American College*, 1978.

15. José Ortega y Gasset, *Man and Crisis*, 1958, p. 151.

16. See Robert Endleman, Joseph Gussfield, and Max Heirich, "The Student Revolt: Afterthoughts and Prospects," 1972, pp. 3-9.
17. Jacques Maritain, *True Humanism*, 1938, P. 202. On dilemmas of social action, see also J. Milton Yinger, *Religion in the Struggle for Power*, 1946, pp. 25-50.
18. Endleman, 1972, p. 6; see also Kenneth Keniston, *Young Radicals*, 1968. For a variety of pictures of ego-alien, rather than ego-integrated protesters, see Robert Liebert, *Radical and Militant Youth: A Psychoanalytic Inquiry*, 1971; Herbert Hendin, *The Age of Sensation*, 1975; and Feuer, 1969 (note 4 above).
19. Endleman, 1972, p. 6.
20. Feuer, 1969, pp. 181-83.
21. Theodore Roszak, *Person/Planet: The Creative Disintegration of Industrial Society*, 1978, p. 197.
22. Hill, 1974, (note 2 above), p. 135.
23. See Roszak, 1978, p. 194.
24. See Joseph Schwab, *College Curriculum and Student Protest*, 1969.
25. Richard Thorne, "A Step Toward Sexual Freedom in Berkeley," 1965, p. 5.
26. Florence Howe, "Mississippi's Freedom Schools: The Politics of Education," 1965.

Chapter Fourteen

Countercultures and Social Change

Gloucester, 'tis true that we are in great danger;
The greater therefore should our courage be. . . .
There is some soul of goodness in things evil,
Would men observingly distil it out. . . .
Thus may we gather honey from the weed,
And make a moral of the devil himself.

Shakespeare, *King Henry V*, before the battle at Agincourt, Act IV, Scene I

Countercultures are variously regarded as engines of social change, symbols and effects of change, or mere faddist epiphenomena. Throughout this book I have argued, by implication, that the last is not true, believing instead that countercultures are of great human significance. This does not mean that many of their manifestations are not dangerous or banal, undeserving of much attention; but altogether, as a continuing part of experience, cultural reversals both symbolize fundamental dilemmas and deeply influence the course of our lives.

In an earlier chapter I discussed the sources of countercultures, seeing them as the effects of numerous social and individual factors. When we turn the question around to ask how and to what degree countercultures are the cause of social change, we come to some of the most critical problems of sociological theory. With respect to recent countercultures, a basically functionalist interpretation is now commonly given, even by some conservatives who have been more inclined to emphasize their dysfunctions. Chief Justice Warren Burger of the United States Supreme Court has declared that "turbulent American youth, whose disorderly acts he once 'resented,' actually had pointed the way to higher spiritual values."[1] Philip Slater writes that a basic characteristic of successful social systems is the presence of devices that keep alive alternatives antithetical to the dominant emphases.

> These latent alternatives usually persist in some encapsulated and imprisoned form ("break glass in case of fire"), such as myths, festivals, or specialized roles. Fanatics continually try to expunge these circumscribed contradictions, but when they succeed it is often fatal to the society. For, as Lewis Mumford once pointed out, it is the "laxity, corruption, and disorder" in a system that makes it viable, considering the contradictory needs that all social systems must satisfy. Such latent alternatives are priceless treasures and must be carefully guarded against loss. For a new cultural pattern does not emerge out of nothing—the seed must already be there.[2]

Well, some of them are priceless treasures and others are lethal bombs; but we may not be able to have one without the other. Slater's argument is Durkheimian. Durkheim referred primarily to crime, but his interpretation can readily be applied to countercultures. Crime, he declared, is necessary to the evolution of morality and law. "In order that the originality of the idealist whose dreams transcend his century may find expression, it is necessary that the originality of the criminal, who is below the level of his time, shall also be possible. One does not occur without the other."[3] And of course Durkheim goes on to say that crime not only implies that new ways are open; it may even be an anticipation of new collective sentiments. Socrates was a "criminal," but he helped pave the way for a new morality.

I am uncomfortable with such unqualified functionalist views. Countercultures may stimulate the growth of highly resistant forces in society that make wise and necessary changes less likely. Opposition to the bizarre may deflect attention from basic needs; it may furnish those most resistant to change with superficially strong moral arguments, not to mention allies.

In the face of opposition, frustration, and the inherent difficulty in establishing new cultural patterns, quietism may become the dominant mood of those most likely to hold deviant values. Thus what might have been an adjustment to new circumstances is unavailable to the larger society; "what had looked . . . as though it might become a counterculture," Hill says of the Ranters, "became a corner of the bourgeois culture whose occupants asked only to be left alone."[4] The same process of withdrawal is strongly at work today.

At another point, Durkheim states the functionalist issue in a more satisfactory way, and, for balance, let me quote him again: "The most barbarous and the most fantastic rites and the strangest myths translate some human need, some aspect of life either individual or social. The reasons with which the faithful justify them may be, and generally are, erroneous; but the true reasons do not cease to exist, and it is the duty of science to discover them."[5]

The impact of countercultures is not automatic. It is filtered through human intelligence—or can be. We can extract "honey from the weed" and we can discover the needs that lie behind "the most barbarous and the most fantastic rites," thus having some chance of meeting those needs in constructive ways. These things we cannot do without taking thought—quiet, contemplative, indeed systematic thought based on observations as objective as we can make them.

In commenting on nineteenth-century French literature and the great clarity with which it revealed the harshness and corruption of social life, Trilling noted how widely that literature was available. "Almost, we might be moved to say, it made itself too available: it is the rare person who can receive the full news of the inherent social immorality without injury to his own morality, without injury, indeed, to his own intellect—nothing can be so stultifying as the simple, unelaborated belief that society is a fraud. Yet with the explicit social intelligence of the great French novels we dare not quarrel—it is a *given* of our culture."[6]

Indeed we cannot quarrel with it, but we can build upon it. We need to take full account of the sweeping critical judgments of modernism, of the adversarial perspective, in literature and in other ways of looking at the world. It enunciates a truth about human life, a powerful truth. But the very fact that so many recognize its power is another truth—a kind of dialectical refutation of the first, because it demonstrates the strength of an intellectual and moral perspective that Trilling believed was threatened.

The confrontation of culture and counterculture is a vital aspect of the process of social evolution. Antithetical groups do not escape each other's influence. We take on the face of the adversary, as the French proverb puts it, whether we wish to or not. (Chacun prend à l'adversaire, qu'il le veuille ou non.) Or, more technically, culture and counterculture are bound together in linked evolution. Although the outcomes vary widely, few societies have avoided collisions between the need for a shared system of values and norms and the need for flexibility and adaptability. The collisions tend to produce "fanatics of both persuasions," as Victor Turner puts it, although in terms somewhat different from those we have been using: "if structure is maximized to full rigidity, it invites the nemesis of either violent revolution or uncreative apathy, while if communitas is maximized, it becomes its own dark shadow, totalitarianism, from the need to suppress and repress in its members all tendencies to develop structural independences and interdependences."[7]

Under conditions of lowered legitimacy and loss of faith, efforts on the part of the dominant society to repress new norms and values can lead to deviation-amplification, not to a reaffirmation of the established norms and values. Efforts to co-opt the deviants can, by legitimating their more moderate practices, have the same effect. Thus we need to complement Durkheim's view of the way deviation strengthens a group with an evolutionary view of the way it modifies a group. In the words of Gerlach and Hine, "if you're not part of a mutation, you are part of the environment which selects for or against it. No one can escape an evolutionary role."[8] Deviant ideas that become the operative values of a group tell us, at the least, something about the stresses faced by the members of that group. On another level, they can tell us something about the larger system, indicating points of inadequacy. On still another level, they can prove to be new values required to meet a new situation.

Countercultures as Mutations

One way to study the connection between social change and oppositional movements is to glance at genetic mutations, which stand as powerful analogies to countercultures. If we take them as suggestive hints about similar processes that occur on the cultural level, study of these analogies can help us to describe, if not to explain, countercultures.

Biological systems are self-reproducing, but they are not closed systems. In addition to natural genetic variations they experience drastic discontinuities. Most mutations are maladaptive; biologists worry about x-rays, untested drugs, atomic testing, and other forces that cause more mutations. Individuals whose genes are thus modified are less likely to survive or reproduce than more standard members of a species, so long as the environment remains stable. If significant changes occur in the environment, however, individuals carrying the mutant gene may have a survival advantage. (A mutant gene can remain recessive for some time.)

In *The Immense Journey*, Loren Eiseley beautifully described the evolution of a deviant fish, the Snout, at a time some 300 million years ago when waters were receding from many parts of the planet. With his stubby fins and mutant lung, he was not a very successful fish, so long as water was everywhere; but in the changing environment, more elegant fish were dying of oxygen starvation in the "primeval ooze." However, descendants of the Snout, that poor bog-trapped failure, dominated the earth millennia later, for "among those gasping, dying creatures, whose small brains winked out forever in the long Silurian drought, the Snout and his brethren survived."[9]

Thus some individuals inherit, by chance, a capacity to resist a new environmental threat or to exploit a new environmental opportunity superior to more "normal" members of the species. Animals with long necks may get nothing for their pains if most of the foliage is near the ground; but if low bushes are destroyed by environmental change or taken over by competitors, it pays to be a giraffe. The trouble is that the environment may continue to change; and the giraffe, who has his neck stuck out for good, can then be in trouble. In terms of our topic, the critical question is: Do modern industrial societies have their cultural necks stuck out too far in a rapidly changing world? Do they have sets of recessive or deviant values, a sufficiently rich supply of cultural mutations, to furnish modes of life appropriate to new environments? Or are most of those mutations harmful?

Most evolutionary change is incremental, produced by a series of small adaptive changes. At times, however, sharp discontinuity, or what G. G. Simpson calls "quantum evolution," occurs. We need to be aware of the possibility that cultural change may also be precipitated, on occasion, by a major transforming mutation, perhaps stated in religious terms.

Recessive genes can be thought of as a kind of gene bank where maladaptive mutations are sometimes stored, a survival resource to be drawn upon if drastic changes of environment make them adaptive.[10] In a similar way, cultural deviations can be seen as the mutations of a society's normative system. They can survive only if they become something more than the idiosyncrasies of individuals, perhaps by being built into the normative systems of subsocieties and passed along through the group's processes of socialization.

The development of a culture that deals with a large share of individual needs and anxieties, facilitates interpersonal relations, accommodates conflicts, and at the same time adapts to new circumstances in an inherently difficult task. It is scarcely surprising that most of the cultural inventions that appear during periods of cultural change not only seem to the majority to be ridiculous or obscene or dangerous, but that they have little staying power. Since it is difficult to believe, however, that the individual-societal-environmental system is as well balanced as the organism-environment system—the result of a long process of evolutionary selectivity—we ought not to assume that most cultural deviation, like most mutation, is maladaptive. Nor should we assume the opposite, after the fashion of those who believe that any kind of change is preferable to stability. Some cultural deviations, like most mutations, are lethal, Or to change the figure, they may be Trojan horses that seem interesting and attractive but contain unimagined destructive forces.

I heard once of a man who bought a mahogany door at a flea market. It was too elegant, too beautiful—and too inexpensive—to resist. He immediately made it the door to his study. The result was, of course, that all the rest of the room looked shabby. He had to redecorate the whole room—which made the rest of the house look shabby. And so the whole house had to be repaired and improved. When a mutation or a cultural deviation is brought into a system, it may be either a Trojan horse or a mahogany door. We need to try to understand the conditions that lead to one or the other.

Most social scientists today believe that rigidity is a greater threat than are cultural mutations. Few share the lighthearted optimism of Charles Reich, who sees Consciousness III as the instrument of a quiet and peaceful revolution that "promises a higher reason, a more human community, and a new and liberated individual."[11] But as Donald Campbell has argued in an important paper, social scientists and psychologists may be overeager "to discover and believe antitraditional, antirepressive theories"; they may be especially receptive to "the prohedonic message of liberation." The disciplines that study human behavior may "recruit persons unusually eager to challenge the cultural orthodoxy. . . . It is a prerequisite to a scientific approach in the social sciences that investigators be willing to challenge the cultural orthodoxy. But a science with this entrance requirement may end up recruiting persons who are not only willing to make this challenge but are in fact overeager to do so."[12]

The old ways, of course, contain social adaptations that have become destructive under new sets of circumstances. In reviewing Robert Heilbroner's *An Inquiry into the Human Prospect*, Campbell emphasizes that "more of the sources of impending disaster which he foresees are due to the persistence of social adaptations now outmoded (such as military nationalism, environmental conquest, and taboos against birth control) than are due to a failure to retain once-functional inhibitory morality systems."[13] Pressure against the traditional cultures, however, comes not only from their failures to adapt to new circumstances but also from the hedonic individualism and self-centeredness that are the product of biological selection. The continuing task, Campbell argues, is to arrive at a minimax solution or a stable compromise between the needs and requirements of the biological and the social systems.

Although tendencies toward altruism furnish some advantages for survival, as we noted earlier, biological evolution has favored the development of self-centered individuals. Had biological evolution selected more strongly for altruism, we would not find the overwhelming emphasis on the social virtues and opposition to selfishness in the world's ethical and religious codes. Social evolution has favored the survival of societies that restrain self-centeredness to some degree. In one way or another, the tension between self-assertiveness and social control, which are manifestations of these two streams of evolution, has been used—as by Freud and Durkheim—to account for social process and social change.[14]

Social norms the world over seek to limit selfishness, greed, and dishonesty, even though it can be argued that biological evolution favors individuals who practice them. "Look out for your own interests" may be as important as "thou shall not covet," Campbell observes, but spontaneous compliance with the former generally makes normative reinforcement unnecessary.

This is a powerful argument, but I would emphasize somewhat more than Campbell does the rigidity built into sociai systems, partly as a result, ironically, of the social virtues ("altruistic genes") that make social life possible. He notes that in Moses' day, as in ours, honoring one's parents could have been carried to dysfunctional lengths, "but such excesses were so little of a social problem that 'Thou shalt show independence from thy parents' was usually omitted from the limited list of reiterated commandments."[15] Usually omitted, perhaps, but not always. Several centuries after Moses, a charismatic prophet with countercultural tendencies declared: "For I have come to set a man against his father, and daughter against her mother, and a daughter-in-law against her mother-in-law; and a man's foes shall be those of his own household."[16]

This quotation prompts me to suggest that major countercultural mutations often—I am tempted to say in the majority of cases—appear as religious movements. That is not to say that they are therefore inevitably good—or that they are bad. Most persons would probably agree that certain prophetic movements with which they identify have been major social forces in transforming an unjust or otherwise inadequate social order. Religions other than ones own are not usually regarded this way, however; and not many persons are inspired with awe by hearing from the Church of Satan that greed, pride, envy, anger, gluttony, lust, and sloth are cardinal virtues, not the seven deadly sins. In noting that many countercultures are religious, I want simply to emphasize that those involved connect them with the fundamental problems of existence. Lewellen describes a small group of Seventh Day Adventists in predominantly Catholic Peru. They were not individually misfits but were culturally deviant in religious beliefs, a quality that prepared them to take the lead in guiding the community through a rapid economic transition. Throughout history, "small and deviant religious sects have, after a period of intense persecution, prospered and ultimately established new social norms."[17]

Some evolutionists emphasize the treasury of adaptive mechanisms, both genetic and cultural, that have been created in a long evolutionary process.[18] Mutations, whether biological or cultural, are in their view, almost uniformly destructive. Innovations, therefore, ought to be opposed.

Others see many elements of accumulated culture not as a treasure but as a trap. Cultural standards may repress inherited needs, at what some believe is a fearful cost; or they may directly threaten health or life itself. Numerous values and norms support war. We can read on a pack of cigarettes: "Warning: The Surgeon General has determined that cigarette smoking is dangerous to your health." It is mainly from counterculturalists, however, not from the Surgeon General, the Attorney General, or a Major General that we hear: "Warning: History has determined that warfare is dangerous to life and limb."

There are those who believe that the evolutionary process has also left us with some genetic traps, when judged against contemporary circumstances. The evolutionary process doubtless selected for those individuals who had strong aggressive (as well as altruistic) and sexual drives. For most of its existence, until a few centuries ago, societies have often felt threatened by extinction from opposite dangers: insufficient food and insufficient population. High capacities for aggression and sex were important parts of the volatile mixture by which those threats were dealt with. One is not likely to win any medals, but may nevertheless be correct, by suggesting that those drives, at their present levels of strength, may now put the species at a survival disadvantage.

If mutations, whether biological or countercultural, survive, they develop in linked evolution along with the system with which they interact. Gerlach and Hine describe a species of moth that changed coloration and behavior in ways that improved its chances for survival. Among its predators, mutations occurred that helped some to detect such changes better, so that they also evolved. In their efforts to repress or to co-opt deviations, societies may, in a similar way, be drastically changed.[19]

The evolutionary analogy can be highly instructive. Cultural change, however, adds the element of conscious creations, of active response to the dominant culture, not simply adaptation to environmental change. Someone asked Thomas Edison why he persisted in attempts to build an incandescent bulb after 10,000 failures. He replied: I don't consider them to be failures; I have discovered numerous ways how not to make one. He worked in "a failure-tolerant environment," as a systems engineer said of the early rocket builders. A society that "accepts the goal of discovering fundamentally new lifeways, adaptive for a post-industrial era," Gerlach and Hine suggest, "might also be willing to subsidize a failure-tolerant environment for experimenting in new social structures."[20]

One ought to note, however, their reference to rigorous scientific planning. Those carrying out the experiments were ready to see the effects, to set aside the failures. They were not fighting an establishment, struggling with oedipal problems, or searching for an identity. Perhaps failure-tolerant cultural experimentation might best be carried out by those over sixty. More seriously, I want to emphasize the place of "rational preselection" in cultural evolution, a process that works alongside blind selection. Mutations can be anticipated only in the statistical sense that certain environments are more and others less likely to produce them. They cannot be planned. Humankind, however, and certain other highly social animals, Boehm writes, "are able to anticipate complex evolutionary problems. They may then beat natural selection to the draw by making their own deliberate adaptive choices." Decisions occur at both the individual and group levels. "Especially in group preselection, the result is an adaptive mechanism of unparalleled flexibility and rapidity of action."[21] We need not proclaim every unilluminating light bulb a success (even if we believe that we are living in the cultural dark). By recognizing, however, the great significance of rational preselection in human experience, we will be encouraged to examine with care alternative ways of doing things, rather than waiting for the harsher process of "natural selection."

Revolutions and Countercultures

The changes in values and norms propounded by countercultures cannot proceed far without concomitant changes in social structure and character. Social change, as I use that term, is the process of movement from one relatively stable structural-cultural-characterological system toward another. This does not imply "that societies move from situations of relative balance, through periods of disruption, into new situations of balance. New forces may enter a system at such a rate that the realignment process cannot proceed rapidly enough."[22] A situation where structural, cultural, and characterological elements are continuously out of phase with each other may now be endemic. It should not be assumed to be either exceptional or pathological. Nor should we assume that change must begin with one part of the system, with structural change in the economy, for example, or with the revelations of a charismatic leader, or with a shared cultural vision of what the new world should be. Whichever part of the social change process occurs first, its impact will be strongly influenced by the extent and direction of changes in the other parts.

These statements are of particular relevance to the study of revolutions. Social revolutions, as I see them, are organized movements designed not just to seize power but to replace one set of values with another and to train individuals to adhere to those values.

The word "revolution" is now used so freely that it is difficult to make much sense of it. When one can buy a "revolutionary new soap" or a revolutionary home movie system, word inflation has greatly reduced the value of the term. Nevertheless, it retains its fundamental place in the analysis of social change and cannot be given up.

The circularity implied in its original meaning—with reference to social change as well as physical processes—is almost entirely absent from current usage. Revolution, in the words of *the Oxford English Dictionary*, is "a complete overthrow of the established government by those who were previously subject to it." In modern Chinese usage, revolution is "a changing mandate"; but earlier, according to Chinese-speaking friends, it indicated renewal, a fresh start, a return to a predetermined point that had mistakenly been left. This was also an early English usage. If one adds the idea of progress, however, as in Rousseau, revolution becomes one-directional—an overturning of the old.[23]

For our purposes it may be wise to keep the older usage partly in view, because the countercultural elements in many revolutions contain values from a pristine past—often substantially imaginary—to which the new society should, it is believed, return.

One of the struggles within every revolutionary movement concerns the extent to which it must encompass not simply changes in the structure of power, but drastic cultural and characterological changes as well. In the early stages revolutions usually emphasize the cultural changes; they contain a counterculture, envisaged in a utopian conception of a new world. As Herbert Blumer has observed, reform movements *use* prevailing values to criticize and seek to change undesired conditions. Their appeal is to public opinion. Revolutions *attack* those values, seeking converts, not the support of the general public, and thus "operate more like a religion."[24]

Rapid changes of values are unlikely to occur without changes in the structure of power. Those whose primary concern is the transfer of power, however, may believe this objective to be threatened by demands for a new culture.[25] A violent battle to win control of a state makes power itself the final value, obscuring, even effacing other values for which the power was sought. Lord Acton's aphorism that power corrupts and absolute power corrupts absolutely is an important truth, or so it seems to me, because absolute power requires enormous coercion and utter dedication to the maintenance of ones position by any means. Other goals are forgotten.

On the utopian level, in Mannheim's sense of a guiding image of the desired new world, the new values are vital to a revolution. Most revolutions demonstrate, however, that structural change is easier to accomplish than cultural change. The former can occur as a result of a fairly brief and decisive series of events, while the latter is more incremental. To be effective, the cultural element in a revolution must not only transform a complex system of values, each part of which reinforces the others, but must also transform individual characters within which those values are embedded. Ideological fervor aids in the necessary conversion of many of the direct participants in the revolution. The fervor is difficult to maintain, however, after the old order is overthrown. Internal competition grows in intensity. The many mute observers of the change have not, in any event, been swept up in the ideological battle. They have hoped only for more justice, the removal of cruel rulers, and a better chance to realize their dreams. Structural changes that have weakened the power of the dominant classes encourage some peasants and other disprivileged persons to revolt and many others to support the revolutionary movement,[26] but for many it is more in the name of traditional aspirations than new values.

After a transfer of power has taken place—carried out in the name of the revolutionary values—the new rulers don't seem very different from the old. From czar to commissar is not so far. Radicals fight the revolution; conservatives write the constitution. The family is attacked, to break the linkage of generations, but usually returns to a pattern quite similar to its prerevolutionary form. The educational system is transformed—often substantially democratized in many instances— but new elites and remnants of the old may reestablish privileged access for their children.

Marx, who dreamed of a full-scale revolution, was dismayed by such tendencies toward cultural reactions:

> The tradition of all dead generations weighs like a nightmare on the brain of the living. And just when they seem engaged in revolutionizing themselves and things, in creating something that has never yet existed, precisely in such periods of revolutionary crisis they anxiously conjure up the spirits of the past to their service and borrow from them names, battle cries and costumes in order to present the new scene of world history in this time-honoured disguise and this borrowed language.[27]

Whether continuing traditions "weigh like a nightmare" or, as some believe, indicate the validity and vitality of the established ways of doing things (both statements seem to me to contain truth), it is difficult to disagree with Marx's judgment that "the spirits of the past" have great tenacity. The Soviet Union is surely as much Russian as it is communist, to the discomfort of the other cultural groups within its borders and often of its East European allies. The influence of its prerevolutionary history has not been turned off. Its geopolitical situation has not changed. Two-thirds of a century has been insufficient time to transform the revolutionary counterculture into the established culture.

Recent Chinese experience indicates equally clearly that the counterculture embodied in a revolution is less easily realized than the seizure of power. In Marxian terms the base changed, but the superstructure did not collapse. As often happens in revolutionary societies, vested interests, individual habits, and deeply learned values persisted, despite the dramatic change in the base of the social structure.

In 1966, at a mass rally of the Red Guards, Mao Zedong put their red band on his own arm, signifying his support for their attack on "the four olds"—ideas, culture, customs, and habits. Paradoxically, the ostensible ruler thus helped promote a fight against those in his own party and government, as well as "bourgeois" elements outside it, who supported old institutions, values, and individual interests. Seeing what had been happening in the Soviet Union, Mao emphasized that established privileges, attitudes, and values did not inevitably change when the power base was changed; a classless society did not automatically appear. The revolutionary counterculture had not dislodged the traditional way of life which, if allowed to continue, could in fact overturn the new socialist base. It had not maintained the "worker-peasant" quality throughout the population nor prevented the development of a large bureaucracy.

"To the historian of the future," Joan Robinson has written, the Great Proletarian Cultural Revolution "will appear as the first example of a new kind of class war—a revolt of a new proletariat of workers in socialist enterprises and peasants turned commune members against the incipient new class of organization men in the Communist Party."[28] This is an argument similar to that of Djilas, who saw the power to control and to profit by control in communist societies as the functional equivalents of ownership, hence *The New Class*, to use the title of his book. In this view, the party apparatus plays a role in communist societies similar to that of the bourgeoisie in capitalist societies.[29]

It was not only the new "organization men," however, who defended personal and class privileges. In China many middle-class persons had welcomed the revolution and worked for its success, in light of what they saw as years of chaos and corruption. They did not, however, deeply share the revolutionary ideology. Many elements of the Chinese tradition, even its Confucianism, and of the earlier class structure persisted, in the minds of some peasants and workers as well as among the gentry.[30]

Focusing particularly on Canton, Ezra Vogel wrote: "The Great Proletarian Cultural Revolution was not only a party purge but a fundamentalist revival of political orthodoxy."[31] Orthodoxy, in his terms, is the dominant ideology of the Chinese revolution. The Cultural Revolution expressed the belief on the part of the ruling group that a strong division persisted between those traveling a socialist and those traveling a capitalist road—thus a continuing "two-line struggle" was involved. It can also be seen as a kind of "witch-hunt," which served to reaffirm the collective identity of the Chinese nation in the face of internal discord and perceived outside threats.[32]

Vogel also remarked, however, that most people, and especially most rural people, tried to "remain outside the struggles." Although millions of young people were involved in the Cultural Revolution, even they were not free from traditional and self-centered values. The Cultural Revolution was, at the same time, a "revival of political orthodoxy" and a sign that its own system of values—countercultural in many ways to the traditional orthodoxy of China and to many of the modernizing sectors of the society—was not easily set in place. It was easier to win power than to create a new culture. During the Cultural Revolution Mao's own remarks seemed to show more opposition to a traditionalism that remained and the need to transform the people (the revolution in values not having occurred), than a fear that an established communist orthodoxy was threatened by "a new class."[33] This distinction should not be sharply drawn, however. Earlier, and to some degree throughout his regime, Mao expressed concern over the power of bureaucrats to block socialist development, partly because of their roots in traditionalism.

It is doubly ironic that the official ideology, which I have suggested can be seen as countercultural, has not itself escaped the opposition of new countercultures. "For some years," Robinson wrote in 1969, "there has been talk of the problem of the third generation, the lucky children who take New China for granted and begin to think of what they can get out of it for themselves more than of what their fathers gave to build it."[34] By giving the Red Guards nearly free rein to criticize and in some instances to attack the "rightists," Mao sought to kill two birds with one stone: to bring the Red Guards back into the Cultural Revolution, with the task of building a new superstructure, and to expost and weaken party members and others who stood in the way of that goal.

Events since Mao's death indicate that his counterculture, although of enormous influence on China, has not swept away the old or blocked the spread of more moderate modernizing values. Less important, but deserving notice, is that some of the "lucky children" of the third generation to which Robinson referred now show some Bohemian trends. "In many ways they seem to deliberately stand Maoist ideals on their head, to parody the pantheon of Communist virtues. They might be called China's counter-culture, for they are a reaction to all the years of stifling restrictions on personal and cultural life. They also represent part of the new sense of rising expectations which is sweeping China's cities, along with a yearning among some for Western ways."[35]

The difficulties in building a revolutionary culture despite the success in creating a new base did not suddenly appear in 1966. (Indeed they go back at least to Lao Zi.) Commenting on the background of the Cultural Revolution, a member of the committee forming the Shanghai "temporary organ of power" noted in 1967 that the Party had launched a strong attack in 1951-52 on "the three evils" among government officials (corruption, waste, and bureaucracy) and "the five evils" among businessmen not yet absorbed into the socialist economy (bribery of government officials, theft of state property, tax evasion, cheating on government contracts, and stealing economic information).[36] The presence of these very old-fashioned evils was a clear indication of how incomplete the reversal of values had been.

Of the numerous other efforts to "complete the revolution" in China, the one most publicized in the West was Jiang Qing's campaign against traditional opera, which she saw as glamorizing emperors and feudalism rather than the valor of the proletariat. This campaign illustrated her important and highly visible role, as wife of the Chairman, in the effort to "turn the world upside down," to build China around a new set of values. Yet after Mao's death her influence was rapidly destroyed. She was one of "the gang of four" who, in the new leaders' view, threatened China's economic development, orderly governance, and ability to defend itself, especially against the Soviet Union. In commenting on the conflict between the goals of the Chinese revolution and the needs of organization, Robinson remarked that the Cultural Revolution "has swung the balance violently against organization towards popular spontaneity; how can it be kept from gradually creeping back in?"[37] Since Mao's death those who emphasize the need for orderly planning and some outside support have come back into power. It is too early to tell how far the pendulum has swung, how much older values have become, once again, acceptable. Shanghai has long been a center of revolutionary pressure for cultural change. Yet an astute observer remarked to me in China in 1979 that Shanghai was a "closet Hong King."

Recognizing the dilemmas and the counterforces, Mao remarked that it might be necessary to have another Cultural Revolution in fifteen or twenty years. Jefferson had made a similar remark about the United States, for he saw that it was easier to win independence than to build a new society. Both had seen drastic changes in the power structures of their societies but fewer changes in values.

Some contemporary observers, perhaps disillusioned by the failure of revolutions to attain new values, believe that the cultural changes can, and perhaps must, occur first. It is not the productive relations, in Marx's term, that drastically need reordering, but consciousness and values.[38] Structural changes, they affirm, will follow.

I would emphasize not the primacy of one or another source of change, but their interdependence. Those who stress one or the other, playing down the interdependence, may be puzzled by the outcomes. To some, the Chinese Cultural Revolution was a great burst of primitive democratic energy that promised a more egalitarian society—a society that could avoid the errors of both Soviet "bourgeois" communism and imperialist capitalism. To others, the movement was a crude attack on essential and orderly development that was building China on a socialist base, within the limits set by resources, organizational needs, and international tensions.[39]

Not with specific reference to the Chinese situation, which I shall not attempt to judge, but as a general principle, both statements about "cultural revolutions" tend to be true, each statement limiting and being limited by the other. I do not want to argue that major cultural reversals, particularly those that define new ultimate meanings of life, cannot be a major factor in social transformation.[40] They do not take hold, however, without accompanying changes of social structure and of individual character. And structural changes lose their revolutionary significance if they are not confirmed by new values. These are not statements of preference. Whether or not one wants the structural and cultural changes to occur, with matching influences on individuals, cannot be stated in general, unless change *per se* is the supreme value. Nor can revolutions be judged simply by reference to utopian goals. It is the culture that unfolds in the revolutionary process, powerfully affected by the means used to attain and maintain power, that should be considered.

Effects of Countercultures on Individual Participants

Don't trust anyone over thirty.

Sooner or later the mirror asks: Did you mean that? Few bother to answer in words, but behavioral answers range from repudiation of the statement—by blending back into the straight world—to tragic reaffirmation that one believes the statement, even as applied to oneself.

The various answers are important, not only for the individuals who give them and those closest to them but also for society generally—for the groups they do or do not join, the causes they do or do not support.

It is probably never literally true that persons who were more than marginal participants in activities slip back into the dominant world without a trace of their former selves showing through.[41] Major role shifts and declarations of values, however, show that changes can be dramatic. I noted earlier that Eldridge Cleaver, a founder of the Black Panthers, is now a political moderate and born-again Christian (but also a supporter of Sun Moon's Unification Church—which is not quite the same thing). He has remarked that the Black Panthers fought for an increase in the number of black policemen. You see a lot of them now "and they don't seem any nicer." From Los Angeles, he "can't even complain about the white racist mayor anymore." At a hearing, when he was in prison, he found himself standing before a black judge—"who upped my bail."[42]

Jerry Rubin, a leader of the hippies and the yippies and participant in encounter groups of many types, once wrote: "To steal from the rich is a sacred and religious act."[43] He now works on Wall Street. Bob Dylan, a clarion voice of the musical and protest countercultures for nearly two decades, after exploring Buddhism, Hinduism, and his own Jewish background, converted to Christianity in 1979.

There is little doubt that Cleaver, Rubin, Dylan, and the thousands less publicly visible who now participate in dominant institutions carry values and goals into their new activities that express their earlier convictions. In a similar way, the shift from Ranterism to Quakerism in seventeenth-century England, although scarcely a shift from counterculture to establishment, did furnish a more secure institutional base for opposition to the dominant society and many of its values. The spread of Quakerism, Christopher Hill observes, "witnessed *both* to the defeat of the political Levellers *and* to the continued existence and indeed extension of radical ideas."[44] So it is with many of those today who have decided to work "within the system" in groups devoted to conservation, opposition to nuclear power and weapons, the women's movement, or other activities in harmony with their values.[45]

Others will fall victim to what I have called the "John Wesley syndrome": When they have become wealthy out of countercultural activities, the accumulation of ever more money—and the power and glamour it brings—will become their primary goal. There are already numerous writers, publishers, personal growth and encounter group leaders, and doubtless—although less publicly visible—producers and sellers of illegal drugs who are millionaires. Their countercultural "piety," to parody Wesley, has led to riches; and their riches, unless some new factor has entered history, endanger piety.

When hope for rapid social change is frustrated or one's chosen vehicle of protest proves unreliable, many persons, still committed to new values, shift from one countercultural group to another. If the establishment changes all too slowly, one can live out his new values in a commune. If a drug-and-sex-oriented group shatters one's selfhood as much as it shatters established values, he can turn to an ascetic religious group that still is experienced as highly countercultural. Although for some these are brief or part-time activities, for a few they become a way of life. Of the thousands of communes that have appeared in the United States in the last twenty years, most have lasted for only a few years. Some have reduced internal conflict, however, and have learned to live with the nonnegotiable demands of the larger society to become established as a way of life.

Finally, one must note the personal tragedies that are the accompaniment, for some, of participation of countercultures. Ellen Goodman has written movingly of the "Sixties Kid" out of step with the world, who "dropped out—not only from college but from gowing up." His "quiet desperation," and that of others like him has not led, with Thoreau, to withdrawal from one life into another, but to resignation, to "a permanent loss of will." "They embraced their lack of purpose, as if it were a benign response to a harsh world."[46]

Some of those who are successful, by dominant standards, are also distressed. A report by Robert Lindsey, based on interviews with psychiatrists and mental health counselors, carries the headline: "Many Rebels of the 1960's Are Depressed as 30 Nears." The perceived failure of their earlier visions and the sense of emptiness from having "done everything" and still feeling depressed have increased their alienation. "I've got a good job, I'm successful, and I want to kill myself. Life doesn't mean anything."[47]

We are doubtless referring to a small minority of those actively involved in recent countercultures. More have transposed their discomfort into reformist activities or have joined one of the new religions. We cannot ignore, however, the higher rate of depression, of alcoholism and other forms of drug addiction, and of suicide. Rates of suicide for young people have increased by more than 200 per cent since 1955. Only a case-by-case study could reveal the extent to which this increase reflects participation in and disillusionment with countercultural activities. Even a high correlation would not demonstrate a causal connection. Perhaps those with high levels of anxiety, an effect of their earliest experiences, were led first into a countercultural protest and then into self-destruction. This was taking place in an increasingly anomic setting, which released suicidal tendencies, as Durkheim has so powerfully argued. Countercultural participation, as I read the evidence, is one ingredient in a complex mixture of forces that have increased the number of suicides.[48]

Similar tragic outcomes occurred among the Bohemians of the post-World War I period, as their youth faded. By 1927, F. Scott Fitzgerald wrote,

> . . . contemporaries of mine had begun to disappear into the dark maw of violence. A classmate killed his wife and himself on Long Island, another tumbled "accidentally" from a skyscraper in Philadelphia, another purposely from a skyscraper in New York. One was killed in a speakeasy in Chicago; another was beaten to death in a speakeasy in New York. . . . These are not catastrophes that I went out of my way to look for—these were my friends; moreover, these things happened not during the depression but during the boom.[49]

(With a few word changes I could have used this statement to describe the 1970s and early 80s.)

Amid these various responses, what seems to me the most crucial aspect of countercultural participation is heightened ambivalence. Old conflicts and antipathies do not disappear; they are seen in a new light. Utopian dreams fade, but the new, more complicated reality doesn't take their place as the promised land. Sadness over goals not attained is often blended with a chastened activism for goals still to be won. Through the range of effects we see a common element, a confirmation of "generational theory": The major experiences of early adulthood are decisive in shaping the issues that dominate a person's life. These become, of course, not simply personal issues but social issues, as those now "over thirty" move more completely into influential positions. Some of them, as Westhues says, are "carrying a vision of what cannot be today or tomorrow but which prompts us to at least leave yesterday behind."[50]

Conclusion

> *Let us learn to apply the insights of science on a human scale, so that people "may learn to live more gently upon the Earth."*
>
> New Alchemy Institute

Stavrianos, to whom I am indebted for this quotation, sees four types of changes, political and economic as well as technical, that constitute, in the words of the title of his book, *The Promise of the Coming Dark Age*. Each of the four has been brought to public attention and tried out, in part, as a result of protests and activities of unorthodox groups. Stavrianos speaks of shifts from aristo-technology to demo-technology, from boss control to worker control, from representative to participatory democracy, and from self-subordination to self-actualization. None of these changes is a panacea, although each has, on occasion, been acclaimed as such. In his thoughtful discussion, Stavrianos largely avoids excessive claims as he examines some of the developments that can help to achieve several goals: to bring technology into a human frame, resource-protecting and smaller in scale; to increase both efficiency and satisfaction in work, through political decentralization, the establishment of counter-institutions, and the development of effective "watchdog" associations; and to open up greater opportunities for self-actualization by the reduction of discrimination and the enlargement of life's goals.

These goals are complimentary to another: recognition of the interdependence of the world's people. The countercultures of recent years, interacting with ecological, economic, political, and spiritual crises—by which they were partly created—have helped to forge a new awareness of our common fate. This is an ancient belief, of course, but one that easily gets buried under the weight of individual and national problems. Today we have some renewal of emphasis on the fact that the world is a single geographical unit. In a phrase popularized by Barbara Ward, Kenneth Boulding, and others, we are all riding on spaceship earth, a total environment containing a single, highly interdependent human community. The depth of the interdependence and the consequences of our failure to act upon it may have increased, but the fact of it has a permanent quality. "No man is an *Island*, entire of it selfe; every man is a peece of the *Continent*, a part of the maine . . . any man's *death* diminishes *me*, because I am involved in *Mankinde*; And therefore never send to know for whom the *bell* tolls; It tolls for thee."

Few can match the eloquence of this familiar passage from John Donne's *Devotions upon Emergent Occasions*, but this generation should count itself fortunate in having an activist as well as a devotional testimony to the interdependence of humankind. It seems to me self-evident that we have, at best, a few generations within which to abolish war as a way of trying to settle disputes. That will occur, however, only if a far greater measure of international, as well as intranational, equality has been attained, the profligate consumption of resources curtailed, and the concentration of power drastically reduced. To those goals, the "Me!" parts of countercultures, whether of the withdrawal or the mystical varieties, will contribute little. Those that look outward, challenging the legitimacy of the dominant institutions and urging drastically different standards, can help to create institutions that correspond more closely to the world's great needs.

A kind of privatism, however, is a major theme, even of the present emphasis on ecology: Save the environment so that I can have a quiet corner. To this must be added a stronger emphasis on a "crowded-earth ecology," a recognition that six or seven billion of us will reside here by the end of the century and ten billion or more only a few decades later. We will be not only mutually dependent, but mutually visible, even beyond the present levels. Dominant institutions seem ill prepared to deal with the impact of this situation.

Perhaps it is only from a countercultural movement that we can expect to hear: The nation-state is not sacrosanct. A few decades ago, British pundits used to say, only partly in just: We are all honorary Americans; we are powerfully affected by American decisions and ought to have a vote. Now we are all honorary world citizens. This is not a matter of "giving up" national sovereignty. It has been taken away by technological developments, enormous population growth, incredibly destructive weapons, and our great interdependence. We only pretend to have it—a vastly dangerous pretense.

Continued economic growth for wealthy nations and wealthy individuals is not the road to salvation.

Our grandchildren (all of them, seen together) have rights, of which we are collectively the guardians.

I would not want to run for Congress on such a platform, unless I needed the exercise. These are countercultural planks. Were they to become rallying points for a new wave of challenges to the social order, we might get from Tom Wolfe, or some other keen-eyed observer, an article on the " 'All of Us' Decade." *1984* would be a good year for it to appear.

With such a large and growing population in the world, it seems unwise, indeed impossible, to give up the productivity of industrialization. This means, in turn, that instrumentalism, large-scale coordination, technical training, and high levels of skill are needed. Yet we know too little of the costs of such industrialization, not only in smothering our sense of play and mystery and sensuality, as its opponents say, but also in its own terms—the pollution, the illness, the exhaustion of irreplaceable resources, and the violent conflicts over dwindling supplies that are among its by-products.[51] We are only beginning to learn to say no to some industrialization, as for example in some forms of highly capitalized farming that is, in fact, less productive, depletes the soil, wastes water and other resources, breeds new pests, and adds trace elements of harmful substances to our food.

In such a situation it seems likely that cultural, as well as political, protests will continue.

In a perceptive paper a decade ago Fred Davis observed that hippies, despite their similarities to earlier movements, were more likely than their predecessors to persist. He saw a large middle- and working-class group living mainly by a set of values essential to an industrialized and technical society, but also a hippie "dropout group," and a "larger, morally aggrieved, economically subsidized and culturally separatist Third World segment (mainly blacks, Chicanos, and Amerindians?" all living in symbiotic relationship. "The hippie contraculture," he wrote, "is not an epiphenomenon—a mere fad, fashion, or temporary aberration." Precisely because the dominant, technically oriented society cannot abandon its values, its reverse image—the hippie contraculture—will continue. The three cultures will not have impermeable boundaries. There will be coming and going, with some of the "third world" members climbing and some of the hedonistic and expressive styles from hippiedom spreading to the larger population.[52]

His predictions are on target. There is now a substantial middle class among America's "third world" population, but the large majority are still on the margins of an affluent society. If hippies, as we came to think of them in the 1960s, are less numerous, there are others living by "reverse images," and the new norms have made some inroads into the mainstream culture. In 1969, 12 per cent of American adults thought marijuana should be made legal; by 1979, 25 per cent held that view. In 1969, 21 per cent believed that premarital sex was not wrong; that percentage had increased to 55 by 1979.[53]

In the United States at the present time, there is some tendency to romanticize the 1960s. The myth that is emerging, forgetting some of the harsher facts, may be more powerful—and more constructive—than the reality. Just as we make our past heroes into something bigger than life, shaping them into what we now need them to be, so we shape our social movements, adapting them to our current requirements.

We cannot regard all segments of highly diverse countercultural movements as if they carried the same implications for social change. Some are irrelevant, others poorly adapted to the world situation or to constants of the human condition, while still others are viable innovations. Like established organizations, groups seeking to live by inverted values face a number of dilemmas and contradictions, which some learn to deal with and others are destroyed by. The deepest contradiction is that between the powerful anarchic impulse and the impulse to organize a new society within which the new values can be protected. It proves to be difficult to do my own thing, escape bureaucratic traps, get release from social conventions, and at the same time to overcome loneliness and find a warm, supportive community in a civilized and well-governed society. "If autocracy is the anarchy of lawless, lonely tyrants, anarchy is the tyranny of lawless, lonely crowds."[54] There are limits to the degree to which one can attain maximum sensual enjoyment, sex without commitment, responsibility, and "hassles," and yet find a situation in which one can love and be loved.

"After attacking definition as such, differentiation as such, ritual as such, it is very difficult to turn about and seek the new definitions, differentiations and rituals which will remedy the case. . . . It follows that the solution to grave problems of social organisation can rarely come from those who experience them."[55] They can alert society to those problems, but it remains for others who can "resist the allurements of millennial thinking," as Douglas puts it, to struggle with solutions.

This may be too limited a view. Viewing the recent past at points seven years apart, Musgrove saw signs that three important lessons had been learned by many participants in countercultures:

> . . . that hard drugs are not ecstatic but soporific and finally lethal: they do not enhance personal relationships, but destroy them; that communes are more difficult to establish and maintain than was initially supposed: instead of promoting "meaningful" relationships, they can often survive only by keeping relationships shallow; and there are limits to a social system's being purely "expressive": "instrumentality" creeps in and may be a condition of survival.[56]

These are only negative lessons, however; and they may not be the correct or the most important ones. They may add to the list of persons, in Mary Douglas's phrase, who can "resist millennial thinking," but they do not of themselves represent the new ideas that are demanded in this age of rapid change.

The indirect effects of countercultures are probably more important than the direct and intended effects. The protest movements of mid-seventeenth-century England created a dissenting *tradition* that has outlasted some of the content of particular dissenting movements. This tradition has strongly influenced English and American history ever since. France and Germany, on the other hand, with much less strong traditions of dissent, have been more subject to revolutionary-counterrevolutionary cycles.[57]

Insofar as some upper-middle-class Wasps and Jews persist in their opposition to and withdrawal from technological society, Berger and Berger observe, they are less likely to modify that society drastically then to create new room at the top for the sons and daughters of manual workers—"The Blueing of America." "If Yale should be hopelessly greened," the Bergers write, "Wall Street will get used to recruits from Fordham or Wichita State. Italians will have no difficulty running the RAND Corporation, Baptists the space program."[58]

The effects of a given form of counterculture depend not only on its own characteristics but on the situation. Suppose that it becomes essential for wealthy societies to shift into a lower consumption, lower resource-using style of life. In the last few years we have discovered, once again, that even a small drop in accustomed levels of living exposes a society to enormous strains. All the political compromises and hard bargains through which a given distribution of resources has been attained are exposed. Without unusual support, lower consumption *values* would come about only from the effects of the slow and painful erosion of necessity. Now into this scene may come (has come), not as a purposive invention but as a cultural mutant, a movement that reduces certain pleasure demands in the name of a powerful ideology that satisfies other needs. The reduction in what was formerly thought to be a high standard of living is not defeat; it is, in fact, the good life. We find "religious" support for the shift rather than sullen, strife-ridden retreat. Communes, ascetically inclined sects, and hippies may help to devalue the pleasure currency, helping those involved and the many others pushed toward the new values by their appraisals of the situation to balance their psychic economies. Without such shifts, we would have to think in terms of a continuously escalating pleasure demand standard. The new values, of course, have a cost: Painfully won disciplines, essential to other values, may be weakened; additional value shifts are tied into the change by the counterculturalists.

Someone has said that every country gets the socialist party it deserves. It is equally true that every society gets the countercultures it deserves, for they do not simply contradict, they also express the situation from which they emerge—pushing away from it, deploring its contradictions, caricaturing its weaknesses, and drawing on its neglected and underground traditions. If we shudder at the illegal drug problem, we ought to study more carefully our rates of alcoholism and lung cancer and the results of the use of other legal mind-altering drugs. If we shudder at the Manson family or the Symbionese Liberation Army we ought to do more than contemplate the violence we do to some of our children, by action and lack of action. If we shudder at the Church of Satan, we should at the same time note the aberrant violations of basic values by "respectable" people, violations that such nonconformist cults have transposed into virtues.

Lest I seem to be confirming only the negative images of countercultures, let me add: If we applaud the emphasis on gentleness and love, on conservation and sharing, on self-reliance and self-discovery that characterizes many oppositional movements today, we should recognize that these too—although expressed in the context of drastic value reversals—borrow from the dominant culture even as they oppose it.

The most important lesson from the study of countercultures is not what it tells us about our times—or any specific time—but what it tells us about the human condition. In some ways such a study underlines the points made by conservatives: The social fabric is delicate, it is based on long experience, it is built on constant factors in human life. Therefore, don't touch. This is often the wrong conclusion, however.

Just because the social fabric is delicate, we need continually to weave in new threads. A cultural—countercultural confrontation, a consequence of changing conditions and inflexible structures, is a costly way to proceed. We need to learn how to respond to early warning signals rather than waiting for overcompensating attacks powered by ambivalence and anger.

Whether we are speaking of cultures or of countercultures, we are confronted by an analog of the old political question: Who guards the guardians?[59] A pyramid of answers has been applied to the political question:

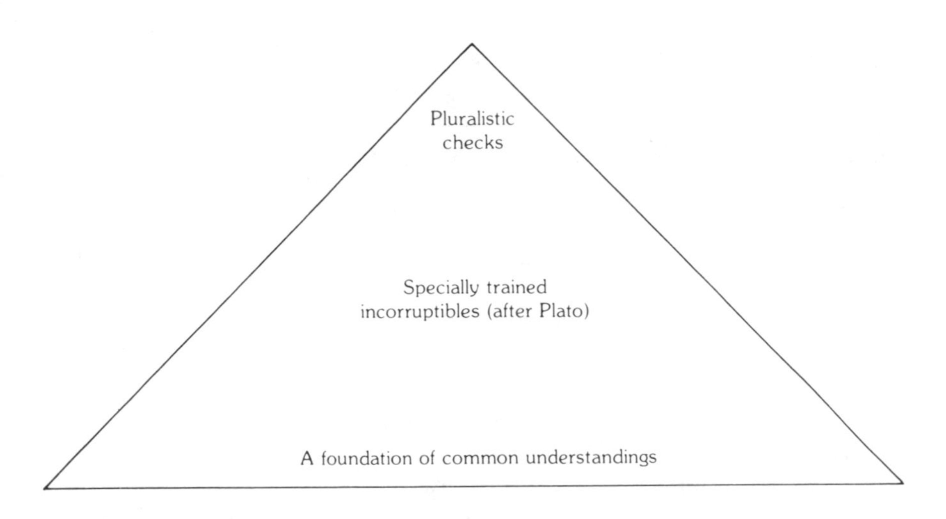

Applying this design to countercultural transitions, we need to ask: Who sets the standards of those who set the standards? What happens when the pyramid of answers has been lost or greatly weakened? Simply to affirm or to oppose either the new or the old is not to answer but to evade the questions. We need continuous and intensive study of the various consequences of the new and old standards.

In my judgment we are in the midst of a major civilizational transformation. The critical issue that humankind faces today is how to create a rolling adjustment to the incredibly rapid and drastic changes taking place on the planet. We're faced with the problem of rebuilding the station, relaying and changing the gauge of the tracks, and accommodating vastly more passengers, while still keeping the trains running. Some say: "Don't change; civilization can be breached too easily; or, in the language of the train analogy, patch up the station a bit, but don't tamper with the basic structure. Others say: Stop the trains; the building isn't worth saving; it's about to collapse; we need a clean field on which to build anew. That is the position taken by countercultures. If we think of them as art forms, we may find that, like other forms of art ranging from the sublime to the ugly, they highlight, dramatize, and anticipate drastic problems. Whether as "voices crying in the wilderness" or as symptoms of major disorders—unintended warnings and illustrations of what may lie ahead—countercultures require the most intensive study, not only by those whose aim and task it is to examine societies and to see them whole, but also by those who strive to improve them. We shall be fortunate if these are in many instances the same people.

Notes

1. *Cleveland Plain Dealer*, May 29, 1976, p. 5-A.
2. Philip Slater, *The Pursuit of Loneliness*, 1971, pp. 110-11.
3. Emile Durkheim, *The Rules of Sociological Method*, 1938, pp. 70-71.
4. Christopher Hill, *The World Turned Upside Down: Radical Ideas During the English Revolution*, 1975, p. 371.
5. Emile Durkheim, *The Elementary Forms of the Religious Life*, 1965, pp. 14-15.
6. Lionel Trilling, *The Opposing Self*, 1955, p. 176.
7. Victor Turner, *Dramas, Fields, and Metaphors*, 1974, p. 268. See also David Felton, editor, *Mindfuckers: A Source Book on the Rise of Acid Fascism in America*, 1972, and Nathan Adler, *The Underground Stream: New Life Styles and the Antinomian Personality*, 1972, pp. 126-32, for description of some of the contemporary dark shadows.
8. Luther Gerlach and Virginia Hine, *Lifeway Leap: The Dynamics of Change in America*, 1973, p. 260. See also Kai Erikson, *Wayward Puritans: A Study in the Sociology of Deviance*, 1966.
9. Loren Eiseley, *The Immense Journey*, 1957, pp. 52-53.
10. Gerlach and Hine, 1973, pp. 224-25.
11. Charles Reich, *The Greening of America*, 1970, p. 4.
12. Donald T. Campbell, "On the Conflicts Betweeen Biological and Social Evolution and Between Psychology and Moral Tradition," 1975, p. 1121.
13. *Ibid.*, p. 1123.
14. See Jay Meddin, "Human Nature and the Dialectics of Immanent Sociocultural Change," 1976.
15. Campbell, 1975, p. 1118.
16. As recorded in Matthew 10: 35-36.

17. Ted Lewellen, "Deviant Religion and Cultural Evolution: The Aymara Case," 1979, p. 249.

18. For example, see Konrad Lorenz, *On Aggression*, 1966.

19. Gerlach and Hine, 1973, pp. 219-60.

20. *Ibid.*, p. 314.

21. Christopher Boehm, "Rational Preselection from Hamadryas to *Homo Sapiens:* The Place of Decisions in Adaptive Process," 1978, p. 265.

22. J. Milton Yinger, *The Scientific Study of Religion*, 1970, p. 477; see also pp. 387-92 and 476-80.

23. See Theda Skocpol, *States and Social Revolutions: A Comparative Analysis of France, Russia and China*, 1979; Lyford P. Edwards, *The Natural History of Revolution*, 1927; and James C. Davies, "Toward a Theory of Revolution," 1962.

24. Herbert Blumer, in *An Outline of the Principles of Sociology*, Robert E. Park, editor, 1939, pp. 269-71.

25. Abner Cohen, *Two-Dimensional Man*, 1974, chap. 3.

26. Skocpol, 1979.

27. Karl Marx, *The Eighteenth Brumaire of Louis Napoleon*, 1963, p. 15.

28. Joan Robinson, *The Cultural Revolution in China*, 1969, p. 28.

29. Milovan Djilas, *The New Class: An Analysis of the Communist System*, 1962. See also John K. Fairbank, *The United States and China*, 1979, chap. 16.

30. Fred Hung in *Moving a Mountain: Cultural Change in China*, Godwin C. Chu and Francis L. K. Hsu, editors, 1979, pp. 419-23.

31. Ezra Vogel, *Canton Under Communism: Programs and Politics in a Provincial Capital, 1949-1968*, 1969, p. 321. See also Marc J. Blecher and Gordon White, *Micropolitics in Contemporary China: A Technical Unit During and After the Cultural Revolution*, 1979.

32. See Lowell Dittmer, " 'Line Struggle' in Theory and Practice: The Origins of the Cultural Revolution Reconsidered," 1977, and Albert J. Bergesen, "A Durkheimian Theory of Witch-Hunts with the Chinese Cultural Revolution of 1966-69 as an Example," 1978.

33. Lowell Dittmer in Chu and Hsu, editors, 1979, pp. 207-36.

34. Robinson, 1969, p. 27.

35. Fox Butterfield, *The New York Times*, October 12, 1979, p. II-3.

36. See Robinson, 1969, p. 47.

37. *Ibid.*, p. 43.

38. Reich, 1970 (note 11 above); Theodore Roszak, *The Making of a Counter Culture*, 1969; and Robert Wuthnow, *The Consciousness Reformation*, 1976b.

39. I shall "hide" my appraisal of the shifting emphases in China—not being certain of my judgment—in a footnote. The three-way pull of recent years might be charted as follows (with the dots representing guesses about comparative locations):

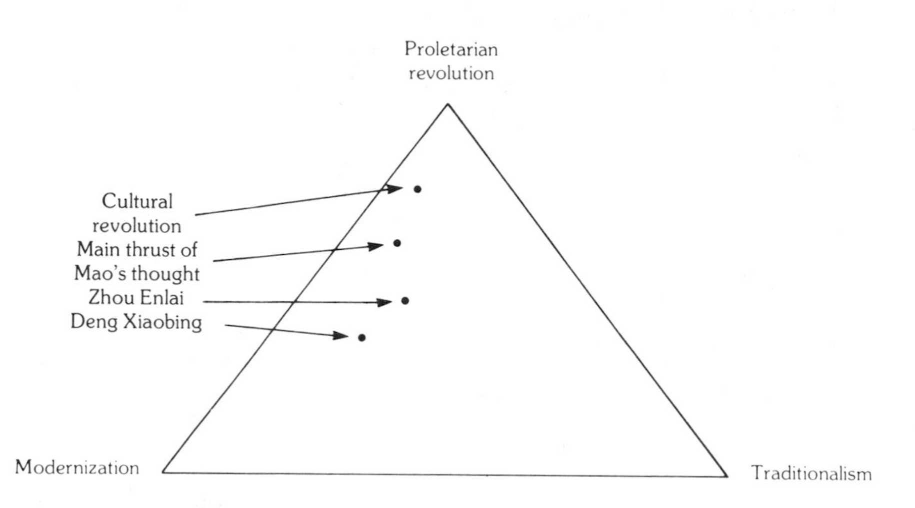

40. See Max Weber, *The Protestant Ethic and the Spirit of Capitalism*, 1930, and Wuthnow, 1976b.

41. See Rex Weiner and Deanne Stillman, *Woodstock Census: The Nationwide Survey of the Sixties Generation*, 1979.

42. *St. Petersburg Times*, January 16, 1977, p. 2B

43. See Jerry Rubin, *Do It*, 1970, and *idem*, *Growing (Up) at 37*, 1976.

44. Hill, 1975, (note 4 above), p. 240.

45. See Robert Reinhold, Tony Schwartz, and Robin Herman, "After Woodstock: The Impact of the Counterculture," 1979.

46. *Cleveland Plain Dealer*, January 28, 1979, p. IV-7.

47. *The New York Times*, February 29, 1976, pp. 1, 40.

48. See Herbert Hendin, *The Age of Sensation*, 1975, chap. 9, and J. Milton Yinger, *Toward a Field Theory of Behavior*, 1965, pp. 279-81.

49. Quoted by Malcolm Cowley, *Exile's Return: A Narrative of Ideas*, 1934, p. 238.

50. Kenneth Westhues, *Society's Shadow: Studies in the Sociology of Countercultures*, 1972, p. 208.

51. See William R. Catton, Jr. *Overshoot: The Ecological Basis of Revolutionary Change*, 1980.

52. See Fred Davis, *On Youth Subcultures: The Hippie Variant*, 1971, pp. 21-26.

53. Robert Reinhold, *The New York Times*, August 12, 1979, p. 38.

54. E. Digby Baltzell, "Epilogue: To Be a Phoenix—Reflections on Two Noisy Ages of Prose," 1972, p. 202.

55. Mary Douglas, *Natural Symbols,* 1970a, pp. 153-54.

56. Frank Musgrove, *Ecstasy and Holiness: Counter Culture and the Open Society,* 1974, p. 26.

57. See Baltzell, 1972, pp. 217-18.

58. Peter Berger and Brigette Berger, "The Blueing of America," 1971, p. 23.

59. Ernest Gellner, *Contemporary Thought and Politics,* 1974, pp. 40-41.

Bibliography

ABELL, TROY, and LARRY LYON. "Do the Differences Make a Difference? An Empirical Evaluation of the Culture of Poverty in the United States." *American Ethnologist* 6 (August 1979): 602-21.

ABERLE, DAVID. *The Peyote Religion Among the Navaho.* Chicago: Aldine, 1966.

———. "The Prophet Dance and Reactions to White Contact." *Southwestern Journal of Anthropology* 15 (1959): 74-83.

———. "Shared Values in Complex Societies." *American Sociological Review* 15 (August 1950): 495-502.

ABRAMS, PHILIP, and ANDREW MCCULLOCH, with SHEILA ABRAMS and PAT GORE. *Communes, Sociology and Society.* Cambridge: Cambridge University Press, 1976.

ACKERMAN, JAMES S. "The Demise of the *Avant Garde:* Notes on the Sociology of Recent American Art." *Comparative Studies in Society and History* 11 (October 1969):371-384.

ADAMS, ROBERT M. *Bad Mouth: Fugitive Papers on the Dark Side.* Berkeley: University of California Press, 1977.

ADELSON, JOSEPH. "What Generation Gap?" *New York Times Magazine*, January 18, 1970, pp. 10-11, 34-36, 45.

ADLER, NATHAN. *The Underground Stream: New Life Styles and the Antinomian Personality.* New York: Harper Torchbooks, 1972.

AIKEN, CONRAD. *Time in the Rock.* New York: Charles Scribner's Sons, 1936.

ALVES, WAYNE M., and PETER H. ROSSI. "Who Should Get What? Fairness Judgments of the Distribution of Earnings." *American Journal of Sociology* 84 (November 1978): 541-64.

ANTHONY, DICK, and THOMAS ROBBINS. *In Gods We Trust: New Patterns in American Religious Pluralism.* New Brunswick, N.J.: Transaction Books, 1980.

ARMYTAGE, W. H. G. *Heavens Below: Utopian Experiments in England, 1560-1960.* London: Routledge & Kegan Paul, 1961.

ARNOLD, DAVID O., editor. *The Sociology of Subcultures.* Berkeley, Calif.: Glendessary Press, 1970.

ARNOLD, MATTHEW. *Poetical Works.* London: Macmillan, 1907.

ARON, RAYMOND. *History and the Dialectic of Violence*. Trans. Barry Cooper. New York: Harper & Row, 1975.

ASHLINE, NELSON F., T. R. PEZZULLO, and C. I. NORRIS, editors. *Education, Inequality, and National Policy*. Lexington, Mass.: Lexington Books, 1976.

AYLMER, G. E., editor. *The Levellers in the English Revolution*. London: Thames & Hudson, 1975.

BABBIE, EARL R. "The Third Civilization: An Examination of Sokagakkai." *Review of Religious Research* 7 (Winter 1966): 101-21.

BABCOCK, BARBARA A., editor. *The Reversible World: Symbolic Inversion in Art and Society*. Ithaca, N.Y.: Cornell University Press, 1978.

BACK, KURT W. *Beyond Words: The Story of Sensitivity Training and the Encounter Movement*. Baltimore: Penguin Books, 1973.

BAINBRIDGE, WILLIAM SIMS. *Satan's Power: A Deviant Psychotherapy Cult*. Berkeley: University of California Press, 1978.

BALANDIER, GEORGES. *Political Anthropology*. Trans. A. M. Sheridan Smith. New York: Random House, 1970.

BALL, RICHARD A. "The Dialectical Method: Its Application to Social Theory." *Social Forces* 57 (March 1979): 785-98.

BALL-ROKEACH, SANDRA J. "Values and Violence: A Test of the Subculture of Violence Thesis." *American Sociological Review* 38 (December 1973): 736-49.

BALSWICK, JACK. "The Jesus People Movement: A Generational Interpretation." *Journal of Social Issues* 30, No. 3 (1974): 23-42.

BALTZELL, E. DIGBY. "Epilogue: To Be a Phoenix—Reflections on Two Noisy Ages of Prose." *American Journal of Sociology* 78 (July 1972): 202-20.

BANFIELD, EDWARD. *The Unheavenly City: The Nature and Future of Our Urban Crisis*. Boston: Little, Brown, 1968. Rev. ed., 1974.

BANTON, MICHAEL, editor. *Anthropological Approaches to the Study of Religion*. London: Tavistock, 1966.

BARAKA, AMIRI (LeRoi Jones). *Selected Poetry of Amiri Baraka/LeRoi Jones*. New York: William Morrow, 1979a.

______. *Selected Plays and Prose of Amiri Baraka/LeRoi Jones*. New York: William Morrow, 1979b.

BARBER, THEODORE X. *LSD, Marihuana, Yoga, and Hypnosis*. Chicago: Aldine, 1970.

BARKER, EILEEN. "Living the Divine Principle: Inside the Reverend Sun Myung Moon's Unification Church in Britain." *Archives de Sciences Sociales des Religions* 45 (January-March 1978): 75-93.

BARKUN, MICHAEL. *Disaster and the Millennium*. New Haven: Yale University Press, 1974.

BARNES, DOUGLAS F. "Charisma and Religious Leadership: An Historical Analysis." *Journal for the Scientific Study of Religion* 17 (March 1978): 1-18.

BARNETT, HOMER. *Indian Shakers: A Messianic Cult of the Pacific Northwest.* Carbondale: Southern Illinois University Press, 1957.

BATES, WILLIAM, and BETTY CROWTHER. *Drugs: Causes, Circumstances, and Effects of Their Use.* Morristown, N.J.: General Learning Press, 1973.

BATESON, GREGORY. *Steps to an Ecology of Mind.* San Francisco: Chandler, 1972.

BATESON, GREGORY, *et al.* "Toward a Theory of Schizophrenia." *Behavioral Science* 1 (October 1956): 251-64.

BECKER, HOWARD P., with CHRISTOPHER BENNETT BECKER. "Normative Reactions to Normlessness." *American Sociological Review* 25 (December 1960): 803-10.

BECKER, HOWARD S. *Outsiders: Studies in the Sociology of Deviance.* New York: The Free Press, 1963.

BECKETT, SAMUEL. *Waiting for Godot.* New York: Grove Press, 1954.

BECKFORD, JAMES. "Through the Looking-Glass and Out the Other Side: Withdrawal from Reverend Moon's Unification Church." *Archives de Sciences Sociales des Religion* 45 (January-March 1978): 95-116.

BEIDELMAN, T. O. "Swazi Royal Ritual." *Africa*, 36 (October 1966): 373-405.

BELL, DANIEL. *The Cultural Contradictions of Capitalism.* New York: Basic Books, 1978.

BELL, WENDELL, and ROBERT V. ROBINSON. "An Index of Evaluated Equality: Measuring Conceptions of Social Justice in England and the United States." *Comparative Studies in Sociology* 1 (1978): 235-70.

BELLAH, ROBERT N. *Beyond Belief: Essays on Religion in a Post-Traditional World.* New York: Harper & Row, 1970.

BELLOW, SAUL. *Herzog.* London: Penguin Books, 1965.

BEN-YEHUDA, NACHMAN. "The European Witch Craze of the 14th to 17th Centuries: A Sociologists's Perspective." *American Journal of Sociology* 86 (July 1980): 1-31.

BERENS, LEWIS H. *The Digger Movement in the Days of the Commonwealth as Revealed in the Writings of Gerrard Winstanley, the Digger* (1906). London: Holland Press and Merlin Press, 1961.

BERGER, BENNETT M., *Looking for America: Essays on Youth, Suburbia, and Other American Obsessions.* Englewood Cliffs, N.J.: Prentice-Hall, 1971.

______. *The Survival of a Counterculture: Ideological Work and Everyday Life among Rural Communards.* Berkeley: University of California Press, 1981.

BERGER, BENNETT M., and BRUCE M. HACKETT. "On the Decline of Age Grading in Rural Hippie Communes." *Journal of Social Issues* 30, No. 2 (1974): 163-83.

BERGER, PETER L. "Charisma and Religious Innovation: The Social Location of Israelite Prophecy." *American Sociological Review* 28 (December 1963): 940-50.

______. *Facing Up to Modernity: Excursions in Society, Politics, and Religion.* New York: Basic Books, 1977.

______. *The Sacred Canopy: Elements of a Sociological Theory of Religion.* Garden City, N.Y.: Doubleday & Co., 1967.

BERGER, PETER L., and BRIGITTE BERGER. "The Blueing of America." *New Republic*, April 3, 1971, pp. 20-23.

BERGER, PETER L., BRIGITTE BERGER, and HANSFRIED KELLNER. *The Homeless Mind.* New York: Random House, 1973.

BERGER, SUZANNE. "Politics and Antipolitics in Western Europe in the Seventies." *Daedalus*, Winter 1979, pp. 27-50.

BERGESEN, ALBERT JAMES. "A Durkheimian Theory of 'Witch-Hunts' with the Chinese Cultural Revolution of 1966-69 as an Example." *Journal for The Scientific Study of Religion* 17 (March 1978): 19-29.

______. "Political Witch Hunts: The Sacred and the Subversive in Cross-National Perspective." *American Sociological Review* 42 (April 1977): 220-33.

BERGSON, HENRI. "Laughter." In *Comedy*, Wylie Sypher, editor. Garden City, N.Y.: Doubleday Anchor Books, 1956, pp. 61-190.

BERKE, JOSEPH, editor. *Counter-Culture: The Creation of an Alternative Society.* London: Peter Owen Ltd., 1969.

BERNSTEIN, EDUARD. *Cromwell and Communism: Socialism and Democracy in the Great English Revolution.* New ed. London: F. Cass, 1963.

BESTOR, ARTHUR EUGENE, Jr. *Backwoods Utopias.* Philadelphia: University of Pennsylvania Press, 1950.

BIALE, DAVID. *Gershom Scholem: Kabbalah and Counter-History.* Cambridge: Harvard University Press, 1979.

BIDDLE, BRUCE, BARBARA BANK, and MARJORIE MARLIN. "Parental and Peer Influence on Adolescents." *Social Forces* 58 (June 1980): 1057-79.

BLAKE, WILLIAM. *Poems.* Edited by W. H. Stevenson. Text by David V. Erdman. London: Longmans, 1971.

BLAU, PETER M., editor. *Approaches to the Study of Social Structure.* New York: The Free Press, 1975.

______. *Exchange and Power in Social Life.* New York: Wiley, 1964.

BLECHER, MARC J., and GORDON WHITE. *Micropolitics in Contemporary China: A Technical Unit During and After the Cultural Revolution.* White Plains, N.Y.: M. E. Sharpe, 1979.

BLOY, MYRON B., Jr. "Alienated Youth, the Counter Culture, and the Chaplain." In Donald R. Cutler, editor, *The Religious Situation: 1969.* Boston: Beacon Press, 1969, pp. 649-63.

BLUMER, HERBERT. Contribution in *An Outline of the Principles of Sociology,*

Robert E. Park, editor. New York: Barnes & Noble, 1939, Part IV.

BODEMAN, Y. MICHAEL."Mystical, Satanic, and Chiliastic Forces in Countercultural Movements: Changing the World—Or Reconciling It." *Youth and Society* 5 (June 1974): 433-47.

BOEHM, CHRISTOPHER. "Rational Preselection from Hamadryas to *Homo Sapiens*: The Place of Decisions in Adaptive Process." *American Anthropologist* 80 (June 1978): 265-96.

BOTT, ELIZABETH. "Psychoanalysis and Ceremony." In J. S. LaFontaine, editor, *The Interpretation of Ritual: Essays in Honor of A. I. Richards*. London: Tavistock Publications, 1972, pp. 205-37.

BOUDON, RAYMOND. *Education, Opportunity and Social Inequality: Changing Prospects in Western Society*. New York: Wiley, 1974.

BOULDING, ELISE. "Adolescent Culture: Reflections of Divergence." In *Social Forces and Schooling: An Anthropological and Sociological Perspective*, Nobuo K. Shimahara and Adam Scrupski, editors. New York: David McKay, 1975.

BOWKER, LEE. *Prisoner Subcultures*. Lexington, Mass.: Heath, 1977.

BOWLES, SAMUEL, and HERBERT GINTIS. *Schooling in Capitalist America*. New York: Basic Books, 1976.

BRADEN, WILLIAM. *The Private Sea: LSD and the Search for God*. New York: Quadrangle Books, 1967.

BRAILSFORD, H. N. *The Levellers and the English Revolution*. Edited and prepared for publication by Christopher Hill. London: The Cresset Press, 1961.

BRAKE, MIKE. "The Skinheads: An English Working Class Subculture." *Youth and Society* 6 (December 1974): 179-200.

BRAND, STEWART, editor. *The Next Whole Earth Catalog: Access to Tools*. Sausalito, Calif.: Point/Random House, 1980.

BRICKER, VICTORIA R., editor. "Intra-Cultural Variation." *American Ethnologist*, Vol. 2, February 1975, whole issue.

BRIM, ORVILLE G., Jr., and STANTON WHEELER, editors. *Socialization After Childhood: Two Essays*. New York: Wiley, 1965.

BROMLEY, DAVID G., and ANSON D. SHUPE, Jr. "Financing the New Religions: A Resource Mobilization Approach." *Journal for the Scientific Study of Religion* 19 (September 1980): 227-39.

BROWN, BERNARD E. *The French Revolt: May, 1968*. Morristown, N.J.: General Learning Press, 1970.

BROWN, CECIL. *The Life and Loves of Mr. Jiveass Nigger*. New York: Fawcett, 1978.

BROWN, JAMES W. "The Values and Norms of the Expressive Student Subculture." *Youth and Society* 4 (June 1973): 483-98.

BROWN, MICHAEL E. "The Condemnation and Persecution of Hippies." *Trans-Action* 6 (September 1969): 33-46.

BROWN, NORMAN O. "Apocalypse: The Place of Mystery in the Life of the Mind." *Harper's* 222 (May 1961): 46-49.

______. *Life Against Death: The Psychoanalytic Meaning of History*. New York: Random House, 1959.

______. *Love's Body*. New York: Random House, 1966.

BRYCE-LAPORTE, ROY S. "Crisis, Contraculture, and Religion Among West Indians in the Panama Canal Zone." In *Afro-American Anthropology*, Norman E. Whitten and John F. Szwed, editors. New York: The Free Press, 1970, pp. 103-18.

BUCK-MORSS, SUSAN. *The Origin of Negative Dialectics*. New York: Free Press, 1977.

BUFFALO, M. D., and JOSEPH W. RODGERS. "Behavioral Norms, Moral Norms, and Attachment: Problems of Deviance and Conformity." *Social Problems* 19 (Summer 1971): 101-13.

BURKE, KENNETH. *Language as Symbolic Action: Essays on Life, Literature, and Method*. Berkeley: University of California Press, 1968.

BURNS, TOM. "The Reference of Conduct in Small Groups: Cliques and Cabals in Occupational Milieu." *Human Relations* 8 (1955): 467-86.

BURRIDGE, KENELM. *Mambu: A Melanesian Millennium*. London: Methuen & Co., 1960.

BUTLER, CHRISTOPHER. *After the Wake: An Essay on the Contemporary Avant-Garde*. New York: Oxford University Press, 1980.

CAMPBELL, DONALD T. "On the Conflicts Between Biological and Social Evolution and Between Psychology and Moral Tradition." *American Psychologist* 30 (December 1975): 1103-26.

CAMUS, ALBERT. *The Rebel: An Essay on Man in Revolt*. Trans. Anthony Bower. New York: Random House, 1956.

CAPLAN, ARTHUR L., editor. *The Sociobiology Debate: Readings on Ethical and Scientific Issues*. New York: Harper & Row, 1978.

CARMICHAEL, STOKELY, and CHARLES HAMILTON. *Black Power*. New York: Vintage Books, 1967.

CARROLL, JACKSON W. "Transcendence and Mystery in the Counter Culture." *Religion in Life* 42 (August 1973): 361-75.

CATTON, WILLIAM R., Jr. *Overshoot: The Ecological Basis of Revolutionary Change*. Urbana: University of Illinois Press, 1980.

CHU, GODWIN C., and FRANCIS L. K. HSU, editors. *Moving a Mountain: Cultural Change in China*. Honolulu: East-West Center, 1979.

CLAMMER, J. R., editor. *The New Economic Anthropology*. New York: St. Martin's Press, 1976.

CLARK, BURTON R. *Educating the Expert Society*. San Francisco: Chandler, 1962.

CLARK, WALTER H. *Chemical Ecstasy: Psychedelic Drugs and Religion*. New York: Sheed & Ward, 1969.

CLARKE, MICHAEL. "On the Concept of 'Sub-Culture'." *British Journal of Sociology* 25 (1974): 428-41.

CLAYTON, RICHARD R., and HARWIN L. VOSS. "Shacking Up: Cohabitation in the 1970s." *Journal of Marriage and Family* 39 (May 1977): 273-83.

CLEAGE, ALBERT B., Jr. *Black Messiah*. New York: Sheed & Ward, 1968.

CLEAVER, ELDRIDGE. *Soul on Ice*. New York: McGraw-Hill, 1968.

CLECAK, PETER. *Radical Paradoxes: Dilemmas of the American Left: 1945-1970*. New York: Harper & Row, 1973.

CLOWARD, RICHARD A., *et al.*, editors. *Theoretical Studies in the Social Organization of the Prison*. New York: Social Science Research Council, 1960.

CLOWARD, RICHARD A., and LLOYD E. OHLIN. *Delinquency and Opportunity*. New York: The Free Press, 1960.

CLUB OF ROME. *The Limits to Growth*. 2d Edition. New York: Universe Books, 1974.

COGSWELL, BETTY E. "Variant Family Forms and Life Styles: Rejection of the Traditional Nuclear Family." *Family Coordinator* 24 (October 1975): 391-406.

COHEN, ABNER. *Two-Dimensional Man*. Berkeley: University of California Press, 1974.

COHEN, ALBERT K. *Delinquent Boys*. Glencoe, Ill.: The Free Press, 1955.

COHEN, ALBERT K., and HAROLD M. HODGES, Jr. "Characteristics of the Lower-Blue-Collar-Class." *Social Problems* 10 (Spring 1963): 303-34.

COHEN, ALBERT K., and JAMES F. SHORT, Jr. "Research in Delinquent Subcultures." *Journal of Social Issues* 14 (1958): 20-37.

COHEN, STANLEY, *Folk Devils and Moral Panics: The Creation of the Mods and Rockers*. London: MacGibbon & Kee, 1972.

COHN, NORMAN. *Europe's Inner Demons: An Enquiry Inspired by the Great Witch-Hunt*. New York: Basic Books, 1975.

______. *The Pursuit of the Millennium: Revolutionary Millenarians and Mystical Anarchists of the Middle Ages*. Rev. and exp. edition. New York: Oxford University Press, 1970.

COLEMAN, JAMES S. *The Adolescent Society*. New York: The Free Press, 1961.

______. "Review Essay: Inequality, Sociology, and Moral Philosophy." *American Journal of Sociology* 80 (November 1974): 739-64.

COLES, ROBERT. *Children of Crisis: A Study of Courage and Fear*. Boston: Little, Brown, 1967.

______. *Privileged Ones: The Well-off and the Rich in America*. Boston: Little, Brown, 1977.

COLLINS, RANDALL. *Conflict Sociology*. New York: Academic Press, 1975.

COMMONER, BARRY. *The Closing Circle: Nature, Man, and Technology.* New York: Knopf, 1971.

CONE, JAMES H. "Black Consciousness and the Black Church: A Historical-Theological Interpretation." *Annals of the American Academy of Political and Social Science* 387 (January 1970): 49-53.

______. *God of the Oppressed.* New York: The Seabury Press, 1975.

CONVERSE, PHILIP, and HOWARD SCHUMAN. "Silent Majorities and the Viet Nam War." *Scientific American* 222 (June 1970): 17-25.

CONWAY, FLO, and JIM SIEGELMAN. *Snapping: America's Epidemic of Sudden Personality Change.* New York: Dell Publishing Co., 1979.

COOK, KAREN S., and RICHARD M. EMERSON. "Power, Equity and Commitment in Exchange Networks." *American Sociological Review* 43 (October 1978): 721-39.

COOPER, DAVID G. *Psychiatry and Anti-Psychiatry.* New York: Balantine Books, 1971.

COSER, LEWIS. *Continuities in the Study of Social Conflict.* New York: The Free Press, 1967.

______. *The Functions of Social Conflict.* New York: The Free Press, 1956.

COSER, ROSE LAUB, and LEWIS COSER. "Jonestown as a Perverse Utopia." *Dissent* 26 (Spring 1979): 158-63.

COWLEY, MALCOLM. *Exile's Return: A Narrative of Ideas.* New York: W. W. Norton, 1934.

COX, HARVEY. *The Feast of Fools: A Theological Essay on Festivity and Fantasy.* New York: Harper & Row, 1970.

______. *Turning East: The Promise and Peril of the New Orientalism.* New York: Simon & Schuster, 1977.

CROSSMAN, RICHARD, editor. *The God That Failed.* New York: Harper & Row, 1949.

CUMMINGS, WILLIAM K. "The Aftermath of the University Crisis." *Japan Interpreter* 10 (Winter 1976): 350-60.

CURLE, ADAM. *Educational Problems of Developing Societies, with Case Studies of Ghana, Pakistan, and Nigeria.* Exp. and updated edition. New York: Praeger, 1973.

CUTLER, DONALD, R., editor. *The Religious Situation: 1969.* Boston: Beacon Press, 1969.

DAHRENDORF, RALF. *Class and Class Conflict in Industrial Society.* Stanford, Calif.: Stanford University Press, 1959.

DALTON, GEORGE, editor. *Studies in Economic Anthropology.* Washington: American Anthropological Association, 1971.

______, editor. *Tribal and Peasant Economies.* Austin: University of Texas Press, 1967.

DAMRELL, JOSEPH. *Search for Identity: Youth, Religion and Culture*. Beverly Hills: Sage Publications, 1978.

DAVIDOV, Y. N. "Counter-Culture—A Symptom of Development or an Indication of Decay?" Paper presented at the World Congress of Sociology, Uppsala, Sweden, August 14-19, 1978.

DAVIDSON, SARA. "The Rush for Instant Salvation." *Harper's Magazine*, July 1971, pp. 40-54.

DAVIES, JAMES C. "Toward a Theory of Revolution." *American Sociological Review* 27 (1962): 5-19.

DAVIS, DAVID BRION. "Some Themes of Counter-Subversion: An Analysis of Anti-Masonic, Anti-Catholic, and Anti-Mormon Literature." *Mississippi Historical Review* 48 (September 1960): 205-24.

DAVIS, FRED, *On Youth Subcultures: The Hippie Variant*. New York: General Learning Press, 1971.

DAVIS, J. C., "Gerrard Winstanley and the Restoraton of True Magistracy." *Past and Present*, No. 70 (February 1976), pp. 76-93.

DAVIS, NANETTE J. *Sociological Constructions of Deviance: Perspectives and Issues in the Field*. Dubuque, Iowa: William C. Brown, 1975.

DAVIS, NATALIE Z. "The Reasons of Misrule: Youth Groups and Charivaris in Sixteenth-Century France." *Past and Present*, No. 50 (February 1971), pp. 41-75.

______. "The Rites of Violence: Religious Riot in Sixteenth-Century France." *Past and Present*, No. 59 (May 1973), pp. 51-91.

DE BERKER, PAUL, and PATRICIA DE BERKER. *Misfits*. London: Pitman Publishing Company, 1973.

DECTER, MIDGE. *Liberal Parents, Radical Children*. New York: Coward, McCann & Geoghegan, 1975.

DEGLER, CARL N. *At Odds: Women and the Family in America from the Revolution to the Present*. New York: Oxford University Press, 1980.

DELEON, DAVID. *The American as Anarchist: Reflections on Indigenous Radicalism*. Baltimore: Johns Hopkins Press, 1979.

DELLA FAVE, L. RICHARD. "The Culture of Poverty Revisited: A Strategy for Research." *Social Problems* 21 (June 1974):609-21.

DEMOTT, BENJAMIN, "The Pro-Incest Lobby." *Psychology Today* 13 (March 1980): 11-16.

DENISOFF, R. SERGE. *Solid Gold: The Popular Record Industry*. New Brunswick, N. J.: Transaction Books, 1975.

DENISOFF, R. SERGE, and MARK H. LEVINE. "Generations and Counter-Culture: A Study in the Ideology of Music." *Youth and Society* 2 (September 1970): 33-58.

DEVEREUX, GEORGE. "Normal and Abnormal: The Key Problem of Psychiatric Anthropology." In *Some Uses of Anthropology: Theoretical and Applied*, J. B. Casagrande and T. Gladwin, editors. Washington: Anthropological Society of Washington, 1956, pp. 3-32.

DeVos, George, and Lola Romanucci-Ross, editors. *Ethnic Identity*. Palo Alto, Calif.: Mayfield Publishing Co., 1975.

Dickstein, Morris. *Gates of Eden: American Culture in the Sixties*. New York: Basic Books, 1977.

Dinnerstein, Dorothy. *The Mermaid and the Minotaur*. New York: Harper & Row, 1976.

Dittmer, Lowell. " 'Line Struggle' in Theory and Practice: The Origins of the Cultural Revolution Reconsidered." *The China Quarterly* 72 (December 1977): 675-712.

Djilas, Milovan. *The New Class: An Analysis of the Communist System*. New York: Praeger, 1962.

Donaldson, Ian. *The World Upside Down: Comedy from Jonson to Fielding*. Oxford: Oxford University Press, 1970.

Dorn, Dean S. "A Partial Test of the Delinquency Continuum Typology: Contracultures and Subcultures." *Social Forces* 47 (March 1969): 305-14.

Dostoevsky, Fyodor. *Notes from Underground* and *The Grand Inquisitor*. Trans. Ralph E. Matlaw. New York: E. P. Dutton, 1960.

______. *Poor Folk*. Trans. Lev Navrozov. Moscow: Foreign Languages Publishing House, 1957.

Douglas, Jack. *Youth in Turmoil*. Chevy Chase, Md.: National Institute of Mental Health, 1970.

Douglas, Mary. *Natural Symbols*. New York: Random House, 1970a.

______, editor. *Witchcraft: Confessions and Accusations*. London: Tavistock Publications, 1970b.

Downes, David M. *The Delinquent Solution*, New York: The Free Press, 1966.

Doyle, Bertram, *The Etiquette of Race Relations in the South*. Chicago: University of Chicago Press, 1937.

Drane, James, *A New American Reformation: A Study of Youth Culture and Religion*. Totowa, N. J.: Littlefield, Adams, & Co., 1974.

Drosnin, Michael. "Ripping Off: The New Life Style." *New York Times Magazine*, August 8, 1971, pp. 12-13, 47-48, 52.

Durkheim, Emile. *The Elementary Forms of the Religious Life*. Trans. Joseph Ward Swain. New York: The Free Press, 1965.

____ *Moral Education*. Foreword by Paul Fauconnet, trans. Everett K. Wilson and Herman Schnurer, edited by Everett K. Wilson. New York: The Free Press, 1973.

______. *The Rules of Sociological Method*. 8th edition. Trans. Sarah Solovay and John H. Mueller. Edited by George E. G. Catlin. Chicago: University of Chicago Press, 1938.

______. *Suicide*. Trans. John A. Spaulding and George Simpson. New York: The Free Press, 1951.

DURKHEIM, EMILE, and MARCEL MAUSS. *Primitive Classification*. Trans. and edited by Rodney Needham. London: Cohen & West, 1963.

DYER, EVERETT D. *The American Family: Variety and Change*. New York: McGraw-Hill, 1979.

EASTERLIN, RICHARD A. *Birth and Fortune: The Impact of Numbers on Personal Welfare*. New York: Basic Books, 1980.

______."What Will 1984 Be Like? Socioeconomic Implications of Recent Twists in Age Structure." *Demography* 15 (November 1978): 397-432.

EDGERTON, ROBERT B. *Deviant Behavior and Cultural Theory*. Reading, Mass.: Addison-Wesley, 1973.

EDWARDS, CHRISTOPHER. *Crazy for God*. Englewood Cliffs, N.J.: Prentice-Hall, 1979.

EDWARDS, LYFORD P. *The Natural History of Revolution*. Chicago: University of Chicago Press, 1927.

EIDUSON, BERNICE T., and JANNETTE W. ALEXANDER. "The Role of Children in Alternative Family Styles." *Journal of Social Issues* 34, No. 2 (1978): 149-67.

EISELEY, LOREN. *The Immense Journey*. New York: Random House, 1957.

EISEN, JONATHAN, editor. *The Age of Rock: Sounds of the American Cultural Revolution*. New York: Random House, 1969.

EISENSTADT, S. N. *From Generation to Generation: Age Groups and Social Structure*. New York: Free Press, 1956.

______. *The Political Systems of Empires: The Rise and Fall of the Historical Bureaucratic States*. New York: The Free Press, 1963.

EKEH, PETER. *Social Exchange Theory: The Two Traditions*. Cambridge, Mass.: Harvard University Press, 1974.

ELIADE, MIRCEA. *Cosmos and History*. Trans. Willard R. Trask. New York: Harper & Row, 1959.

ELLENBERGER, HENRI F. *The Discovery of the Unconscious*. New York: Basic Books, 1970.

ELLWOOD, ROBERT S., Jr. *The Eagle and the Rising Sun: Americans and the New Religions of Japan*. Philadelphia: Westminster Press, 1977.

ELSHTAIN, JEAN BETHKE. "Feminists Against the Family." *The Nation* 229 (November 17, 1979): 481, 497-500.

EMERSON, RICHARD. "Social Exchange Theory." In *Annual Review of Sociology*, Vol. 2, Alex Inkeles, James Coleman, and Neil Smelser, editors. Palo Alto, Calif.: Annual Reviews, 1974.

EMPEY, LAMAR T., and STEVEN G. LUBECK. "Conformity and Deviance in the 'Situation of Company'." *American Sociological Review* 33 (October 1968): 760-74.

ENDLEMAN, ROBERT, JOSEPH GUSFIELD, and MAX HEIRICH. "The Student Revolt: Afterthoughts and Prospects: Review Symposium of *The University Crisis Reader*" (Immanuel Wallerstein and Paul Starr, editors. Two Vols. New York: Random House, 1971). *Contemporary Sociology* 1 (January 1972): 3-18.

ERIKSON, ERIK. *Childhood and Society*. Rev. ed. New York: W. W. Norton, 1963.

______. *Identity: Youth and Crisis*. New York: W. W. Norton, 1968.

______."Reflections on the Dissent of Contemporary Youth." *Daedalus* 99 (Winter 1970): 154-76.

______. *Young Man Luther: A Study in Psychoanalysis and History*. New York: W. W. Norton, 1958.

______. Editor, *Youth: Change and Challenge*. New York: Basic Books, 1963.

ERIKSON, KAI. *Everything in Its Path: Destruction of Community in the Buffalo Creek Flood*. New York: Simon & Schuster, 1970.

______. *Wayward Puritans: A Study in the Sociology of Deviance*. New York: John Wiley & Sons, 1966.

ERLANGER, HOWARD. "The Empirical Status of the Subculture of Violence Thesis." *Social Problems* 22 (December 1974): 280-92.

ERRINGTON, FREDERICK. "Indigenous Ideas of Order, Time, and Transition in a New Guinea Cargo Movement." *American Ethnologist* 1 (May 1974): 255-67.

ESSIEN-UDOM, E. U. *Black Nationalism*, Chicago: University of Chicago Press, 1962.

ESSLIN, MARTIN, *The Theatre of the Absurd*. Rev. ed. Woodstock, N. Y.: Overlook Press, 1973.

FAIRBANK, JOHN K. *The United States and China*, 4th edition. Cambridge, Mass: Harvard University Press, 1979.

FANON, FRANTZ. *Black Skin, White Masks*. New York: Charles Lamm Markmann, 1967.

______. *The Wretched of the Earth*. New York: Grove Press, 1963.

FEATHERMAN, DAVID L., and ROBERT M. HAUSER. *Opportunity and Change*. New York: Academic Press, 1978.

FEINSOD, ETHAN. *Awake in a Nightmare*. New York: W. W. Norton, 1981.

FELTON, DAVID, editor. *Mindfuckers: A Source Book on the Rise of Acid Fascism in America*. San Francisco: Straight Arrow Press, 1972.

FENDRICH, JAMES M. "Activists Ten Years Later: A Test of Generational Unit Continuity." *Journal of Social Issues* 30, No. 3 (1974): 95-118.

FESHBACH, NORMA D., and SEYMOUR FESHBACK, editors. "The Changing Status of Children: Rights, Roles, and Responsibilities." *Journal of Social Issues*, Vol. 34, No. 2 (1978), whole issue.

FESHBACH, SEYMOUR, and NEAL MALAMUTH. "Sex and Aggression: Proving the

Link." *Psychology Today* 12 (November 1978): 111-17, 122.

FEUER, LEWIS. *The Conflict of Generations: The Character and Significance of Student Movements.* New York: Basic Books, 1969.

FINE, GARY A., and SHERRYL KLEINMAN. "Rethinking Subculture: An Interactionist Analysis." *American Journal of Sociology* 85 (July 1979): 1-20.

FINESTONE, HAROLD. "Cats, Kicks, and Color." *Social Problems* 5 (July 1957): 3-13.

FIRESTONE, SHULAMITH. *The Dialectic of Sex: The Case for Feminist Revolution.* New York: Bantam Books, 1971.

FIRTH, RAYMOND, editor. *Themes in Economic Anthropology*, New York: Tavistock, 1967.

FLACKS, RICHARD. *Youth and Social Change*, Chicago: Markham, 1971.

FOCAULT, MICHEL.*The History of Sexuality*, Vol. I: *An Introduction.* Trans. Robert Hurley. New York: Pantheon Books, 1977.

FOX, GEORGE. *Journal.* Rev. edition by John L. Nickalls. Cambridge: Cambridge University Press, 1952.

FOX, RICHARD G., editor. "Political Economy." *American Ethnologist*, Vol. 5 (August 1978), whole issue.

FRANK, JEROME D. "The Bewildering World of Psychotherapy." *Journal of Social Issues* 28, No. 4 (1972): 27-43.

FRAZER, JAMES G. *The Golden Bough.* New York: Macmillan, 1922.

FREE (see Hoffman, Abbie).

FREIRE, PAULO, *Education for Critical Consciousness.* New York: The Seabury Press, 1973.

______. *Pedagogy of the Oppressed.* Trans. Myra B. Ramos. New York: Herder & Herder, 1970.

FREND, W. H. C. *Martyrdom and Persecution in the Early Church.* Oxford: Oxford University Press, 1965.

FREUD, SIGMUND. *The Basic Writings of Sigmund Freud.* A. A. Brill, editor. New York: Random House, 1938.

______. *Civilization and Its Discontents.* Trans. James Strachey. New York: W. W. Norton & Co., 1962.

______. "Wit and Its Relation to the Unconscious." In *The Basic Writings of Sigmund Freud.* Trans. and edited by A. A. Brill. New York: Modern Library, 1938.

FRIED, M. H. *The Evolution of Political Society.* New York: Random House, 1967.

FRIEDENBERG, EDGAR Z. *The Anti-American Generation.* Chicago: Aldine Publishing Co., 1971.

FROMM, ERICH, and MICHAEL MACCOBY. *Social Character in a Mexican Village: A Sociopsychoanalytic Study.* Englewood Cliffs, N. J.: Prentice-Hall, 1970.

FROUDE, JAMES ANTHONY. *Short Studies on Great Subjects*, Vol. 4, "Origen and Celsus," pp. 361-431. London: Longmans, Greene & Co., 1917.

FRYE, NORTHROP. *The Educated Imagination*. Bloomington: Indiana University Press, 1964.

FURST, PETER T. *Hallucinogens and Culture*. San Francisco: Chandler & Sharp, 1976.

GARDNER, HUGH. *The Children of Prosperity: Thirteen Modern American Communes*. New York: St. Martin's Press, 1978.

GEERTZ, CLIFFORD. "Deep Play: Notes on the Balinese Coockfight." *Daedalus* 101 (Winter 1972): 1-38.

______. "Religion as a Cultural System." In *Anthropological Approaches to the Study of Religion*. Michael Banton, editor. London: Tavistock, 1966, pp. 1-46.

GELLNER, ERNEST. *Contemporary Thought and Politics*. London: Routledge & Kegan Paul, 1974.

GENNEP, ARNOLD VAN. *The Rites of Passage*. Chicago: University of Chicago Press, 1960.

GERGEN, KENNETH, MARTIN GREENBERG, and RICHARD WILLIS, editors. *Social Exchange: Advances in Theory and Research*. New York: Plenum, 1980.

GERLACH, LUTHER P., and VIRGINIA H. HINE. *Lifeway Leap: The Dynamics of Change in America*. Minneapolis: University of Minnesota Press, 1973.

GIBBS, M. A. *John Lilburne the Leveller: A Christian Democrat*. London: Lindsay Drummond Ltd., 1947.

GIDDENS, ANTHONY. *The Class Structure of Advanced Industrial Societies*. New York: Barnes & Noble, 1973.

GINSBERG, ALLEN. *Howl and Other Poems*. San Francisco: City Lights Pocket Bookshop, 1956.

GIRAUDOUX, JEAN. *The Madwoman of Chaillot*. New York: Random House, 1947.

GLAZER, NATHAN. *The Social Basis of American Communism*. New York: Harcourt Brace Jovanovich, 1961.

GLENN, NORVAL D. *Cohort Analysis*. Beverly Hills, Calif.: Sage, 1977.

GLOCK, CHARLES Y., editor. *Religion in Sociological Perspective: Essays in the Empirical Study of Religion*. Belmont, Calif.: Wadsworth, 1973.

GLOCK, CHARLES Y., and ROBERT N. BELLAH, editors. *The New Religious Consciousness*. Berkeley: University of California Press, 1976.

GLOVER, T. R. *The Conflict of Religions in the Early Roman Empire*. 12th edition. London: Methuen & Co., 1932.

GLUCKMAN, MAX. *Order and Rebellion in Tribal Africa*. New York: The Free Press, 1963.

______. *Rituals of Rebellion in South-East Africa*. Manchester: Manchester University Press, 1954.

GLUECK, SHELDON, and ELEANOR GLUECK. *Family Environment and Delinquency*. Boston: Houghton Mifflin, 1962.

———. *Predicting Delinquency and Crime*. Cambridge, Mass.: Harvard University Press, 1959.

———. *Unraveling Juvenile Delinquency*. New York: The Commonwealth Fund, 1950.

GOFFMAN, ERVING. *Asylums: Essays on the Social Situation of Mental Patients and Other Inmates*. New York: Doubleday, 1961.

———. *Stigma: Notes on the Mànagement of Spoiled Identity*. Englewood Cliffs, N.J.: Prentice-Hall, 1963.

GOOCH, G. P. *English Democratic Ideas in the Seventeenth Century*. 2d edition. Cambridge: Cambridge University Press, 1927.

GOODE, ERICH. *The Marijuana Smokers*. New York: Basic Books, 1970.

GOODE, WILLIAM. *The Celebration of Heroes: Prestige as a Social Control System*. Berkeley: University of California Press, 1978.

GOODMAN, FELICITAS D., JEANNETTE H. HENNEY, and ESTHER PRESSEL. *Trance, Healing, and Hallucination: Three Field Studies in Religious Experience*. New York: John Wiley & Sons, 1974.

GOODMAN, PAUL. *Compulsory Mis-Education*. New York: Horizon Press, 1964.

———. *Growing Up Absurd: Problems of Youth in the Organized Society*. New York: Random House, 1960.

GOODY, JACK. *Death, Property and the Ancestors: A Study of the Mortuary Customs of The Lodagoa of West Africa*. London: Tavistock Publications, 1962.

GOULDNER, ALVIN W. *The Coming Crisis of Western Sociology*. New York: Basic Books, 1970.

GOVE, WALTER R. *The Labelling of Deviance*. New York: John Wiley, 1975.

GRANT, GERALD, and DAVID RIESMAN. *The Perpetual Dream: Reform and Experiment in the American College*. Chicago: University of Chicago Press, 1978.

GREENFIELD, JEFF. "They Changed Rock, Which Changed the Culture, Which Changed Us." *New York Times Magazine*, February 16, 1975, pp. 12 ff.

GROSS, ALAN E., and CHRISTINE CROFTON. "What Is Good Is Beautiful." *Sociometry* 40 (March 1977): 85-90.

GUSFIELD, JOSEPH. *Utopian Myths and Movements in Modern Societies*. Morristown, N. J.: General Learning Press, 1973.

HALLIDAY, M. A. K. "Anti-Languages." *American Anthropologist* 78 (September 1976): 570-84.

HAMPSHIRE, STUART, editor. *Public and Private Morality*. New York: Cambridge University Press, 1978.

HARMON, JAMES E. "The New Music and Counter-Cultural Values." *Youth and Society* 4 (September 1972): 61-83.

HARNER, MICHAEL J., editor. *Hallucinogens and Shamanism*. London: Oxford University Press, 1973.

HAUSKNECHT, MURRAY, LIONEL ABEL, GEORGE P. ELLIOTT, CYNTHIA FUCHS EPSTEIN, IRVING HOWE, and DAVID SPITZ. "The Problem of Pornography." *Dissent* 25 (Spring 1978): 193-208.

HEATH, ANTHONY. *Rational Choice and Social Exchange: A Critique of Exchange Theory*. New York: Cambridge University Press, 1976.

HEGEL, G. W. F. *Science of Logic*. 2 Vols. Trans. W. H. Johnston and L. G. Struthers. New York: Macmillan, 1929.

HEIRICH, MAX. "Change of Heart: A Test of Some Widely Held Theories About Religious Conversion." *American Journal of Sociology* 83 (November 1977): 653-80.

______. "Cultural Breakthroughs." *American Behavioral Scientist* 19 (July-August 1976): 685-702.

HENDIN, HERBERT. *The Age of Sensation*. New York: W. W. Norton, 1975.

HENSLIN, JAMES M., editor. *Deviant Life-Styles*. New Brunswick, N. J.: Transaction Books, 1977.

HERNTON, CALVIN. "Blood of the Lamb: The Ordeal of James Baldwin." *Amistad 1*. New York: Vintage, 1970.

HESSE, HERMAN, *Steppenwolf*. Intro. by Joseph Mileck. Revision of Basil Creighton's trans. by J. Mileck and Horst Frenz. New York: Holt, Rinehart & Winston, 1963.

HEWITT, JOHN P. *Social Stratification and Deviant Behavior*. New York: Random House, 1970.

HILL, CHRISTOPHER, *Change and Continuity in Seventeenth-Century England*. London: Weidenfeld & Nicolson, 1974.

______. *Milton and the English Revolution*. New York: The Viking Press, 1977.

______. *The World Turned Upside Down: Radical Ideas During the English Revolution*. Harmondsworth, Middlesex, Eng.: Penguin Books, 1975.

HINCKLE, WARREN. "The Social History of the Hippies." *Ramparts* 5 (March 1967): 5-26.

HINDELANG, MICHAEL J. "Moral Evaluations of Illegal Behaviors." *Social Problems* 21, No. 3 (1974): 370-85.

HOFFMAN, ABBIE (Free). *Revolution for the Hell of It*. New York: The Dial Press, 1968.

HOLLOMAN, REGINA E. "Ritual Opening and Individual Transformation: Rites of Passage at Esalen." *American Anthropologist* 76 (June 1974): 265-80.

HOLT, JOHN. *Instead of Education.* New York: Dutton, 1976.

HOMANS, GEORGE C. "Bringing Men Back In." *American Sociological Review* 29 (December 1964): 808-18.

______. *Social Behavior: Its Elementary Forms.* Rev. edition. New York: Harcourt Brace Jovanovich, 1974.

HORI, ICHIRO. *Folk Religion in Japan: Continuity and Change.* Edited by Joseph M. Kitagawa and Alan L. Miller. Chicago: University of Chicago Press, 1968.

HORNEY, KAREN. *The Neurotic Personality of Our Time.* New York: W. W. Norton, 1937.

HOROWITZ, IRVING, editor. *Science, Sin, and Scholarship: The Politics of Reverend Moon and the Unification Church.* Cambridge, Mass.: The MIT Press, 1978.

HOROWITZ, IRVING L., and MARTIN LIEBOWITZ. "Social Deviance and Political Marginality: Toward a Redefinition of the Relation Between Sociology and Politics." *Social Problems* 16 (Winter 1968): 280-96.

HOSTETLER, JOHN A. *Hutterite Society.* Baltimore: Johns Hopkins Press, 1974.

HOWE, FLORENCE. "Mississippi's Freedom Schools: The Politics of Education." *Harvard Educational Review* 35 (Spring 1965): 144-60.

HOWE, IRVING, editor. *The Idea of the Modern in Literature and the Arts.* New York: Horizon Press, 1967.

HOWELLS, WILLIAM W. *The Heathens: Primitive Man and His Religions.* Garden City, N. Y.: Doubleday, 1948.

HOYLAND, JOHN. "The Long March Through the Bingo Halls." *Oz*, Vol. 46, January-February 1973.

HUNT, MORTON. *Sexual Behavior in the 1970s.* New York: Playboy Press, 1975.

HUNTINGTON, SAMUEL P., editor. *Changing Patterns of Military Politics.* New York: The Free Press, 1962.

______. *Political Order in Changing Societies.* New Haven: Yale University Press, 1968.

HURN, CHRISTOPHER J. *The Limits and Possibilities of Schooling.* Boston: Allyn & Bacon, 1978.

HUXLEY, ALDOUS L., *Brave New World.* New York: Harper Bros., 1946.

______. *Doors of Perception and Heaven and Hell.* New York: Harper & Row, 1954.

ILLICH, IVAN. *Deschooling Society.* New York: Harper & Row, 1971.

INGLEHART, RONALD. *The Silent Revolution: Changing Values and Political Styles Among Western Publics.* Princeton, N. J.: Princeton University Press, 1977.

INKELES, ALEX, and DAVID H. SMITH. *Becoming Modern: Individual Change in Six Developing Countries*. Cambridge: Harvard University Press, 1974.

IRWIN, JOHN, and DONALD R. CRESSEY. "Thieves, Convicts, and the Inmate Culture." *Social Problems* 10 (Fall 1962): 142-55.

JENCKS, CHRISTOPHER. *Inequality: A Reassessment of the Effect of Family and Schooling in America*. New York: Basic Books, 1972.

JENNINGS, H. S., *et al. Scientific Aspects of the Race Problem*. New York: Longmans, Green, 1941.

JESSOR, SHIRLEY L., and RICHARD JESSOR. "Maternal Ideology and Adolescent Nonconformity." *Developmental Psychology* 10 (May 1973): 246-54.

JOHNSON, BRUCE D. *Marihuana Users and Drug Subcultures*. New York: John Wiley & Sons, 1973.

JOHNSON, CHARLES S. *Patterns of Negro Segregation*. New York: Harper & Row, 1943.

JOHNSON, FRANK, editor. *Alienation: Concept, Term, and Meanings*. New York: Seminar Press, 1973.

JOHNSON, RICHARD E. *Juvenile Delinquency and Its Origins: An Integrated Theoretical Approach*. Cambridge: Cambridge University Press, 1979.

JONAS, HANS. *The Gnostic Religion: The Message of the Alien God and the Beginnings of Christianity*. Boston: Beacon Press, 1958.

JONES, LEROI (see also Amiri Baraka). *Black Magic: Collected Poetry, 1961-1967*. Indianapolis: Bobbs-Merrill, 1969.

JUDAH, J. STILLSON. *Hare Krishna and the Counterculture*. New York: John Wiley & Sons, 1974.

JURICH, A. P., and J. A. JURICH. "The Effect of Cognitive Moral Development upon the Selection of Premarital Sexual Standards." *Journal of Marriage and the Family* 36 (1974): 736-41.

KAGAN, JEROME. "The Child in the Family." *Daedalus* 106 (Spring 1977): 33-56.

KAHN, HERMAN, WILLIAM BROWN, and LEON MARTEL. *The Next 200 Years: A Scenario for America and the World*. New York: William Morrow & Co., 1976.

KANDEL, DENISE B. *Longitudinal Research on Drug Use: Empirical Findings and Methodological Issues*. New York: Wiley, 1978.

KANDEL, DENISE B., and GERALD S. LESSER. *Youth in Two Worlds*. San Francisco: Jossey-Bass, 1972.

KANTER, ROSABETH MOSS. *Commitment and Community: Communes and Utopias in Sociological Perspective*. Cambridge, Mass.: Harvard University Press, 1972.

______. *Men and Women of the Corporation*. New York: Basic Books, 1977.

KANTER, ROSABETH MOSS, D. JAFFE, and D. K. WEISBERG. "Coupling, Parenting and the Presence of Others: Intimate Relationships in Communal Households." *The Family Coordinator* 24 (1975): 433-52.

KAPLAN, HOWARD B. "Self-Attitudes and Deviant Response." *Social Forces* 54 (June 1976): 788-801.

______. "Sequelae of Self-Derogation: Predicting from a General Theory of Deviant Behavior." *Youth and Society* 7 (December 1975): 171-197.

KAPLEAU, PHILIP, editor and Trans. *Three Pillars of Zen: Teaching, Practice, and Enlightenment*. New York: Harper & Row, 1969.

KATZ, MICHAEL. *Class, Bureaucracy, and Schools*. New York: Praeger, 1971.

KAVOLIS, VYTAUTAS. "Post-Modern Man: Psychocultural Responses to Social Trends." *Social Problems* 17, No. 4 (1970a):435-48.

______. "The Social Psychology of Avant-Garde Cultures." *Studies in the Twentieth Century* 6 (Fall 1970b):13-34.

KEEN, SAM. "A Voyeur in Plato's Cove." *Psychology Today* 13 (February 1980): 85-101.

KEIL, CHARLES. *Urban Blues*. Chicago: University of Chicago Press, 1966.

KELLEY, DEAN M. *Why Conservative Churches Are Growing*. New York: Harper & Row, 1972.

KELLEY, KEN. "Blissed Out with the Perfect Master." *Ramparts* 12 (July 1973): 32-35, 50-57.

KENISTON, KENNETH. *The Uncommitted: Alienated Youth in American Society*. New York: Harcourt Brace & World, 1965.

______. *Young Radicals*. New York: Harcourt Brace & World, 1968.

______. *Youth and Dissent: The Rise of a New Opposition*. New York: Harcourt Brace Jovanovich, 1971.

KEROUAC, JACK. *On the Road*. New York: The Viking Press, 1957.

KESEY, KEN. *One Flew over the Cuckoo's Nest*. New York: Viking Press, 1962.

KILDUFF, MARSHALL, and RON JAVERS.. *The Suicide Cult: The Inside Story of the Peoples Temple Sect and the Massacre in Guyana*. New York: Bantam Books, 1978.

KLAPP, ORRIN E. *Collective Search for Identity*. New York: Holt, Rinehart & Winston, 1969.

KLINEBERG, OTTO, MARISA ZAVALLONI, CHRISTIANE LOUIS-GUÉRIN, and JEANNE BENBRIKA. *Students, Values, and Policies: A Crosscultural Comparison*. New York: The Free Press, 1979.

KLUCKHOHN, CLYDE. *Culture and Behavior*. Edited by Richard Kluckhohn. New York: The Free Press, 1962.

KOBRIN, SOLOMON. "The Conflict of Values in Delinquency Areas." *American Sociological Review* 16 (October 1951): 653-61.

KOCH, SIGMUND. "The Image of Man in Encounter Group Theory." *Journal of Humanistic Psychology* 11 (Fall 1971): 109-28.

KOMAROVSKY, MIRRA. *Dilemmas of Masculinity: A Study of College Youth.* New York: Norton, 1976.

KONVITZ, MILTON. *Religious Liberty and Conscience.* New York: Viking Press, 1968.

KOPKIND, ANDREW. "Mystic Politics: Refugees from the New Left." *Ramparts* 12 (July 1973): 26-27, 47-50.

KRAMER, HILTON. *The Age of the Avant-Garde: An Art Chronicle of 1956-1972.* New York: Farrar, Straus & Giroux, 1973.

KRAUSE, CHARLES A., with LAWRENCE M. STERN, RICHARD HARWOOD, and FRANK JOHNSTON. *Guyana Massacre: The Eyewitness Account.* New York: Berkeley, 1978.

KRAUSS, IRVING. *Stratification, Class and Conflict.* New York: The Free Press, 1976.

KVARACEUS, WILLIAM, and WALTER B. MILLER. *Delinquent Behavior.* Washington: National Education Association of the United States, 1959.

LABARRE, WESTON. *The Ghost Dance: Origins of Religion.* New York: Dell, 1972.

______. "Materials for a History of Studies of Crisis Cults: a Bibliographic Essay." *Current Anthropology* 12 (February 1971): 3-44.

LABOV, WILLIAM. *Language in the Inner City: Studies in the Black English Vernacular.* Philadelphia: University of Pennsylvania Press, 1972.

LADD, E. C., Jr., and S. M. LIPSET. *The Divided Academy: Professors and Politics.* New York: McGraw-Hill, 1975.

LADURIE, EMMANUEL LEROY. *Carnival in Romans.* Trans. Mary Feeney. New York: George Braziller, 1979.

LA FONTAINE, J. S., editor. *The Interpretation of Ritual: Essays in Honour of A. I. Richards.* London: Tavistock Publications, 1972.

LAING, R. D. *The Facts of Life: An Essay in Feelings, Facts, and Fantasy.* New York: Pantheon Books, 1976.

______. *The Politics of Experience.* New York: Random House, 1967.

LANGER, SUZANNE K. *Philosophy in a New Key: A Study in the Symbolism of Reason, Rite, and Art.* 3d edition. Cambridge, Mass.: Harvard University Press, 1972.

LANGMAN, LAUREN, RICHARD L. BLOCK, and INEKE CUNNINGHAM, "Countercultural Values at a Catholic University." *Social Problems* 20 (Spring 1973): 521-32.

LANTERNARI, VITTORIO. "Ethnocentrism and Ideology." *Ethnic and Racial Studies* 3 (January 1980): 52-66.

______. *The Religions of the Oppressed: A Study of Modern Messianic Cults.*

Trans. Lisa Sergio. New York: Alfred A. Knopf, 1963.

LAPPE, FRANCES MOORE, and JOSEPH COLLINS. *Food First: Beyond the Myth of Scarcity*. Boston: Houghton Mifflin, 1977.

LAQUEUR, WALTER. *Terrorism*. Boston: Little, Brown & Co., 1977.

______. editor. *The Terrorism Reader: A Historical Anthology*. Philadelphia: Temple University Press, 1978.

LASCH, CHRISTOPHER. *The Agony of the American Left*. New York: Alfred A. Knopf, 1969.

______. *The Culture of Narcissism: American Life in an Age of Diminishing Expectations*. New York: W. W. Norton, 1978.

______. *Haven in a Heartless World*. New York: Basic Books, 1979.

LASSWELL, HAROLD D. *World Politics and Personal Insecurity*. New York: The Free Press, 1965.

LAVEY, ANTON S. *The Satanic Bible*. New York: Avon Books, 1969.

LAWRENCE, PETER. *Road Belong Cargo*. Manchester: Manchester University Press, 1964.

LAYMAN, EMMA MCCLOY. *Buddhism in America*. Chicago: Nelson-Hall, 1976.

LEACH, E. R., editor. *Dialectic in Practical Religion*. Cambridge: Cambridge University Press, 1968.

______. *A Runaway World*. London: Oxford University Press, 1968.

LEARY, TIMOTHY. *High Priest*. New York: New American Library, 1968.

LEBRA, TAKIE SUGIYAMA. *Japanese Patterns of Behavior*. Honolulu: The University Press of Hawaii, 1976.

LECLAIR, E. E., and H. K. SCHNEIDER, editors. *Economic Anthropology: Readings in Theory and Analysis*. New York: Holt, Rinehart & Winston, 1968.

LEFKOWITZ, BERNARD. *Breaktime: Living Without Work in a Nine to Five World*. New York: Hawthorn Books, 1979.

LEIGHTON, DOROTHEA, *et al. The Character of Danger*. New York: Basic Books, 1963.

LENSKI, GERHARD E. "Status Crystallization: A Non-Vertical Dimension of Social Status." *American Sociological Review* 19 (August 1954): 405-12.

______. "Marxist Experiments in Destratification: An Appraisal." *Social Forces* 57 (December 1978): 364-83.

LERMAN, PAUL. "Argot, Symbolic Deviance and Subcultural Delinquency." *American Sociological Review* 32 (April 1967a): 209-24.

______. "Gangs, Networks, and Subcultural Delinquency." *The American Journal of Sociology* 73 (July 1967b): 63-72.

LERNER, DANIEL. *The Passing of Traditional Society*. New York: Free Press, 1958.

LERNER, MICHAEL. "Anarchism and the American Counter-Culture." *Government and Opposition* 5 (Autumn 1970): 430-55.

LERNER, ROBERT E. *The Heresy of the Free Spirit in the Later Middle Ages.* Berkeley: University of California Press, 1972.

LESSER, ALEXANDER. "Cultural Significance of the Ghost Dance." *American Anthropologist* 35 (January -March 1933): 108-15.

LEVI-STRAUSS, CLAUDE. *Structural Anthropology.* New York: Doubleday, 1967.

______. *Tropical Sadness.* New York: Antheneum, 1974.

LEVINE, R. A., and DONALD T. CAMPBELL. *Ethnocentrism: Theories of Conflict, Ethnic Attitudes and Group Behavior.* New York: Wiley, 1972.

LEVITAS, RUTH. "Sociology and Utopia." *Sociology* 13 (January 1979): 19-33.

LEWELLEN, TED C. "Deviant Religion and Cultural Evolution: The Aymara Case." *Journal for the Scientific Study of Religion* 18, No. 3 (1979): 243-51.

LEWIS, GEORGE H. "Capitalism, Contra-Culture, and the Head Shop: Exporations in Structural Change." *Youth and Society* 4 (September 1972): 85-102.

______. "The Structure of Support in Social Movements: An Analysis of Organization and Resource Mobilization in the Youth Contra-Culture." *British Journal of Sociology* 27 (June 1976): 184-96.

LEWIS, OSCAR. *The Children of Sanchez.* New York: Random House, 1961.

______. "The Culture of Poverty." *Scientific American* 215 (October 1966a): 19-25.

______. *Five Families: Mexican Case Studies in the Culture of Poverty.* New York: Basic Books, 1959.

______. *La Vida: A Puerto Rican Family in the Culture of Poverty.* New York: Random House, 1966b.

LEWY, GUENTER. *Religion and Revolution.* New York: Oxford University Press, 1974.

LICHTER, S. R. "Young Rebels: A Psychopolitical Study of West German Male Radical Students." *Comparative Politics* 12 (October 1979): 27-48.

LIEBERMAN, MORTON A., *et al. Encounter Groups: First Facts.* New York: Macmillan, 1973.

LIEBERT, ROBERT. *Radical and Militant Youth: A Psychoanalytic Inquiry.* New York: Praeger, 1971.

LIEBMAN, ARTHUR. *Jews and the Left.* New York: Wiley, 1979.

LIEBOW, ELLIOT. *Tally's Corner, A Study of Negro Streetcorner Men.* Boston: Little, Brown, 1967.

LIETZMANN, HANS. *A History of the Early Church.* 2 Vols. Trans. Bertram L. Wolfe. Cleveland: World, 1961.

LIFTON, ROBERT JAY. *Thought Reform and the Psychology of Totalism: A Study of "Brainwashing" in China.* New York: Norton, 1961.

LINCOLN, C. ERIC. *The Black Muslims in America.* Boston: Beacon Press, 1961.

LINTON, RALPH. *The Cultural Background of Personality.* New York: Appleton-Century, 1945.

______. *The Study of Man: An Introduction.* New York: Appleton-Century, 1936.

LIPSET, SEYMOUR MARTIN. *Rebellion in the University.* Boston: Little, Brown, 1971.

______. editor, *The Third Century: America as a Post-Industrial Society.* Stanford, Calif.: Hoover Institution Press, Stanford University, 1979.

LIPSKY, MICHAELS. "Protest as a Political Resource." *American Political Science* Review 62 (December 1968): 1144-58.

LOFLAND, JOHN. *Doomsday Cult: A Study of Conversion, Proselytization, and Maintenance of Faith.* Enlarged edition. New York: Irvington Publishers, 1977.

LOFLAND, JOHN, and RODNEY STARK. "Becoming a World-Saver: A Theory of Conversion to a Deviant Perspective." *American Sociological Review* 30 (December 1965): 862-75.

LORENZ, KONRAD. *On Aggression.* New York: Harcourt, Brace, & World, 1966.

LYMAN, STANFORD M. *The Seven Deadly Sins: Society and Evil.* New York: St. Martin's Press, 1978.

LYMAN, STANFORD M., and MARVIN B. SCOTT. *A Sociology of the Absurd.* New York: Appleton-Century-Crofts, 1970.

LYNCH, FREDERICK R. " 'Occult Establishment' or 'Deviant Religion'? The Rise and Fall of a Modern Church of Magic." *Journal for the Scientific Study of Religion* 18 (1979): 281-98.

LYNESS, JUDITH L., MILTON E. LIPETZ, and KEITH E. DAVIS. "Living Together: An Alternative to Marriage." *Journal of Marriage and Family* 34 (May 1972): 305-11.

MACCOBY, ELEANOR. "The Choice of Variables in the Study of Socialization." *Sociometry* 24 (December 1961): 357-71.

MACKLIN, ELEANOR D. "Heterosexual Cohabitation Among Unmarried College Students." *The Family Coordinator* 21 (October 1972): 463-72.

MACRAE, DONALD G. *Weber.* Glasgow: Fontana-Collins, 1974.

MAILER, NORMAN. *The Armies of the Night.* New York: The New American Library, 1968.

______. *Genius and Lust: A Journey Through the Major Writings of Henry Miller.* New York: Grove Press, 1976.

MAIR, LUCY P. "Independent Religious Movements in Three Continents." *Comparative Studies in Society and History* 1 (January 1959): 113-36.

MALAMUTH, NEAL, SEYMOUR FESHBACH, and YORAM JAFFEE. "Sexual Arousal and Aggression: Recent Experiments and Theoretical Issues." *Journal of Social Issues* 33 (Spring 1977): 110-33.

MALCOLM X, with ALEX HALEY. *The Autobiography of Malcolm X*. New York: Grove Press, 1966.

MANNHEIM, KARL. *Essays in the Sociology of Knowledge*. New York: Oxford University Press, 1952.

______. *Ideology and Utopia*. Trans. Louis Wirth and Edward Shils. New York: Harcourt, Brace & World, 1936.

MANNING, FRANK E. "Celebrating Cricket: The Symbolic Construction of Caribbean Politics." *American Ethnologist* 8 (August, 1981): 616-632.

MANUEL, FRANK E., and FRITZIE P. MANUEL. *Utopian Thought in the Western World*. Cambridge: Harvard University Press, 1979.

MARCUSE, HERBERT. *Eros and Civilization: A Philosophical Inquiry into Freud*. 2d edition. Boston: Beacon Press, 1966.

______. *One Dimensional Man: Studies in the Ideology of Advanced Industrial Societies*. Boston: Beacon Press, 1964.

______. *Reason and Revolution: Hegel and the Rise of Social Theory*. 2d edition. New York: The Humanities Press, 1954.

MARITAIN, JACQUES. *True Humanism*. Trans. M. R. Adamson. London: Geoffrey Bles, Centenary Press, 1938.

MARTIN, DAVID A. *The Dilemmas of Contemporary Religion*. New York: St. Martin's Press, 1978.

MARTIN, JAMES J. *Men Against the State: The Expositors of Individualist Anarchism in America: 1827-1908*. DeKalb, Ill.: Adrian Allen Associates, 1953.

MARTY, MARTIN. "The Occult Establishment." *Social Research* 27 (Summer 1970): 212-30.

______. *A Nation of Behavers*. Chicago: University of Chicago Press, 1976.

MARX, JOHN H., and JOSEPH P. SELDIN. "Crossroads of Crisis: I. Therapeutic Sources and Quasi-Therapeutic Functions of Post-Industrial Communes." *Journal of Health and Social Behavior* 14 (March 1973): 39-50.

______. "Crossroads of Crisis: II. Organizational and Ideological Models for Contemporary Quasi-Therapeutic Communes." *Journal of Health and Social Behavior* 14 (June 1973): 183-91.

MARX, KARL. *Capital: A Critique of Political Economy*. Trans. Samuel Moore and Edward Aveling from 3d German edition. New York: The Modern Library, 1906.

———. *Early Writings*. Trans. and edited by T. B. Bottomore. New York: McGraw-Hill, 1964.

———. *The Eighteenth Brumaire of Louis Napoleon*. New York: International Publishers, 1963.

———. *Selected Writings in Sociology and Social Philosophy*. Edited by T. B. Bottomore and Maximilien Rubel. New York: McGraw-Hill, 1964.

MARX, LEO. "The Uncivil Response of American Writers to Civil Religion in America." In Russell E. Richey and Donald G. Jones, editors, *American Civil Religion*. New York: Harper & Row, 1974, pp. 222-51.

MATZA, DAVID. *Becoming Deviant*. Englewood Cliffs, N. J.: Prentice-Hall, 1969.

———. "Subterranean Traditions of Youth." *Annals of the American Academy of Political and Social Science* 338 (November 1961): 102-18.

MATZA, DAVID, and GRESHAM SYKES. "Juvenile Delinquency and Subterranean Values." *American Sociological Review* 26 (October 1961): 712-19.

MAURER, DAVID W. "The Argot of the Dice Gambler." *Annals of the American Academy of Political and Social Science* 269 (May 1950): 114-33.

MAUSS, ARMAND L., issue editor. "The New Left and the Old." *Journal of Social Issues*, Vol. 27, No. 1 (1971), whole issue.

MAUSS, MARCEL. *The Gift*. Trans. Ian Cunnison. London: Cohen & West, 1954.

MCCREADY, WILLIAM C., with ANDREW M. GREELEY. *The Ultimate Values of the American Population*. Beverly Hills, Calif.: Sage, 1976.

MCDONALD, MARCI. "Le Nouveau Nazism: A Rightist Fashion from France." *Saturday Review*, February 2, 1980, pp. 13-16.

MCEWEN, CRAIG A. *Designing Correctional Organizations for Youths: Dilemmas of Subcultural Development*. Cambridge, Mass.: Ballinger, 1978.

MCFARLAND, H. NEILL. *The Rush Hour of the Gods: A Study of New Religious Movements in Japan*. New York: The Macmillan Company, 1967.

MEAD, MARGARET. *Culture and Commitment*. Rev. edition. New York: Doubleday, 1978.

MEDDIN, JAY. "Human Nature and the Dialectics of Immanent Sociocultural Change." *Social Forces* 55 (December 1976): 382-93.

MEIER, AUGUST, ELLIOT RUDWICK and FRANCES BRODERICK, editors. *Black Protest Thought in the Twentieth Century*. 2d edition. Indianapolis: Bobbs-Merrill, 1971.

MELTON, J. GORDON. *The Encyclopedia of American Religions*. 2 Vols. Wilmington, N. C.: McGrath Publishing Co., 1978.

MELVILLE, KEITH. *Communes in the Counter Culture: Origins, Theories, Styles of Life*. New York: William Morrow, 1972.

MERTON, ROBERT K. "Insiders and Outsiders: A Chapter in the Sociology of Knowledge." *American Journal of Sociology* 78 (July 1972): 9-47.

______. *Social Theory and Social Structure*. 3d edition. New York: The Free Press, 1968.

______. *Sociological Ambivalence and Other Essays*. New York: The Free Press, 1976.

MERTON, ROBERT K., LEONARD BROOM, and LEONARD COTTRELL, Jr., editors. *Sociology Today*. New York: Basic Books, 1959.

MERTON, ROBERT K., and ROBERT A. NISBET, editors. *Contemporary Social Problems*. 2d edition. New York: Harcourt, Brace & World, 1966.

MEYER, EDUARD. *Ursprung und Anfänge des Christentums*. 3 Vols. Darmstadt: Wissenschaftliche Buchgesellschaft, 1962.

MICHAELS, LEONARD, and CHRISTOPHER RICKS, editors. *The State of the Language*. Berkeley: University of California Press, 1980. (Published in association with the English-Speaking Union).

MIDDLETON, JOHN. *Lugbara Religion: Ritual and Authority Among an East African People*. London: Oxford University Press, 1960.

MIDDLETON, THOMAS H. "Light Refractions: Me, Myself, and I." *Saturday Review*, October 28, 1978, p. 56.

MILES, MICHAEL W. *The Radical Probe*. New York: Antheneum, 1971.

MILLER, HENRY. *Tropic of Cancer*.New York: Grove Press, 1961.

MILLER, RICHARD. *Bohemia: The Protoculture Then and Now*. Chicago: Nelson-Hall, 1977.

MILLER, WALTER B. "Lower Class Culture as a Generation Milieu of Gang Delinquency." *Journal of Social Issues* 14 (1958): 5-19.

______. "White Gangs." *TransAction* 6 (September 1969): 11-26.

MILLS, C. WRIGHT. *White Collar: The American Middle Classes*. New York: Oxford University Press, 1951.

MILLS, RICHARD. *Young Outsiders: A Study of Alternative Communities*. London: Routledge & Kegan Paul, 1973.

MINOGUE, KENNETH. "The Doctrine of Violence" (a review essay). *Times Literary Supplement*, November 7, 1975, pp. 1318-20.

MITCHELL, WILLIAM E. "The Baby Disturbers: Sexual Behavior in a Childhood Contraculture." *Psychiatry* 29 (November 1966): 367-77.

MOODY, EDWARD J. "Magical Therapy: An Anthropological Investigation of Contemporary Satanism." In *Religious Movements in Contemporary America*, Irving I. Zaretsky and Mark P. Leone, editors. Princeton N.J.: Princeton University Press, 1974: 355-82.

MOONEY, JAMES. *The Ghost-Dance Religion and the Sioux Outbreak of 1890*. Chicago: University of Chicago Press, 1965.

MOORE, JOAN W., with ROBERT GARCIA, CARLOS GARCIA, LUIS CERDA, and FRANK VALENCIA. *Homeboys: Gangs, Drugs, and Prison in the Barrios of Los Angeles*. Philadelphia: Temple University Press, 1978.

MORIOKA, KIYOMI. *Religion in Changing Japanese Society*. Tokyo: University of Tokyo Press, 1975.

MORIOKA, KIYOMI, and WILLIAM H. NEWELL. *The Sociology of Japanese Religion*. International Studies in Sociology and Social Anthropology 6. Leiden: E. J. Brill, 1968.

MORTON, A. L. *The World of the Ranters: Religious Radicalism in the English Revolution*. London: Lawrence & Wishart, 1970.

MÜHLMANN, WILHELM E., *et al. Chiliasmus and Nativismus: Studien zur Psychologie, Soziologie und historishchen Kasuistik der Umsturzbewegungen*. Berlin: Dietrich Reimer Verlag, 1961.

MUMFORD, LEWIS. *The Story of Utopias*. New York: Boni & Liveright, 1922.

MUNCY, RAYMOND LEE. *Sex and Marriage in Utopian Communities: Nineteenth Century America*. Baltimore: Penguin Books, 1974.

MURDOCK, GEORGE P. *Social Structure*. New York: Macmillan, 1949.

MURDOCK, GRAHAM, and GUY PHELPS, "Youth Culture and the School Revisited." *British Journal of Sociology* 23 (December 1972): 478-82.

MURRAY, GILBERT. *Five Stages of Greek Religion*. 2d edition. New York: Columbia University Press, 1925.

MURVAR, VATRO. "Messianism in Russia: Religious and Revolutionary." *Journal for the Scientific Study of Religion* 10 (Winter 1971): 277-338.

MUSGROVE, FRANK. *Ecstasy and Holiness: Counter Culture and the Open Society*. Bloomington: Indiana Univ. Press, 1974.

NAKANE, CHIE. *Japanese Society*. Berkeley: University of California Press, 1972.

NATIONAL CHILDREN'S BUREAU. *Britain's Sixteen-Year-Olds*. London: National Children's Bureau, 1976.

NEEDHAM, RODNEY, editor. *Right and Left: Essays on Dual Symbolic Classification*. Chicago: University of Chicago Press, 1973.

NEEDLEMAN, JACOB. *The New Religions*. Garden City, N. Y.: Doubleday, 1970.

NEEDLEMAN, JACOB, and GEORGE BAKER, editors. *Understanding the New Religions*. New York: Seabury Press, 1978.

NIETZSCHE, FRIEDRICH. *Twilight of the Idols*. Trans. with an introduction and commentary by R. J. Hollingdale. Harmondsworth, Middlesex, England: Penguin Books, 1968a.

———. *The Anti-Christ*. Trans. with an introduction and commentary by R. J. Hollingdale. Harmondsworth, Middlesex, England: Penguin Books, 1968b.

———. *The Will to Power*. Trans. by Walter Kaufmann and R. J. Hollingdale. New York: Random House, 1967.

NISBET, ROBERT. *The Sociology of Emile Durkeim*. New York: Oxford University Press, 1974.

NORBECK, EDWARD. "African Rituals of Conflict." *American Anthropologist* 65 (December 1963): 1254-79.

NORDHOFF, CHARLES. *Communistic Societies of the United States*. New York: Schocken Books, 1965.

OFFER, DANIEL, RICHARD C. MAROHN, and ERIC OSTROV. *The Psychological World of the Juvenile Delinquent*. New York: Basic Books, 1979.

OKEN, DONALD. "Alienation and Identity: Some Comments on Adolescence, the Counterculture, and Contemporary Adaptations." In *Alienation: Concept, Term, and Meanings*. Frank Johnson, editor. New York: Seminar Press, 1973: 83-110.

OLSEN, MARVIN E. "Perceived Legitimacy of Social Protest Actions." *Social Problems* 16 (Winter 1968): 297-310.

ORTEGA Y GASSETT, JOSÉ. *Man and Crisis*. New York: W. W. Norton, 1958.

ORTIZ, SUTTI. "The Structure of Decision-Making Among Indians in Colombia." In *Themes in Economic Anthropology*, Raymond Firth, editor. London: Tavistock, 1967, pp. 191-228.

ORWELL, GEORGE. *Nineteen Eighty-four*. New York: Harcourt, Brace, 1949.

O'TOOLE, ROGER. *The Precipitous Path: Studies in Political Sects*. Toronto: Peter Martin Associates, 1977.

PAGELS, ELAINE. *The Gnostic Gospels*. New York: Random House, 1979.

PARKER, SEYMOUR, and KLEINER, ROBERT J. "The Culture of Poverty: An Adjustive Dimension." *American Anthropologist* 72 (June 1970): 516-27.

PARSONS, ELSIE C., and R. L. BEALS. "The Sacred Clowns of the Pueblo and Mayo-Yaqui Indians." *American Anthropologist* 36 (1934): 491-516.

PARSONS, TALCOTT. *Essays in Sociological Theory*. New York: The Free Press, 1954.

______. *The Social System*. New York: The Free Press, 1951.

PARSONS, TALCOTT, and EDWARD A. SHILS, editors. *Toward a General Theory of Action*. New York: Harper Torchbooks, 1962.

PATRICK, TED, and TOM DULACK. *Let Our Children Go!* New York: E. P. Dutton, 1976.

PARTRIDGE, WILLIAM L. *The Hippie Ghetto: The Natural History of a Subculture*. New York: Holt, Rinehart & Winston, 1973.

PAUL, ROBERT A. "Dumje: Paradox and Resolution in Sherpa Ritual Symbolism." *American Ethnologist* 6 (May 1979): 274-304.

PEARSON, GEOFFREY. *The Deviant Imagination: Psychiatry, Social Work and Social Change*. New York: Holmes & Meier, 1975.

PECKHAM, MORSE. *Man's Rage for Chaos: Biology, Behavior, and the Arts*. Philadelphia: Chilton, 1965.

PERLIN, TERRY MICHAEL, editor. *Contemporary Anarchism*. New Brunswick, N. J.: Transaction Books, 1979.

PERRUCCI, ROBERT. *Circle of Madness: On Being Insane and Institutionalized in America*. Englewood Cliffs, N.J.: Prentice-Hall, 1974.

PETEGORSKY, DAVID. *Left-Wing Democracy in the English Civil War: A Study of the Social Philosophy of Gerrard Winstanley*. London: Victor Gollancz, 1940.

PFEFFER, LEO. *God, Caesar, and the Constitution: The Court as Referee of Church-State Confrontation*. Boston: Beacon Press, 1974.

PICON, GAETAN. *Surrealists and Surrealism 1919-1939*. Trans. James Emmons. New York: Skira/Rizzoli International Publications, 1977.

PIETROPINTO, ANTHONY, and JACQUELINE SIMENAUER. *Beyond the Male Myth*. New York: Times Books, 1977.

PILARZYK, THOMAS, "The Origin, Development, and Decline of a Youth Culture Religion: An Application of Sectarianization Theory." *Review of Religious Research* 20 (Fall 1978): 23-43.

PLATO. *The Dialogues of Plato*. 2 Vols. Trans. B. Jowett. New York: Random House, 1937.

PRUESS, JAMES B. "Merit and Misconduct: Venerating the Bo Tree at a Buddhist Shrine." *American Ethnologist* 6 (May 1979): 261-73.

PUNCH, MAURICE. "The Sociology of the Anti-Institution." *British Journal of Sociology* 25 (September 1974): 312-25.

PYE, LUCIAN W. *Politics, Personality, and Nation-Building*. New Haven: Yale University Press, 1962.

RADIN, PAUL. *The Trickster: A Study in American Indian Mythology*. New York: Philosophic Library, 1956.

RAINE, KATHLEEN. *Blake and Tradition*. 2 Vols. London: Routledge & Kegan Paul, 1969.

______. *Yeats, the Tarot and the Golden Dawn*. Dublin: The Dolmen Press, 1972.

RAINWATER, LEE. "The Problem of Lower Class Culture." *Journal of Social Issues* 26 (Spring 1970): 133-48.

RAMPARTS Editors. *Conversations with the New Reality: Readings in the Cultural Revolution*. San Francisco: Canfield Press, 1971.

RAPPAPORT, ROY A. "Nature, Culture, and Ecological Anthropology." In *Man, Culture, and Society*, Rev. edition, Harry Shapiro, editor. New York: Oxford University Press, 1971, pp. 237-68.

RAWLS, JOHN. *A Theory of Justice*. Cambridge: Harvard University Press, 1971.

REDL, FRITZ, and DAVID WINEMAN. *Children Who Hate*. New York: The Free Press, 1951.

REICH, CHARLES A. *The Greening of America*. New York: Random House, 1970.

______. *The Sorcerer of Bolinas Reef*. New York: Random House, 1976.

REICH, WILHELM. *The Sexual Revolution*. 3d edition. New York: Orgone Institute Press, 1945.

REINHOLD, ROBERT, TONY SCHWARTZ, and ROBIN HERMAN. "After Woodstock: The Impact of the Counterculture." *New York Times*, August 12, 1979, pp. 1, 38; August 13, 1979, p. A-15; and August 15, 1979, p. A-20.

REISCHAUER, EDWIN O., *The Japanese*. Cambridge, Mass.: The Belknap Press, 1977.

REISS, IRA L. *The Social Context of Premarital Sexual Permissiveness*. New York: Holt, 1967.

RESTON, JAMES, Jr. *Our Father Who Art in Hell*. New York: New York Times Books, 1981.

RICHARDSON, JAMES T., editor. *Conversion Careers: In and Out of the New Religion*. Beverly Hills, Calif.: Sage Publications, 1978.

______."People's Temple and Jonestown: A Corrective Comparison and Critique." *Journal for the Scientific Study of Religion* 19 (September 1980): 239-55.

RICHARDSON, JAMES T., MARY W. HARDER, and ROBERT B. SIMMONDS. "Thought Reform and the Jesus Movement." *Youth and Society* 4 (December 1972): 185-202.

RICHTER, HANS. *Dada: Art and Anti-Art*. Trans. David Britt. New York: Harry N. Abrams, 1965.

RIEFF, PHILIP. *Freud: The Mind of the Moralist*. New York: The Viking Press, 1959.

RIESMAN, DAVID, with NATHAN GLAZER and REUEL DENNEY. *The Lonely Crowd*. Rev. edition. New Haven, Conn.: Yale University Press, 1961.

RIGBY, ANDREW. *Alternative Realities*. London: Routledge & Kegan Paul, 1974a.

______. *Communes in Britain*. London: Routledge & Kegan Paul, 1974b.

RIGBY, PETER. "Some Gogo Rituals of 'Purification': An Essay on Social and Moral Categories." In *Dialectic in Practical Religion*, E. R. Leach, editor. Cambridge: Cambridge University Press, 1968, pp. 153-78.

RILEY, MATILDA W. "Aging and Cohort Succession: Interpretations and Misinterpretations." *Public Opinion Quarterly* 37 (Spring 1973): 35-49.

ROACH, JACK L., and ORVILLE R. GURSSLIN. "An Evaluation of the Concept 'Culture of Poverty'." *Social Forces* 45 (March 1967): 383-92.

ROBBINS, THOMAS. "Eastern Mysticism and the Resocialization of Drug Users: the Meher Baba Cult." *Journal for the Scientific Study of Religion* 8 (Fall 1969): 308-17.

______. "Even a Moonie Has Civil Rights." *The Nation* 224 (February 26, 1977): 238-42.

ROBBINS, THOMAS, and DICK ANTHONY. "Cults, Brainwashing, and Counter-Subversion." *Annals of the American Academy of Political and Social Science* 446 (November 1979): 78-90.

______. "Getting Straight with Meher Baba: A Study of Mysticism, Drug Rehabilitation and Postadolescent Role Conflict." *Journal for the Scien-*

tific Study of Religion 11 (June, 1972): pp. 122-40.

ROBERTS, KEITH A. "Toward a Generic Concept of Counter-Culture." *Sociological Focus* 11 (April 1978): 111-26.

ROBINSON, JAMES M., director. *The Nag Hammadi Library in English.* San Francisco: Harper & Row, 1977.

ROBINSON, JOAN. *The Cultural Revolution in China.* Harmondsworth, Middlesex: Penguin Books, 1969.

ROBINSON, PAUL A. *The Freudian Left: Wilhelm Reich, Geza Roheim and Herbert Marcuse.* New York: Harper & Row, 1969.

RODMAN, HYMAN. "The Lower-Class Value Stretch." *Social Forces* 42 (December 1963): 205-15.

ROHEIM, GÉZA. *Pychoanalysis and Anthropology: Culture, Personality, and the Unconscious.* New York: International Universities Press, 1950.

ROHNER, RONALD P. *They Love Me, They Love Me Not: A Worldwide Study of the Effects of Parental Acceptance and Rejection.* New Haven, Conn.: Human Relations Area Files, 1975.

ROHRER, JOHN, MUNRO EDMONSON, *et al. The Eighth Generation: Cultures and Personalities of New Orleans Negroes.* New York: Harper & Row, 1960.

ROKEACH, MILTON. *The Nature of Human Values.* New York: The Free Press, 1973.

ROOF, W. CLARK. *Community and Commitment: Religious Plausibility in a Liberal Protestant Church.* New York: Elsevier, 1977.

ROOM, ROBIN. "Ambivalence as a Sociological Explanation: The Case of Cultural Explanations of Alcohol Problems." *American Sociological Review* 41 (December 1976): 1047-65.

ROSENHAN, D. L. "On Being Sane in Insane Places." *Science* 179 (January 19, 1973): 250-58.

ROSSI, ALICE S. "A Biosocial Perspective on Parenting." *Daedalus* 106 (Spring 1977): 1-31.

ROSZAK, THEODORE. *The Making of a Counter Culture.* Garden City, N. Y.: Doubleday, 1969.

______. *Person/Planet: The Creative Disintegration of Industrial Society.* Garden City, N. Y.: Doubleday, 1978.

______. *Where the Wasteland Ends: Politics and Transcendence in Postindustrial Society.* Garden City, N. Y.: Doubleday, 1973.

ROTH, GUENTHER. "Socio-Historical Model and Developmental Theory: Charismatic Community, Charisma of Reason, and the Counterculture." *American Sociological Review* 40 (April 1975): 148-57.

ROTHCHILD, JOHN, and SUSAN BERNS WOLF. *The Children of the Counter-Culture.* Garden City, N. Y.: Doubleday, 1976.

ROTHMAN, STANLEY. "Group Fantasies and Jewish Radicalism: A Psychodynamic Interpretation." *Journal of Psychohistory* 6 (Fall 1978): 211-39.

ROTHMAN, STANLEY, and S. R. LICHTER. "Power, Politics and Personality in 'Post-Industrial Society'." *Journal of Politics* 40 (August 1978): 675-707.

RUBERT DE VENTÓS, XAVIER. *Heresies of Modern Art*. Trans. J. S. Bernstein. New York: Columbia University Press, 1980.

RUBIN, HERBERT J., and IRENE S. RUBIN. "The Function of Liminal Events in the Succession to a Position of Power: The Transfer of the District Officer in Thailand." *American Ethnologist* 2 (May 1975): 329-46.

RUBIN, JERRY. *Do It*. New York: Simon & Schuster, 1970.

______. *Growing (Up) at 37*. New York: Warner Books, 1976.

RUBIN, VERA, and LAMBROS COMITAS. *Ganja in Jamaica: The Effects of Marijuana Use*. Garden City, N. Y.: Doubleday, 1976.

RUSSEL, JEFFREY BURTON. *Dissent and Reform in the Early Middle Ages*. Berkeley: University of California Press, 1965.

SAGARIN, EDWARD, editor. *Deviance and Social Change*. Beverly Hills, Calif.: Sage, 1977.

SALGÃDO, GÃMINI, editor. *Cony-Catchers and Bawdy Baskets: An Anthology of Elizabethan Low Life*. Harmondsworth, Middlesex: Penguin Books, 1972.

SAMPSON, EDWARD E., editor. "Stirrings out of Apathy: Student Activism and the Decade of Protest." *Journal of Social Issues*, Vol 23 (July 1967), whole issue.

SAPIR, EDWARD. "Fashion." *Encyclopedia of the Social Sciences* 6: 139-44. New York: Macmillan, 1931.

SARTRE, JEAN-PAUL. *Critique of Dialectic Reason*. Trans. Alan Sheridan-Smith. Atlantic Highlands, N. J.: Humanities Press, 1976.

______. *Nausea*. Trans. L. Alexander. New York: New Directions, 1964.

SCARPITTI, FRANK R., and SUSAN K. DATESMAN, editors. *Drugs and the Youth Culture*. Beverly Hills, Calif.: Sage, 1980.

SCHACHT, RICHARD. *Alienation*. Garden City, N. Y.: Doubleday, 1971.

SCHAMA, SIMON. "The Unruly Realm: Appetite and Restraint in Seventeenth Century Holland." *Daedalus* 108 (Summer 1979): 103-23.

SCHEFF, THOMAS J., editor. *Labeling Madness*. New York: Prentice-Hall, 1975.

SCHNEIDER, LOUIS. "Dialectic in Sociology." *American Sociological Review* 36 (August 1971): 667-78.

SCHUMACHER, E. F. *Small Is Beautiful*. New York: Harper & Row, 1973.

SCHWAB, JOSEPH J. *College Curriculum and Student Protest*. Chicago: University of Chicago Press, 1969.

SCHWARTZ, GARY. *Youth Culture: An Anthropological Approach*. Reading, Mass.: Addison-Wesley, 1972.

SCHWARTZ, GARY, and DON MERTEN. "The Language of Adolescence: An Anthropological Approach to Youth Culture." *American Journal of Sociology* 72 (March 1967): 453-68.

SCOTT, GINI GRAHAM. *Cult and Countercult: A Study of A Spiritual Growth Group and a Witchcraft Order.* Westport, Conn.: Greenwood Press, 1980.

SCOTT, ROBERT A., and JACK D. DOUGLAS, editors. *Theoretical Perspectives on Deviance.* New York: Basic Books, 1972.

SEALE, BOBBY. *Seize the Time: The Story of the Black Panther Party.* New York: Random House, 1970.

SEARS, ROBERT, ELEANOR MACCOBY, and HARRY LEVIN. *Patterns of Child Rearing.* New York: Harper & Row, 1957.

SEIKYO PRESS. *Sōka Gakkai.* Tokyo: The Seikyo Press, 1960.

SENNETT, RICHARD. *Authority.* New York: Alfred Knopf, 1980.

———. *The Fall of Public Man.* New York: Alfred Knopf, 1977.

———. *The Uses of Disorder: Personal Identity and City Life.* New York: Alfred Knopf, 1970.

SEWELL, WILLIAM H., and ROBERT M. HAUSER. *Education, Occupation and Earnings.* New York: Academic Press, 1975.

SHAW, CLIFFORD. *Delinquency Areas.* Chicago: University of Chicago Press, 1929.

SHEEHAN, THOMAS. "Italy: Behind the Ski Mask." *The New York Review of Books,* August 16, 1979, pp. 20-26.

———. "Italy: Terror on the Right." *The New York Review of Books,* January 22, 1981: 23-26.

SHILS, EDWARD. "Charisma, Order, and Status." *American Sociological Review* 30 (April 1965): 199-213.

———. *Center and Periphery: Essays in Macrosociology.* Chicago: University of Chicago Press, 1975.

SHIMAHARA, NOBUO K., and ADAM SCRUPSKI, editors. *Social Forces and Schooling: An Anthropological and Sociological Perspective.* New York: David McKay, 1975.

SILVERMAN, SYDEL. "Agricultural Organization, Social Structures, and Values in Italy: Amoral Familism Reconsidered." *American Anthropologist* 70 (1968): 1-20.

SIMMEL, GEORG. *Conflict.* Trans. by Kurt Wolff. New York: The Free Press, 1955.

SIMON, WILLIAM, and JOHN H. GAGNON. "The Anomie of Affluence: A Post-Mertonian Conception." *American Journal of Sociology* 82 (September 1976): 356-78.

SIMPSON, GEORGE E. *Religious Cults in the Caribbean: Trinidad, Jamaica, and Haiti.* Rev. and enl. edition. Rio Piedras: Institute of Caribbean Studies, University of Puerto Rico, 1970.

———. *The Shango Cult in Trinidad.* Rio Piedras: Institute of Caribbean Studies, University of Puerto Rico, 1965.

SIMPSON, GEORGE E., and J. MILTON YINGER. *Racial and Cultural Minorities.* 4th edition. New York: Harper & Row, 1972.

SKOCPOL, THEDA. *States and Social Revolutions: A Comparative Analysis of France, Russia and China.* New York: Cambridge University Press, 1979.

SLATER, PHILIP. *The Pursuit of Loneliness: American Culture at the Breaking Point.* Boston: Beacon Press, 1971.

______. *The Wayward Gate: Science and the Supernatural.* Boston: Beacon Press, 1977.

SLOTKIN, J. S. *The Peyote Religion: A Study in Indian-White Relations.* New York: The Free Press, 1956.

SMITH, ADAM. *Powers of Mind.* New York: Random House, 1976.

SMITH, STEVEN R. "The London Apprentices as Seventeenth-Century Adolescents." *Past and Present* 61 (November 1973): 149-61.

SOHM, RUDOLPH. *Kirchenrecht.* Leipzig: Duncker & Humbolt, 1892.

SOLOMON, TED J. "The Response of Three New Religions to the Crisis in the Japanese Value System." *Journal for the Scientific Study of Religion* 16 (March 1977): 1-14.

SONTAG, SUSAN. *Against Interpretation and Other Essays.* New York: Farrar, Straus & Giroux, 1966.

______. *Styles of Radical Will.* New York: Farrar, Straus, & Giroux, 1969.

SPATES, JAMES L. "Counterculture and Dominant Culture Values: A Cross-National Analysis of the Underground Press and Dominant Culture Magazines." *American Sociological Review* 41 (October 1976): 868-83.

SPATES, JAMES L., and JACK LEVIN. "Beats, Hippies, the Hip Generation and the American Middle Class: An Analysis of Values." *International Social Science Journal* 24 (1972): 326-53.

SPIRO, MELFORD E. *Children of the Kibbutz.* 2d edition. Cambridge: Harvard University Press, 1975.

______. *Gender and Culture: Kibbutz Women Revisited.* Durham, N. C.: Duke University Press, 1979.

______. "Is the Family Universal?" *American Anthropologist* 56 (October 1954): 839-46.

______. *Kibbutz: Venture in Utopia.* 2d edition. Cambridge: Harvard University Press, 1971.

STARK, WERNER. *The Sociology of Religion: A Study of Christendom.* Vol. 2: *Sectarian Religion.* New York: Fordham University Press, 1967.

STARR, JEROLD M. "The Peace and Love Generation: Changing Attitudes Toward Sex and Violence Among College Youth." *Journal of Social Issues* 30, No. 2 (1974): 73-106.

STAUB, ERVIN. *Positive Social Behavior and Morality.* 2 Vols. New York: Academic Press, 1978.

STAVRIANOS, L. S. *The Promise of the Coming Dark Age.* San Francisco: W. H. Freeman, 1976.

STE. CROIX, G. E. M. DE. "Why Were the Early Christians Persecuted?" *Past and Present* 26 (November 1963): 6-38.

STEEGMULLER, FRANCIS, editor. *The Letters of Gustave Flaubert, 1830-1857.* Cambridge: Harvard University Press, 1980.

STEINFELS, PETER. *The Neoconservatives: The Men Who are Changing America's Politics.* New York: Simon & Schuster, 1979.

STERLING, CLAIRE, *The Terror Network.* New York: Readers Digest Press (Holt, Rinehart & Winston), 1981.

______. "The Terrorist Network." *The Atlantic* 242 (November 1978): 37-47.

STONER, CARROLL, and JO ANNE PARKE. *All God's Children: The Cult Experience—Salvation or Slavery?* New York: Penguin Books, 1977.

STOODLEY, BARTLETT H., editor. *Society and Self.* New York: The Free Press, 1962.

STRATHERN, ANDREW. "The Red Box Money-Cult in Mount Hagen 1968-71." *Oceania* 50 (December 1979): 88-102, Part I; *Oceania* 50 (March 1980): 161-75, Part II.

STREIKER, LOWELL, D. *The Jesus Trip: Advent of the Jesus Freaks.* Nashville, Tenn.: Abingdon Press, 1971.

SUMNER, WILLIAM GRAHAM. *Folkways.* Boston: Ginn, 1906.

SWIDLER, ANN. "What Free Schools Teach." *Social Problems* 24 (December 1976): 214-27.

SYKES, GRESHAM M., and DAVID MATZA. "Techniques of Neutralization: A Theory of Delinquency." *American Sociological Review* 22 (December 1957): 664-70.

SZASZ, THOMAS. *Heresies.* New York: Doubleday, 1976.

______. *The Myth of Mental Illness.* New York: Hoeber-Harper, 1961.

TALESE, GAY. *Thy Neighbor's Wife.* New York: Doubleday, 1980.

TALMON, YONINA. "Pursuit of the Millennium: The Relation Between Religious Change and Social Change." *Archives Européennes de Sociologie* 3 (1962): 125-48.

TASHJIAN, DICKRAN. *Skyscraper Primitives: Dada and the American Avant-Garde, 1910-1925.* Middletown, Conn.: Wesleyan University Press, 1975.

TAYLOR, A. E. *Plato: The Man and His Work.* New York: Meridian Books, 1957.

THOMAS, CHARLES W., and SAMUEL C. FOSTER. "Prisonization in the Inmate Contraculture." *Social Problems* 20 (Fall 1972): 229-39.

THORNE, RICHARD. "A Step Toward Sexual Freedom in Berkeley." *Berkeley Barb*, February 4, 1965.

THORNER, ISIDOR. "Prophetic and Mystic Experience: Comparison and Consequences." *Journal for the Scientific Study of Religion* 5 (Fall 1965): 82-96.

THRALL, CHARLES A., and JEROLD M. STARR, editors. *Technology, Power, and Social Change.* Lexington, Mass.: D. C. Heath, 1972.

THRASHER, FREDRIC M. *The Gang.* 2d Rev. edition. Chicago: University of Chicago Press, 1936.

TIRYAKIAN, EDWARD A., editor. *On the Margin of the Visible: Sociology, the Esoteric, and the Occult.* New York: John Wiley & Sons, 1974.

______. "Toward the Sociology of Esoteric Culture." *American Journal of Sociology* 78 (November 1972): 491-512.

TOURAINE, ALAIN. "The Voice and the Eye: On the Relationship Between Actors and Analysts." *Political Psychology* 2 (Spring 1980): 3-14.

TRILLING, LIONEL. *Beyond Culture: Essays on Literature and Learning.* London: Secker & Warburg, 1966.

______. *The Opposing Self.* New York: The Viking Press, 1955.

TRIVERS, R. L. "The Evolution of Reciprocal Altruism." *Quarterly Review of Biology* 46, No. 4 (1971): 35-57.

TRUZZI, MARCELLO. "The Occult Revival as Popular Culture: Some Random Observations on the Old and Nouveau Witch." *Sociological Quarterly* 13 (Winter 1972): 16-36.

TSURUMI, KAZUKO. *Social Change and the Individual: Japan Before and After Defeat in World War II.* Princeton, N. J.: Princeton University Press, 1970.

TURNER, RALPH H. "The Public Perception of Protest." *American Sociological Review* 34 (December 1969): 815-30.

______. "The Real Self: From Institution to Impulse." *American Journal of Sociology* 81 (March 1976): 989-1016.

______. *The Social Context of Ambition.* San Francisco: Chandler, 1964.

TURNER, RALPH H., and LEWIS M. KILLIAN. *Collective Behavior.* Englewood Cliffs, N. J.: Prentice-Hall, 1957.

TURNER, VICTOR W. *Dramas, Fields, and Metaphors.* Ithaca, N. Y.: Cornell University Press, 1974.

______. *The Ritual Process: Structure and Anti-Structure.* Chicago: Aldine, 1969.

TYLER, LAWRENCE L. "The Protestant Ethic Among the Black Muslims." *Phylon* 27 (Spring 1966): 5-14.

UNDERWOOD, BARBARA, and BETTY UNDERWOOD. *Hostage to Heaven: Four Years in the Unification Church, By an Ex-Moonie and the Mother Who Fought to Free Her.* New York: Clarkson N. Potter, 1979.

UNITED STATES, PRESIDENT'S COMMISSION. *Campus Unrest.* Washington: Government Printing Office, 1972.

UNITED STATES COMMISSION ON OBSCENITY AND PORNOGRAPHY. *The Report of the U. S. Commission on Obscenity and Pornography.* Washington: Government Printing Office, 1970.

UNITED STATES DEPARTMENT OF COMMENCE, BUREAU OF THE CENSUS. *American Families and Living Arrangements.* Washington: Government Printing Office, 1980.

UYS, STANLEY. "South Africa's New Black Puritans." *New Stateman* 92 (November 19, 1976): 702-3.

VALENTINE, BETTYLOU. *Hustling and Other Hard Work: Life Styles in the Ghetto.* New York: The Free Press, 1978.

VALENTINE, CHARLES. *Culture and Poverty.* Chicago: University of Chicago Press, 1968.

VEYSEY, LAURENCE. *The Communal Experience.* New York: Harper & Row, 1973.

VOGEL, EZRA F. *Canton Under Communism: Programs and Politics in a Provincial Capital, 1949-1968.* New York: Harper Torchbooks, 1969.

______. *Japan as Number One: Lessons for America.* Cambridge, Mass.: Harvard University Press, 1979.

VOGET, FRED. "The American Indian in Transformation: Reformation and Accommodation." *American Anthropologist* 58 (April 1956): 249-63.

WALLACE, ANTHONY F. C. *The Death and Rebirth of the Seneca.* New York: Alfred A. Knopf, 1970.

______. *Religion: An Anthropological View.* New York: Random House, 1966.

______. "Revitalization Movements." *American Anthropologist* 58 (April 1956): 264-81.

WALLERSTEIN, IMMANUEL, and PAUL STARR, editors. *The University Crisis Reader.* 2 Vols. New York: Random House, 1971.

WALLIS, ROY. *The Road to Total Freedom: A Sociological Analysis of Scientology.* New York: Columbia University Press, 1977.

______, editor. *Sectarianism: Analysis of Religious and Non-Religious Sects.* New York: John Wiley & Sons, 1975.

WALZER, MICHAEL. *Just and Unjust Wars.* New York: Basic Books, 1977.

WARING, JOAN M. "Social Replenishment and Social Change: The Problem of Disordered Cohort Flow." *American Behavior Scientist* 19 (December 1975): 237-56.

WATTENBERG, BEN J. *The Real America: A Surprising Examination of the State of the Union.* New York: G. P. Putnam's Sons, 1974.

WATTS, ALAN. *This Is It, and Other Essays on Zen and Spiritual Experience.* New York: Collier, 1967.

WEBER, MAX. *From Max Weber.* Trans., edited, and with an introduction by H. H. Gerth and C. Wright Mills. New York: Oxford University Press, 1946.

______. *The Protestant Ethic and the Spirit of Capitalism.* Trans. Talcott Parsons. London: George Allen & Unwin, 1930.

______. *The Rational and Social Foundations of Music*. Trans. and edited by Don Martindale, Johannes Riedel, and Gertrude Neuwirth. Carbondale: Southern Illinois University Press, 1958.

______. *The Sociology of Religion*. Trans. Ephraim Fischoff. Boston: Beacon Press, 1963.

______. *The Theory of Social and Economic Organization*. Trans. A. M. Henderson and Talcott Parsons. New York: Oxford University Press, 1947.

WEINER, ANDREW. "Political Rock." *New Society*, No. 487, January 27, 1972, pp. 187-89.

WEINER, REX, and DEANNE STILLMAN. *Woodstock Census: The Nationwide Survey of the Sixties Generation*. New York: The Viking Press, 1979.

WESTBY, DAVID L. *The Clouded Vision: The Student Movement in the United States in the 1960s*. Lewisburg, Pa.: Bucknell University Press, 1976.

WESTHUES, KENNETH. *Society's Shadow: Studies in the Sociology of Countercultures*. Toronto: McGraw-Hill Ryerson, 1972.

WESTLEY, WILLIAM A., and NATHAN B. EPSTEIN. *The Silent Majority*. San Francisco: Jossey-Bass, 1969.

WHEELER, STANTON. "Socialization in Correctional Institutions." In *Handbook of Socialization Theory and Research*, David A. Goslin, editor. Chicago: Rand McNally, 1969, chap. 25.

WHITE, RALPH, and RONALD LIPPITT. *Autocracy and Democracy: An Experimental Inquiry*. New York: Harper & Row, 1960.

WHITMAN, WALT. *Leaves of Grass*. Edited by Malcolm Cowley. New York: Viking Press, 1959.

WIEDER, D. LAWRENCE, and DON H. ZIMMERMAN. "Becoming a Freak: Pathways into the Counter-Culture." *Youth and Society* 7 (March 1976): 311-44.

______. "Generational Experience and the Development of Freak Culture." *Journal of Social Issues* 30, No. 2 (1974): 137-61.

WILENSKY, HAROLD L. *The Welfare State and Equality*. Berkeley: University of California Press, 1975.

WILLENER, ALFRED. *The Action-Image of Society: On Cultural Politicization*. Trans. A. M. Sheridan Smith. New York: Random House, 1970.

WILLIAMS, ROBIN, Jr. *American Society*. 3d edition. New York: Alfred A. Knopf, 1970.

______. "The Concept of Values." *International Encyclopedia of the Social Sciences* 16:283-87, David L. Sills, editor. New York: Macmillan, 1968.

WILLIS, PAUL E. *Profane Culture*. London: Routledge & Kegan Paul, 1978.

WILSFORD, ENID. *The Fool: His Social and Literary History*. New York: Farrar & Rinehart. 1935.

WILSON, BRYAN R. *Magic and the Millennium*. New York: Harper & Row, 1973.

______. *The Noble Savages: The Primitive Origins of Charisma and Its Con-*

temporary Survival. Berkeley: University of California Press, 1975.

WILSON, W. CODY, and HERBERT I. ABELSON. "Experience with and Attitudes Toward Explicit Sexual Materials." *Journal of Social Issues* 29, No. 3 (1973): 19-39.

WILSON, W. CODY, and MICHAEL J. GOLDSTEIN, editors. "Pornography: Attitudes, Use, and Effects." *Journal of Social Issues*, Vol. 29, No. 3 (1973), whole issue.

WINSTANLEY, GERRARD. *Law of Freedom and Other Writings*. Edited by Christopher Hill. Harmondsworth, Middlesex: Penguin Books, 1973.

WISPÉ, L. G., editor. "Positive Forms of Social Behavior." *Journal of Social Issues*, Vol. 28, No. 3, (1972), whole issue.

WOLFE, TOM. *The Electric Kool-Aid Acid Test*. New York: Farrar, Strauss & Giroux, 1968.

______. "The 'Me' Decade and the Third Great Awakening." *New York*, August 23, 1976, pp. 26-40.

______. *Radical Chic and Maumauing the Flak Catchers*. New York: Farrar, Strauss & Giroux, 1970.

WOODEN, KENNETH. *Weeping in the Playtime of Others: America's Incarcerated Children*. New York: McGraw-Hill, 1976.

WOOLF, LEONARD SIDNEY. *Sowing: An Autobiography of the Years 1880-1904*. London: The Hogarth Press, 1960.

WORDSWORTH, WILLIAM. *Lyrical Ballads*. London: N. Douglas, 1926.

WORSLEY, PETER, *The Trumpet Shall Sound: A Study of "Cargo" Cults in Melanesia*. London: MacGibbon & Kee, 1957.

WRIGHT, RICHARD. *Native Son*. New York: Harper, 1940.

______. *White Man, Listen!* Garden City, N. Y.: Doubleday, 1964.

WRIGLEY, E. A. *Population and History*. New York: McGraw-Hill, 1969.

WRONG, DENNIS. "The Oversocialized Conception of Man." *American Sociological Review* 26 (April 1961): 184-93.

WUTHNOW, ROBERT. "Astrology and Marginality." *Journal for the Scientific Study of Religion* 15 (June 1976a): 157-68.

______. *The Consciousness Reformation*. Berkeley: University of California Press, 1976b.

______. "Recent Patterns of Secularization: A Problem of Generations." *American Sociological Review* 41 (October 1976c): 850-67.

______. *Experimentation in American Religion: The New Mysticisms and Their Implications for the Churches*. Berkeley: University of California Press, 1978.

WUTHNOW, ROBERT, and GLEN MELLINGER. "Religious Loyalty, Defection, and Experimentation: A Longitudinal Analysis of University Men." *Review of Religious Research* 19 (Spring 1978): 234-45.

YABLONSKY, LEWIS. *The Hippie Trip*. New York: Pegasus, 1968.

______. *The Violent Gang*. New York: Macmillan, 1962.

YANKELOVICH, DANIEL. *The New Morality: A Profile of American Youth in the 70's*. New York: McGraw-Hill, 1974.

YATES, FRANCES A. *Giordano Bruno and the Hermetic Tradition*. Chicago: University of Chicago Press, 1964.

YEATS, WILLIAM BUTLER. *The Collected Poems of W. B. Yeats*. New York: Macmillan, 1924.

YINGER, J. MILTON. "Anomie, Alienation, and Political Behavior." In *Handbook of Political Psychology*, Jeanne Knutson, editor. San Francisco: Jossey-Bass, 1973, pp. 171-202.

______. A Comparative Study of the Substructures of Religion." *Journal for the Scientific Study of Religion* 16 (March 1977): 67-86.

______. "Contraculture and Subculture." *American Sociological Review* 25 (October 1960): 625-35.

______. "Countercultures and Social Change." *American Sociological Review* 42 (December 1977): 833-53.

______. *A Minority Group in American Society*. New York: McGraw-Hill, 1965.

______. "On Anomie." *Journal for the Scientific Study of Religion* 3, No. 2 (1964): 158-73.

______. *Religion in the Struggle for Power*. Durham, N. C.: Duke University Press, 1946.

______. "Salvation and Witches in a 'Secular' Age." *Contemporary Sociology* 9 (July 1980): 472-77.

______. *The Scientific Study of Religion*. New York: Macmillan, 1970.

______. *Toward a Field Theory of Behavior*. New York: McGraw-Hill, 1965.

YINGER, J. MILTON, and STEPHEN J. CUTLER, editors. *Major Social Issues*. New York: The Free Press, 1978.

YOUNG, FRANK W. "Reactive Subsystems." *American Sociological Review* 35 (April 1970): 297-307.

ZABLOCKI, BENJAMIN D. *Alienation and Charisma: A Study of Contemporary American Communes*. New York: The Free Press, 1980.

______. *The Joyful Community*. Baltimore: Penguin Books, 1971.

ZAENER, R. C. *Our Savage God: The Perverse Use of Eastern Thought*. New York: Sheed & Ward, 1975.

ZARETSKY, IRVING I., and MARK P. LEONE, editors. *Religious Movements in Contemporary America*. Princeton, N. J.: Princeton University Press, 1974.

ZURCHER, LOUIS A., Jr. "The Poor and the Hip: Some Manifestations of Cultural Lead." *Social Science Quarterly* 53 (September 1972): 357-76.

Name Index

Subject Index